Judy and I

Judy and I

MY LIFE WITH JUDY GARLAND

SID LUFT

With a foreword and additional material by
RANDY L. SCHMIDT

CHICAGO
REVIEW
PRESS

An A Cappella Book

Published by Chicago Review Press Incorporated
814 North Franklin Street
Chicago, Illinois 60610

ISBN 978-1-61373-583-1

Library of Congress Cataloging-in-Publication Data
Is available from the Library of Congress.

All photos courtesy of Royal Rainbow Productions LLC
Typesetting: Nord Compo

Printed in the United States of America
5 4 3 2

Contents

Foreword
by Randy L. Schmidt

I love Judy. I want to protect her from the trauma she once knew. I don't want her to be bewildered or hurt again. I want her to have happiness.

—Sid Luft

He's the kind of person you can lean against if you fall down. He's strong and protects me. I respect him. And most important, I like him as much as I love him.

—Judy Garland

"ANY WOMAN WHO'S a real woman wants a man to protect her and love her. That's what Sid Luft does for me." Closing night, backstage at New York's legendary RKO Palace Theatre in 1952, Judy Garland beamed as she spoke of her newfound love. Her stint at the Palace had begun as a modest four-week run but quickly turned into a triumphant nineteen-week, record-breaking engagement of 184 performances grossing nearly $800,000. "We have accomplished so much together," Judy said. "This whole thing at the Palace has been magical. Sid has done it for me. That's my fella!"

Act 1 of Judy Garland's immense career encompassed her beginnings in vaudeville, followed by sixteen years at Metro-Goldwyn-Mayer. It was there that she made more than two dozen feature films, including

The Wizard of Oz, Meet Me in St. Louis, and *Easter Parade.* That curtain closed on Judy in 1950, and she found herself out of work and unemployable at the age of twenty-eight. It was a frustrating and hopeless year until Sid Luft entered the scene. Ushering in a fresh sense of confidence and energy in Judy, Sid was the impresario who pushed her to play the Palace. That success marked the beginning of Judy's act 2, when the star was reborn in a series of comebacks as legendary as the living legend herself.

Judy would marry five times in her short life of just forty-seven years. Her marriage to Sid lasted the longest, probably because Sid was so drastically different from the others. "Yeah, well, I was no Minnelli, that's for sure," Sid told Michael Shelden, a writer for the *Telegraph*, in 2001. "I grew up in a rough New York neighborhood and didn't put up with shit from anyone. I'm a survivor, with the scars to show for it, and I think that appealed to Judy. She needed someone to lean on who wouldn't crack."

The self-proclaimed Hollywood tough guy was a former amateur boxer they called One-Punch Luft, who had a reputation for drinking and gambling. He was a test pilot turned producer with a strong build and even stronger Bronx accent. In a December 2005 piece for the *Atlantic*, titled "The Least Worst Man," writer Mark Steyn distinguished Sid from Judy's other husbands by saying he was "a rare friend of Judy who wasn't a friend of Dorothy. . . . Unlike his predecessor [Vincente Minnelli], he was not 'musical,' in either the artistic or the euphemistic sense; unlike his successor [Mark Herron], he was not voraciously gay."

The Lufts were married for thirteen years (1952–1965), but together—on and off and on again—for two decades. One gossip columnist joked, "So Sid Luft is what a girl finds over the rainbow?" Some saw Sid as Judy's savior, the person who scooped her up from the depths of despair and gave her a second chance. Others thought he was a shady opportunist riding the coattails of his famous wife and milking her for all she was worth. But when you look at the big picture of Judy's creative output during their time together, it's hard to deny that they were obviously doing something right. The Palace, *A Star Is Born*, Carnegie Hall, *The Judy Garland Show*—some of her finest performances and greatest triumphs—all came during the Luft years.

———— ∞∞∞ ————

Judy and I: My Life with Judy Garland is a book that was in the works for more than thirty years. In November 1963, newspapers reported that Sid Luft was writing his autobiography. It was to be titled *I'll Laugh Saturday*, in reference to a private joke between him and Judy. The project continued intermittently with a range of ghostwriters and working titles, including *Good Girl, Bad Girl* and *Star Light, Star Bright*.

Just two months after Judy's untimely death on June 22, 1969, there was news that Sid was at it again, this time working with Leo Guild on a book for Holloway House. Even though he and Judy had been divorced for four years and she had remarried twice, Sid turned out to be the sharpest steward of her legacy. *A Star Is Born*, their mutual masterpiece, was beautifully and painstakingly restored and rereleased in 1983. Sid later produced *Judy Garland: The Concert Years*, an award-winning PBS documentary. Additionally, Judy's TV specials from the 1950s and '60s, as well as the twenty-six episodes of *The Judy Garland Show*, were issued on DVD under his guidance.

Sid remained in Hollywood and remarried twice, first in 1970 to Patti Hemingway in a marriage that lasted less than a year, and later to actress Camille Keaton. The last time he acquired a book deal for this project was in 1992 with HarperCollins, but the deal fell through when the manuscript wasn't delivered in a timely manner. Sid never gave up on his plan to tell the story of his life with Judy Garland, but the manuscript remained unfinished at the time of his death on September 15, 2005, at the age of eighty-nine.

The late Coyne Steven Sanders, author of the outstanding book *Rainbow's End: The Judy Garland Show*, knew Sid Luft for many years and contributed to his obituary in the *Los Angeles Times*. "Sid was a great showman," Sanders said. "I think he understood Judy better professionally than anyone else did. He knew how to produce her shows, which were lavishly full-blown productions. I'd say he was the most important male figure in her adult life. He certainly was the most sustained relationship she had in her adult life. They had a great love affair."

—✷—

The original manuscript for *Judy and I* comes to a halt in 1960. This is quite telling, for it was that year that marked a turning point in the couple's marriage: the arrival of Freddie Fields and David Begelman, Judy's new agents. This was to be the beginning of the end for Sid, who soon witnessed a swift succession of steps in which he was gradually and strategically removed from Judy's life, both professional and personal.

It is with the blessing and encouragement of the Sid Luft Living Trust that I have crafted the final sections of this book (parts VI and VII) with artistic license, using quotes mined from various interviews and conversations with Sid. My sincere thanks to Joe Luft and his partners John Kimble and Phil Sandhaus of Royal Rainbow Productions for this honor, and to Yuval Taylor, senior editor at Chicago Review Press, for the opportunity.

The primary sources include a 237-page transcript of notes from extensive interviews between an unknown interlocutor and Sid (circa 1996–1997), Sid's quotes from *Judy*, the 1975 book by Gerold Frank (currently owned by Royal Rainbow Productions), and an eighty-page transcript of notes from a taped conversation between Sid Luft, Freddie Fields, and David Begelman (recorded August 22, 1963).

Other materials sourced include an audio recording of an interview conducted by Mike Wallace for *Mike Wallace at Large*, CBS Radio Network, 1974; a transcript for "Judy," a *60 Minutes* profile produced by Igor Oganesoff for CBS News, August 3, 1975 (volume VII, number 29), with special thanks to Barbara Dury; Jeanie Kasindorf's cover story for *New West*, "The Incredible Past of David Begelman," February 13, 1978; an audio recording of an interview conducted by Lawrence Schulman (recorded September 15, 1993), with special thanks to John

H. Haley; and Michael Shelden's June 2001 feature for the *Telegraph*, titled "I Couldn't Stop Judy Falling Apart."

———— ⌘ ————

Love him or hate him, Sid Luft was Judy's "fella," and *Judy and I: My Life with Judy Garland* is the man's long-lost "love letter" to his legendary wife. It's a rich and intimate portrait of their lives and creative work together, and one that captivatingly explores the couple's very public marriage as well as their private moments and shared struggles. That classic era of silver screen glamour from the days of *A Star Is Born* is gone, but it comes back to life in true Vicki Lester–Norman Maine fashion through Sid's chronicles. Here you'll find a wealth of information on one of Hollywood's stormiest up-and-down relationships, and a fresh insight into a larger-than-life show business power couple. It's a vivid illustration of how, at least for a time, Judy Garland and Sid Luft shared something sincere and special.

PART I

Manhattan, 1950

I

NEW YORK WAS A SCORCHER. It was September, and the entire Eastern Seaboard was having a heatwave.

I'd returned to the city from Media, Pennsylvania, where I'd met with Sam Riddle, the owner of the great racehorse Man o' War. I'd been working for a month to put together a film about the near mythical golden-red horse, a post–World War I symbol of greatness like Babe Ruth or Gene Tunney. Man o' War had won the Lawrence Realization Stakes by as much as one hundred lengths. I'd been driven, in spite of the long odds on independent producers at the time, to make this Technicolor film. With two profit-making grade-B Monogram movies under my belt, I was eager to continue climbing the show-business mountain. I had no fear of heights.

Bob Agins, a lawyer I'd come to know during my not-yet-finalized divorce from the actress Lynn Bari, had accompanied me to Media. We needed script approval from Riddle before we could continue with the project. The screenplay had been written by W. R. Burnett, author of such megahits as *Asphalt Jungle*. We had high hopes.

However, Riddle had just nixed the Burnett script. It was the first of many vetoes. "It didn't happen this way!" was Riddle's favorite response.

As I ducked into the air-conditioned refuge of the 21 Club to meet my golf pals Jock and Neddie McLean for lunch, I was thinking maybe I should have just stayed in Los Angeles. I was early and the bar was half filled. I ordered a double martini with olive and cooled off while reading the *Daily News*.

Theater legend Billy Rose had devoted his entire column, Pitching Horseshoes, to Judy Garland. The column headline, Love Letter to a National Asset, was addressed to Judy at the Calvena Lodge in Lake Tahoe, where she was vacationing, and made reference to her recent "bout with the jim-jams." Rose extolled Judy's talent in a folksy story, telling how he'd recently wandered into her latest hit (and final film for MGM), *Summer Stock*. "A hundred minutes later I walked out of the projection room with a slaphappy grin on my face." He finished off the lengthy piece with this advice to Judy:

> One thing more: Next time you're down in the dumps—if there has to be a next time—it might help you to remember that you're only feeling the way most of us feel a good part of the time. Unfortunately, we're in no position to ease your headache. You, on the other hand, through the medium of the neighborhood theatre, can do more than a million boxes of aspirin to ease ours.
>
> Your devoted fan,
Billy Rose

MGM had recently suspended the country's favorite daughter. I'd been aware of the press reports: Judy's attempt at suicide was considered unimportant, a bid for attention. I was all too familiar with the stress and strains of performers. I had a built-in reflex not to credit the press with accuracy.

⁂

You couldn't live in Hollywood, as I did, and not be aware of "little Judy Garland." In fact, our lives had crisscrossed a couple times over the years. On both occasions she sang, and I thought how talented she was.

I'd seen Judy out on the town several times, once with Louis B. Mayer at the Trocadero nightclub, another time with her mother and friends at Victor Hugo's, a popular supper club in the heart of Beverly

Hills. But the first time we actually met was the day I visited my lover Eleanor Powell on the set of *Broadway Melody of 1938*. It turned out to be Judy's fifteenth birthday. We were introduced. I thought she was full of beans, but she seemed a child.

In 1940, exactly a year before Pearl Harbor, I married Marylou Simpson, a Los Angeles debutante and an aspiring actress. It was also the year Judy Garland's engagement to musician/composer David Rose was announced. "I'm Always Chasing Rainbows" was a hit song, and Judy's rendition of the Chopin melody lifted by songwriter Harry Carroll seemed to be playing everywhere. Three MGM films starring Judy Garland were box office successes throughout the nation: *Andy Hardy Meets Debutante*, costarring Mickey Rooney; *Strike Up the Band*, directed by Busby Berkeley; and *Little Nellie Kelly*, in which Judy played both the child and the mother (George Murphy's wife). She was allowed to grow up in this film.

I understood it's not the content that's so important for an artist as much as how the artist uses it. That's the difference between a genius and somebody who has some talent. Judy was a good example of genius. She performed in ordinary story lines, but the one distinguishing element was her tremendous gift: she was a great lyric reader and had the natural ability to coordinate her dance skills with her acting and voice. There was a reason George and Ira Gershwin, as well as Irving Berlin, wrote songs especially for her.

The second time I met Judy was several years later, when I joined Peter Lawford at the Hillcrest bowling alley, near the Beverly Wilshire Hotel. Judy was part of the gang. By then I was married to Lynn Bari and Judy to Vincente Minnelli. She wore bobby socks and saddle shoes, reflecting the juvenile image she projected to the public.

I was not at first attracted to her. Anita Loos said, "Gentlemen marry brunettes," which was certainly true in my case. When I fell in love I got married. I thought my wives sophisticated, glamorous types, not wholesome apple-pie girls. So Judy Garland was not an erotic fantasy. How could it occur to me our lives would in any way be connected?

And yet some invisible cord was shortening with every contact, no matter how casual or distant the meeting.

———— ⌇⌇ ————

The McLean brothers, whom I was meeting for lunch that day in September 1950, shuttled between Palm Beach, New York, and Hollywood. Eastern Seaboard playboys, they came from a wealthy family that had owned the *Washington Post*, among other assets. Their mother, Evalyn, was eccentric, famous for owning the Hope Diamond. Neddie and Jock were constantly attempting to interest their pal Henry Ford II in putting up money for one thing or another. The brothers smarted from Henry's refusals, as though someone had spanked them. Now, at the 21 Club over a London broil, they were attempting to persuade me to invest in a cemetery on Long Island. I told them, holding back the laughter, that maybe it was the way I grew up but the idea depressed me. Neddie and Jock seemed dejected by my negative response, but I suggested they keep me in mind for something else.

I proceeded to tell them about my deal, *Man o' War*. I would be meeting with Ted Law, a Texas oilman, in Saratoga the following week to shoot sample footage. Ted, who was my partner in Walfarms, our stable outside of Los Angeles, was also one of the investors in *Man o' War*. I'd arranged for jockeys Eddie Arcaro and Sam Renick to ride, and we were going to re-create the 1919 Sanford Stakes, an allegedly fixed race that Man o' War lost to the racehorse Upset. It was the only race that Man o' War ever lost. I held Neddie and Jock's interest through another martini, but I could see the idea of a racetrack movie didn't thrill them as much as a cemetery. We made a golf date for later on in the month and went our separate ways.

That Saturday night, I took a date to Billy Reed's Little Club in the East Fifties and ran smack into screenwriter Freddie Finklehoffe sipping daiquiris with the "national asset," Judy Garland. Oh, I thought, she's left Lake Tahoe. Judy looked very different from the last time we'd met in the Beverly Hills bowling alley. Freddie, who was a pal of mine, would have to say hello and introduce me to Judy. And Freddie could be extremely territorial.

I'd become drinking buddies with him as a result of a bet. We both used to hang out at Ciro's, an "in" watering hole on the Sunset Strip, but somehow we'd never talked to one another. Then one day as I was leaving for the Santa Anita track, Freddie asked if I'd place a bet for him. I did, and he won a considerable amount of money. Freddie was very impressed. By 1950 we'd shared a few adventures.

Harvard-educated, small, bookish, Freddie dressed in a sort of sloppy, Ivy League fashion as opposed to my Savile Row style. He covered his prematurely balding pate with a jauntily worn fedora, giving him a devil-may-care appearance. Freddie had worshipped Judy from the early MGM years, when he wrote and collaborated on many of her films, including *Strike Up the Band*, *Babes on Broadway*, *For Me and My Gal*, *Girl Crazy*, and *Meet Me in St. Louis*.

Everyone who worked with Judy respected her talent, and most everyone, including Freddie, was a little in love with her. Judy could memorize a script in one read, dance after simply watching the choreography, and perform in front of the camera in one take. In those years her coworkers were in awe. Joe Pasternak, who produced *Summer Stock*, said, "Judy Garland half dead was better than anyone else."

At the moment Freddie was not happy. In the middle of a divorce from singer Ella Logan, he was actually going with a beautiful blonde, whom he eventually married. But for a long time he'd had a crush on Judy, whom he called "chocolate drop." Their relationship was more of a hallucination on Freddie's part, mesmerized as he was by Judy's talent. It was one of those mythical romances.

Shortly before I left for New York I'd been out drinking with Freddie in Los Angeles. Just as Judy was finished with MGM, her manager, Carlton Alsop, whom Judy called "Pa," was also leaving Hollywood, this time for good. His marriage to the actress Sylvia Sidney was ending, and as an ex-CIA man he was returning to Washington. Freddie knew Carlton was eager to sell his black Cadillac, and I wanted to buy it. So we went over to Carlton's house for a late drink. I paid Carlton cash for his Cadillac, "the black teardrop job," and he gave me the keys. There were other people around, enjoying themselves. At one point Carlton left the party room with a young woman. When it came time to go I looked around to say good-bye and wish Carlton luck, but we couldn't find him. Freddie and I left the house by way of the front door. On our way out I spotted Carlton under the dining room table making love to his date, a young woman who went on to marry a Heinz, of ketchup fame.

Alsop was a rangy man with longish, blond hair, a deep baritone voice, and a twinkle in his eye. He was an articulate person who seemed to be interested in producing films, although I never quite knew what Carlton did other than that he had personally managed Judy Garland in her later career at MGM. When I bought his Cadillac, I was unaware that the previous year he had been by Judy's side in Boston, during her hospitalization at the Peter Bent Brigham hospital, a wing of the Harvard Medical Center.

When I actually fell in love with Judy, I knew nothing of her medical history other than her recent problems at MGM. Apparently Judy had ignored her doctor's advice and left the hospital too soon. She was feeling so much better and was eager to return to work. She shot *Summer Stock*, but she hadn't confronted her substance abuse; right in the middle of work on her next film, *Royal Wedding*, she broke with MGM forever due to irreconcilable differences. Again, the rigors of staying "camera slim" became the excuse to return to medication—Judy's direct path to chaos. Only in rare situations was she ever able to acknowledge the toxic effect of pills on her nervous system.

At the Little Club in New York City, Freddie reluctantly invited me to sit down. I demurred and thanked him, explaining I was about to leave the club with my date. But I sensed a kind of electrical force coming from the small, voluptuous Garland. She was glowing like a ripened cherry in the smoke-filled martini atmosphere. Judy's brown-black eyes were made up to appear even larger, and they caught me in a kind of fierce, laughing eye contact. I noticed her hair was cut unconventionally short, like a boy's, creating a disarming contrast. The plunging neckline on her black cocktail dress revealed alabaster white skin, and she wore ruby red lipstick. I thought her lips were more beautiful than Hedy Lamarr's.

I remembered the reaction I had when I saw Judy in *For Me and My Gal* in 1942, costarring with Gene Kelly. She appeared glamorous to me for the first time, only to have MGM return her to the Miss Wholesome America image. Of course, there was a war on, and she was more valuable to the studio as a morale booster than as a sexpot. In Hollywood, sexpots were a dime a dozen.

Judy's eyes darted all over me, through me. I hovered at the table locked into some sort of unexpected mutual attraction, which left Freddie muttering under his breath. When I returned to my date I felt as though I'd been through something I didn't quite understand. Judy's eyes coming on, her sensual lips, the small sleek head, the round, alabaster breasts showing off, all of it a heady potion to swallow.

The next day Freddie called me at the Hotel Ritz Carlton, where I was staying. "Join us tonight?" Judy and several friends—all men, as it would turn out—were planning to hear Billy Daniels sing at the Riviera Club in New Jersey. Without hesitation I said, "Sure."

Freddie explained Judy was on her own, although she was still married to Vincente Minnelli. She was staying at the Hotel Carlyle along with two attendants and her four-year-old daughter, Liza. I said, "Isn't it strange you coauthored *Meet Me in St. Louis*, which Minnelli directed, now six years later Judy's left MGM, Vincente's preparing *An American in Paris*, and neither of you are involved in the production?"

"And Sid," came Freddie's response, "neither of us gives a fuck."

That night Judy's limo picked me up in front of the hotel. She looked as glamorous as she had the night before. The two of us carried on a banter that excluded everyone. It drove Freddie crazy. I'd attempt to include others in the conversation, but Judy would find a way to single me out. I could tell it was a game. Again, her eyes were seductively penetrating.

Later, I was to become conscious of her eyes in other ways. When our relationship eventually developed into a commitment, I could detect

Judy's pill intake by their expression, the pupils changing like a cat's in the noonday sun. They would seem to cast long shadows as easily as the brilliant sparks that were flying over the table at the Riviera club. In the background there were the sound of altercations, disgruntled customers requiring "good" tables busily stuffing bills in the captain's pocket, but we only had eyes for each other. We'd already had our photographs taken by news photographers who waited at the door for celebrities.

Freddie was so jealous it was funny. He was warning Judy, "Watch out for this guy." He didn't have to worry. I was not going to run after Judy Garland, the big movie star who was a little cuckoo, a little exotic. But when I sat down next to her I thought, *I'm going to help her.* I don't know why I thought that. I saw her profile, and I caught a certain look in those eyes, so beautiful and yet so sad. My head was full of thoughts. It was, in any case, out of my hands. And it definitely was out of Freddie Finklehoffe's, because Judy had already taken aim.

Back in the hotel, I read the newspapers, smoked, and roamed about in my pajamas. I couldn't get Judy's image out of my mind. I kept seeing her small hands, the unpolished nails short and smooth, the better to run her fingers through her hair, which she frequently did. With tiny feet in very high heels, she was barely five feet tall. Her legs were very developed, shapely, and she had a rhythmic kind of walk. Her voice was melodic, with a hypnotic effect, just like when she performed. Not self-conscious either.

All of this would have been of no consequence had she not focused her attention so exclusively on me, and had I not been so taken in. She had cast a spell, no question. I was certainly not wishing for any kind of involvement. I was not rushing into anything except the door of my hotel room, anxious to leave my $300 custom-made shoes out in the hallway to be shined. I took a deep drag on a Chesterfield, slammed down a shot of Jack Daniels, and went to sleep.

———— ◦≈≈◦ ————

A few days later I picked up my date at a Broadway theater where she'd been performing. We were on our way to a party at Jackie Gleason's apartment when the Checker cab got caught in a nasty traffic jam. We were stopped near the Capitol Theatre's big neon lights beaming *Summer Stock*. It was the sort of movie I rarely watched: Judy allows her sister to use Judy's barn for a summer theater; Judy not only falls in love with the lead actor (Gene Kelly) but becomes a performer herself. Movie houses were not doing well that summer, but *Summer Stock* was pulling in the crowds because of Garland. Judy performed a memorable routine wearing a tuxedo jacket, black tights, high heels, and nothing else but a man's felt hat pulled over her brow. It was styled like an early Eleanor Powell production number.

"What's the holdup?" I asked the driver.

"Judy Garland," he answered. "She's in a car by the Winter Garden at Fifty-First. I just came from there. Fans stopped her."

I had a visceral response. "Is she OK?"

My date observed my interest, saying, "I didn't know you were such a Garland fan!"

I waited for the answer from the cabbie: "Yeah. She loves it." The driver talked like a relative. "She's signing autographs out the car window."

Edward Albee, the American playwright, would later remember:

> Once upon a time. . . . I was sitting in the balcony of what was probably the Capitol Theatre, in New York, watching a Judy Garland movie which my memory tells me was *Summer Stock*. . . . When Garland finished singing, the audience watching that film was breathless for a moment and then, to a person, burst into sustained applause . . . Nothing has instructed and gratified me more than the time she convinced a bunch of afternoon movie watchers that a strip of celluloid was the real thing.

After our previous meeting, Judy had asked me to ring her at the Carlyle. I was attracted, perhaps too much, and so I'd managed to put off the telephone call. When I finally did place the call one night, I didn't get through. It was very late, and I'd been drinking at the Russian Bear. A scuffle ensued and I found myself in a brawl outside the club. My expensive watch was lost in the melee. Pulling myself together, I rang Judy at the Carlyle again, and this time I got through. She was incredibly supportive of my woes and immediately left her hotel and came to assist me in searching for my watch. We found it—crushed to bits. We laughed and went over to the St. Regis for a nightcap. We made a date, but it got postponed, and we hadn't talked since.

When the cab finally got through the traffic jam and arrived at Jackie Gleason's, I saw Judy was there. I thought, *My date is going to discover I'm a fan.* Once again, Judy focused on me and excluded the rest of the world. She was enjoying the game. Judy found a way to keep dancing with me, and we danced well together. (I had been well trained by Eleanor Powell.)

Now we were making another late night rendezvous. MGM had assigned a driver to Judy who, at three in the morning, cheerily took us wherever we wanted to go. Judy was wearing one of her plunging-neckline black cocktail dresses and a black onyx ring with a pearl in the center. I again noticed her hands, which will forever remind me of Willie Shoemaker's—small and strong. She also wore a gold chain bracelet with a mesh charm containing a lucky penny.

"That's not the bracelet Gable gave you on your fifteenth birthday?"

"How'd you know?"

"I was on the set the day of your birthday. You were showing it off to everyone, including me."

"Showing off anything else?"

"No."

"Well, I'm sorry, Mr. Luft, I don't remember you."

Judy looked fresh, as though she was starting out the evening. "I know a place you'll like," she said.

It was an after-hours club in a Midtown brownstone, a duplex, posh and dark. When we came in, Johnny Mercer was playing the piano. He was another golf buddy of mine from the California Country Club, where I'd been in the habit of going immediately after knocking off work in midafternoon when I was a test pilot for Douglas Aircraft. Judy sat down next to Johnny and began to sing with him.

Standing by the piano was an obnoxious patron. He was drunk and proceeded to insult Judy. I would never instigate anything, but it wasn't in my nature to ignore a slur, drunk or sober. It was a holdover from my old barroom habit of belting anyone who was unduly offensive. In this case, I could see the owner was aware that the man was bothering other patrons, so I wrestled him to the exit and threw him down the stairs.

"What did you do?" Judy giggled.

"I threw him out." She loved it—here was someone willing to protect her on the spot. Punch and Judy!

Judy and I knew many people in common, including Roger Edens. MGM's musical supervisor was perhaps the single most creative influence in her life, at once both a mentor and a disciple. I told Judy how Roger, who was also a close friend of Eleanor Powell's, would insist on driving me home from parties if he thought I drank too much. This was before the war, and Desi Arnaz was my neighbor at the time. Desi, a highly charged person, had a lot of charm. His energy overwhelmed me. He laughed a lot with his hands, and I had the impression he never heard anything I said. Desi wasn't your average bongo player. It seemed he was on a fast escalator moving up, while I was on the one that got stuck. One night Roger was dragging me up the stairs to my apartment and Desi happened to be getting in at the same early hour. He glanced over, and despite my debilitated condition I noticed he was speechless at the sight. He wondered what I was doing with Roger, who was known to be gay.

"He should've known the difference," Judy flirted when I told her this story. We had left the after-hours club on foot just before dawn. The car trailed us as we walked along Fifth Avenue, window shopping. The stores were filled with merchandise, the New Look—Dior's invention—and other goods the likes of which we hadn't seen for over a decade.

It was postwar, rebirth. I was thirty-four and Judy was twenty-seven. I'd been married twice. Judy was on her second marriage. She had married Vincente when she was twenty-four and he was forty-two.

As we strolled the avenue, Judy would take my arm or we'd hold hands. It was warm, affectionate. I sensed that she was emotionally tied up. She'd indicated that she and Vincente were not getting along—he was a company man, he couldn't "protect" her. I wasn't sure what she meant by "protect." She never said she didn't love him, but she was testing the waters.

"Where do you get *your* clothes?" Judy asked.

I explained how Leonora Luft, my mother, had weaned me on hand-tailored suits—handmade everything, in fact—a habit I never kicked.

We sat for a moment in the square at the Plaza. Judy said she'd never felt more free. We continued to hold hands, and she rested her head on my shoulder. Judy Garland was not usually allowed to go anywhere, because she would be mobbed by fans; it was not possible for her to take a walk, to shop. But the world was empty now except for us, and we seemed to be filling the space pretty good.

I later learned that Judy's personal makeup assistant Dottie Ponedel wrote about this episode in her unpublished book. "Judy ran in [to the Carlyle Hotel]. . . . 'Dottie, I met a guy, Sid Luft, and I'm in love and I'm going to have him. You see, Dottie, he was a pilot like your husband, and I'm going to see him again tonight.'"

2

AFTER DAVID ROSE, Judy had gone through crushes and love affairs and wound up married to Vincente Minnelli, a creative, self-absorbed person who was apparently not able to focus his life around her. In my case, I'd felt I'd fucked up with Marylou, I'd fucked up with Lynn. These were fabulous failures in that they could have been repaired if I'd been so motivated. My gut feeling had been that these relationships were not destined to succeed. Lynn loved me but did not believe in me. I knew she would be difficult if and when I fell in love again. She was a vindictive person. Lynn was separated from her first husband when we met, and she was determined to leave him; she hated him. Whereas, clearly, Judy did not hate Vincente.

Judy introduced me to her favorite bistro, Charles à la Pomme Soufflée. It was our first formal date. I picked her up around eight and was presented to her entourage: Liza, who was an adorable four-year-old with huge, luminous eyes, and "Tully," who was married to Jim Tully, the so-called "hobo writer." She was a wonderful, warm woman, as devoted to Judy as was Dottie Ponedel, who did her makeup and had replaced Judy's mother in her affections.

Judy had made a reservation and preordered the menu, which included coq au vin. The management was well prepared. We were seated in a booth and given the royal treatment. It was romantic: candlelight and flowers. After a bottle of Dom Perignon, Judy said softly, "I was told about you, Sid."

Encouraging her, I said, "Tell me about it."

Again in her irresistibly melodic voice: "You're a very tough guy." Then she added, "But a very well-dressed tough guy."

I could see Judy was serious in her lighthearted way. "You mean I'm a guy who flies off the handle as a way of life? Do I have to belt guys to know I exist?"

"Yeah," she said, her eyes telling me lots of other things.

"Well, I couldn't turn the other cheek—I'm not Jesus Christ, I'm another kind of Jew."

"You do have a reputation around town." She sipped her champagne. "Freddie warned me to stay away from you."

We laughed at that. "Judy," I said, "I've been in at least a dozen fights on the Strip, or in nightclubs. It's not in my nature to let an insult slide by." I explained I was from the rough-and-tumble school. Since childhood I'd always been attracted to what society would label macho interests: Wrong Way Corrigan was my hero. I respected derring-do. I hadn't been a test pilot for nothing. And I'd had my share of publicity in Hollywood. I was a sitting duck for gossip columnists. I knew it was a hype, and deep down I wasn't interested in whether the press presented me as Mr. Nice Guy. I wasn't running for political office.

"I think you're nice, Sid. How about going to El Morocco?"

Patrons were squashed against the Morocco's purple velvet ropes, and the waiters kept bringing out tables, reducing the dance floor to a dime. We danced until it was not wise to hold one another in public. I wasn't eager to be pegged Judy's "boyfriend," which, of course, is what happened anyhow.

Later, over a coffee at the Brasserie, she explained she'd been working on the film of the Broadway hit *Annie Get Your Gun* when she was overcome with insecurities, insomnia, and a general state of anxiety that she felt was irreversible. She was taken off the film and admitted to the hospital, and she'd been replaced by an old friend of mine, Betty Hutton.

After Judy returned from the Peter Bent Brigham hospital in Boston, feeling wonderful, she was asked to lose weight. That meant not eating. She wasn't going to take pills anymore, and this was a problem, so in part of *Summer Stock* she appears round and in another part she looks thin. "Couldn't control my appetite to their requirements. Then they took me off *Royal Wedding*. At which point I made a scene." I knew she was referring to the scratch on the neck reported as a suicide attempt. "Of course, it was the wrong thing to do. Such ominous reports: 'It remains to be seen if she ever faces the camera again.'" She dropped her voice to a sort of bogeyman tone. "So I went to Lake Tahoe for a vacation."

"And New York," I added. "Very much New York, and very much a vacation." I felt this tremendous wave of caring. I wanted to keep her from harm's way. I looked at the young woman—a robust, high-spirited, hearty, strong person who was clearly not on any kind of medication. It didn't occur to me she should curb her appetite in any way. I agreed with Judy that nonstop performing in front of the camera could be a terrible pressure to withstand. I never took pills myself. I enjoyed booze, but it was generally in a social context.

Judy had represented the home front, worked in uplifting films, sung chin-up, hope-filled tunes for a country that was losing its youth to a cruel war. Not to mention the bond tours, propaganda for Roosevelt, entertaining the boys. All this while I'd been testing aircraft for Douglas and flying for the Royal Canadian Air Force, delivering bombers to Europe and Russia. I thought, hell, I survived two marriages. And I was still young. I'd gotten through the insanity of the war. It was a new decade, and I was allowing myself to believe in the possibility of a new life.

Judy asked me so many questions. She was clever in extracting information. There were moments I thought she might open up, tell me what was true. I'd noticed the fine scar lines on the inside of her wrists and I thought, well, she has really harmed herself to some degree. Somehow I wasn't able to ask her about those tracks. It was simply inappropriate. And if I mentioned her mother, Ethel, she'd switch the subject. It was easy for her to redirect: she merely had to hold me in a long gaze. I knew nothing about the inner machinations of Judy's life. As we sat together in the middle of the night in a public yet sequestered niche of the Brasserie, I listened to Judy talk, in the most general terms, about events leading up to the present moment.

It would take some years before she recorded, in her unfinished autobiography, what actually had happened the year before we came together:

> My mother called me at night many times and said, in a very quiet voice, [that she thought] I had a brain tumor and the only chance I had would be to have an operation. I never heard from my sisters. I never heard from anybody, except for Carlton [Alsop] and [his wife,] Sylvia [Sidney]. They were really standing by, since I had been ill; Carlton was there all the time. This was after he had worked at the studio. But he believed in me, and he hated what they were doing to me. I was fired from *Barkleys of Broadway*. Sylvia took me down into her house on Beverly Drive, because that house on the hill was so lonely, and she moved me into her bed and cooked for me and fed me and, you know, was wonderful to me. Carlton too, but the press kept pounding away at me every day in the newspapers and on the front page.
>
> One day I thought, between the calls from my mother, no help from my husband, [Vincente Minnelli,] no telephone calls from a soul, I thought, I can't take it anymore. So I, in a burst of complete irrationality . . . it was morning, right after the morning papers had come in and nobody was there. So, I went in the bathroom and I took a razor . . . I went into bed and laid down, and I got weaker, weaker . . . there was blood all over the place and so the cook happened to come in. . . . I wanted to go to sleep. I just wanted to go to sleep. And so she was horrified, she called the doctor. . . . There were a series of doctors and he came up and . . . the nurse got in touch with Carlton and Vincente and anyway they kept me out of the hospital and there was no publicity about it. . . .
>
> I suffered a terrific feeling of guilt and awful shame after trying that, because actually I didn't want to die. I had a baby to live for. It was just that the pressure had been too much for a minute. [In

hindsight Judy was suffering from postpartum depression along with a dependency on pills.] I'd heard this doctor say that I was "suicidal." My mother said there was something wrong with my brain. It was just too much for me.

Jimmy Tarantino in the *Hollywood Nightlife* started calling me a dope addict. It was a little scandal sheet in town, but it was a rotten thing in this town, because people really stayed away from me, as though I were a leper then. Of course, the first thing Carlton said: "You've got to get out of this house and you've got to go right down to Romanoff's with me for lunch and walk in and just face the whole damn town and let them see you, because you look fine and let them know that you're not some kind of a nut the way they've printed in the papers," and so he started taking me out . . . three or four days later. I was wearing tall collars. We walked into Romanoff's . . . but nobody would come to our table. When I walked in there'd be a kind of a hush that would fall over the room. The only one who would come to the table who was marvelous was Mike [Romanoff]. And he always came over and never mentioned anything. His expression for me was "great dame."

I kept going out and Carlton and Sylvia were tremendous help for me. Eventually Metro called me in and said how do you feel and I said I feel great. I didn't. I still wasn't right. I hadn't had my year or six months off. . . . I weighed about a hundred pounds. They informed me they bought *Annie Get Your Gun* for me. There was an enormous banter, because MGM paid more money for that than they had ever paid for any property to date. Irving Berlin came out and there was pictures in all the papers and big announcements with Berlin and [Arthur] Freed and myself—I was going to do *Annie Get Your Gun.*

I started rehearsal and I was still very tired and a very distressed woman. The first thing that happened was I started to lose my hair. My hairline started to recede badly. I went to the rehearsals and the costume fittings and unfortunately they put Buzz Berkeley on the picture. I think he's a wonderful director. I think he did a fine job with the earlier pictures but psychologically Buzz Berkeley represented all of the years of Benzedrine, to work as hard as we could, and just exhaustion. To tell the truth he was in a very bad mental state himself doing *Annie Get Your Gun.*

I said, "I don't think we're a very good combination right now," but they said, "Oh, we know what we're doing, you just do as you're told." So we started the picture and we did a couple of scenes and I knew I wasn't good. The prerecordings were pretty good. But I was just in a daze. My head wouldn't stop aching. . . . They called a new doctor in, Fred Pobirs. He walked in the room and I was sitting there, very charming and really with the birds. Pobirs took one look at me and decided on shock treatment for me.

I went through a series of twelve shock treatments and it brought me out of it just fine, and after that I went with a nurse and my baby [Liza] and secretary to Sun Valley for a week, then I went to Lake Tahoe for a week, then I came home. I had put on maybe five or eight pounds but again I was back on pills for *Annie Get Your Gun.* . . . At any rate I went through it and we started to shoot and I was very bad. I wasn't good and I knew it. I was really pitiful, because they had to keep putting black in my hairline because of my hair falling out badly and I had these heavy costumes and trying to play a terribly funny role. I kept plugging away and . . . I'm an Indian girl. Bob Alton was directing and I started being late again. I didn't know what the hell I was doing. I didn't know, and I was trying to take direction from both Buzz Berkeley and Bob Alton and all of the music and the costumes and the chorus boys and everything were confusing me. I had a migraine headache constantly. So I went back to my dressing room one day for lunch and they had evidently looked at the rushes and I wasn't good, I was being late, so they sent me another notice dismissing me at noontime. I really blew my top. [MGM publicist] Les Peterson, that rat, came to the door saying here's a message for you. I opened it and read it. It said don't bother to report back to work after lunch because you are dismissed from the picture.

They put Betty Hutton in the picture. By then I decided to go to Boston but I didn't have the money. After so many years at Metro, perhaps they'll lend me the money to get well. . . . I went to Louis Mayer's office and told him that I felt I had to go to Boston, and he agreed. [Mayer's personal physician] Jessie Marmorston and Carlton accompanied me, and Louie B. said, "That's the least we can do for you is to pay for your hospital bills . . ." To clear it he picked up the phone, confident, and talked to Mr. [Nicholas] Schenck [president of Loew's, parent company of MGM]. He put the phone down. "Mr. Schenck suggests you go to a charity hospital, because we're not in the money lending business." He looked at me, I'll never forget what he said, he said, "You know, if they do this to you, they'll do it to me too."

Louis got the train tickets for Carlton and myself. . . . He would go with me to Boston so I wouldn't have to go all by myself. He [Mayer] said send all your bills to me. [MGM paid the hospital expenses: $40,000.]

All of these tests had to be made and no one called, except Frank Sinatra. He sent flowers every day and so forth. It was very sweet, as he is with all his people. But anyway he was very kind, he sent a record player and records and flowers and bed jackets and perfume and all kinds of stuff.

Carlton was standing by every day and it was summertime in Boston and boy it was hot. And all he had to do was either stay at the hospital during visiting hours or sit in that hotel. We came to the last test and they said we're going to take an electro-encephalogram. I thought oh my God, I've passed all the tests, now they're going to record my brain and they're going to get down on paper my thoughts. I'm a dead pigeon because they'll never let me out of here. . . .

I was in Boston four months. In the meantime, one day Frank did bring a lot of people up to see me. I got well enough to have a press reception at the hotel.

I didn't hear from my mother or my sisters. I heard from Vincente. Carlton and I would go on visits for the weekend, we'd go to different people's houses. They finally said I could go on a two- or three-week holiday on Cape Cod. My little girl [Liza] was with me.

Hugh Martin, who had done the songs for *Meet Me in St. Louis*, had a show, *Best Foot Forward*, running in a little theater on Cape Cod. We all went over to the theater, and of course Hugh was playing the piano—they didn't have an orchestra, it was just a little road company. And the lights went on and there I was. Hugh and the whole cast just about died. We went out into the garden afterwards, where we had hot dogs, and then Hugh asked if I would sing for them. I hadn't sung in four months. It was the first time in years that I really felt good. I had weight on me, I was sleeping and eating, I felt marvelous. I started to sing and I discovered an entirely new voice: a much more powerful voice. I've had that voice ever since.

All night long we continued to exchange stories about our past (though some were edited). A few of my tales struck Judy as hilarious, and she'd giggle or chortle, which was infectious, and soon we'd both be laughing uncontrollably as though we'd been smoking grass. She told me that in 1940 there'd been a kidnap threat against her. A young man, Robert Wilson (she'd not forgotten the name), had phoned the Los Angeles Police Department and threatened to kidnap her unless a ransom of $50,000 was handed over. Thursday was the maid's day off, and Wilson and a friend were planning on breaking into her home on Stone Canyon Road in Bel Air. A teenage Judy had commissioned the home in 1938 and lived there for nearly a decade with her mother. Apparently the police captain arrested the boy right where he was calling from. "Imagine what kind of condition I'd be in if I'd ever been kidnapped!" She was sardonic.

Judy talked about her early years at MGM with Mickey Rooney. She said in her mid-to-late teens she was obsessed by boys. She'd had a romantic nature, and neither her mother nor the moguls could subdue her imagination. She wrote poetry to express her passions. They couldn't keep her altogether a performing slave. Mickey had taught Judy to play

Ping-Pong. And she was a good player, but Mickey was table tennis champ from 1935 to 1940 in California.

Judy and Mickey were shipped out on promotional tours, going from theater to theater. Tumultuous crowds waited for them. There were autographs to be signed, executives to meet, theater owners to be courted, luncheons, and press interviews, and their health was constantly threatened by overwork.

Judy loved Mickey, but they were never boyfriend and girlfriend. Having known Mickey from my early years in Hollywood, I knew he went for the glamour gals, like Ava Gardner, who later became one of his wives. Mickey's mother would have preferred her son to love and marry someone like Judy. Mickey was multitalented like Judy. And they were very much like brother and sister, equal in every way—except in the salaries they received. Mickey earned three times more per picture than Judy, and eventually he quit MGM to form his own company.

Back in my suite at the Ritz Carlton, in the early morning light, everything I thought about Judy began to take on a definite shape. Her hair was silky, very fine on her forehead. Touching her continued to be altogether a new experience. Her white skin seemed to wrap around her limbs like satin. At the same time, there was nothing unformed about Judy: Her body had musculature. Judy was self-conscious about her shoulders, which she considered too round. Her legs were hard, and long for her size. She was short waisted, had full breasts with strong nipples. Other than her skin and her hair, she was not soft.

It was her enormous rib cage that gave her the advantage while performing—all the juice came from there. She was never to be winded onstage when at times, by all appearances, she might have been the walking dead. Her voice was bell-like, whether she was acting, reading a script, or just chatting. Her dialogue was thought out and very definite. She was not lazy in her speech. I could never mistake anything she said or did. Judy did not sound like any other woman, nor, as I would find out, did she make love like any other woman.

Unlike my soon-to-be ex-wife, Lynn, who put down my projects, Judy was interested, especially about *Man o' War*. She knew nothing about horses, and the idea of owning a stable as a business intrigued her. I told her the common perception that a person must be a millionaire to own horses was false. This was the beginning of her fascination with jockeys, racehorses, and people who are attracted to the world of racing. I'd have preferred to tell Judy of my exploits as a macho bomber pilot. Instead she wanted to hear about horses.

———— ⌾ ————

Judy's entrance to what Walter Winchell called the "New York-iest" spot, the Stork Club, was equal to a coronation. First an army would lead us to our seats. Owner Sherman Billingsley would send over champagne, along with French perfume that Judy would keep for Tully and Dottie. She had her own preferences, two different musky scents: Balmain's spicy Vent Vert and Patou's Joy, heavy with jasmine.

Billingsley was quite a tyrant. He had a famous ongoing feud with Toots Shor, and he had eighty-sixed Jackie Gleason and Humphrey Bogart from the club. The Stork was later to take a dive from which it would never recover when Billingsley refused to serve Josephine Baker in 1951, an incident that grew into a widely publicized scandal.

I was becoming restless under the glare, and we decided to leave the Stork for Harlem to listen to blues. In the car, her eyes pinning me, Judy said, "Sid darling, you do know I'm a black Irish witch?"

"Baby," I said, "I know you're not Dorothy from the Yellow Brick Road." We were both bombed while making an attempt to appear sober.

"Darling, say 'darling'?" she asked.

"I'd rather hear about the black Irish witch."

"Say 'darling' first."

"Darling," I groaned.

"*Hnnn.* That's awful."

"Can we work on it later?"

———— ⌾ ————

As the nights passed, we continued to dance, talk, and hold hands. We'd count per minute the smoke rings coming out of the Camel billboard sign at Times Square, usually en route to an exclusive nightspot where Judy was greeted like royalty. Chocolate mousse cake at Chauveron, the Latin Quarter, Voisin, Chambord: we were everywhere, laughing, dancing, drinking. Manhattan, or Gotham, as some columnists preferred to call New York City, was alive with the new chic. From the clank of the Third Avenue El so near to P. J. Clarke's to the cheerful, reassuring red double-decker buses on Fifth Avenue, life was a bowl of cherries with a few diamonds thrown in.

Underlying the social activity was an intense subtext of sexual attraction, but neither of us were about to act upon it. I wasn't going to wake up at the Carlyle in Judy's bed, and she wasn't going to wake up at the Ritz Carlton in mine. She was too famous, and too married.

Our dating was primarily in the evening so that I was free during the day to work. I had managed, however, to manipulate my project, *Man o' War*, into our "fling."

Tully would call in advance to set up the evening. And so a dinner had been arranged at Seymour and Eleanor Lambert Berkson's elegant Upper East Side apartment. Judy had cultivated the friendship with the Berksons through Vincente. Seymour was the publisher of the *New York Journal-American*, and Eleanor was a fashion authority, creator of the Best Dressed List. Clearly, Judy admired the Berksons' sophistication.

That night I was to meet Judy at the Berksons' apartment. One of the big pop song hits that year was Anton Karas's theme from the film *The Third Man*. It had a hypnotic effect, and it seemed to be following me through airports, taxi rides, even floating up to where I sat in the Fifth Avenue double-decker bus on the way to the Berksons'. I was beginning to feel wonderful. Judy bolstered my spirits. She seemed very different from Lynn, who was a tall, sultry, attractive woman. Lynn remained a "good joe," but her negativity about my work had come between us.

I had agreed to the evening at the Berksons, but I wasn't comfortable. There was too much chatter about the black poodle that ran away and, of course, Vincente. Seymour wasn't enthralled by my presence either, although later we did become friends. The apartment was spacious, beautifully decorated, with a butler and a maid in attendance. I didn't know anyone. I didn't even know Judy that well. It was a sit-down dinner. I suppose Judy wanted the Berksons to meet me. She ate very little of the fashionable menu: salmon mousse, rare roast beef, asparagus hollandaise, tiny potatoes, and, for dessert, cherries jubilee, Eleanor's favorite. The cherries jubilee was served flaming in highly polished silver goblets. (Eleanor frequently ordered the extravagant dessert when dining out; at a later date she was to watch a waiter flame the dish at her table and, unfortunately, drop dead when he inhaled the fumes. This incident may have changed her affection for the dessert.)

Aline de Romanones, a close friend of Eleanor's, was often a guest at the Berksons'. Aline was an American girl who married a Spanish count, became an agent for the OSS during the Second World War, and wrote the memoir *The Spy Wore Red*. She was present at Eleanor's table that night, and later I'd see her with the Duke and Duchess of Windsor. Laddie Sanford and Mary Lasker were there, part of the café society crowd that seemed to adore Judy. This group was not interested in horses. I was overly sensitive to the fact that these were Judy's friends with Vincente. The most exciting exchange I'd had all evening was with a gentleman who had fixated on my shoes and was interested to learn that they were custom made from a shop on Madison Avenue.

Judy and I had been in one another's company every night at one place or another, and after the Berksons' I thought it a good idea to change the pace. I took her back to her hotel instead of on to any of the clubs. My attitude was *Listen, baby, I've just gotten out of a marriage, you've got your own private army, but I'm not a walker.* The undercurrent of attraction was a good feeling, but in a few days I'd be in Saratoga shooting and the fling would have to wind down.

I strolled over to P. J. Clarke's to have a nightcap and think things over. For the past two decades Judy had been working in a glistening white tower, unskilled in life's ordinary aspects. Her least need had been provided for by servants, hairdressers, secretaries, agents, lawyers, and accountants—all the accoutrements of fame that I'd come to label "pop-ups." But it was a hothouse atmosphere that was presently chilling out. She'd been wined, dined, and indulged, and now she was more in the cold than she realized. MGM was only temporarily supplying the limos, along with the escorts she'd ditched to be with me.

Judy was not exhibiting any signs of rejection, however. She'd already disclosed bits and pieces of her MGM history. Apparently Louis B. Mayer didn't sign Judy at age thirteen for any particular project; he'd just heard her sing and signed her up. It was Roger Edens who had accompanied her on the piano for the final audition. After she appeared in *Every Sunday* in 1936, Edens arranged for her to sing on the popular Jack Oakie radio broadcast. A 20th Century Fox talent scout then borrowed Judy for *Pigskin Parade*. Edens wrote a special version of "You Made Me Love You" for Judy to sing to Clark Gable on his birthday. Metro had pushed Judy into *Broadway Melody of 1938*. In 1939 Arthur Freed wanted Judy to play Dorothy in *The Wizard of Oz* while Mayer preferred Shirley Temple, but 20th refused to loan Shirley and so Judy got the part. Although at the time the film played to mixed reviews, *Oz* has become an American classic. Judy's portrayal of the L. Frank Baum character has yet to be matched.

The mix of Judy's impish yet seductive charm was totally operative off screen as well. As I downed my last bourbon for the night, I thought, *Where is it built into a contract that a star must function in a society with which she has no practical understanding but paradoxically happens to be the focus of?* Certainly I'd perceived this fundamental split the year I worked as an agent for Zeppo Marx's theatrical agency.

I was now in the midst of a terrific lark with Judy Garland, movie star. She thinks I'm a big test pilot. She's clearly looking, and I'm on the rebound. I felt I'd been decent to Lynn, and she thought I was crazy to believe I could be a producer. Now Judy was saying, "I think you're great." She was pretty and wholesome and a lot of fun. This one doesn't want me, this one says, "Hey, you're some kind of guy. You're funny. What're you doin' tomorrow? Want to take me to dinner? Hey, give me a kiss." Judy's bubbly laugh was contagious, and her comic streak was completely natural. It was hard to believe someone so beautiful could be so funny.

We seemed to have the same kind of electrodes, and together we were making quite a spark around town. I was not about to walk away.

⸙

Edith Piaf, the "little sparrow," was in New York performing at the Versailles, backed up by nine male singers, Les Compagnons de la Chanson. The stage set of pink and white plaster representations of famous Paris landmarks somehow managed to look fancy and urbane. It was the start of Piaf's publicized romance with the French boxer Marcel Cerdan, who was very much married. She'd been in America shortly after the war ended and was not a success, but now she was playing to a sell-out crowd and rave reviews. The audience was filled with her peers: Judy, Marlene Dietrich, Charles Boyer.

Judy was eager to meet Piaf and congratulate her on her performance. As the divas embraced backstage, I was struck by the similarity: both were petite women with powerful voices and impassioned private lives. Yet Piaf was all soul, serious, life was not to be treated lightly; Judy would cheerfully kibitz with the audience and comment on issues the French generally held sacred. Judy interpreted the songs other people wrote, while Piaf sang songs she'd written alone or in collaboration. It was clear Judy not only admired other performers, she was genuinely entertained by them as well. If there was jealousy or competitiveness, it was not visible.

The following night, sitting in the red velour "Royale" section reserved for the elite at Le Pavillon, I mentally gave Judy a makeover. Her makeup was intense and to my mind not necessary. I thought the severe haircut intriguing but not soft enough for such an angelic face, and the pillbox hats could go too. I was never able to persuade her out of those: she even wore one to the premiere of our film *A Star Is Born*. (Maybe if they'd been called something else . . .)

Judy was content, munching away on the finest of gray caviar and sipping Dom Perignon, tokens of appreciation from chef Henri Soule, whose haughty air was misleading. Soule was to create the popular restaurant La Côte Basque, but he never considered it important or equal to his jewel, Le Pavillon. I was mesmerized by Judy that night, but time was running out. I needed to finish organizing a sound and camera crew for Saratoga. *I'm working*, I kept telling myself.

One afternoon, Bob Agins and I were going to take Judy out to the racetrack in Jamaica, Long Island. We arrived at the Carlyle to pick her up only to discover that Judy had somehow misunderstood the invitation and was prepared to leave with me for the island of Jamaica. She had in fact visited designer Hattie Carnegie and ordered various outfits she thought appropriate for the trip. The bills had been automatically sent on to California. Her relationship with MGM may have ended, but the world was at Judy Garland's feet and it was clear she assumed it would remain there. In reality, she owed the US government $80,000 and didn't know it.

The misunderstanding over the Jamaicas was an embarrassment for her. I just thought she was being funny, and off we went to the racetrack. It was much later that I realized in hindsight what an error of communication it had been: she was ready to be with me even at that early date, and at any cost.

Nevertheless, I left for Saratoga, and Judy returned to Hollywood. Our attraction for one another was accelerating, and my bill at the Madison Avenue florists was $700. Judy loved flowers, especially yellow roses.

PART II

The Boy from Bronxville

3

FRANCES ETHEL GUMM, a name that was to appear on sundry legal documents for most of my life, was born June 10, 1922, in Grand Rapids, Minnesota, the very year I achieved local notoriety as the sole witness to a payroll holdup in Bronxville, New York, where my father had a jewelry store. I was six years old, and my sister, Peri (Pearl in those days), was a year older. The Bronxville High School and Elementary School were under construction. The payroll office was located in a shack, where salaries were dispensed in cash. I've always had photographic sense: I look at colors and shapes and they imprint. And I happened to see the getaway car that held up the payroll office. I remembered two or three of the last digits of the license plate, plus the colors of the vehicle: a green touring car with a black top and black wire wheels. Actually, I had seen men go into the shack with guns. I'd been a bystander along with my sister, who didn't notice anything.

The police were there within minutes. I was able to go up to them and say, "I saw it." This was the Bronxville police's introduction to me. Over the years they would come to know me better.

Around 1924 we moved to Bronxville ourselves. A square mile with nothing left to build on, no land to develop, Bronxville was surrounded closely, on one side by Mt. Vernon, another by Yonkers, and another by Tuckahoe. Every inch was accounted for. Previously, my father, Norbert Luft, would commute to Bronxville from our home in Mt. Vernon. I remember going to kindergarten in a big sleigh with four donkeys, flying over snow, innocently pushing into a new society, an environment of elitism and racial hatred.

Father was a watchmaker, and he also sold fashionable jewelry. The customers entered from the arcade side. The glass partition featuring the sign NORBERT LUFT, JEWELER faced Kraft Avenue, a short street that started at the Bronxville River Parkway and ended at Pondfield Road.

Bronxville was an upper-class WASP community dominated by the Mudd and Rickenbacker families. Father's customers were bankers, stockbrokers, Wall Streeters who daily grabbed the half-hour ride into Grand Central Station. Bronxville had a population of about five thousand, a hardware store, a funeral parlor. There were two drugstores, one owned by Harry Liden and the other by our neighbors the Steinmans, and the Bronxville Hospital. On the opposite side of the train tracks was barren flatland.

Pondfield Road was the longest street in Bronxville. It crawled from Yonkers almost up to Sarah Lawrence College, through Bronxville to Post Road, cutting across the middle of the city. We had the last house on Kraft Avenue. Altogether there were three Jewish families in the vicinity. The Steinmans lived on the south side, right on the border of Mt. Vernon.

My mother, Leonora Luft, was born Lena Krasnakutsky. During the Russian pogroms she lived with a Meyers family; subsequently, when she came to America, she assumed their name. While Father called her Lena, the outer world knew her as Leonora. She was barely five feet tall, a little chunky, a very strong person. She was, you might say, a specialty.

Mother had come to America at the age of thirteen. She lived with her brother in the Bronx, where she found work in a blouse factory sewing on buttons. I never got to know her brother, my uncle, but he was famous for his daredevil antics. Once, back in Russia, he jumped off a roof on a dare and broke both legs. In New York he rode a motorcycle everywhere. When he got hurt in an accident his little boy, Max, spent a few months with us in Bronxville. If there was a wife, I didn't know her. I inherited a lot from this uncle I never knew. Cousin Maxie was a cute little six-year-old when he stayed with us on Kraft Avenue, but he was naughty by Luft standards. Maxie was wild and refused to mind Mother.

At the time, Mother was strictly a housewife devoted to the family. But that would soon end when she became dissatisfied with my father's earning capacity. She went into Manhattan, as the story goes, and on her own, visited some dress manufacturers. She told them where she lived and took a few dresses on consignment. Right away she sold one to my piano teacher, a French woman (I hated the piano and Peri loved it), and another to our neighbor Mrs. Steinman, whose husband owned the drugstore. Mother sold directly from the house. Within a month's time she knocked down one of the walls in a bedroom and had a long mirror and shelves installed, and hired a seamstress.

Mother had struck oil. There were no dress shops in Bronxville. Women had to travel to New Rochelle or Mt. Vernon to shop.

Six months later, mother opened her fashion boutique, Madame Leonora's, right in front of Alger Court next to the railway station: Bronxville, Fleetwood, Mt. Vernon, 125th Street, and Grand Central! About a year later, the railway company allowed the construction of more stores: a village tavern, a Buick agency with cars in the window, a large realty office. Madame Leonora's was right smack in the middle of the mini mall. All the storefronts faced the Bronxville Railway Station. A customer might step off the platform less than a hundred yards from Madame Leonora's. She eventually outgrew this space, and her next shop, designed by a German architect, was in Bronxville proper.

Leonora would dress women who didn't know how to dress. She would travel to Grasse in the south of France, where she'd mix her own perfume, "Leonora." She'd also bring back samples of fabric and dress designs to be made at the shop. She fashioned all the silk pajamas for composer Jerome Kern, who lived a block away from us. At the age of eight, I would personally deliver the clothes to his wife in my wooden car made out of an ash can and four wheels. I felt terribly important doing this. What a sight I must have been for clients, coming and going in that contraption.

My father was a good-looking man. He had grayish-green eyes; he was about five nine, medium build. Basically a mild-mannered fellow who spoke in a low tone with a hint of an Austrian accent. He never knew what to do with me.

When we lived on Kraft Avenue, I built a hut out of wood with some pals. We made a wooden chimney tall enough to stand up in. We had a door on the hut and a bench inside. We'd smoke cigarettes in there. We'd climb up into the chimney and peek out. Once I shot a kid in the ass with a BB gun (and my father had forbidden me to have a BB gun). The kid's father, a Hungarian, came to our house at night to see my father. I tried to explain to my father that we had to have the BB gun to protect our hut. I had warned the boy not to come near, but he started to turn around and I hit him. The kid was a big baby, I thought; he had to run home to show his father the blue mark on his behind. I certainly didn't feel I'd done anything wrong. My father bit his fingers so as not to hit me. I was all of eight years old.

Our gang also had a crank-up Model T Ford without tires. It was on rims. I wasn't strong enough to crank it alone. I'd advance the spark to get it going and control the ignition. And if I didn't get the handle in the right place, because of the compression, the cylinder would flip the starting device backward. It was in this way that I broke my thumb. There were a lot of kids walking around with broken thumbs. The Model T had a hell of a kick to it, and once we got it going we drove it all over the area. We had a swimming hole, the Model T, and the hut. That was our gang's world.

The drugstore owner's son, Freddy Steinman, was officially the first Fred in my life. Curiously, there were many Freds, and they all played pivotal roles. He was six months my senior and a good student, but he topped me as a hell-raiser. In the second grade I used to follow him around. One afternoon we ran away from home on his bike. We pedaled all the way to Fleetwood on the Bronx River Parkway. Freddy hated his father, but I had no reason to run away from home myself. We had traveled about three miles when I got real uncomfortable. I don't remember how I got home, but I returned without Freddy.

Father was born an only child in Austria, and he learned watchmaking in elementary school. So he was an apprentice watchmaker when he came to New York at the age of eighteen. As a youth he had read so much about the Wild West, and he was eager to go out there. He didn't particularly like New York City, and as soon as he could he moved to San Antonio, Texas, where he worked for a jewelry store. Whatever his fantasies had been about Texas, they were not realized. Father quickly saved enough money to return to New York. I could never get him to tell me much about his adventures in the wild, wild West, except he'd say it was the best drinking water he'd ever had, just like spring water.

More importantly, he said, "There's one thing in this life: I don't ever want to work for anybody again. I want my independence." That impressed me. Sometimes I'd be at Father's shop, watching him handle pincers like a surgeon, expertly picking up the minuscule parts. I was fascinated by his patience and skill as he put a watch together, the incredible attention to detail. He had graceful hands, and he used them in an artistic manner. He taught Peri to string pearls, and she'd earn extra allowance money working on beads in the store.

His clients were fond of him. "Hi, Norbert." "Nice boy you've got—little Sidney." Mother had named me Mischa at birth, after a brother. At times, and, to my horror, she called me Mischa. I changed it to Michael, as it sounded less foreign. Then I rejected Michael altogether in favor of Sidney. I thought "Sid" sounded more American. And for years I harbored resentment toward my father for settling in an environment hostile to Jews.

I first noticed Beans McGyver when I was in front of the Bronxville movie house waiting for the doors to open. I caught him vandalizing my father's sign with a piece of soap. He was knocking out the letters ELER from JEWELER. I must have tackled him, because we didn't get into slugging it out. In a flash I spun him around, and we were rolling around in the gutter until he was out, so his head must have hit the curb.

My father, seeing the blood on Beans's forehead, grabbed me and took me inside the shop, where he proceeded to slap me hard on the face. "What the hell are you doing?" he demanded. This was my father, a quiet, nonviolent man. "Go in the back of the store and stay there," he ordered. It was very confusing to me. He didn't ask why we were fighting, and I didn't tell him. He said if I went around beating up kids in the street, it would call attention to ourselves. He didn't care about my reason.

The Bronxville Police Department protected Father's store in exchange for gifts. During the Christmas holidays he'd give the police captain a wristwatch or maybe the second lieutenant a signet ring. Norbert was friendly with the police, but he didn't respect them. The police chief, O'Connor, was an Irishman, as were the motorcycle cops.

Beans was eleven years old when he was rubbing out letters on my father's sign. Years later, I ran into him in Pelham at the home of W. W. Hawkins, who was the editor of the *World-Telegram*. Hawkins's son Ewing and I were classmates at the Hun School, and Ew had invited me to their house for a Christmas party. I hadn't seen Beans since we were children. He was a freshman at Yale, a football player, a big guy, over six one; he weighed about 185.

Every Christmas, W. W. Hawkins threw an elaborate affair. This year he had engaged Ella Logan as the entertainer, along with a big band. There must have been a thousand people at the party. It was very Eastern Seaboard. Ew had an older brother, John, who lived with Richard Halliday in an apartment at the Warwick Hotel in Manhattan. Halliday later married Mary Martin, and not long after that, John died.

I was mingling at the Hawkins holiday bash and ran into Beans. McGyver said, "So, how's the li'l Jew boy?"

I thought, *Jesus, this is seven years later. We're adults, and he's still talking that crap.* I said, "Hey, it's a big night, let's not scuffle here, Beans. Let's go outside." We went out on the grounds, and a couple of his friends followed. The lawns were frozen solid under layers of freshly fallen snow. An enormous winter moon lit up the icy landscape.

"Beans," I said, "listen." I saw he'd been drinking heavily. I'd had one drink. "I don't want a fight, Beans."

Beans decided to take off his jacket. We both wore gray pants, rep ties, tab collars, and J. Press jackets. He wasn't going to listen, and I hit him hard, right in the solar plexus. I saw his tongue fly out of his mouth and his eyes go up. He fell forward onto his knees. My wrath took over. I got hold of his head and I kept hitting him. His friends stopped me. They carried Beans indoors. Guests were milling all over; they thought Beans had passed out from too much booze. A girl came up and asked, "What happened to Beans?" I said, "He got hit by a car." While they were putting him down I ripped his watch off. I put it in my pocket as a souvenir, the way a soldier takes a dead man's gun. I was actually scared I'd killed him. I hit him so quick and I was very strong. The end of the vendetta.

Some years later I was told Beans had become a World War II pilot and was killed in action. In the end, he died for the Jews.

<hr>

When Mother became successful, we moved north across the river to Armour Villa Park. It was up the hill from Bronxville and therefore over-looking the city. There were about twenty other homes in the vicinity. As a kid, whenever I'd walk over the hill and see home, I'd breathe a sigh of relief. There were some wonderful families around the neighbor-hood. There were the Tuarts; Dr. Tuart, a surgeon, was a single parent bringing up three boys on his own. At Halloween he'd throw a big party in the cellar of their house. He'd pair us off and hand each kid a glove. The right hand would be strapped to the other's left hand. Two against two—it was a funny game. We'd dunk for apples with money in the water. Dr. Tuart's son Peter was a close pal; he was a half grade ahead of me and played football. Peter named me the "stalker": not that different from the "starker," a Yiddish term some of my Hollywood friends would later call me around the golf course.

Our next door neighbors were the Leos, who owned a coal and lumber company in Bronxville. They were a family of French descent with five kids, four boys and one girl; one of the boys, Johnny, became another good friend. One day Johnny and I went to get a haircut. On Saturday, we usually went to Pete the barber down Pondfield Road. Italian Pete loved to hunt and fish, and the magazines in the barber

shop were all about the outdoors, fishing, hunting. After Pete finished
my haircut I took him aside, and from deep inside my possum-collared
leather jacket I pulled out a loaded revolver. I flipped open the cylinder
and there were four bullets in the chamber.

I had bought the gun for a dollar and a half from Woody Sex-
ton, a freckle-faced little guy with a turned-up nose and reddish-
blond hair. One day we were playing somewhere and Woody told
me about a gun he found. Johnny Leo and I had taken Woody's
gun—we thought it was a starter pistol—put a .22 in it, took it up
into the woods, tied it to the fork of a tree, got behind a boulder,
and pulled the trigger. We'd seen guys shooting off a starter gun for
boat races and track meets. But we didn't know what this gun was.
I was showing off.

Here was my chance to be equal to the Leos. Johnny and his older
brother, Charlie, always had guns. Their house, too, was filled with
sporting magazines: *Field and Stream*, the *Outdoors*. The Leo kids made
their own fly rods, their own trout flies. Old Man Leo took them fishing
and hunting for quail and pheasant in the Mt. Kisco area, which was
blocked off for hunting. My father was dead set against guns. Norbert
didn't go into the local saloon and have a beer with the boys. At best, he
would have a shot of whiskey at night. Old Man Leo—well, you could
always smell that breath of his. He had a deep cigarette-and-whiskey
voice. He sounded like Orson Welles with a twang.

I was impressed by and probably envious of the attention Mr. and
Mrs. Leo paid to their children. To me the Leos were the ideal American family. While their kids hunted and fished with their father, had
guns and knew how to use them, I had a broken-down fishing reel.
My father abhorred killing and violence of any kind. My appetites
embarrassed him. The Leo household boasted a kind of bustle alien to
the Luft house, where tangos and opera filled the air when Mother and
Father were at home.

Johnny and I left Pete's and walked under the bridge where the
Grand Central Railroad goes right through the middle of Bronxville,
all the way up to White Plains and beyond. We were leaving the town

and returning home. I saw a motorcycle cop come in our direction, but I didn't pay any attention. He'd spotted us walking through the tunnel. He immediately got off his motorcycle and said, "Who's Luft?"

"I am."

"Where's the gun?"

"What gun?" I weakened.

Pete the barber had turned me in.

"Look kid, I want the gun." The policeman felt my coat and found the nickel-plated revolver with a white handle, small and neat. "Both of you come with me." He left his motorcycle and marched us into the nearby Yonkers police station. But not before he had made me dump the bullets.

"Gimme those." He grabbed my hand. "You," he instructed, "stay right here." He went in to call my mother: "We've your son here."

I pictured mother walking across the bridge. It would take her about five minutes. Then he called my father. I imagined them separately leaving their shops to converge in the local precinct. How was I going to get out of this one?

Johnny was allowed to go home. When my father walked in the police station, the first thing he did was to whack me across the face. Leonora shouted, "Stop it," and she got between us. They were told, "Your son has been carrying a revolver." It was an emotional scene. I'd begun to cry before the parents arrived. I had been snotty when the policeman arrested me, and I'd also made up my mind that he had called me "a little Jew."

I was booked on the Sullivan Act. I was well aware it was against the law to carry arms. And there were never any revolvers in the Leo house. There were .22s, shotguns, but not handguns. I used to brag to the Leos that I had shot a cat one night on the fence, but it was a lie, conceived out of my need to feel equal to the Leo boys.

The police sent me home with my parents. I was to appear in front of a junior appellate judge in Mt. Vernon a week later. That night the headline in the *Yonkers Statesman* read, BOY WALKING ARSENAL.

I was still crying when we returned home, ashamed that I had disappointed my parents. So the family drove to Mt. Vernon after dinner and bought me two pairs of new shoes, and we went to a movie. They were trying to cheer me up, but everything stayed downbeat; we drove in silence.

My father accompanied me the day I was to appear before the judge. The report read that I had kicked the cop. The judge said, "Have you anything to say for yourself?" I said, "I do. I apologize." I explained that I kicked him because he attempted to lift me up and he called me a "dirty little Jew boy." But, of course, I'd learned to employ this excuse whenever I got in trouble. It was my way of turning the insult around, putting it to good use. The judge gave me six months' probation. The incident had a positive result: it pushed me back into my books. I studied hard and the teacher took a shine to me—for a while, at least.

4

WHEN WE MOVED TO Armour Villa Park, we bought a corner lot from an army veteran who owned a beautiful piece of property there. We built a large redbrick colonial-style house. The front lawn had a sumptuous cherry tree that flowered in season. The land had been altogether richly landscaped with pine and other flowering shrubs.

Our neighbor was an eccentric man. I have no memory of a wife. It might very well be that nobody but us wished to live next door. For example, on either side of the man's steps leading to his front door were two tremendous bomb shells, three or four feet high. He was a World War I veteran. Some people have jockeys or pink flamingoes on their lawn. This character had bombs. He was always running his lawn mower and planting trees. My parents were at their respective stores, so I was the one who had the chance to observe. He had a huge aerial like a mast attached to the top turret of his house, and he flew the American flag up there, day in and day out. There were also wires that went down to the ground—for his shortwave radio, a superheterodyne. In those days it was the most powerful radio there was. He could pull in foreign stations with that aerial.

This man had big biceps. You could see his veins when he was pulling out roots and things. He looked about six three, and he never seemed to remove his creased, cloth army cap. Slowly, I perceived that the spiked iron gates around his house were more than decorative, that he was a paranoid type, but we kept up an excellent relationship as neighbors.

<hr />

From the age of seven on, I'd been fascinated by a big World War I picture book we had on our sunporch. It was filled with sepia photos taken from the *New York Times* that vividly captured the horrors of war: a French soldier hanging on barbed wire with part of his face shot off, men who suffered terrible burns from mustard gas—in fact, every possible example of destruction to a human as a result of war. I was especially intrigued by the Battle of Verdun, by foreign names, places outside of North America. I'd study the morbid images over and over, scrutinizing the faces of the Belgian troops, the American fighters, and the Germans. The saintly appearance of those Red Cross volunteers in the heat of battle. The aviators with their leather helmets and goggles. As ghastly and unimaginable as war seemed, the airplanes and the pilots looked glamorous. I experienced a great surge of wanderlust. One day, I dreamed, I would actually leave Bronxville and travel, and maybe even become a pilot, see foreign lands, and have all sorts of major adventures. Ripping through those grisly introductions to life, I vowed if there was ever to be a war in my lifetime, I would never see a trench. Those photos triggered dreams of glory, moments of death and destruction, a sense of heroism in goggles and leather helmet, sartorial splendor, aviator chic.

My love affair with engines started about a year later, when my father's half brother, Israel Rappaport, gave me a one-cylinder steam engine one Christmas. The engine sat there for another year, until I was nine, and then I began to figure out how to use it. It had a little tank that held alcohol to drive the motor. The tank was wedged under the mechanism and the alcohol would heat up the boiler—the same principle as a locomotive engine. I'd light the alcohol with a match, and the boiler produced sufficient steam to make it hot enough to drive. My buddy Peter Tuart's older brother, Bob, helped me.

I became fascinated by engines of all kinds. I was especially intrigued with building model airplanes, and this interest would develop into a passion for flying. I understood the principle of flight from working on the models, how air flows up a vacuum that lifts the aircraft off the ground, and so on. I'd take the train into Manhattan for pieces of copper tubing at Hammacher Schlemmer to fashion exhaust pipes for my model of the Curtiss Hawk. Yonkers Boys' Week awarded me a medal for my efforts. I had dreams of owning a boat and a plane. I'd build these models at home and in school. Hours on end I'd be sanding wings to a thousandth of an inch. The contour would have to be perfect; the fuselage would have to be perfect. When the material dried I'd sand it off and paint it again. I was a perfectionist.

I was also sensitive to animals, and I drew and painted them. I had a part–German shepherd mutt I loved, but horses were my favorite. I was captivated by the rhythm and beauty of the horse's anatomy.

Uncle Israel was a distinguished heart doctor. When he came to stay with us for a few months after his arrival from Europe, he wrote for the *American Medical Journal*, translating French, German, and Hungarian into English. It wasn't long before he was able to develop a private practice.

He was a nice-looking man with a thin, straight nose and a mouth that I perceived to be in a perpetual pout. He had piercing dark brown eyes and bushy eyebrows, and an altogether exotic mode of dress. His style was very different from the Bronxville dudes: he wore knickers made of a gray worsted fabric, black silk hose, and highly polished shoes. His jackets were belted in the back, single breasted with leather buttons and elbow patches. Mother thought the outfit stylish; I thought it odd.

Later that year, he married one of five sisters from Romania, and they lived on Fifth Avenue in Manhattan. The first floor was his office, which he would share with his daughter who also became a physician. The second floor was his study, and the third floor was where the sisters lived. The fourth floor was a custom drapery and curtain business run by his wife and her sisters. None of the sisters-in-law were ever to marry. They had big circles under their eyes and thick black hair. As a youngster, I found this harem of Uncle Israel's remarkably unattractive. He was more interested in brains than beauty. As a noted physician, he treated Harpo Marx, among others. Eventually he was to diagnose and cure Judy when she hovered between life and death with a life-threatening liver disease.

Uncle Israel was very serious. He never exercised and he had no apparent hobbies: his entire life was devoted to medicine. I'd eavesdrop on my father and uncle talking way into the night about subjects well over my head. I had the sense they were philosophizing. I could tell father looked up to him. Israel was conscious of my hyperactivity. He'd comment to Mother, "This kid is so active, he should do something physical, be a carpenter, a bricklayer." I didn't appreciate that, since my sights were set so high. But I was forever climbing, running, rushing to an activity, driving the family nuts with my energy level.

Leonora liked to occasionally tease me: "Remember, Uncle Israel thinks you should be a dockhand." One of the more salutary effects he had on the Luft family was eventually convincing my mother to let go of fatty foods in our diet. Israel stressed protein, and we entered into a routine of either baked or broiled meals. We rarely ate desserts—only on special occasions. Steaks were consumed every three months. I wasn't permitted hamburgers. It was fish and fowl and veal, salads mixed with Mazola oil, lemon, and a little vinegar . . . In retrospect, I attribute the family's general good physical stamina to Uncle Israel's influence.

In those years I was virtually unsupervised, with both parents hard at work. In a way I had an ideal childhood: so much time on my hands and so much trouble to get into! One day Johnny Leo and I grabbed a block of tar from a nearby roofing job. I had made a barge-like boat out of stolen lumber. The construction was about six feet long and three feet wide. We didn't know if it would float or not. My idea was to use the tar to waterproof it.

I knew I'd have to melt the tar first. We got the block downstairs near the furnace room, where the maid did the laundry. While I was stirring it and talking to Johnny some tar flew in my face. Boiling tar. I started to scream. Johnny ran over to get his mother. Once tar hits the face it stays there. Mrs. Leo immediately took me down to Bronxville Hospital. On the way I pleaded, "Don't tell my mom."

In the emergency room, doctors poured something over the tar and quickly bandaged me up. I peered out of two holes, something out of a horror movie, with an extra hole for the mouth. I spluttered, "Mrs. Leo, please tell Mom it's not that serious."

At home mother shouted, "Oh my God!"

"Don't worry, Mrs. Luft, I've seen Sid's face. It's not that bad." Mrs. Leo explained how they couldn't remove the tar or the skin would come off with it. "It's got to fall off," Mrs. Leo reassured. Four days later the outer skin began to fall off with the tar and I was fine. The barge, however, did not get down to the river.

Frightening as this experience was, it didn't deter my appetite for mischief. It also eerily presaged a more dangerous exploit that occurred years later, when as a test pilot I was to suffer third-degree burns.

———— ∞ ————

My parents didn't bother to educate me about sex or religion. They avoided these subjects. Like most kids of my generation, I learned about the ways of the world from the other boys. But my parents loaded me down with a sense of respect for older people and women. And Mother hated to hear me swear. I obliged by never using four letter words around the house. I wouldn't dare to call anyone a "bastard." Later, if I swore around my mother, she'd remark, "Sidney, you shouldn't talk like that!" Only once did I hear my father swear: he called O'Connor, the chief of police, a "son of a bitch," and that was radical for my father.

Whenever I was worried or made uncomfortable by Norbert's disapproval, I'd run out of the house, usually as he was in midsentence. One night he chased after me. It was dark and he couldn't find me. I slept in the car that night, age nine. The house was locked, but if I wanted I could always climb one of the two pillars and get in a window, which was left open to accommodate my caprices.

We were not a religious family. The nearest synagogue to our house was in Mt. Vernon. And we never attended services. We always had a Christmas tree. My parents thought it was a very American thing to do, and we exchanged presents. Mother's one nod to Hanukkah was the baking of challah bread. She was not one to cook, but she enjoyed baking. Mother and Father were proud of their Jewish identity, unlike myself. It would take some years for the self-hatred to disappear.

I was thrilled when we moved to Armour Villa next to the Leos and the other Catholic families. Although there were exceptions, in general they were warmer, not so elitist or intimidating.

Whenever I called for Johnny, Mrs. Leo would more often than not say, "He's learning his catechism." I finally got up enough nerve to ask Johnny just what catechism was. He answered, "Prayers." Once, on a Wednesday night, I went with Johnny to the local church. I sat next to him in the third row, and Father McCann picked me to answer a question: "Why is Catholicism the one true church?" When he pointed to me, I thought, wrong kid. I froze and muttered something. Johnny looked real embarrassed. The father didn't know who I was, just a new face that evening. I never expected to participate. When I finally spoke up, I said, "I don't know." He moved away. I was waiting for some kid to snicker and humiliate me, but it didn't happen.

Norbert and Father McCann became friends. They'd have long conversations I wouldn't understand. As threatened as I was during childhood by the WASP boys, I was totally at home on the hill in the Catholic community. These kids were my close friends.

Nevertheless, ignominy seemed to lie in wait for me in Bronxville—it never subsided. A boy in my fourth grade class, Tom Nasworthy, had a habit of calling me "a dirty Jew." One day at recess when I could take it no longer I hit him. We rolled around in the playground's mud until one of the teachers stopped us. He asked, "Do you really want to fight?"

I said, "Yeah, I do."

So we removed ourselves to the cafeteria, blocked off some tables to simulate a ring. The teacher put boxing gloves on both of us. Tom was three inches taller then I, but he couldn't see without his glasses and he was cross-eyed, so I was able to punch him all over the place.

Jack Dempsey was a hero of mine. One night we were gathered in the Leos' living room for the heavyweight championship between Jack Dempsey and Gene Tunney. I bet fifty cents on Dempsey, and lost. Tunney got up to win the fight on points. He didn't actually knock Dempsey out, but Dempsey went to the wrong corner. Years later Dempsey and I were on the same plane from New York to Los Angeles, and we sat together. I was impressed by his enormous, smooth, ungnarled hands.

I had other idols. Tom Mix was one, along with the writer Jack London, aviator Doug Corrigan, and Lindbergh, of course. I went down to New York on my own when Tom Mix made a personal appearance. Parked in front of the theater, roped off by police guards, was Mix's black Duesenberg convertible. It had wicker trim on the doors, with horns and other decorations. I reached out and touched it; I thought it was the most fabulous automobile in the world. Mix was a major star. He'd come out onstage with his lariat and horse, Tony. Later, when I moved to Hollywood, I discovered he was an egomaniac, insisting his initials, TM, had to be on everything in his house, including toilet seats.

———— ⧜ ————

Shortly after we moved into our new home in Armour Villa Park, Johnny insisted, "Come up to Kessler's pond to skate." I was still a bumpkin when it came to competitive sports. I wore my sister's awful brown skates; instead of a blunt toe they had a steel plate. The boys already skating on the pond wore authentic hockey shoes. I looked like a fucking idiot, and I wasn't prepared for the local jocks.

The Leo kids had skates, and hockey sticks that were properly taped, and genuine hockey gloves. I wore mittens. As I energetically made my way out on the ice, Don Miller greeted me with "No Jews on the ice."

My response was to thwack Miller with my pathetic hockey stick, whereupon he went nuts. I was no match for Miller. He commenced to kick the shit out of me. I was spitting saliva from the struggle. He cut me up by skating over my leg and my back. My hands, face, and lips were bleeding. One eye was black. When the fight started there was about an eighth of an inch of water, and as the sun began to set I started to chill. I was soaking wet. I was left exhausted at the side of the pond, where I sank into the snowbank trying to gain strength enough to drag my ass home. The gang had skated off. I was humiliated. Miller had been ruthless.

I refused to tell my father who had beaten me to a pulp. I couldn't stand any further embarrassment of my father going over to the Millers' house, which he surely would have done. I didn't want anyone to fight my battles.

After the Miller episode I worked out once a week in the ring at the Eastchester Police Department, and sometimes we'd go over to Westchester. There was always an assortment of boys around the Eastchester area. I began to develop. I responded to the policemen's instruction. I had the rhythm and I kept going and going until I became local boxing and wrestling champion in Westchester County. There was no stopping my aggression. I ran at least two or three miles daily. This was part of the bodybuilding program, motivated by the idea of revenge: I had to get back at Miller.

Three years later I had my chance. Hank Richards, the principal of Roosevelt High, called my father from his office and put me on the phone. I said, "I just killed Don Miller."

Richards told my father that Miller was seriously injured and that he'd better come to school immediately. I reminded Norbert of the time I came home half dead, cut up, bleeding, black and blue. "Now we're even." That was my mentality. For the first time Norbert said, "Mr. Richards, I must tell you I'll support Sidney in this incident."

I was expelled from school. To be reinstated I needed to go before the Yonkers Board of Regents. I was to tell the board the origin of my contempt for Miller, how it began on the ice pond three years earlier. True to his word, my father supported me, and eventually, I was readmitted.

5

WITH SO MANY FANTASIES in mind, the first thing I built in shop class was a sailboat that I named the *Get Away*. Mother's chief seamstress, Vera, made the sails and did the stitching. I polished and painted the hull, rubbed down the paint until it was slick. The following year I built a motorboat with a proper motor. Every year I won medals for the airplane models, the boats. I suppose I inherited some of father's manual dexterity.

My parents were very busy with their respective businesses, and my little victories went by like water off a duck's back. Westchester Interscholastic Athletic Association awarded me over and over again for things boys can do. If it wasn't for the model airplanes, it was for painting or boxing. Neither parent paid attention to these small honors. But there I was winning one medal after another.

My sister and I both painted. My work was stiff, very flat, illustrative. Peri was more inventive. I worked on a twelve-foot mural, a backdrop for a high school Shakespeare production. Later I stashed it in a secret hiding place beneath our sunporch along with a gun and an airplane propeller.

Peri suffered more from our parents' lack of attention. She was an overachiever who tried to please through her intellect, and she felt totally shut off. Leonora's fastidiousness, her insistence on plumping a pillow rather than noticing Peri's good marks, was perceived as rejection. Peri's silent fury went into her books, while I was still possessed by unleashed energy. As much as I enjoyed my friendship with the kids from Catholic backgrounds, I was an outsider in that environment too. I was looking for something to distinguish myself, to be noticed.

I tried showing off my strength. By the time I was a teenager I'd perform eye-catching acts such as "watch me" walks on my hands from the cellar up the stairs to the kitchen. I drove my mild-mannered, opera-loving father nuts. I'd plead, "I can walk up to the second floor on my hands."

"No, Sidney, I think this is good enough."

As devilish as I may have been, father was proud of how I looked. He'd comment at dinner to mother, in German, "Look at him, how handsome he is." And I began to think I was something. I wore corduroys and lace-up boots. Most kids had a corduroy coat with fake fur on the collar. I wore leather and possum.

Peri didn't look like the all-American Sarah Lawrence girl either. She had curly hair, a good figure, and a warm smile. In Bronxville, a girl had to have a turned-up nose to be popular. Everyone in those years was nose conscious. Mother had a rounded nose, Father a straight one. I had a widow's peak, and lots of hair. No glasses, thank God. They'd have called me four eyes. More fights.

In Peri's case, she was not chosen to go to school proms. She was rejected by those boys in Bronxville. She had a crush on Dick Rossiter. Dick had a brother who went to Cornell, a dumpy little guy, but brilliant. Dick was tall and handsome, like a movie actor, and not so brilliant. He was nice to her, but competition was too rough, and he didn't ask her out. Peri's revenge was that she was super smart and would graduate high school early. From there she'd go on to Skidmore College and graduate in three years.

I admired the style of the men who lived in Bronxville, the commuters who were the advertising agents, big brokers, corporate lawyers. Very social. Their daughters would make their debut at the Waldorf, the

Plaza, in the coming-out cotillions. A few of them went to Bronxville High School, but the majority of the Bronxville children went to Lawrenceville, or to Hanover, and to prep schools. We didn't have "good schools" nearby. Though the Mudds, the Rickenbackers, were mother's customers, and they adored "Madame Leonora" because they didn't have to get on a train and go into Lord & Taylor or to the Tailored Woman, it was an era when their kids were not interested in democratic social behavior. They saw us, of course, as "tradespeople," and I was determined to live down the "townie" designation.

The dude syndrome set in early. I enjoyed good clothes, and Mother allowed me to have charge accounts at A. G. Spalding and Comstock men's haberdashery in Bronxville. I didn't violate that trust. I'd tell her, "I'm going down to Comstock's to buy trousers" or "I'm going to Spalding's to buy football pads or hockey skates." And it was perfectly fine.

It was Mother, not Dad, who taught me how to dress. "Keep it simple" was her motto. Her taste could be described as classic elegance, never flamboyant. Perhaps a handsome, colorful scarf or maybe a pin, not a lot of jewelry.

One afternoon, mother was giving a fashion show at the Bronxville Women's Club. I knew she was going to come home with her number-one customer: Mrs. Erskin, tall, slender, well groomed, and socially correct. She was the quintessential WASP: she and her Aryan daughters appeared to me to be from another world with white ice fjords where anything brown or amber or gray couldn't live. I was warned I must make a good impression on the woman. I was in the bathroom trying to open up a can of black shoe polish to shine my shoes. Somehow, I slammed it onto the floor, where it blew up like a goddamned black fire bomb, spattering all over the wall, on the rugs, on a piece of priceless tapestry. I was grabbing towels, running water in the bathtub, when my sister announced, "I'm gonna tell Ma." I said, "You've gotta help me clean up this mess." Peri said, "No, I'm gonna call her and tell her what you did." I ripped the phone away from her, shoving my sister aside. Under certain circumstances, I had a vicious temper, with no intention of controlling it.

———— ✕✕✕ ————

For two summers Peri and I were sent away to a camp we hated. We ran away when they fired the only counselors we liked, a young married couple. We knew they were staying in the village, and we went to their house. They called our parents and Mother and Father came up and got us.

The second camp we were sent to was in Rutland, Vermont. I was captain of the "blues," and a kid named Bobby Williams was captain of the "grays." Bobby was to become a successful businessman in California. We were intense about sports. I was either running, pole vaulting, broad jumping, or boxing. Accidents were always happening, endless situations that no doubt drove the staff nuts. I once dug shoe spikes into the inside of my ankle and tore a big hole. I had to be taken to the hospital for a tetanus shot.

Years later I ran into Bobby in Hollywood. He first worked for Warner Bros. as a publicist before marrying and starting a pasta company. He became a big golfer, and we'd run into one another on various fairways. He went on to walk with Palmer and Nicklaus on the green.

The next summer, our parents didn't know where to send us. They were concerned that we be safe. So we wound up at kosher Camp Jened in the Catskills for the months of July and August. Jenny and Ed Fine owned the camp. We had to shop for the right clothes, to get the blue and gold shorts with the blue and gold CJ initials. We each had our own trunk, but there was an error on my blue trunk: it read SID LUST, in large gold lettering.

I resisted the camp's regimentation. Among other rules, on Friday nights the kids put on their yarmulkes and a white shirt, a blue tie, and a blue jacket with the CJ initials on it, and white knickers to go to shul. It was mandatory. However, I refused to go, and my Bronxville friend Freddy Steinman, whom I could always count on to be more outrageous than me, was a partner in crime. Freddy had a bad mouth.

We'd sneak off to a stream that fed the lake where we swam. We'd go way the hell up in the woods and dam up the stream and catch trout, and cook them up instead of attending shul.

Certain activities were prohibited on Saturday, because a lot of these kids were Orthodox Jews. Most of them could speak Yiddish, and the prayers were all in Hebrew. Freddy and I, having grown up in Bronxville, knew nothing about Jewish culture. On top of that, unfortunately, we were ashamed of anything Jewish.

I despised discipline of any kind in those years. The Leo kids were Eagle Scouts. I was never a Boy Scout. They said, "Why don't you join the Scouts?" Not me. Those innocent organizations represented repression to me. I couldn't see their value.

Freddy and I were the curse of Camp Jened. We were bad, bad. The counselors made a plan: one afternoon we were led about three hundred yards from the camp to a vacant field usually reserved for campfires. Waiting for us were two or three counselors and the camp doctor, a young man in his last year of medical school. We were going to be hypnotized in the hope it might help change our outlaw actions.

The doctor-to-be said, "Freddy, I want you to concentrate on this pen." He kept bringing the pen closer to Freddy's nose. Freddy concentrated until he actually went under. I couldn't believe it! Two counselors lifted him on the chair: "Freddy, be rigid." Freddy was rigid. They placed his neck on the back of the chair and the medical student said, "Now Freddy, you're going to be a different camper. You're going to stop swearing, and you're going to pay attention. You're *not* going to run off when you should come to shul." And he added, "When I snap my fingers, you'll wake up."

Freddy woke up, shook his head. He looked pretty groggy, and I knew he wasn't faking.

Now they turned their attention on me. They gave me the same line as they gave Freddy. "Put out your hand, Sid." I raised my hand, someone took a nail file and stuck my hand. I didn't flinch. Afterward, the experiment completed, we walked up to the tents (four bunks to a tent). The path was obstructed by an exposed tree root, and Freddy tripped over it. "Fuckin' root!" he yelled out. I had to control my laughter. Freddy's going under hadn't done a bit of good.

I had a grudge fight with another camper: Red Lerner, a kid I couldn't beat. He was a sturdy boy. Red was from Upstate New York, and he had looked like a skinny punk to me. I didn't like him. The counselors took us up the hill in back of the bunks and we fought ten rounds. I couldn't knock the turkey down. We could hardly hold our hands up, and wound up hitting each other with our arms and butting our heads. I still couldn't knock him down. I began to have a lot of respect for Red. Our instructor, a man named Mike, was a Hungarian from the University of Alabama. I'd watch him skip rope and work out. He'd match me with Red and we'd go three rounds for an exhibition at camp. I fancied myself "big gloves," and then when I returned home I'd always get the shit kicked out of me by the bigger guys. Mike's brother also wanted to be a boxer, but he didn't have the speed and he incurred serious brain damage in a match at college. Tragically, Mike was in a fatal auto accident not long afterward.

It was at Camp Jened that I experienced my first thrill at being high up. The flag rope got stuck and we couldn't lower it for taps in the evening, so I volunteered to shinny up the flagpole. I was in shorts and got chafed on the inside of my legs. I was proud of those burns. I looked down at the camp staff and the campers and realized I loved it up there. The counselors rewarded me with a large bowl of chocolate ice cream, but I would have gladly gone up for nothing.

———— ❦ ————

In high school my energy got channeled into sports. I ran in the early morning light. I loved the speed, the feel of my track shoes on concrete. I was developing muscles. I was the best quarter miler in the school. I pole vaulted and broad jumped; you couldn't keep me down. My wrestling coach, Andy Thomas, saw I was fast and well-built for a kid. I was developing into an amateur athlete. I ran the hundred, 220, and 440 in high school, and later in college. Andy took a personal interest in me, we got along, and he inspired me. Every year I attended the ten relays. I began to excel.

Andy was able to get a lot out of an individual. He also coached basketball, track, and football, and my freshman year I nearly made the varsity football team. (I wasn't interested in basketball—or baseball or tennis, for that matter. Bats, caps, and white shorts didn't appeal to me.) That year I got hurt in the opening game, and Andy screamed at me. I broke my thumb. It was a very fast play. I was in the backfield, an off-tackle play. Andy shouted, "Dig in." I ended up playing the backfield in high school, prep school, and college. I was all-county in the Westchester Interscholastic Athletic Association.

In those days, being a professional athlete didn't carry weight, as there was no real money in athletics. It was more of a gentleman's pursuit, for the honor. But I did make some money with my boxing skills. By the time I was fifteen I could spar well enough that parents would hire me to teach their kids how to work out in the ring in the hope they would exercise, lose weight. I got two dollars per lesson.

I continued to drive my father crazy with accidents. Once I cut my hand just before a swimming meet. I'd been splitting a two-by-four with an ax when it happened. I was used to nicks from working with airplane models, but this time I was near split to the bone. I insisted on competing with a poultice over the wound. Reluctantly, Norbert drove me to the meet. How was I going to win? I didn't place at all. I felt like I was dragging a bowling ball along.

I was well developed by fifteen, so it was a horrendous experience for me when I contracted chicken pox, just as I was getting to feel grown up and independent. I came home from football practice and noticed I was covered by nasty little red marks: on my tongue, in my nostrils and ears, in fact all over my body. I threw myself in the bath, which turned out to be the worst thing I could have done for my condition. Eventually I was swabbed down with Vaseline and forced to wear cotton flannels.

It was extremely uncomfortable and I was irritable. I was not taking the illness well.

During my confinement mother had awakened especially early, five thirty in the morning, to bake. She'd put the dough in the icebox overnight. By noon there was the rapturous odor of her pastries: napoleons, eclairs, tarts. Elaborate and rich pastries for her rich customers. She'd send them along in a fancy box, with whatever clothes they'd purchased. That particular noontime father drove home for lunch. He noticed that the baked goods were gone from the cabinet in the dining room. "Sid, what did you do with the pastries?" I said, "I don't know what you're talking about." He answered, "Son, I don't want you to lie to me." I said, "But I didn't touch the pastries." His jaw started to clench. He was thinking, *This damn kid is defying me.* It was clear he didn't believe me. I knew Peri had packed the goodies up and taken them to school after my mother left the house for the shop. Peri did it in defiance of Mother and to give them to her friends in the hopes of gaining their interest.

I repeated, "I didn't take the desserts." But father wanted a confession out of me. Instead I put up my fists. He looked down at me and said, "Are you showing your fists against your father?" I said, "Yes, sir." I was able to drive a car, but here I was with a children's disease, and my father accusing me of stealing pastries.

"What were you going to do?"

"If you kept it up I was going to belt you." And I walked out of the room. In a strange way, in defying my father I suddenly felt grown up, a man. I thought he should have known better; he should have trusted me. Mother didn't make a big deal about the pastries; she knew her daughter.

In general, they were lenient parents. One winter's night, shortly after the pox disappeared, Norbert, Leonora, and Peri went off to the opera. It was always an opportunity for me when the family was out of the house. I took Mother's car to Mt. Vernon to the movies. Coming back, there was about a foot of snow. It was one of the harshest blizzards in years. My luck! I crept along the Bronx River Parkway from Mt. Vernon to Bronxville. Nearly three hours had passed. I was a half mile from home when a car hit me head-on. The front left fender was smashed, bending the wheel out of kilter. I had to call a neighbor to tow the car back to the garage.

I admitted to Father I'd taken the car. He was calm about it, and this time he was on my side. In the morning, he told mother that the car wasn't working. Maybe by now he was afraid of me.

6

ONE SUMMER I SPENT a month with the Warren family on Schroon Lake in their log cabin. Bill and Mac Warren were pals. Their sister was married to a Jew, and Bill had a way of saying "You know, my brother-in-law the kike," which was kind of Lenny Bruce funny, and I was never offended. He did that to tease me, because he thought I was overly sensitive. He was my good, loyal friend, a fearless fellow hell-raiser. Old man Doc Warren was a minister.

A mile or so down the other side of the lake was a nightclub, with an emcee and four chorus girls. Beer was available. Every Saturday night there was entertainment and dancing to a small band. The personable band leader sang and told jokes. The girls had a routine. They wore blue shorts, bright yellow blouses, campy hats. They tap danced and sang. Ruthie was one of the performers, and I took a shine to her. I had heavy competition in a lifeguard from one of the nearby summer camps who also had a crush on Ruthie. One Saturday night, Ruthie and I, after a few pints of beer, carried on a mock marriage. The lifeguard, a big fellow, made a negative remark. And with my reactive and explosive nature I said, "Let's go outside."

We were both drunk. He threw a punch at me, and I began kicking the shit out of him. He fell down, near unconscious, when someone cracked me in the back of the head with what felt like a fist. Too late I heard Mac scream, "He's got a blackjack!" My head started to bleed over my white linen jacket. The drunk lifeguard was wavering on his knees. I didn't feel the impact of the blackjack right away. Bill had managed to knock my assailant down by the time the sheriff arrived and broke it up. Back in the car one of the Warrens said, "Your scalp is ripped. We gotta find a doctor." We found one in the local Jewish summer camp. He shaved the back of my head, stitched me up. Doc Warren was waiting for us in early morning light on the front porch of the log cabin. "Where you boys been?" We told him what happened. I was loony from the beer and the fight. I said, "I'm married. I'll have to get the marriage annulled."

We were privileged teenagers, able to participate in sports, given presents from caring parents, although we may not have perceived them as kindly at the time. We whiled away our evenings playing competitive poker games, talking sports, visiting gyms, thinking about girls.

There'd been a girl in the high school band when I was in junior high. She was kind of a flashy bleached blonde, a little knock-kneed. I used to neck with her, heavy petting, as it was called, on her porch, but that's all it was. My one sexual exploit had happened in my freshman year, at age fourteen. I went with a group of boys to a house of ill repute on the boundary of Mt. Vernon and Bronxville. Three of us had the same girl. She was in her twenties, and we were drunk from downing beer all night.

My first real love, Charlotte Lunken, was naturally blonde. I was in love with her the last two years of high school. Our first date was at the Glen Island Casino. All the big bands played there. I wore white flannels, white shoes, a blue blazer, white shirt, and blue tie. I felt ridiculous. I had two big boils on my forehead—adolescent nerves. I tried to cover them up with powder. It didn't work.

Charlotte Lunkenheimer was from that class I perceived to be golden. Her father had shortened their name from Lunkenheimer to Lunken. He owned the Lunkenheimer Valve Company in Cincinnati, Ohio, although the family lived in Scarsdale. There'd been two Mrs. Lunkens—Charlotte had an older brother from a different mother.

Charlotte was a few years younger than I, and she resembled a young Bette Davis—large eyes and small face.

Around this time I got a secondhand Hudson Terraplane Eight that I would drive to school. To be free of asking for money all the time I worked in a Yonkers department store wrapping packages, and I also delivered for my mother's shop. I was rarely without money in high school. I needed it to support my lifestyle of dating and going out well dressed. And if I didn't have enough money for a tire for my car, I'd put five bricks under the rear axle of some guy's Ford, let the air out, and take his. Johnny Leo would help me.

A black couple, Mr. and Mrs. Jim Bolling, worked for us. Jim would chauffeur my mother to work; my father preferred to walk. Jim had a good enough salary to buy himself a brand new little Ford. The first day he brought it home, I lifted the wheel off the back. I was incorrigible.

On Saturdays I'd play football, and Jim would cook me a big steak and baked potatoes. I'd eat this at ten in the morning before I ran to the field. Jim enjoyed cooking, and he taught me how to prepare food. We had a wonderful time together. Jim's special sandwich of chopped-up lettuce, crisp bacon, tomatoes, and homemade mayonnaise on toast remains my favorite.

I was sixteen when I took my first flying lesson for five dollars. I'd save up and drive out to the airport in Armonk, a half hour from Yonkers, taking the back roads. I'd wrecked two cars by then, but now I was in love with the Terraplane Eight and I was careful. I bought it for $300 and fixed it up. It was the fastest little car of its time. Dillinger owned one, and this had impressed me.

My virgin flight in the air was with a flight instructor in a two-seated, open-cockpit, single-engine plane. I was mimicking a pilot in goggles and leather jacket. I took about four or five lessons, no longer than a half an hour each, and soon I was able to handle the controls with some confidence. I shot some landings with the instructor. I was in heaven, more and more eager to fly solo.

I loved the sensation of soaring; diving 30 feet into the sound was one of my big thrills. I liked to climb trees as a kid, so it was a natural evolution from trees to high-dive platforms to airplanes. The motivation to be different was there, but aviation genuinely fascinated me. I experienced a sense of power looking down at the crazy world, and for that brief, splendid moment I was afforded a sensation of serenity in an open cockpit, seemingly in command of my fate.

Roosevelt High was a melting pot: Jewish boys from other parts of Yonkers attended the school. There was also a Jewish orphanage nearby, and some of these kids were in our classes. They'd arrive in old, beat-up clothing. It was cruel, but these kids couldn't gain anyone's respect.

There were several black athletes on our football team. These guys were well liked, but behind their back the fraternity boys would call them "niggers," as the Italians were called "wops" or "guineas" and the Jews were "kikes" or "sheenies." And not in a playful manner—it was intended to be demeaning. But generally, Roosevelt High was so mixed that pejorative words were the exception. I'd been raised by Jim Bolling, who was like an older brother, so I escaped from ignorant prejudices early on. My parents made it a point of never using any kind of racial epithet.

One of my closest pals was a transplanted Virginian, J. B. Rebling. His family lived in Lynchburg, Virginia. We hitchhiked there one time, easily catching rides all the way. On our arrival we learned that Lynchburg had just survived the worst fire in its history: one hundred or more black men were burned to death in a housing project. It was a terrible disaster, and it happened as we were on the road, ruining our holiday and the fantasy of courting southern belles. As it turned out, I was actually uncomfortable listening to all the racist talk and could hardly wait to get back to stuck-up Bronxville.

In my last year at Roosevelt High I became the captain of the track team, as well as captain of the football team. Along with the latter came an invitation to pledge a Christian fraternity. At first I was honored. I'd come a long way from the runt on the ice to gaining respect by excelling in athletics. The evening of my initiation, two frat boys came to my house to pick me up. I invited them both inside and proceeded to explain how I couldn't become a member, since they excluded other boys of my faith. I thought it unfair for me to participate in such an organization. I explained how I didn't like the Boy Scouts either, or any of the other boys' clubs, not only because of the dreaded regimentation but also because I had come to believe that they bred prejudice.

I had thought a lot about the isolation of a bunch of guys, and said that I wondered why they didn't include the Oppenheim boy, or the black boy, or the Italian? I was polite; I said I was grateful and felt privileged to have been selected. "No hard feelings." I felt a kind of liberation when I told them I was not joining. I liked the guys, not the organization.

Meanwhile, the relationship I had with my football coach, Andy Thomas, was developing into a lifelong friendship. He was my mentor, filling the gap I suffered from Father's indifference to my interests. Andy was a cool kind of guy with a great sense of humor, and he loved vaudeville. This appealed to me. Andy and I would go to the Palace Theatre or to the Lotus on 125th Street and watch Milton Berle or Tom Mix. His wife stayed at home with their daughter and Andy Jr.—the typical American family.

Coach Thomas received mail daily from various schools that were scouting athletic talent. Eventually he introduced me to another important Fred in my life: Fred Mann, who sponsored athletes for the University of Pennsylvania. Fred became the president and owner of the American Paper Box Company. He was affluent. He was also a gifted pianist of Russian descent. Fred saw me play the day I made a long touchdown. I was cornered, away from my team, and somehow came out of the pile and ran the rest of the sixty yards. The *Yonkers Student* ran a story on how I emerged miraculously to run the winning touchdown.

Mann wanted me for Penn, but my marks were lousy—I hated to study—and I needed a few points to graduate. So he arranged for me to go to the Hun School in Princeton, New Jersey. A prestigious institution restricted to ninety students, Hun was the preparatory school for students aspiring to Princeton University. A handful of the students were offspring of Hun instructors, and twenty were on athletic scholarship.

I received a weekly stipend, but with my taste I needed more money, so I rented out my car, which I kept off school grounds. By this point the Depression had stamped out the market for eight-cylinder cars, so I considered myself lucky to own one. The wealthy boys would rent it on weekends to drive their dates to Manhattan.

While I was at Hun we won the New Jersey title in football. Richard Bokum and James Aubrey at Princeton were two all-American football players who came out of Hun. Bokum would go on to discover the most prolific uranium areas in New Mexico. He created a company called United Nuclear and eventually sold out for millions. He was an exemplary person. His parents died when he was quite young, so he took on the family responsibilities, supporting his kid brother. He was a great tackle at Hun and a winning fullback at Princeton. And Aubrey would become president of CBS and later MGM.

It was at Hun that I became friends with Nick Du Pont and others who figured much later in my life. I was impressed by Nick's family. We were to have business schemes together much later, our friendship remaining strong throughout our lives. When I was estranged from Judy, I went into a business with Nick, and later I was able to help him out when he was the victim of an international financial scam.

After one year at Hun I'd made up the necessary points to enter the University of Pennsylvania, so I moved into a Philadelphia fraternity house, TEΦ (Tau Epsilon Phi), and played one year of freshman ball at Penn. Our coach was Harvey Harman.

My introduction to Penn was paved by a line guard. He was large, about 250 pounds, and he'd grab me every time I was in the shower. He'd pinch me on the nipples. He was so tough, so macho, his behavior couldn't possibly be interpreted as an advance. Locker politics, maybe, but it didn't appeal to me. When he tried it again, I knocked him out cold. We did become friends, however. His ambition in those days was to make fifty dollars a week as a coach. Eventually he owned a lumber yard, became a millionaire, and retired young to Milwaukee.

One of my mentors, Ken Strong, was with the New York Giants. I'd go down to Ohio Field, where the NYU guys trained. I learned to punt there. A wonderful old man (he seemed old at the time), Strong was the best punting coach for colleges in the area.

Jews were not supposed to be pilots, athletes, or drinkers. Jews were in books or selling *schmattes* as far as the Christian world was concerned. Well, I wasn't going into my mother's business, or my father's. I wanted to fly, to see the world, to remove myself from the stereotypical prejudices of what a Jew should be. I was interested in becoming recognizable for my best attributes. I had stamina, looks.

But I no longer had Charlotte Lunken. My first romance had ended when I left high school, after meeting with resistance from Charlotte's mother. One evening Mrs. Lunken said right out, "You two kids are getting too serious. I'm not too pleased with you staying up all night either."

Mrs. Lunken was up against a popular kid. If she had disapproved of Charlotte's relationship with me from the beginning, I wasn't aware of it. But she sent her off to school in Tarrytown. And when I went away to Hun school, Charlotte had written me a "Dear John" letter.

By the time I got to the University of Pennsylvania, I learned that she had married. I was devastated. I thought, *Fuck this, I'm skipping out on school.*

I let people down by doing so. They'd had high hopes for me as an athlete.

7

IT WAS DURING a family weekend visit to Atlantic City that my life took a radical swerve. I'd taken a stroll on my own by the boardwalk when I encountered an extraordinary-looking woman. She was wearing an expensive outfit unlike any women's fashion I'd as yet been exposed to: a navy blue blazer and white flannel slacks, black-and-white spectator shoes, a Scotch beret with a large red pom-pom. She looked wonderful, and there was something completely glamorous about her. I'd never been that intrigued. We chatted, and the mystery woman told me she lived near Armour Villa Park in Crestwood. As we began to walk and talk she told me her name was Eleanor Powell, she lived with her mother, and she was a dancer. She was older than me by a few years, enough to fall in the category of "older woman." She was rather boyish to my thinking, flat chested, slim hipped; nevertheless, my new friend had a great smile, her lips were painted a seductive red to match her pom-pom, and her eyes held a Latin glint.

I was muscled but young, and too naive to realize I'd been picked up. Later when I sat in the audience of a Broadway theater I was impressed by Eleanor's presence onstage—the grandness of the setting, the orchestra in the pit, and the curtain opening to reveal a dazzling performer. She had great legs; they were powerful and at the same time sexy. This was her greatest asset—this, and a kind of powerful charm she exuded when she performed. She was Miss Show Biz to me—and, as it turned out, to a million others once she became an MGM star. Eleanor and I would meet backstage after the show and go dancing. We'd kiss, be affectionate, but not have sex. She'd introduce me to Broadway actors—Ray Bolger and many others. I'd accompany her, always in the role of "younger brother" when introduced, but when we dined and danced it would turn intimate.

I was a good ballroom dancer. My mother preferred dancing with me rather than Norbert. I was frequently obliged to escort her onto the dance floor. So in a way, Leonora prepared me for Eleanor, who enjoyed dancing with me almost as much as my mother did. When we were out for an evening, Eleanor was able to avoid men she really didn't want to spend time with. I was smitten by my new friend, who confessed to me she had been born out of wedlock. She never knew a father.

I got to know the Powell family of women, the mother and grandmother, and I observed that Eleanor was a workaholic. She was already a Broadway name when we met on the boardwalk, but I didn't know show business.

Our friendship cooled off when she went to Hollywood and I went to Europe with my mother and sister. But she was the first person I looked up when I moved to Los Angeles a few years later. By then she was a big movie star.

———— ✕✕✕ ————

My sister, Peri, had returned home from Skidmore a college graduate. She was rebellious and didn't get along with Mother. It was war between them, and it was out in the open now. She'd gone on a charging spree all over New York.

But now Mother was taking both Peri and me to Europe and Russia. I was eighteen, and I had never been abroad. The idea was for our grandparents in Russia to meet their American grandchildren. Afterward, Mother planned on her usual buying trip in France to update herself on the latest fashions in Europe.

Though the US economy had crashed in 1929, the Depression did not have much effect on Bronxville. By the summer of 1934, Bronxville's people still saw no need to tighten up. "Madame Leonora" had been so successful that she persuaded Dad to sell his business and run one of her stores in Scarsdale. This would prove a mistake: apparently women were not happy to see a man around a dress shop. Mother lost a lot of money that year.

Neither the Depression nor the Scarsdale loss entered her mind the day we boarded the elegant ship *Conte di Savoia*, bound for Italy. As we were leaving the Hudson River, Guy Lombardo came out on the deck of his own boat with a sign reading, BON VOYAGE MARY AND JACK. Jack and Mary Benny, along with their best friends, George Burns and Gracie Allen, were actually aboard our ship. First, touching Tom Mix's Duesenberg, second, my friendship with Eleanor Powell—and now the Bennys. My heart beat faster and faster.

Father was not taking the trip with us, so I'd be escorting mother and Peri, and they'd be dependent on me. Further, I was free from hearing my parents argue; Mother certainly wouldn't be shouting "*SID-NEY!*" aboard ship. How Norbert disdained Leonora's outbursts. Mother was generous, not affectionate. A warm personality, and witty too, but she was not physically loving. Father would kiss, embrace me, but not Mother. However, nothing could dampen my excitement as we pulled away from everything familiar, and from a country financially going down the tubes.

Soon American radios would provide another avenue of escape, something to swell the spirits of people going further and further into debt. It was in 1934 that the twelve-year-old performer billed as "Baby Gumm" changed her name to "Judy Garland." Within a year she was enthralling radio listeners with her cheery, uplifting, bell-like voice. She was so sunny, and her timing was so perfect for a youngster. She was a jewel of a find, as she demonstrated on the popular *Jack Oakie's College Show*:

> JUDY GARLAND: *My, but you're looking well.*
> JACK OAKIE: *Looking well? Well, I ain't, honey, I'm a pretty*
>   *sick man. . . .*

JUDY (giggles): I'll bet you live to be 150.
JACK: What odds would you give? . . .
JUDY: Cheer up, you look fine—you ought to feel fine.
JACK: Yes?
JUDY: Certainly. Let me see you smile.

She adds her devilishly funny laugh, then breaks into song. Little Judy Garland sings in an amazingly developed voice with such emotion: "There are smiles that make us happy, there are smiles that make us blue . . ."

While Ethel, Judy's mother, was carefully watching over Judy's every move, Leonora, my mother, was requesting I lead her in a fox-trot to the mellow strains of the ship's first-class orchestra. The two mothers were never to know one another.

We docked in Italy and proceeded to Rome, where we stayed at the Excelsior Hotel and enjoyed the usual American tourist activities. Next we visited the Lido in Venice, arriving by speedboat. I felt very glamorous pulling up with two Swiss guards and walking a red carpet into the hotel. Chez Vous, the nightclub, was magically lit from under the glass floor, tables arranged in tiers of three, with candlelight and exotic flowers. The men were dressed in black tie and the women in ball gowns. The room was oval shaped. At the narrow end of the oval sat the orchestra. It was something out of a film, only it was for real. The maître d' looked like Valentino in a black shirt and tie and suit of white gabardine. After Venice we went to Genoa, where we boarded an Italian ship that sailed through the Dardanelles with a stopover in Turkey. We were on our way to Russia: we sailed the Black Sea to Odessa.

This was the Stalin era. When we docked in Odessa, mother was looking for her parents through a barbed wire fence. But after we went through customs, we were immediately bustled into an open touring car. The three of us were squeezed into the backseat, the luggage in front with the driver. We drove sharply out of the dock area when mother shouted, "Stop the car!" She still wanted to find her parents. The driver replied in Russian, "I can't." She actually shook his shoulders. He brushed her aside, "I cannot stop the car." I remember these two rather elderly people, my grandparents, running after the car with posies in their hands. That image tears at my heart. They showed up at the New London Hotel two or three hours later. They had walked all the way from the Odessa seaport.

Mother's brother in Russia was head of a bank. He lived quite well, and we visited his house, but we were never to see the way my grandmother and grandfather lived. They were too embarrassed about how poor they were. Grandfather ran a school and he spoke some English, as well as German and French. He was still teaching at the time. My grandmother gave piano lessons in her son's house with one hand. The other was paralyzed. My uncle had rebuilt the piano to accommodate the disability.

Mother had sent money to her parents every month. Now they explained how the police had arrested both of them for "hoarding." Saving was against the law.

Mother's only sister had married a Greek Orthodox nobleman living in Russia. She had converted to Catholicism. The photos of my aunt in a cassock outfit struck me as very appealing. Unfortunately, we were never to meet. I suspected Auntie had disassociated herself from the family.

We were in Odessa for about six days. One incident that took place during our short stay at the New London Hotel was especially memorable: the balcony in my room broke off, right down to the ground. Had I been standing on it at the time, I'd have died. I was happy to leave Russia even though we'd been there barely a week. Of course, thinking back, there was something laughable about it. In any case, we were eager to be on our way, hard as it was for mother to leave her people. I couldn't say the balcony's crashing was the reason to go; in some way it was more of a sign: anything could happen under Stalin and none of it good, especially for Jews. Was I ever going to escape my birthright? Here on the other side of the world, as in Bronxville, I was feeling the pinch of racism, and it was soon to eerily intensify in Austria.

But first we went by train on an overnight trip to Poland. We were told to lock the windows, because train robbers would steal luggage when the train was at its stops, using a pole with a hook. I slept fitfully, lying in wait for the thieves. It was a filthy, dirty old train, and very stuffy with the windows locked. Poland had signed a nonaggression pact with the Soviet Union in 1932 and had recently signed one with Nazi Germany as well. By 1939 the Soviet Union and Germany would carve up Poland between them. A dark age was roiling around us, as we naively continued on our holiday, going from one luxury hotel to the next, getting annoyed if we suffered the least inconvenience.

On the Russian side of the border, a big guard stood with a bayonet. He was a burly guy with a red star vibrating off his helmet. It struck me funny that on the Polish side stood a little guy with a bayonet and no helmet. We ate at the restaurant in the station. I had a huge steak and was allowed to drink a bottle of black beer. It was a welcome feast.

From Poland we went to Bad Gastein, a health resort in the Austrian Alps. Mother thought it would be good for her high blood pressure. The name of the hotel was the Excelsior Palace, and it was extremely picturesque, overlooking a white stone cliff and rich green landscapes. One morning I got up and saw an enormous white swastika being painted on a granite wall.

I'd become friendly with some young people around the hotel pool where I liked to swim and dive, hoping to impress women. They were Austrian Jews. I found out that these kids were originally from Berlin, and not vacationers—they were not going to return. Apparently their families had removed their personal wealth to Austria. It was explained to me that the führer, Germany's chancellor, had taken away the rights of German citizens who were Jewish. In fact, the government was confiscating all Jewish wealth. These kids felt lucky to be in Austria, and at the same time they were ready to leave Austria should the situation become threatening. All of this had an air of adventure for me, the idea of having to leave a country because of political reasons, and here they were at an expensive spa, beautifully dressed and enjoying life.

A charming young woman told me about Hitler. I listened more because of her beauty. At the same time, I was flirting with the girl who ran the photo shop. She was older, extremely attractive, and I found her sexy. I was looking for some action. I could escort my mother and sister for so long, but now I wanted my time. I was working away at the photo shop girl when I was warned by one of the pool group that, yes, she was pretty, but she was a *Nazi*. This soaked in somewhat, enough for me to drop the flirtation but not enough for me to fully understand the implications of being a Nazi.

We left Bad Gastein for Vienna, where I ran into Jack and Mary Benny and George Burns and Gracie Allen. They were sitting in a horse-drawn carriage at one of the squares in town, laughing, also seemingly unaware of the political brew. I waved to them and they happily returned the gesture. After all, we'd been shipmates, and they'd seen me high diving into the ship's pool.

In later years I got to know Jack, a close friend of Judy's—in fact he frequently wrote her notes. Whenever I ran into Jack I'd say, "Remember me, the kid on the diving board?"

Mother took snapshots of me with the Bennys and the Burnses from that trip. Years later I was at a fundraiser in Los Angeles and George was the keynote speaker. Someone introduced me to George after his speech. "Do you know Sid?"

George replied, "Sid Luft? I've known him all my life." It had a bittersweet ring to it.

The week we ran into our former shipmates in Vienna, mother took Peri and me to a posh restaurant, formerly a wing of a famous palace. While we were dining in the regal Viennese atmosphere, Austria's chancellor was assassinated. I immediately thought of my friends in Bad Gastein. How would this affect their lives? There was a sense of panic everywhere, and mother arranged for us to leave for France. I would continue to correspond with my new Austrian friends after I returned to America, and then slowly, their answers stopped arriving.

8

ON THE RIVIERA, we based ourselves at the Carlton Hotel in Cannes. From here mother could motor to Grasse to search out new perfumes or visit Juan-les-Pins or Biot for ceramics or Nice for the latest in resort wear. I would go with mother to Grasse, if she asked, for by now she looked to me for many things.

Peri had decided to enter the Cannes Rose Parade, called "Battle of the Roses." The parade meandered through the main part of town, circling back down and around, continuing in this way throughout the day. The day of the event I'd gone with mother to Grasse. We returned around midafternoon. I stood on the street watching until Peri came by on a float. I waved. The next float in view was bearing the most beautiful girl in the world. She had black hair, violet eyes shaded by thick black lashes, and a gorgeous body. Nature had been kind to Frieda Roberts. And destiny, working in its auspicious mode, presented a fellow standing next to me who exclaimed, "She is beautiful!"

I said, "Do you know her?"

Amazingly, he replied, "Yes, I have a date with her sister." In this way I met the girl of my wet dreams through another American on holiday. When the float came around again my new pal invited the sisters to join us in an outdoor café. The sun was setting—it was definitely aperitif hour. Frieda and her sister ordered Pernod. I said I'd have the same. I was thirsty. I didn't know what I was drinking. I threw it down and they said, "You can't drink Pernod that fast. You're allowed one." I said, "Don't worry." I managed two before they wouldn't let me have another. I got so drunk I didn't know where the hell I was. I suggested we go swimming. So we raced over to the Carlton Hotel. I ran up the stairs, gathered up four thick cotton towels featuring attached hoods, tumbled halfway down the three flights, fell on my ass, jumped over a hedge . . . and in minutes we were in the Mediterranean, swimming in the nude.

I fell in love with Frieda. She was British, sophisticated, and sexy. I wound up living with her at the villa she shared with her sister overlooking Cannes' harbor. I decided I'd call the hotel and explain to Mother I was staying with friends for a while. I'd been the perfect son all trip long, now it had to be my turn. I would insist at any cost. So I stayed with Frieda, making love in the scarlet bougainvillea-covered stone house, drinking the occasional Pernod, swimming naked. For three days I thought I was the stud-about-the-world at last. Frieda was in her twenties. When she asked my age, I lied and said I was nearing my twentieth birthday.

We mingled with individuals I thought might impress even Eleanor Powell. I met Willie Donahue of the Woolworth family; his cousin Barbara Hutton and brother Jimmy Donahue were more well-known socialites. Jimmy was gay, and he and Wallis Simpson, soon to become the Duchess of Windsor, were confidantes for most of their lives. Willie was straight and going with a friend of Frieda's, an English actress. They stayed at the Hotel Martinez and sported a pet ocelot.

As fate would have it, the first day Frieda and I descended from our idyll we ran right into my mother. I considered she may have been camping out, waiting. She ignored me and turned directly to Frieda: "Do you know how old he is?" Frieda responded in her cool, soft English voice, "No. I really don't care, either, Mrs. Luft." Mother stood there unable to speak. There was nothing to say. I patted mother on the shoulder, explained we were off to the beach, and said that I would call the hotel later to make plans. And we took off, leaving Leonora contemplating, no doubt, what a bad boy I really was. It was a scene right out of an adolescent's masturbatory fantasy. Only I hated to masturbate. I've always thought it more worthwhile to have sex.

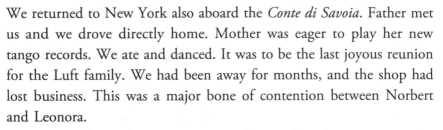

We returned to New York also aboard the *Conte di Savoia*. Father met us and we drove directly home. Mother was eager to play her new tango records. We ate and danced. It was to be the last joyous reunion for the Luft family. We had been away for months, and the shop had lost business. This was a major bone of contention between Norbert and Leonora.

Not too long after our return mother awakened me at six in the morning. "Sid, get up."

"What's the matter, Ma?"

She spat out the heartbreaking news: "Your father's not living with us. He's left the house." I got dressed as she nervously explained that he'd been living with another woman while we were away. I challenged her, and she assured me she could prove it. "I found a love letter when I was putting his socks in the drawer." She was devastated. "The letter explains everything. I'm going to divorce him."

I couldn't believe what I was hearing. I mumbled something like *Well, before you do, Mom, give yourself some time.* As though I were calm and thoughtful. Mother told me that when confronted, my father had told her he came upon the letter while driving back from New York on business. "It was a windy day and this letter blew into the car window." It was a miracle of coincidence, he explained, that the message was addressed to someone else named Norbert. He assured mother it wasn't his. He must have been desperate because he didn't want to break up the family.

"I can't swallow that it blew into the window of the car, Sid. It's too much, I'm going to divorce him." I thought if only she'd pretend it blew in. I didn't want them to separate, let alone divorce.

I'd bought two men's silk scarves in Rome to bring home. Both celebrated an Italian military victory in Ethiopia; one in black silk with white letters, the other black letters on tan. I was intending to give one to my father. Now it would be an act of treason. I was so upset and confused by what was happening I wound up keeping both for myself.

Father moved out, and one day I met the woman in question. He said it wasn't love, but she was an attractive brunette, years younger, with a pretty smile and big eyes. He kept trying to communicate with Leonora to patch things up. He even threatened suicide, and then he wrote a heartbreaking letter pleading with her: "You can't divorce me. It'll wreck you and the kids, the family. What will the kids think of you and I'm going to kill myself if you don't take me back." He tried everything. Nothing worked, and the family was broken.

I didn't blame Father for his romance. Mother was rigid, tough, and unforgiving. When my parents divorced, Leonora had money and Norbert had nothing. But he pulled himself together and found a shop in Scarsdale, a small business that suited him. It was next to a real estate office on Scarsdale Road, and he lived nearby at the Scarsdale Lodge until he remarried a pleasant woman who worked as an executive secretary in the office of United Artists in Manhattan. Though Norbert and I had affection for one another and spoke frequently on the telephone, our lives were essentially separate.

Not so with my mother, who would circle in and out of my life until her death in 1972. Mother had an appetite for the good life. She'd introduced me to music, to dancing, to travel, to handmade clothing and a fine lifestyle. She was determined, and often wouldn't budge in her points of view. By the late '30s, with a war coming, her customers were no longer eager to spend $200 for a frock. They encouraged her to save her shop by selling ready-made dresses at affordable prices. But she was only interested in Madame Leonora's as long as there were beaded dresses, ball gowns, furs, expensive perfume, and jewelry to sell. She didn't want to run a practical, affordable shop. The irony was Leonora's business had been a success for many years based on sheer ingenuity, but now it drove her into bankruptcy. She moved to New York City, where she took a job in a fashionable shop on Park Avenue. She met a man somewhere in Europe and he followed her to America. But she never remarried.

My sister, meanwhile, had a nervous breakdown. I was not close with Peri, but I was sympathetic; I knew she was suffering not only the stress of the family breakup but also her own loss of the guy she loved. It was her old crush on Dick Rossiter did her in, when he fell in love and married Peri's friend Pinky Ward. Peri broke out in boils and had to be wrapped in cold sheets. She completely fell apart. She stayed at the Bloomingdale Clinic in Westchester County for one year. When I visited her, it was a desperate thing to witness. I wanted to rid my brain of the image, it was so painful: my gifted older sister restricted to an institution weaving little baskets.

Peri didn't belong in a mental sanitarium. Uncle Israel understood that and arranged for Peri to live with his family in New York City, where she attended the Art Students League and developed her talent, as well as her emotional strengths. Very soon Peri met Lou Fleishman, a young doctor from Johns Hopkins in Baltimore, and they married and moved to Florida.

Unlike Peri, I had the ability to remove myself, have an adventure. I didn't want to stay in one place and study. I had a lot of bravado, false ego. If I couldn't handle it one way, I'd handle it another. I'd find a way to survive.

I tried to go back to school, but my grades were not good enough for the Wharton School of Business. So I got a job in the paper mill. I'd get up at six o'clock in the morning to go down to the factory and work with big corrugated columns, like giant rolls of toilet paper. My job was to first cut them, then stack the rolls in three-foot-long sections on top of each other, at least eight feet in the air. When I got tired I'd climb up, make a little place where I could sleep. I'd take off my white University of Pennsylvania sweater and roll it up into a pillow. One day a worker caught me. "You're fired," he said. I didn't care. I went to pick up my check. Someone in payroll said, "You can't fire this guy, he's one of Fred Mann's men."

I said, "Give me my money."

I went down to the garage where my car was up on blocks, took it out, and drove to Florida. I took my scrapbooks over to the University of Miami to show them to Irl Tubbs, the football coach. I thought I might qualify for a scholarship right away. But I got in a brawl in Miami with two guys. I got a cut on the eye, a blow to the mouth. I should have kept quiet, because they were going to kill me. I was screaming, "Southern motherfucker." Coach Tubbs bailed me out of jail, and I was fined five dollars. I was looking for trouble, defiant, and filled with aggression. After I was out, I ran into a Mike and Joe Luft, unrelated, from Detroit. They'd read the piece in the *Miami Herald*, and they wanted to meet me because of the name.

Tubbs quickly found me a job working in construction in Coral Gables. I made thirty cents an hour, carrying a hod. I'd load the mortar up and carry about seventy pounds' worth up a ladder. I enjoyed physical labor, but this felt more like a chain gang.

Every Sunday the hotel Miami Biltmore in Coral Gables had a pool show. Aquacades were popular fare, and there were two springboards and a big grandstand. For fun I auditioned and was hired. I would dive off a 10-meter platform for twenty dollars a day.

One of the other performers was an Indian who would wrestle a mean alligator that was lying in wait at the bottom of the pool with its mouth tied up. The Indian would jump in the pool and struggle to get the alligator over to the side. Once that was accomplished he'd free its mouth and put the rope around the body of the beast and continue to wrestle.

Bob Howard and his wife were the best trick divers off a 10-meter platform. The Howards would jump from one platform to another springboard, performing triples and quadruples. There was also a demeaning act featuring a $100 bill tied to the end of a greased pole suspended out over the pool. The idea was for us to get out there and grab the bill, but it was an impossible trick.

There were some other great divers: Pete Desjardins, who had won two gold medals at the 1928 Olympics, and Marshall Wayne, a huge man with big muscles, six feet tall, blond, who would go on to win at the upcoming Olympic Games in Berlin. He was also working as a lifeguard in Miami. Johnny Cawthray, another of the young men working with me, was the national Canadian diving champion. I was not a professional diver, but I was a good amateur. I wore a crazy bathing suit, yellow and red stripes with sleeves, like a clown.

It turned out that Johnny had a singing act as well. He had a good tenor voice, and he did impersonations. The one he did best was Walter Winchell. It was now late spring, and Johnny had ambitions to make the Canadian Olympic team, so he would practice during the day while I schlepped cement and played football, mostly scrimmaging in shorts. At night Johnny and I would hang out around Miami and meet girls. We became good friends.

I knew that Walter Winchell vacationed in Miami. And the Royal Palm Casino was a nightclub he frequented. I went to the casino's bandleader, Joe Condolli, and persuaded him to hire Johnny. The entertainment was primarily a chorus line, but somehow I was able to book Johnny for a short singing and impersonation act in exchange for food. No money was involved. However, as a result of this act Winchell wrote Johnny up in his column. Winchell had also been to the pool show and was impressed by the fact that Johnny was a national Canadian diving champion.

9

Joe Condolli was slight in build with thick black curly hair and eyes like a bullfrog. He was a good-looking mobster type with feminine hands. He played the fiddle and sang and spoke in a raspy, New York Italian kind of voice. His brother was also in the band and played the guitar.

Joe was constantly on the lookout to see who was eyeballing his girlfriend, Connie, and just who she might be looking at. Connie was a big, voluptuous girl with natural red hair and huge tits. I thought about women all the time, and she was a sexy number. I looked at her, and she didn't reject the unspoken message. One night while Joe was at work Connie invited me up to her apartment and we began a torrid romance. She was about ten years older than I, and we both understood that Joe was on the watch. Although he was married, Connie was his chick on the road. He worked Florida's sunny winter and then went to Cleveland for another gig before returning to New York. I felt so guilty fucking his old lady that I gave him one of my precious Italian silk scarves celebrating the Italian victory in Ethiopia.

One night Johnny Cawthray and I wound up at the Roney Plaza Hotel, where Walter Winchell was sitting at his special table with his pals. He spotted Johnny and invited us to join them. Winchell playfully referred to me as "Mr. Olympus." I was all muscle and bravado at the pool show, but I was no champion. We were excited to sit with Walter

Winchell. In fact, it was the biggest thrill we'd had. People kowtowed to us—we felt important. Johnny thought he might seriously try to make it as a performer. I decided I wouldn't go back to college after all. I'd embark on a career in show business.

I was a nobody when Winchell sardonically referred to me as Mr. Olympus. However, I reminded myself, I was sitting with the famous, influential Walter Winchell, and Johnny had been the conduit to such power. Columnists were powerful people. Therefore, why not continue to manage my talent?

Around this time, Judy Garland was finally getting her big break in an MGM two-reel short subject called *Every Sunday*. She appeared with Deanna Durbin, who sang light opera, while Judy sang "swing." Walter was to become one of Judy's most avid fans, and one day his exuberance over her talents would get in the way. I could never have dreamed that I would one day be calling Winchell up to reprimand him, and that he would have to accept Mr. Olympus's admonitions.

Sometime in June 1936, Johnny and I drove to Canada to attend the Olympic Trials in Hamilton, Ontario. We stayed with his family in Ottawa. Johnny placed second in the three-meter springboard events and second in the ten-meter platform. Unfortunately, the Canadians did not have enough money to send two men to the Olympics. They chose a young fellow about sixteen years old who placed first in the platform diving, even though Johnny had amassed more points on the springboard.

I got the notion to raise money to ostensibly send Johnny to the Olympics. I wanted to produce a pool show like the one in Florida. I made an appointment with the mayor of Ottawa. "This is one of the best divers in the world," I said. I suggested the mayor call whoever owned the Clearview Pool outside of Ottawa and see if he'd rent it to us, and His Honor agreed. I went to the local Ys to research swimmers. We were in luck. There were girls who performed in an aqua ballet. The Clearview didn't have a 10-meter platform, but they had a premier springboard. I prevailed upon the manager of their professional hockey team to send out a thousand folding chairs so people could be seated around the pool. I went to the newspaper. They would give us eight hundred lines of free advertising if we sold X number of lines and persuaded local business people to take out ads. We had an entire page devoted to people who donated money to the cause, with such statements as "Sending Johnny Cawthray to the Olympics," and "Good Luck to Johnny."

The Boy Scouts policed the event and managed the traffic. We were to perform Saturday and Sunday in the afternoon. Saturday arrived, and the cars were stuck for miles down the road—people had to abandon their cars and walk along the road to get to the pool for the show. I'd organized a small band: piano, bass, trumpet, and guitar. Johnny, the star, appeared in a sweater, trousers, and gym shoes. He stood high on the platform and sang three popular tunes. He then impersonated Walter Winchell, imitating the sounds of the Morse code that preceded Winchell's broadcasts. He finished with a rendition of "Trees": "I think that I shall never see / A poem as lovely as a tree . . ." Johnny sang "Trees" while peeling off his clothes in preparation for his spectacular descent. It was during Johnny's high-tenor presentation that I began to laugh and got a little hysterical. It seemed like he was still singing "Trees" underwater.

I knew Johnny would never win over someone like Marshall Wayne on the world stage. Furthermore, neither of us wanted to attend an Olympic Games in Nazi Germany, especially me. We rationalized that our pool show might be a scam, but everyone would be highly entertained. And they were. We charged $2.50 for adults and $1.00 for kids. We also took half the action from the guys selling hot dogs. In two days, we earned over $14,000, which we considered a fortune. I felt like a millionaire. We'd pulled it off! We collected some of the monies the first night. The pool owner observed me as we left the locker room with a big tin can filled with cash. Originally, he'd agreed the pool rental would cost nothing. After the last show, as we were leaving, he approached me. "I want $2,000."

"Well, didn't you agree this is money to send Johnny to the Olympics?"

He was a burly man, trying not to get angry. "But you've made enough money to send twenty guys to the Olympics. Besides, you left these chairs out overnight. Three hundred are warped. Who's responsible for that?" It was true the Scouts did not collect all the chairs and some of them had buckled. He repeated, "Who's gonna pay for these?"

He was pushing all the wrong buttons, so instead of offering him money, I said, "We'll work it out with the hockey club, don't worry about it."

"Well," he answered, "there's three hundred seats, it's $1.75 to change them, that's another five hundred dollars." Meanwhile, Mr. Cawthray, Johnny's father, was waiting for us in my Hudson Terraplane. "I want the money right now," the pool owner said. "You've got it, hand it over."

"We'll come back tomorrow for an estimate."

His wife, who joined him by the pool where we were standing, decided to speak up. "Hon," she said, "I think he's an American gangster." At which point I gently pushed both of them in the pool. Johnny and I made a beeline for the car.

Mr. Cawthray came with us as far as the US border, where Johnny and I caught a ferry to the States. When we got to New York, I traded the Hudson for a new model with the gearshift in the control column. It was a jazzy-looking car. We drove up to Westchester and stayed at my mother's house for a few days before pressing on to Cleveland.

Cleveland was hosting the Great Lakes Exposition from 1936 to 1937, plus Joe Condolli was working for Pony Boy Cohen at his nightclub in the city. Pony Boy had a reputation around New York. A small guy with a glass eye, he was known to be "one tough little hombre." Pony Boy was married to a big blonde two heads taller with a son, Harry, from a previous marriage. Harry looked like a greaseball heavy straight out of a gangster movie. Pony Boy's club was an after-hours place featuring gambling, particularly a dice game, which used silver dollars as chips. One day Harry asked me to go with him to pick up a suitcase full of silver dollars. He came out of the office with a .38, the long barrel stuck on his belt. We went into a cigar store that fronted a huge, gymnasium-type space holding about thirty Vegas gambling tables. It was a casino catering to blacks. All craps shooters. I thought this was exciting, the real world.

The Great Lakes Exposition featured an aquacade produced by Billy Rose. We could work for the show and keep earning good money at Pony Boy's club. Rose billed Johnny as the national Canadian diving champion, and I worked the twenty-meter platform. We wound up diving into Lake Erie way into November. We made fifty dollars a night, but I began to think, high up on that platform, freezing my ass off, that perhaps diving into cantaloupe rinds and banana peels was not the way to go. Johnny had a better experience: he sang on weekends backed by Joe Condolli's violin and an eight-piece band. He wore a dinner jacket and his hair was longer; he looked like an entertainer. However, I was getting restless.

I returned to Miami and Coach Tubbs. Maybe it was time to finish college. The second day I was in town, I accidentally drove into the exit of the Miami Biltmore Hotel. A huge Rolls-Royce was coming out and we collided. Nobody was hurt. My car had a dent in the bumper, and the Rolls-Royce didn't have a scratch. The driver, a rich entertainer and successful businessman, immediately filed a complaint against me. He was severe. I was arrested for reckless driving and thrown into jail for two nights. I was wearing a gabardine suit I was especially fond of—but not fond enough to stay in it for forty-eight hours. The guy in the cell next to mine was drunk as a skunk and he'd shout at me, "Hey you . . . gimme a cigarette."

I'd foolishly reply, "Please, old buddy, behave like a human being."

This only infuriated him. The drunkard was a little man filled with whiskey aggression. "Fuck you, when I get out of this fuckin' cage I'm going to tear you to pieces." He proceeded to put on an act: he pulled out his eye! I was dumbstruck until I realized it was a glass eye. I began to laugh and finally I said, "That's impressive, old buddy," and gave him a cigarette through the bars. He sobered up a bit. "Son, when we get out of here, give me a call." He handed me a business card.

The warden invited me to walk the beat with him, but not before he had my word that I wasn't "gonna make a run." I assumed I'd be in the slammer until morning, but in the middle of the night the cops made a raid and brought in a lot of black men. I was transferred to a jail in south Miami next to a busy firehouse. There was a bare room with a broom and a bunch of tin plates. It was early morning. I'd not slept. I began to play golf with the broom and tin plates. I obsessively occupied myself in this fashion, using the tin plates for golf balls, scaling them against the bars. My fellow inmates yelled: "Quiet!" "Put that fuckin' broom down!"

To which I'd answer, "Oh, go fuck yourself."

I didn't have a clue who I was talking to. The sheriff came in, and I quieted down. He offered me some food his wife had cooked up. I said, "I don't eat grits," and he admitted he didn't either. I was angry at this point—there was no reason to be in jail. I began whacking more tin plates against the bar with the broom handle. It drove people crazy. Eventually a fireman, a sheriff, and a cop came in, nailed me up against the wall, and told me to calm down. They pushed me around a bit, and I sweated out my incarceration.

I knew now I was not going back to college. If I was so attracted to the world of entertainment, why not go to the source?

PART III

Lost in the Stars

IO

O N THE ROAD TO HOLLYWOOD, I stopped to visit with a friend in Louisiana whose family was in the sugar business. As I slowly approached the plantation my head filled up with molasses: the air was permeated by an overpowering, sickly sweet smell. I knew I wouldn't be visiting for long. The plantation-like atmosphere was novel and comfortable, but it rained most of the time and there was absolutely nothing to do. The weather and the suffocating smell forced me to leave earlier than planned.

I continued on to California. As yet, I didn't know about Beverly Hills, Bel Air, or even Santa Monica. Coming off Route 66, I stopped in Glendale and checked into a motel. Thinking Glendale was the place, I soon rented an apartment. I decided to wait until I had my footing before calling Eleanor Powell, who was under contract to MGM. I didn't want to appear totally green.

I met a guy who also drove a Packard 12 Roadster. (I'd traded in my Hudson Terraplane for a Packard 12.) One night we attended a fancy Glendale party filled with valley debutantes, and the local dudes were not happy with our presence, particularly our flashy cars. A fight broke out and it spread onto the street. I was in the middle of the street fighting, and as I was picking one of the boys off the road someone came from out of nowhere and whacked me in the face. I never knew where that blow came from. He hit me so hard I was forced into a backflip.

In the distance I could hear the sound of police sirens headed in our direction. We somehow managed to hop in our cars and speed off. I had a healthy mouse within minutes. It was around eleven at night, and my left eye was closed in such a way I thought I might have lost it—the area was swollen up like a tennis ball. We went looking for leeches. I was used to them from my days in the ring at the Eastchester Police Department. The pro boxers in the gyms would get treated with these rather disgusting-looking creatures, dark brown with a rough texture. I knew you could buy them at a drugstore, but there wasn't one open in Glendale at that hour. We found our way to an all-night pharmacy, Horton & Converse, in Beverly Hills—and this was my introduction to Tinseltown. I purchased a cobalt blue jar filled with four unattractive slugs. The boys watched in horror as I threw my head back and attached one bloodsucker to the damaged area. My eyelid was still hammered shut. I explained how they work, sucking the blood out of your skin, and how the inflammation disappears within a few hours. When the leech filled with blood it fell off and I applied another.

Horton & Converse was located on Wilshire Boulevard near Rodeo Drive. Cruising around, I took in the streets and the shops and decided I was not living in the right neighborhood. I got back to Glendale at around five o'clock in the morning, packed up, and drove right back to Beverly Hills. On the way, I stopped at a drive-in restaurant with my top down, and there were two guys with a girl between them sitting in a convertible eating hamburgers. They looked at me and one of the fellows said, "Should've ducked."

"You're so right" was my reply. The boys were the multitalented Heasley twins, Bob and Jack. They were actors and also professional ice skaters. For a long time, they had their own act on the roof of the St. Regis Hotel in New York, and I was soon to be working with them on Eleanor Powell's movie *Rosalie*. Bobby would later become my second assistant producer on *A Star Is Born*. We all became pilots as well, and the Heasleys even had a flying school. They went on to manufacture sophisticated metal components for the aircraft industry.

In the all-night drive-in we began to talk back and forth from our cars. They were currently working on a film with Sonja Henie, the star on ice. After winning the '28, '32 and '36 Olympics she'd become a movie star, and she was now under contract at 20th Century Fox.

Eleanor was finishing her first MGM film, *Broadway Melody of 1938*, when I looked her up. She and her mother had always been warm and receptive to me, but we hadn't seen one another for three years. I didn't anticipate I'd have an affair with her. I was not sophisticated enough to make a pass when we'd known one another in New York. But by now I'd slept with women older than myself. I enjoyed experienced women, and they appreciated a young man, which worked out well for both parties.

I began to spend time at the Powell house, at 727 North Bedford Drive in Beverly Hills. I noticed Eleanor expended her energy avoiding men who were chasing her, men like Roy Del Ruth, the director of *Broadway Melody of 1938*. Another suitor was an important art director at MGM, another a film executive who daily sent her roses and costly presents.

I was impressed by Eleanor's discipline. She had a portable dance floor with a special veneer on which she practiced for hours every day. Later, when we traveled together, Eleanor would always bring the board along.

Eleanor's interest in me was flattering, and I was infatuated. However, I continued to date many girls, and Eleanor encouraged me to do so. She preferred that our relationship appear to be casual.

Through Eleanor and the Heasley twins I was introduced to the younger Hollywood actors. We hung out at the popular clubs: the Mocambo, Victor Hugo's, and the Trocadero. Mickey Rooney was going with Ava Gardner, at the time a pretty unknown MGM starlet. Mickey was the star. We'd double date, and Mickey told funny stories about himself and his little costar, Judy Garland. Of course Mickey married Ava, his first of eight wives.

I met Jack Warner Jr., and with our dates we'd attend private screenings at the Warner family manse. To me it was a big deal. I was sporting

a pipe at the time, and Jack Warner Sr., with whom I would one day
be partners, sharply requested, "Put the pipe out or get out." My ears
rang red with embarrassment that evening. I was not used to commands,
but under the circumstances I was not going to react. Jack Jr. seemed
unfazed by his father's behavior. I'd begun to affect a pipe at the Hun
School and kept it up. I thought it made me look mature, important.
It seemed to go over good with the girls but aggravate the guys.

———— ⚌ ————

Eleanor was now even more glamorous to me now than when I'd first
seen her in Atlantic City. She wore luxurious mink coats and expensive
jewelry, drove handsome cars—the accoutrements of a Hollywood star.
She liked to say she thought of me as her brother, and I'd be dancing
with her holding her very close and telling her to forget the brother stuff.
I'd press her body into mine and turn her on, just as she had turned me
on. Later when we were lovers and our relationship developed, I had
my first taste of privilege and fame. I could blame Eleanor for turning
me on to a lifestyle I would never be able to kick, even as it kicked me.

I was introduced as her "assistant" or "secretary." When we were
returning from a particular cruise from Los Angeles to Cuba, the press
caught up with us as we docked in New York. We'd enjoyed ourselves
immensely in Cuba, dancing through the exotic Latin nights, all perfume
and stars over Havana, enjoying the elite pre-Castro pleasures. We drank
and ate at the lavish casinos with Meyer Lansky and other celebrities.
Nobody questioned my presence. And then we hit New York. Eleanor
was photographed aboard ship, wrapped in mink, my figure lurking in
the background.

Once the story broke Eleanor and her mother immediately returned
to Hollywood by train, leaving me on my own. I was put out. I was
egotistical—in a sense, I felt equally important. I was not to be pushed
under the carpet.

MGM was outraged by the publicity. One of the columnists wrote,
"Doesn't look like any secretary to me." The press played up the notion
of "boy secretaries" as the latest Hollywood fad. Who was Eleanor Powell

kidding? The cruise had been romantic. Neither of us were in love; we were, however, very much attracted to one another.

I suffered a momentary feeling of having been used, but I knew MGM feared a scandal, and it was silly of me to expect Eleanor to defy the studio. Despite the fuckups and scandals in Hollywood, the mores of the country were conventional, and the studios tried to cover up anything unsavory. In some instances, MGM stars were protected beyond the law. The Canadian-born actor Walter Pidgeon was accused of raping a fourteen-year-old girl, and MGM kept the incident entirely from the media. Walter's penchant for pigeon was notorious. MGM was always bailing him out to protect his public image and their investment in a leading man. Young women's parents were bought off time and time again.

In New York, Jack Jr. introduced me to a lovely starlet, Joanne Dru. A beautiful southern belle, she was temporarily living with her mother on Riverside Drive. She was also the sister of Peter Marshall, an actor who became a successful game show host. Unfortunately, my evening was spent listening to how she was an admirer of Adolf Hitler. Clearly, she was not aware that I was Jewish. I wondered who she thought Jack Warner was.

The Heasley twins persuaded me to bring my date up to the St. Regis roof, where they were working. Their ice skating act, performed in tux and black tie, included Bea, Bobby Heasley's girlfriend, who skated and sang. She later married the prominent attorney Sidney Korshak but remained friends with the Heasleys. And when they became fliers and owned a school for flight instructors, Bea also became a pilot. Bob and Jack were intrigued by my date; however, Joanne's conversation was so limited, filled with such silly prejudices, we wondered how she was going to make it in Hollywood, where she and her mother were headed.

I remained in New York three months before returning to the West Coast. "Hi, Ellie, I'm back."

"Come over," came the instant response. But thereafter, as eager as Eleanor was to see me, I was kept under wraps.

I was drawn to Eleanor, but I never considered her my type. She wasn't the voluptuous fantasy like my next-door neighbor Pat Dane, who lived in the apartment between Desi Arnaz's and mine. Pat must have been all of seventeen, and I thought she was gorgeous. We went to bed on the second date. She made it clear, however, that I was not going to be her boyfriend. Pat was like so many of the young women who came to Hollywood—exceptional looking, with stardom and/or a famous, rich man as their goal. In this case, Pat wanted both a contract and someone of note. I thought she was perfection except for her little, whiny voice, which I'm certain she tried to change. Pat didn't need me. She got what she wanted in spades when, after a stint as a contract player with MGM, she married Tommy Dorsey, the bandleader.

Aspiring actresses were plucked off immediately by the local agencies. Most often the young women wouldn't get much further than a stock contract player. The Ava Gardners headed for MGM, the favored studio for the would-be stars streaming into Hollywood seeking fame and fortune. MGM made the best pictures—*Gone with the Wind, The Wizard of Oz*. MGM had the best directors. MGM was it! Clark Gable, Spencer Tracy, the Barrymores, Mickey Rooney, Judy Garland—their list of superstars went on and on.

MGM starlets were all rather gorgeous showgirls. They'd be under contract for fifty to seventy-five dollars a week, going to school, getting coached in drama, dance, and singing, and out of the whole group might come a star or two. Generally they remained in secondary and bit parts, locked into seven-year contracts with agents watching their every move. It was not uncommon for one starlet to say to another, "Don't go in his office, he'll chase you," or "Better bring your agent along if you don't want to be jumped." The casting couch was infamous—but then there was Billy Grady, the head of casting at MGM, who was not a woman chaser. He was considered a tough number, and not one to seduce or be seduced. I was impressed by MGM when I became an agent and had access to the studios. Metro, a world unto itself, had a private police force, as well as security connected to the Los Angeles Police Department and national law enforcement agencies.

MGM had tremendous power. Actors were treated like inmates. Louis B. Mayer, for all his authority, was just another employee. The boss of bosses, Nick Schenck, lived in New York. His brother, Joe Schenck, was head of 20th Century Fox and one of Pat DiCicco's closest friends and sponsors.

DiCicco was Gloria Vanderbilt's first husband. His local credibility was based in large measure on his association with Joe, which is well documented in Vanderbilt's book *Black Knight, White Knight.* In fact, Lynn Bari, my second wife, had been a contract player from age thirteen at Fox, and she'd complained that DiCicco had tried to rape her when she was fifteen.

MGM was to ruin Clark Gable and Robert Taylor. These stars were let go in a cruel way, after having been their greatest draws. Louis B. Mayer himself came to fear he'd also be axed. "I'm afraid for my own job," he'd say. Sure enough, when Dore Schary became production head at MGM, he fired Mayer.

⸻

On a Sunday night Victor Hugo's was the in place to bring a date. Eleanor naturally wasn't going out to the popular clubs with me. One Sunday I left her house and, dateless, went to Victor Hugo's.

There was some element of karma that night. Judy Garland was at the club with Louis B. Mayer and her sisters Jimmie and Susie. I'd heard Judy sing earlier in the year at the Trocadero, also a popular supper club. I'd run into Lester Linsk, an agent and acquaintance of mine and close friend of Bette Davis, at one of Joe Pasternak's afternoon parties. Lester, Bette, and I went on to the Trocadero. Billy Wilkerson was the proprietor; later he became the publisher of the entertainment trade paper the *Hollywood Reporter.* It was a Sunday night, and Judy gave a spontaneous performance. She brought the house down.

Now, at Victor Hugo's, Judy was introduced by the orchestra leader. She belted out a song for the customers. The little plump charmer again captivated everyone with her amazing voice.

In the men's room, I bumped into Lee Siegel, a physician with whom I'd struck up a casual friendship after having seen him around the club. We were both pretty stoned that night and decided it might be a kick to continue on to Tony Cornero's gambling boat, the *Rex*, docked three miles off the Santa Monica pier. The *Rex* featured slot machines and craps and roulette tables. Small motor launches waited to swoosh you from land to sea and back. The croupiers dressed in tuxedos. Customers were served whiskey whether they gambled or not. Lee was without cash, so I advanced him $500.

Before World War II broke out, Lee went into the army as a captain in the medical corps. He was an attractive person, and he returned from the war to what was essentially a celebrity practice in Los Angeles, with patients who included Franchot Tone and Orson Welles, among others. He would be one of Judy's doctors, and I would be one of her husbands. He never sent me a bill. But that particular night we were all strangers.

My introduction to "little" Judy Garland came soon after, while visiting Eleanor on the set of *Broadway Melody of 1938*. The Broadway Melody series of musical films was a big hit for MGM, and a way to introduce new talent. Eleanor costarred with Robert Taylor, and Judy had a scene-stealing role. She would make an indelible impression on the public when she sang "Dear Mr. Gable: You Made Me Love You" to his photograph. The routine had been created for her by Roger Edens.

Though Judy was celebrating her fifteenth birthday on the day of my visit, she looked closer to twelve. She was thrilled with the gold charm bracelet given to her by the "King," Clark Gable, and she went around the set displaying the cherished birthday present to everyone, including me. So I actually met Judy Garland the year I arrived in Los Angeles.

———— ∞ ————

Eleanor arranged for me to be an extra in the film *Rosalie*. The musical had been a Broadway hit. This time, she costarred with Nelson Eddy, who lived in a small apartment with his mother and a big police dog, which Nelson took everywhere.

Our production number required cumbersome uniforms resembling Britain's Coldstream Guards. Happily, the Heasley twins were part of the cast. The choreographer had designed an unusual number: our shoes were nailed to the floor to facilitate a kind of Raggedy Ann–doll movement as we bent in different directions; the rifles we carried remained stationary; all this while Eleanor, high up on a platform, stood on a drum tapping her heart out for America in her sequined halter, bare legs, and top hat.

Nelson Eddy drove Eleanor crazy. Eddy was plagued by nervous stomach gas all through shooting. He was a humorless person. Filming is boring, tedious work, so Eleanor and I would find ways to amuse ourselves. Not Nelson. One of his bad habits was to belch and blame it on his big police dog. He seriously believed we bought it. Eleanor got to the point where she'd imitate him and shout to an imaginary dog, "Stop it!"

Eleanor had been born with gorgeous legs and the gift to use them. A vivacious presence on screen, her compelling smile sparkled from the screen into your heart—not unlike Judy's.

Eleanor and her mother encouraged me to learn camera work, thinking I had an eye for it. Eleanor thought this was the road up in the industry, as moviemaking was such an inside business. But I had this idea that I might go to war, and furthermore I didn't see myself working for a weekly salary.

I may have been the quintessential entertainee, but I also had a burning desire to fly, to become a professional pilot. I spent a good deal of time receiving private flight instructions. Once out of the Santa Monica airport I'd get up to a thousand feet and look over Los Angeles and Pasadena—both natural dust bowls for the prevailing winds coming off the desert—and think what a charming, marvelous town Hollywood was.

No matter how much Eleanor and her mother tried to shape my interests, I turned to other vistas. I hit on the idea of Custom Motors. I enjoyed engines, and customizing automobiles was a Hollywood fad.

It was right up my alley. Eleanor invested $5,000. I found a well-located storefront to work out of, and within the year I was able to buy the property.

Custom Motors flourished. I hired a man away from the Cadillac agency who was a good metalworker. A skillful, well-known body designer, Alex Tremulis, came in one day to see what the hell I was doing. He was out of work. I fell in love with his sketches of futuristic cars, which look like our sports cars of today. He loved speed and so did I. Alex was a rather intellectual-looking individual, prematurely balding, slender, sporting a mustache, and wearing glasses. Duesenberg had folded, so he came to work for Custom Motors.

I wasn't a big operator, but I had an unusual little business going. It was creative, and that was what appealed to Tremulis. I gave him a little American Austin to redesign. Roy Evans, who owned the Palm Bay Club in Florida, thought the American Austin was going to be the car of the future. It was small, not as sturdy as the Volkswagen bug but in that category.

Alex redesigned the Bantam, a small car we transformed from a coupe into a convertible. Alex was driving one back from the company in Pennsylvania when he was blown off the New Jersey turnpike in a storm. We were anxious, but he delivered it in time for us to repaint it and sell it to the customer. Alex went on to become a top designer. I ran into him much later, when he was retired and living in Ventura. Ironically, he is best known for designing Evel Knievel's motorcycle.

The Duesenberg had been the most expensive American car built, and many movie stars wanted to drive this particular automobile. Clark Gable owned one; so did Gary Cooper. Eventually Georgie Stoll, the musical director, bought Clark's and brought it to us. We gave it a new interior of English luggage leather and created a khaki paint color for the exterior. The car has been preserved and remains part of a private collection.

Sooner or later, everyone in town visited Custom Motors. Prince Alexis Mdivani, Barbara Hutton's husband, tragically died in an auto crash in Spain. He willed his fancy Mercedes-Benz roadster to his brother David. It was a custom-built Mercedes by Figoni & Falaschi, a rare model. David asked me to sell the car because he needed cash. I sold it to someone in the Texas Hunt family for an appropriate amount of money.

A colorful character came into the shop one afternoon wearing a trench coat and a pulled-down fedora like Spencer Tracy. He introduced me to a distributor of Cadillacs in Indiana who turned out to be Jewish. Feldstein was a rare bird, as few Jews were granted automobile distributorships in those restrictive days. I flew to South Bend to meet with Feldstein, a jolly, heavyset man with a big Santa Claus belly. From then on I was able to order directly from him. And there was no import tax—it was legal to carry on this kind of business.

My specialty became redesigning these Cadillacs. A roadrunner would deliver them to us. We'd remove the grille, reshape it to look ultramodern. Then we'd drop the entire top section of the car about six inches, recut the windows to make the car look very sleek. I'd sell them for $1,800, lower than the dealer's price.

I sold one of my Cadillac specials to Tony Cornero from the *Rex*. He was a tough guy, short and stocky. He dressed in a dark suit and tie and a wide-brimmed gray felt hat. He looked like a mug Eddie Robinson might portray. Pointed collars, big diamond ring, and cigar—central casting. Tony's girlfriend noticed one of the cars dramatically lit in the show window and had to have one. She too was a stereotype: a mobster's gal, bleach blonde, big breasts, a short chorus girl in five-inch heels. The day Tony and friend were to pick up their car I had put a piece of metal through the hood, and the car buckled under the weight of the lead in it. Frantically we worked at straightening out the buckle, quickly closed up the grille, and put the wooden skirts on the back of the very fancy looking modern car just in time for Cornero to pick it up.

I switched to LaSalles because they were cheaper, with the same engine as the Cadillac. We photographed the cars in front of mansions and then displayed the pictures. That and word of mouth was the extent of my advertising.

Sadly for Cornero, he got indicted. Apparently the girlfriend's car was still in his name; he sold it to Billy Wilkerson when he went off to jail.

II

HOLLYWOOD WAS LIVING UP to all my great expectations. I got word that Columbia was looking for an unknown to play the lead in the film version of Clifford Odets's hit play *Golden Boy*. On a lark, overcome by the phrase "movie star/pilot" as a means for history to describe me, I sent glossies of myself over to the studio. Of course, I was never called. It was to be William Holden's big break. I didn't think of acting as a serious career; in any case, flying was my central interest.

Bud and Doug Ornstein's flying school at Clover Field at the Santa Monica airport was a haven for me. Bud was my first instructor there. I earned my private license with him. He'd married Mary Pickford's niece; Mary's husband Buddy Rogers flew there on weekends, so I was never very far away from show business.

Since World War I, I'd heard that Germany would never rise again as a military power. Now the commercial pilots were sure we were headed toward war. Everything began to feel impermanent. I wouldn't be hanging on to Custom Motors for much longer. I played all the harder at night. I'd frequent the clubs—the Cinegrill and Chasen's. Dave Chasen was a warm person who drew clients to his moderately priced restaurant with excellent American food. It was a small place with a steam room in the rear. The guys in the steam room would be Humphrey Bogart and Billy Grady, people who ate there every night. It was a home away from home: the steam was basically for personal friends of Dave. During the war when I became a test pilot at Douglas Aircraft, I frequented another steam room in the Crosby Building on Sunset Boulevard. It took down the stress. I'd run into film directors like Jimmy Wong Howe, Lewis Milestone. It was a mix of industry people and two or three test pilots trying to relax.

I'd see Errol Flynn around some of the gyms and clubs I favored. In those days, I'd run into him several times a week at the Beverly Hills Athletic Club. I understood Errol wished to enlist but he had a bad heart, "a hole in his pump," so he was unable to fight. Since he knew he had a defective heart, his lifestyle was rather reckless. I thought he was dashing. I certainly bought his act, and liked him very much. Errol was popular—he was invited to all the parties. I admired his attitude toward his limitations: a physical man who could not really be an athlete. Decades later, documents and books were released pointing to Flynn as a fascist sympathizer, aiding and abetting German spies, using his celebrity status to gain certain government favors so he could help close Nazi ties. It's very difficult for me to think of Errol in this context.

I saw A-20 bombers flying out of Clover Field. Bombers with red, white, and blue circles stamped on the bulkhead were marked for delivery to France. Later on, the same aircraft were delivered to Russia stamped with a red star. I'd watch military aircraft running in and out of the field all the time.

In the beginning, it was fun and games, being able to hang out with the commercial pilots at Norms on Olympic Boulevard, where we'd gather to drink beer and talk. We wore leather jackets, goggles, and the famous aviator scarf, which was used to protect against the cold. Women seemed to love the uniform. For me it was an out-and-out ego trip. "Here comes Sid Luft. You know he's a pilot." Hollywood was a town filled with specialists in glamour, and I seemed to be developing my own rather different style.

Periodically, the old World War I photos from my childhood sunporch would flash through my mind: the ominous spiked helmets, the big bayonets. I remembered my youthful vow never to get caught up in a marching war. As I wandered around Yorkville in New York, the

American Nazis displaying their swastikas frightened the hell out of me. Hadn't I been to Europe and met lovely people forced to flee their native country because of the Nazis? The idea of being crushed by a hostile power was despicable. I'd grown up listening to my parents' stories of their escape from tyranny. It was unsettling to hear why Mother came to this country—the descriptions of life during the Russian pogroms were still vivid. Yet she'd been proud of her Russian heritage, as I was presently proud of my American identity. Father, too, left Austria because life had been precarious. I couldn't see why a guy should have his head blown off because he was not in the right place at the right time. I was going to make every effort to be in the right place, and that was not going to be on the ground. So I auctioned off Custom Motors. Eleanor had long since been paid back for her investment, and now there was a hefty profit to share. I immediately concentrated on piling up flying time.

In 1938 I bought a Monocoupe airplane in Burbank for $1,500. I financed it through the Bank of America. The Monocoupe was yellow with bluebirds on the fuselage, orange wings, and a black tail. Lindbergh had one exactly like it, later displayed at the Lindbergh museum in St. Louis.

One of my flight instructors, an actor, was going with a very attractive widow who was the mother of the singer Margaret Whiting. The Whitings lived in a lovely house in Bel Air with a great swimming pool. Mrs. Whiting enjoyed having kids around, and there was always a mix of her friends and the younger generation. I began hanging out there, and I met the woman who became my first wife, Marylou Simpson, a local debutante who also aspired to be an actress. Her mother, Gussie, didn't exactly approve of me, and Eleanor and her mother tried to talk me out of that relationship. But Marylou and I began to go steady, and my intimate relationship with Eleanor faded as a result.

Around this time I had my driver's license revoked. I had raced a friend, Tommy Lee, from the veteran's home in Westwood. It was around three in the morning; I was driving a hopped-up Cadillac, and Tommy was in a small Duesenberg sports car that could drive like the wind. We whipped through Beverly Hills at about a hundred miles an hour. There was nobody on the streets at that hour but the police. I spent a few days in jail and found a lawyer with the wonderful name of Judge Hazzard. He took $500 and the courts took another $500. My license was revoked for six months, so I had to hire a driver. The man was a few years older than me and he called me "boss." He was from Oklahoma and looked like a variation on Li'l Abner, with a thin face and hair falling over his forehead. He was the personification of the pejorative term "Okie," but he was lovable, and an excellent driver even if he never got beyond the second grade. I wasn't permitted to drive a car, but I could still fly an airplane.

———— ∞ ————

It was 1939 and Lindbergh had flown to Germany, met with Göring, and returned to the United States to relate to President Roosevelt the might of the German Luftwaffe. My hero was rapidly falling in my eyes. His isolationist views didn't make sense to me—unless he wanted Hitler to win. I had a lot of anger, because I thought I saw through Lindbergh's machinations. The isolationists were running the country, and Roosevelt would wait until the Japanese bombed Pearl Harbor to declare war on Japan, by which time Hitler was all over Europe. We didn't know about the death camps as yet. I was outraged at the super-Americanism proliferating around the country. What did it mean: was it simply patriotism, or was it a cover up for prejudice of all shapes and varieties?

Meanwhile, Marylou confessed she was in love with me. I was considering marriage, but I wanted to be certain. I remembered Peggy Mitchell, a little girl from home who would be all grown up by now. I was curious to see how she'd matured. I had some wild oats to sow in any case and decided to fly my Monocoupe east to see Peggy in Bronxville and my childhood friends the Leos in Armour Villa Park. I thought I'd make a dramatic return to the old hometown, arriving in my own airplane. I arranged for Johnny Leo to meet me at Armonk.

I kept in mind the Mitchells' serene, rose-colored house a block away from Sarah Lawrence College and the sweet little girl who could be waiting there for me. Peggy had been a beautiful girl, wonderfully Irish, with black hair and blue eyes. Marylou was spoiled, an only child, high strung. I was crazy about her, but I got to thinking Peggy might be more suitable for me.

The flight across the country was insane. I was to encounter one harrowing episode after another. I traveled with a mechanic from Clover Field who wanted to hitch a ride to Des Moines, Iowa. I hadn't been trained sufficiently in instrument flying, and we took off in lousy weather; we were soon forced down in Socorro, New Mexico. I'd been flying along the railroad tracks, which we called flying the steel beam, and I couldn't find an airport; we were running out of gas. I was not experienced enough to read the quadrants—dash, dot, dot, dash. I'd been flying six hundred feet above the ground, and it was around three in the afternoon. We put down in a field, where we happened to find a mobile motion picture unit traveling to an army base to show movies, and they sold us some gas. We were really happy to see them, and they were kind folk. They told us there was a small airport about fifty miles away. In order to get airborne, I had to unload as much weight as possible, so I had to leave my passenger with the traveling picture show. We took out his luggage and tools and made arrangements to meet in town. I had to keep my compass on a certain heading for what seemed like twenty hours instead of twenty minutes through the ominous mountains. It was pitch black and I was flying through a valley with a quarter tank of gas left. The Monocoupe was able to fly a maximum of nine thousand feet with a light load of fuel. The plateau around New Mexico averages seven thousand feet and the peaks go up to thirteen thousand feet. I had to needle my way through these mountains. Finally I spotted some dots on an airstrip and worked the radio for landing instructions. I had no night flying experience. I was floating up there, making turns, waiting for a response. Nothing was coming in. I decided to go for it and brought the aircraft down to the ground in darkness. I made a circle, and there was a tiny white house with an old pump in front of it. I was soaking wet from fear. The wind was up now and blowing, so much so that I thought the airplane was going to tip over. I was looking for a way to tie it down. It was cold as hell. Two lights appeared. "Ho ho, son, I'm the airport manager." To me he was Santa Claus. "Thank Christ I heard you up there, son." So we tied the airplane down. He told me I had landed on an auxiliary airfield that the army used for maneuvers. The actual army base was several hundred miles away. I asked him for the nearest gas pump and the man replied, "Pie Town, and one at Datil."

"Where are we?"

"Right in the middle." I thought, that's the truth! We drove into town in the man's truck, where I located my pal and promptly got incredibly drunk. We took off at eight o'clock in the morning with a full tank of gas and hangovers.

The next mishap led us to a Midwest cornfield. I brought the airplane down in a bumpy landing. The force of it knocked the air scope loose from its two bolts. My passenger didn't have any tools to drill out the two bolts. We managed to repair the airplane, but I decided not to take off. In the morning we got up early and saw that we could take off easily enough if we knocked down some of the fences. We were busy pulling the poles out when a gruff-voiced farmer with a big shotgun aimed squarely at me said, "Who the hell do you think you are?"

I answered fast: "I'm from the United States government. We must remove this plane."

"You're tearin' down my fence."

"We'll repair it. Just give me the bill." I offered him my license, adding, "The government will pay." Then he bought it. He allowed us to tear the entire fence down. About ten miles down the road we found the airport and gassed up. I flew directly to Des Moines, where I dropped off my bemused, good sport passenger. I stayed long enough to have a romance with a girl he introduced to me. She was the daughter of the man who owned the Packard auto agency. I just loved Packards.

I was on my way to Pittsburgh from Des Moines with just five hundred miles' worth of fuel capacity, so I had to refuel somewhere along the way. Flying at five thousand feet, I hit a bluish-gray sheet. I could barely see, so I dipped the airplane into it thinking, *I can go through this.* Suddenly I was turned upside down and I felt like a meat-chopper had me. I thought I was going to be spat out. North looked like certain death, so I quickly turned south. *Luft,* I asked myself, *what the fuck are you doing now?*

I wound up following the White River into St. Louis, where I was able to land. It was a hot, humid night and hundreds of people were out at the airport. Apparently the airport was the place to hang out on hot nights. I had the illusion of Lindbergh coming in on a wing and a prayer. The weather cleared, but I spent the night there.

The next day I figured I'd look for the confluence of the Monongahela and Allegheny Rivers, which is located in Pittsburgh. When I reached the Monongahela, I was low on fuel and once again looking for a place to land. The hills around Pennsylvania and the Continental Divide are known as the "graveyard" to pilots, nothing but one rolling hill after another. I spotted a field and people waving at me. I made three passes around the field, throttled back, and yelled "Pittsburgh" into space as I fast glided. I was completely cuckoo. The fuel indicator was nearly zero, but I made a nice landing in that field. It was a lovely, big farm, and the family was very nice to me. There was a voluptuous young girl, brothers, mother, and father, and they were talking over breakfast about Wendell Willkie, the Republican candidate for president. After breakfast the next morning, they cleared the cows, and I took off with Mexican ethyl taken out of a tractor. I was the nutty pilot. My experience had been aerobatics, short trial solos, but no cross country. I was showing off, and so far, I'd had just enough luck not to get killed.

I finally cracked up in a tree. I was flying the steel beam, and I never did get up enough flying speed and stalled right into the tree. I climbed out, but the tail was stuck in the ground with the engine about ten feet in the air. I had made it across the Continental Divide only to crash into a tree! Some local boys pulled me out unharmed. We dismantled the entire airplane: the motor, the instruments (which were costly), the bank indicator, the compass, and the fuel gauge. My Monocoupe was wrecked beyond saving. Now I had to get from Pittsburgh to Bronxville for my rendezvous with Peggy. I hitched a ride in a little pickup truck with all my salvage. We arrived at Armonk in the late afternoon. I sold the parts for about the same amount of money I'd originally paid for the Monocoupe. I was able to buy a Dart, a low-wing aircraft, on the spot for the flight back west. It had not been a very impressive return to home turf.

Before I contacted Peggy or Johnny Leo, I called Marylou. Her mother, Gussie, came on the line and told me Marylou was hysterical. Somehow she'd heard about one of my crashes. I thought, *She really does care for me.*

In New York, Johnny and I took a nostalgic tour of our old haunts. I romanced Peggy at the Waldorf Astoria, where I was staying, and we had a good time. Peggy had grown up, but I could see she wasn't the girl for me. I found myself looking forward to getting back to Los Angeles to see Marylou.

The return flight to California in the Dart was a piece of cake in comparison to my barnstorming antics going east.

12

IT WAS COMING TOWARD the end of 1939 and the Canadians were looking to enlist pilots. To this end they opened a recruitment office in Los Angeles. I thought, prepare yourself, baby, because the world is really going to war now. I was determined to be a qualified pilot even though I hadn't packed in the proper amount of time.

The way I'd acquired my commercial license was by faking my logbooks with Doug Ornstein's signature. I made a stamp for myself and built up more time than I actually had by marching down to the stationery store and concocting a stamp that looked very much like the Clover Field Flying School stamp. When my faked logbook showed three hundred hours, I had enough to go for my license. I went to the FAA office, a twenty-minute drive from Clover Field, and they took me up and put me through the exercises. The actual flight test was not hard—lazy eights, turning the airplane over at 360 degrees while keeping the nose above the horizon, straight and level flying, take off, landing, and Immelmann, a 180-degree turn. I had to be precise with the stalls and spins. During this period, I was also learning aerobatics from former navy pilots. We'd put the aircraft through maneuvers like slow rolls, figure eights, and loops. We performed usually in an open-pitted aircraft with a good-size engine. I enjoyed the Ryan ST, an all-metal, low-wing craft that I could turn every which way. These maneuvers frightened a lot of people, but I was attracted to this kind of mischief like a moth to light.

The written exam for the commercial license was lengthy and comprehensive: I would have to know not only about engines but about navigation as well. I was able to understand everything, but I was not a test person. I'd hurriedly prepared. I wasn't one hundred percent ready—there were several questions that stymied me. I excused myself to go to the john. Once outside the classroom I got on the pay phone and called Clover Field, where a pal was waiting on the other end of the line. My friend had a lot of experience and gave me the needed correct answers. This kind of unethical behavior was unheard of, but I was too ambitious not to take this opportunity and use it for what I thought was for the best. I was taking risks because I felt the world was closing in on me and I didn't have much time to act.

But to qualify for officer status in the Royal Canadian Air Force, I'd need five hundred hours in my logbook, and it now stopped at four hundred. I was one of a number of guys my age who were building up flight time at Clover Field so we could join the RCAF. We all thought we were going to be the equivalent of squadron leaders—dreams of glory—or at least earn a commission of captain with airline experience, which I didn't have. I'd been flying a little aircraft with a little engine. Nevertheless, of the guys who hung around the flying school, I was one of the few who actually made the RCAF.

I really was learning to fly by trial and error, half derring-do and a semi-ignorant lust for thrills. Once I was at Clover Field taxiing in a little Luscombe, a training airplane. I was on the taxi strip and a guy was holding up a sign: Don't Taxi Back of Airport. I didn't see the sign, it was so small. And I wasn't aware that in the Douglas Aircraft hangars, they were revving up the engines of a cargo aircraft, a DC3. They should have had a red flag waving at the tail section. I got caught in the prop wash from the DC3 and it flipped me on my back.

It was Ornstein's airplane, and Douglas paid for all the repairs.

⸻ ⁂ ⸻

Marylou defied her parents by marrying me. We eloped to Las Vegas in December 1940, with a ring borrowed from Maggie Whiting, Margaret

Whiting's aunt. Three days after our marriage we still had not slept together as man and wife. Gussie had noticed Marylou's car parked in front of my apartment and called me up. "I want to talk to you kids—now."

I'd perceived Lou Simpson—Marylou's father, a rugged, red-faced man—as rather narrow-minded. He was an executive at Pioneer Flintkote, a division of Shell Oil that manufactured roofing materials. He had plans for his daughter to marry someone from a wealthy family with whom he could play golf on weekends at the Los Angeles Country Club, a place that barred "kikes," "niggers," and dogs. His idea of a son-in-law may have been someone from Bronxville, but not a Jewish kid. I was certain he'd been avoiding meeting me for months. Now we both had to face the music.

We sent my driver out for a bottle of whiskey. Marylou was especially nervous and felt she needed to shore up her courage. We belted down some shots, and when we were up to it we made our way over to the Simpson home, where I proceeded to tell Gussie that Marylou and I were deeply in love—in fact, married. Gussie looked as though she was going to have a breakdown. I said, "Please calm down. Marylou and I are married, but we haven't consummated the marriage. She's your daughter." It's two in the afternoon and both mother and daughter are crying.

This went on four more hours, with Marylou trying to assure her mother: "I love Sid."

About a quarter of six I heard whistling. It's Lou, walking to the living room. "What's going on here?" He looked puzzled.

Gussie sobbed, "They're married."

His reaction was to turn and say, "Who are you?"

I was not going to overlook the slight. I'd been around the house steadily for the last five months. I blurted out, "I've been seeing Marylou for some months, and we've gotten married, but we haven't consummated it."

Lou coughed. "Sit down, let's talk this over. What do you do?"

"I'm a pilot and I've just joined the Royal Canadian Air Force. I'll be in Canada in about a week."

He countered, "My cousin is Admiral Simpson. I'll have you on a carrier in a month's time. Enlist in the navy, boy, don't go to Canada."

I was so recklessly defiant at that age that I knew I'd never get along in the US military. If I'd been in the army I'd have been court martialed, hung, or shot. I thought, *This bastard is going to have me killed one way or the other.*

I didn't want to enlist, and I certainly didn't want to be drafted. The first to be drafted were kids not in college; the second were men who were single. The third classification was married men. Had it not been wartime Marylou and I probably would not have married so quickly.

"Look, Lou, I understand how you feel, but your daughter's in love with me. I'm in love with her. Things do happen."

"Well, I don't approve."

"If you can talk your daughter out of marriage, I'm on my way."

The three Simpsons left the room and went upstairs to confer.

Not much time passed before the three of them returned to announce we were going out to celebrate. Amid tears we went for dinner and drinks at the Tropics on Rodeo Drive. For our wedding present Lou and Gussie booked us a suite at the Beverly Wilshire Hotel, where Marylou and I became husband and wife. A few days later we were on a plane to Ottawa.

I became a pilot officer with one stripe on both wrists, equivalent to a second lieutenant, and cloth wings stitched on my tunic. The visor cap was like the UK's RAF. The first day, there was a big party and someone got drunk and screamed at me, "You fuckin' American, coming up here and flying . . ." Before he was finished I had him hanging out the window with my hands around his throat. I thought, is it going to be me against the Royal Canadian Air Force, too?

The pay was $300 a month. To live decently I sold a lot I owned on Rodeo Drive, and Gussie sold my Packard 12 Roadster and sent me the money.

I started my career with the RCAF at Thunderbird Field, School Conversion Training Squadron, Edmonton, Ontario. When we were sent to Edmonton it was forty degrees below zero, an ice palace, but Marylou and I had a good time. There was an indoor armory where we played polo, and at night we'd often take the horses for a gallop in the moonlit snow. We met civilians we enjoyed spending time with, and we were very much in love. This was our honeymoon, but I was concerned about getting Marylou pregnant. It was the era of the soapy douche, and it seemed to work; it did break the afterglow, however, as the woman had to apply this method immediately after making love.

Marylou seemed to adore our new life, the snow's brilliance, the sheer force of nature at night. The purity of the intense winter landscape fed our relationship, so much in contrast to our accustomed palm-lined streets and the smoky ambience of near-tropical nights at the beach.

I worked from six in the morning until three in the afternoon. I piloted wireless air gunners, made for noncommissioned men who were going to be tail gunners and receive instructions by code. The flights were half-hour stints for the kids to practice their inflight exercises. Later that winter I was sent to the number-one wireless gunnery school in Montreal. I flew a Noorduyn Norseman, a single-engine, Canadian-built bush plane with a high wing that was used during peacetime for transporting mining equipment and able to carry a good-size load, with wheels and pontoons. It was a solid workhorse. Instead of one gunner in the rear it had four.

I got into a brawl in Montreal and hit another officer, Pilot Officer Jennings. We were having luncheon and I signed a chit thinking that was the thing to do. It was $1.40. I wrote down my number and where I was stationed. No sooner had I signed the chit than Jennings's voice invaded my eardrum: "You fuckin' Americans come up here and sign those chits."

Again, my reactive nature blasted, "What'd you say?"

"You heard me," came the defiant reply. I pounded him as he finished his retort. I was put under open arrest and sent back to the dormitory on the facility. While I was waiting to be paraded in front of the commanding officer for striking another officer I saw the door to his office was ajar. I overheard an Aussie who was a squadron leader say, "Wing Commander, go fuck yourself, you old cocksucker." He couldn't stop swearing, continuing, "Fuck you, you dirty old son of a bitch," and then he walked out. I thought, *This is going to be a tough act to follow.* I was aware that the Aussies were treated like shit. They were fighter pilots sent in directly from Australia. A division of non-commissioned men, they'd arrive in Canada already half nuts from the strain of flying bombers. They were high strung and some of them broke down; others became drunks. It was a dangerous, tough life for these overworked young men. When I was officer of the day I found a kid locked up in the local precinct. He was an Aussie picked up dead drunk. A nice guy, he was reduced to sobbing. I saw right away that these kids' nerves were shot.

"Officer Luft." My name was barked out. I explained what had happened, that I had misunderstood, that I thought I could sign the chit, and that I regretted hitting the officer. The wing commander was not sympathetic. "You'll have to see the air force marshal in Toronto."

"Yes, sir," I replied, surprised that they were making this into an issue; I knew they couldn't court martial me. As an American, I was in the Canadian Air Force but was not obliged to take the oath. I could quit and walk across the border at any time.

The wing commander told me to report to a warrant officer, who would be accompanying me by train from Montreal all the way to Toronto. I was being treated like a prisoner. Fortunately, the warrant officer was a nice guy and the trip to Toronto, besides being a waste of time, was not a hardship.

The air force marshal sat behind a large desk, and his uniform displayed more spaghetti than I'd seen to date. He made a little speech about my behavior from the papers on his desk. Again, I explained I was very sorry, I lost my temper, it was a misunderstanding. I went on to say I was actually outraged that I'd been insulted as an American who came to Canada in good faith. He then asked me where I'd like to be stationed. I said I'd like to advance myself, and that Picton, Ontario, would be OK. He told me I had a fine record and I said, "Thank you." The marshal was the opposite of the wing commander. He was grateful that Americans came up and enlisted.

Around March 1941 I was transferred to Picton, across the river from Rochester, New York, on Lake Erie. The following summer was lovely, with beautiful weather every day. I was flying something that looked like a Spitfire but was twice as big. It carried the same engine. Now the cadets were working with targets.

Once, though, I was returning to Saint-Hubert Airport in Montreal when, from out of nowhere, a violent snowstorm blew in and I was unable to land. I could only approximate the distance. I was in a Noorduyn Norseman, ferrying training pilots. I remained out of the area for twenty minutes, hoping the front would move on. Airplanes were trying to line up for a landing at the end of their exercises, and there was a great deal of confusion. I made a pass over the airport and saw a red light indicating danger: get out of the area. I nearly collided with another airplane. I was instructed to reduce my speed and land downwind. I came in too fast and the runway was packed with deep snow. I'd never landed in snow. I'd disobeyed my instructions and came in too high over telephone wires. I hit the end of the runway and went into a snowbank and slowly turned over on my back. Luckily, the aircraft didn't catch fire. I loosened the safety belt and promptly fell on my head. Before I could even walk away from the airplane, the tail section crumpled the rudder, and there was some damage to the top of the wing. The emergency trucks and ambulance were at the ready. I helped the kids out. Fortunately, no one was hurt. I'd had experience flying in Edmonton where there was snow, but it was lightweight compared to this situation. I was not as experienced as the guys who were bush pilots delivering mail and supplies infield to the prairie country of Canada. They flew in any weather. I was a nutcase from California who was still learning.

Another time I was delivering a Lockheed Ventura back to Montreal with a navigator and copilot. I took off from Dallas. It was fall and the weather around Nashville was consistently rainy in that season, with fog and storm fronts. A front was closing down on me and I was running out of fuel. The ground was soggy, and I stuck the airplane in a field near Charleroi, Pennsylvania, about the size of a postage stamp. We got out of the airplane and there were farmers and local townspeople swarming around us. The airplane wasn't damaged, but I knew I couldn't fly it out, so I locked it and walked away. I got conscripted to give a talk at the local high school that night. Eventually the RCAF had to haul the airplane away.

I made six flights with a navigator across the North Atlantic from Newfoundland. We'd receive instructions to take off in Montreal. I'd open up the envelope, read the instructions, and fly out and back. Sometimes it would be a false mission. Out of Newfoundland we'd fly to Prestwick, Scotland; to France; and to a region of Finland, where I encountered the women's Russian ferrying command. Both the Americans and Russians were in Finland.

I delivered the first modified A-20 bomber, painted all black. It was used for special operations. The female Russian pilots would pick up these planes in Finland and fly them at tree level over northern Prussia at night. They wouldn't talk to the American pilots. They were strong, masculine women who often didn't survive. They were very courageous. The modified A-20 was but a small step beyond experimental stage, equipped with night-flying restricted gear. Germany had an entire fleet of destroyers in Norway right across the North Sea. And the British engaged Germans in combat over the English Channel. Generally, after delivering an A-20, I flew back in a Lancaster, a heavy bomber. I was not interested in actual warfare. It didn't appeal to me. Some men had to be fighter pilots. But for me, there were enough risks flying the North Atlantic.

Jim Mitchell, one of the former navy pilots who taught me aerobatics at Clover Field, had also joined the RCAF. A quiet, serious guy, he was a mechanic and a great instructor. Flying aerobatics had given me a strong sense of control; precision flying, as it were, helped me become more proficient. As he was older and more experienced, I looked up to Jim and considered him a friend. One morning in Canada, he took an aircraft on a mission that I'd been scheduled to fly, a delivery across the North Atlantic. Jim disappeared on that run. We figured he must have iced up and crashed. I was devastated over the loss of a great friend, and I began to think that if it weren't for Jim, I'd be dead. Over the years I often thought of Jimmy Mitchell as my involuntary guardian angel. I've never stopped thinking about him. He was a top pilot with three times more expertise than me. It was a huge personal loss.

Four pals got stranded on an ice cap in Greenland for a month. These pilots were flying from Gander to Greenland on instruments when they experienced intense turbulence. Luckily, they survived, living inside the fuselage until they were rescued. The winds were too strong for the rescue airplane to land, so supplies were dropped in for them. I half expected a disaster to happen to me—it was all around me, and there was always that taste of danger in my mouth every time I took off.

13

THE DAY I ARRIVED in Picton in 1941, I'd walked into the officers' mess and Harry Arbick, an officer, came up to me and said, "So, you're the tough guy? You like to fight, Officer Luft?"

To which I replied, "No, sir, I'm not tough, but if you want to take the tunic off, I'll knock your fuckin' brains out." The mess hall had emptied out and it was just the two of us. When he took off his tunic, I said, "Officer Arbick, I don't want to hurt you."

He continued, "You think you're a tough guy, take your first shot."

Quite a gentleman, I thought. "Take yours," I offered.

He threw a punch, and I returned it by knocking him right on the jaw. It was all over. His mouth was cut up. I stood him up and we shook hands. He said, "You'll do."

Harry Arbick was my commanding officer and formerly with the North West Mounted Police. He looked like the old movie actor Jack Holt—mustached, sturdy, ready for duty. Arbick and I became good friends. He eventually went overseas, and when he left he gave me a photo and signed it, "To my dear friend, Sid Luft, the best winger I ever had." I treasure that memento of my early life. He retired after the war, and I invited him and his wife to New York to spend a week as my guest when Judy opened the RKO Palace in 1951.

Marylou took my brawling in stride, mostly because I reassured her that people seemed to love to challenge me. Those brawls didn't last long, and there wasn't any severe damage to anyone. We didn't pack guns or use knives; it was the acting out of the brawler as romantic hero. The times were different, and guys had other goals. We were all under pressure—we didn't know if we were going to survive. We were young and it was war. And there was tragedy all around us. My buddies went off on missions and some never came back. Pilot Officer Holden got bored with flying cadets and went overseas. He was in a fighter group that got blown out of the sky and, like many other men, he left a wife and children behind.

While I was wondering who was going to challenge me next, my wife was playing bridge with the officers' wives. This diversion was not very satisfying for her. She spent her days and nights waiting for me to come off duty. It began to be tough on her to sit around in a small town. There were a few other Americans, and we made a point of going out with them and their wives at night dancing, to movies, to parties in the officers' mess. Nevertheless, she was finding life as a pilot's wife confining.

It didn't help her that I was constantly studying. Harry Arbick had motivated me: I studied celestial navigation and flying under the hood (instrument flying). I now had the opportunity to gain more experience than any of my peers.

Marylou decided she was homesick and went back to Los Angeles. When my four-week furlough came up I followed her. We sublet a house on Beverly Glen Boulevard. I could easily see Marylou was back in the routine of lunch with friends and her mother. One night she confided to me she actually had come to hate her life in Canada. I began to think Marylou would be a hell of a lot nicer if I could work nearer to her. I'd heard about a training program for pilots in Oxnard, halfway between Los Angeles and Santa Barbara.

I drove up to Oxnard to see the commanding officer, who was later married to Hollywood star Constance Bennett. He greeted me with "Glad to have you aboard. Come on back tomorrow and we'll check you out." The next morning, I got up there by 8:00 AM. I was to be checked by an army pilot to become a flight instructor. At four in the afternoon I was still warming the bench. Finally I piped up, "Pardon me, sir, I've been here since eight o'clock." He said, "You could warm it another four days!" A surge of anger came over me and I said, "You don't get me up at five o'clock in the morning and talk to me that way. Shove it up your ass." Disgusted, I returned to Canada.

A cold settled in my ears and wouldn't go away. I was retaining fluid behind the inner ear. On one flight I had to make a quick and dangerous descent. I shouldn't have been flying in that condition. The ear drained for weeks and weeks. I was put on a three-week leave to recuperate in Phoenix, Arizona. I stayed at the Camelback Lodge near the Arizona Biltmore, a nice little hotel, and Jimmy Van Heusen and Sammy Cahn were both there. Jimmy was already a private pilot. We were in the bar drinking when a guy yelled out, "Pearl Harbor bombed!" I thought, now it's official. I was actually relieved.

Marylou was tired of Canada and of playing the wife of a pilot officer. She had designs on acting and did not want a restricted life, no matter how much in love she may have believed she was. I didn't think she wanted a separation. I had planned on leaving Phoenix and spending my remaining time in Los Angeles with Marylou before returning to my duties with the RCAF. We were still a couple as far as I was concerned. Jimmy asked me, "What're you going to do?"

"I guess I'll go back to Canada."

"Did you ever think of flying for ATC? It's a private company run by civilians out in Long Beach." Jimmy explained that ATC was in the business of delivering aircraft. "The commanding officer is a friend of mine; with your experience they'd love a guy like you working for them."

I considered it but decided to return directly to Canada and put both ATC and Marylou on hold for the moment. When I came back from Newfoundland a letter from Marylou was awaiting me. She wanted a divorce. I immediately called Max, a lawyer I knew in Los Angeles.

"Is there any property?" he asked. There wasn't. Max said, "Well, if you don't want to contest the divorce, in six months you'll be divorced. Park the papers in the trash."

I hadn't come to Hollywood to be in the automobile business, nor did I ever have it in mind to marry a movie star. It was wartime; I didn't know what was ahead of me. I was in a day-to-day existence. I'd married a little local society girl who was not willing to wait out the war. She hankered after the movies, and she was attached to her parents. She thought it was too rough being married to a pilot, and so we said bye-bye.

As for me, there wasn't much better in life than crawling into a medium bomber, knowing that I could fly up fifteen thousand feet, look down at the cockeyed world, and for one brief, shining moment be captain of my ship. It seemed in those moments that there were no limits to where I might go in life—assuming I'd survive the war.

I quit the RCAF and went to work for ATC. The commanding officer turned out to be a relative of Nicky Du Pont, my old classmate from Hun.

America was knocking out pilots by the minute. Civilians were flying huge, expensive military aircraft. We were paid triple what I was making in Canada. Officially I was a civilian, living in Beverly Hills. I'd pick up assignments to deliver airplanes. It was a straightforward kind of work, leaving me free to chase dames and have them chase me. Marylou showed up at my apartment one night while I was working for ATC. She stayed over, and in the morning I said, "Now go back to Mom and Dad." I wasn't enthusiastic about sleeping with an ex-wife in a casual way. I was already quite used to bachelorhood and glad to be free.

Hollywood, as elsewhere, was overloaded with young women during the war years. They were invariably taking acting and singing lessons and dance classes, and they enjoyed living in the fast lane. I'd make the conquest, but if I wasn't in love, I'd go on to someone else. So there was Sheila Ryan, under contract to RKO, and then June Lang. I thought June was gorgeous. She had beautiful legs and a great face and lived with her mother, who seemed overly protective. This didn't strike me as unusual. As our romance flourished June's mother advised me to leave her alone, as she was being kept by Johnny Roselli, one of the Italian kingpins. "You'll get a bullet in your head." Roselli was associated with Meyer Lansky and Bugsy Siegel. It was the beginning of gangster intrigue: mob men, Vegas, and the motion picture industry. I told June's mother I wished she'd spoken up earlier.

I dropped her fast, telling myself she wasn't that fantastic. She wasn't exactly a college graduate. Years later Johnny Roselli was found floating in an oil drum in a Miami bay.

ATC was a big change from the military constraints and discipline of the RCAF. When you became an ATC pilot you were issued two leather fur-lined jackets bearing the round ATC insignia and supplied with a .38 caliber gun.

The first airplane I flew for ATC was an A-20. The second flight was in a Ventura, and I was copilot. The rest of the time I was a captain with a copilot. I flew all over the United States for three months delivering bombers to different military bases.

I experienced one wonderful show-off moment when I flew a B-24 from Long Beach, California, to Newark, New Jersey, where the army was going to pick it up. My parents, although divorced, got together and came out to see me in my captain's uniform, waving from the pilot's seat of the four-engine bomber.

I flew Lockheed Hudsons, Venturas, B-24s and B-25s. Most often I flew the Ventura, a medium twin-engine bomber. I delivered them everywhere on this continent, from Georgia to Montreal.

Once I lost an engine minutes after takeoff. It stopped dead. I had just cleared eight hundred feet up in Long Beach when I had to return to the airport. The mechanic thought they could repair the problem. Time went by and I picked up another assignment while I was waiting around. A bunch of us took off for Dallas. The next morning was gray, and we were to fly to Nashville. I received a report at Texarkana that Nashville was closing in. I wasn't about to fly on instruments. I was shaky, not having flown "under the hood" for some time. Instead

I flew up the Mississippi Valley and landed in St. Louis. I gassed up in St. Louis and delivered the plane to Detroit, where I grabbed a transport plane back to Long Beach.

I was next assigned another Ventura. The instruction was to fly to Palm Springs. Here I taxied the airplane up to where another aircraft was parked. I shut off the ignition and stepped out. A kid, fresh out of school, was opening the door with a key. I yelled, "Whaddaya' doin'?" He told me he was going to repark the airplane.

"Listen," I said, "do me a favor, don't rev this engine. Leave it alone, and get out of the airplane." He continued to ignore me.

I grabbed him and threw him out. "Go near this airplane, I'll kill you."

The next morning at five o'clock I got a call at the hotel to come down to the airport. I arrived and asked a mechanic, "Where's my airplane?" He told me to jump in the jeep and he'd show me.

About a thousand feet down the runway I saw my airplane, cut in half. On the other side of the runway I saw a Beechcraft, totally demolished. "What the fuck happened?"

"The kid you threw out of the airplane got into the Beechcraft, revved up those engines, and the brakes broke loose. He jumped out of the fuckin' airplane just in time. He's in the hospital. The Beechcraft cut your airplane in half."

I was speechless. I knew that kid was a dunce, but I didn't figure him for plain stupid. Those fresh-out-of-school kids were famous for driving the pilots nuts.

From this incident I was brought up on charges before a Colonel Spake in Long Beach. The fact that I physically threw the kid out counted against me. They seemed to be ignoring that it was the kid who trashed the airplane.

Colonel Spake was irate. He'd been in the roofing business in Texas before recently donning a uniform. He announced, "We've got a charge of assault by Private Benson."

"You do?"

I was shocked. It was on the record that the kid was responsible for what happened. Spake continued: "You physically assaulted an army private."

I said, "Yes, sir, I was captain of the airplane."

"You're not a captain, you're a civilian."

I had to control my fury. "I'm trusted to an airplane, captain of the aircraft, carrying out classified work, and you tell me I can't be in charge of my aircraft?"

With this last question he responded, "You're fired. I'll give you ten minutes to get off this post."

With my reactive nature I retorted, "Can I have twelve, Colonel?"

Now he was howling. "Furthermore, I'll have you in the infantry in forty-eight hours." Shades of my ex-father-in-law.

"No shit," I said, and then turned to his stunned secretary. In a polite voice I asked, "Would you please put in writing what you have witnessed? And by the way, what's your name?"

Spake growled, "Yeah, put it in writing."

I then asked her to read it back to us, and she did.

I'd learned in Canada after another American had been similarly threatened that coercion or threats of any kind were not acceptable. Out of control, I turned to Spake before I left the room and said, "Listen you dumb cocksucker, you can't coerce me."

The next day I went up to Douglas Aircraft. I was interviewed by Win Sargent, one of the top test pilots. Two days later I was working for Douglas as a test pilot.

Win took me aside. "What the hell did you do at Long Beach? There's a colonel who's got it in for you."

I said, "Fuck that colonel." I explained the situation. Win contacted a general who had considerable power. Colonel Spake was sent far away to a cold climate, definitely not like Texas or California.

The Douglas Aircraft industry was headquartered at Clover Field in Santa Monica. They manufactured the DC-3, a forerunner of the DC-10 and the workhorse of the US Army and Navy. The DC-3, unlike its predecessor, the DC-2, had retractable landing gear and a twin-engine cargo. It was to be used by commercial airlines for transcontinental work.

By the time I began working at Douglas I was a serious, seasoned pilot. I'd flown in every condition by now, and knew instruments. Many mornings we'd take off under zero weather conditions. The local weather around Santa Monica was usually dense fog, zero visibility, until midday when the sun rose high enough to burn off the fog. We'd take off on instruments until we were at least two hundred feet above ground and able to climb through that stuff.

Training for this was on the ground under a black cloth over the canopy of a simulated cockpit. This contraption was about six feet long and two and a half feet wide, controlled by hydraulics and motors, simulating every possible movement.

The amount of horsepower a pilot could legally fly was on the license. I was now qualified to fly on instruments and unlimited horse-power, which meant I was finally able to fly airplanes of any size.

14

DOUGLAS PILOTS CAME from all walks of life—navy fliers, former airline pilots. I was the youngest of the Douglas aviators. My childhood hero Doug Corrigan also worked for Douglas Aircraft. A great test pilot, he was also a grade A master mechanic. He was never seen dressed in anything but his bomber jacket, work shoes, pants, a frayed shirt, and string tie. He carried a black lunch pail to work every day. He was a small, unassuming guy who parted his hair in the middle and had the look of Mortimer Snerd, with a loveable quality.

On July 17, 1938, he'd earned his nickname, Wrong Way Corrigan, when he took off from Floyd Bennett Field, Long Island, and landed near Dublin, Ireland, where he removed his goggles and simply announced he'd "lost his way." Corrigan had been warned not to attempt a transatlantic flight in his rickety plane. Corrigan's flight, lasting twenty-eight hours and thirteen minutes, won him worldwide acclaim. He rejected the modern compass and map that were presented to him (on the basis that he'd never finished high school) and said instead he would "fly low, near the railroad station, and read the name of the town." Much the same technique I'd adopted in my barnstorming years.

Whenever I ran into him I'd jokingly corner him by the sleeve of his bomber jacket. "Doug, before this is over you're going to tell me the truth."

Corrigan would laugh and say, "Sid, I *was* going to fly to California." And he never changed his response.

------ ✺ ------

One of the aircraft I tested for Douglas was the A-20. The variant I flew had a French designation on the fuselage; when it reached the hands of the French it was renamed the DB-7 (dive bomber). It was used for low-level bombing, and the cockpit could accommodate a gunner in the back and bombardier and pilot in front. The ground procedure for testing the airplane was to take it for a forty-five-minute flight, checking controls, instruments, hydraulic and electrical functions, looking for anything that might need an adjustment or modification. If there was a malfunction of any kind the airplane was returned and fixed and tested again.

When a Douglas test pilot returned the airplane and signed his sheet, it signified the craft was free of any problems and ready to be turned over for purchase. We delivered the tested aircraft to one of the two air force depots in the United States: Daggett, California, which was in the desert about forty-five minutes from Santa Monica; or Las Vegas, a little hick town in those days—just one hotel, El Rancho, and a few motels.

Once there was an alarm at Clover Field that the Japanese were in the vicinity. We had to remove every C-54 bomber from the field. Pilots were all over the place, jumping in everything. We flew the aircraft to Mines Field, now Los Angeles International Airport, and then on to Las Vegas. On our return flight to Santa Monica, Jimmy Haizlip, a former navy pilot who was famous for setting speed records, was aboard the cargo ship. I noticed Haizlip seemed disoriented—unusual behavior for him. By the time we landed at the field he'd flipped out. He ran from the aircraft yelling, "Whaddaya know, it's snowing!" Bolting across the runway, grasping at imaginary snowflakes, shouting, "Snow at last!" He'd gone berserk.

Many men could not withstand the stress. There was another pilot, Tommy Chastain, who happened to have married the sister-in-law of

Lynn Bari, my soon-to-be second wife. He put a .22 to his head and blew his brains out.

I suppose I was able to withstand tremendous pressure because I had a streak of hell-raising in my genes. I sure didn't avoid taking risks. Once when I was in the midst of a takeoff in an A-20 and the winds changed, I decided to take off from west to east, opposite of the general direction in a normal takeoff. I held the airplane down, waiting for maximum speed, and when there was a drop-off I flew it off an edge. I was only two seconds from the end of the runway when I raised the landing gear.

When I got back to the pilot's house there was a message from Jake Moxness, my chief pilot, to come to his office. I went up there right away.

Moxness barked, "You know where I was when you pulled that stunt?" He was angry.

I said, "Where were you?" I felt like an ass.

"I was on the end of the runway with General 'Cockombottom' and you pulled that stuff. Last year, O'Leary bent six prop blades and he paid for them, six thousand bucks."

"Sir, I'll never let it happen again."

Jake was kind to me: "Please don't, for your own safety."

"My word, sir."

The conversation changed and Moxness began telling me about an engine that he thought was the future of aeronautics. He asked me if I'd like to take a look. I didn't have a clue as to what he was talking about. We walked through locked doors, a series of catwalks, and several buildings. Jake had to give a secret code to enter the restricted building where, on a long work table in an isolated chamber, rested the first captured Messerschmitt jet engine—aviation's future. The Germans were more successful in developing equipment than we were. However, the ground war was currently going against them. The Russian front had proved fatal to the German infantry. I beheld the jet engine, agreeing with Jake that it was indeed an awesome sight. Our top-speed aircraft, the P-51 and P-38, loaded up with cannons, machine guns, and fuel, could travel up to 325 miles an hour, while the German fighters were doing 500 miles an hour, running rings around us.

Jake said, "There it is, Sid, the future. Stick with it!"

At Mines Field I knew a French engineering test pilot who was chosen to fly the first "flying wing" aircraft. He had a lovely wife; we'd have a bite to eat and a couple of drinks, the three of us. I thought they were an interesting couple, and I'd made a mental note to look them up again in future. Later the Frenchman went to Muroc Lake and got killed when the wing crashed during a test flight. This abrupt termination of life happened all too often. These losses were always a jolt to the system, and they seemed to happen to the most experienced pilots, men whom I admired and respected. It left me with a bitter taste, and always the question: why should a lowly pilot like myself still be here?

—❊❊❊—

Once I started working for Douglas Aircraft, though, my own life fell into place. I joined the California Country Club, which was started by Fred MacMurray, Johnny Weissmuller, and John Wayne. Bo Roos was their business manager. The men bought the land, refurbished the run-down grounds, and had a drive for membership—and I signed up. I was off work at three o'clock in the afternoon, and nearly every day I went directly to the club to play golf. I played with some amazing people: Babe Didrikson, who loved to gamble, Johnny Mercer, Harold Arlen, Ira Gershwin, and Swifty Lazar, among others. It was Arlen who dubbed me the "starker." I was obsessive about the game, and after a year or so my handicap was down to about six, but I had to keep working at it.

I came to admire my golf chums as I'd admired certain pilots. I had an out-and-out desire to live well, and these men, so entrenched in the entertainment field, seemed to be doing just that. The test pilots at Douglas, on the other hand, were generally rugged individualists, not show business dudes. Wrong Way Corrigan, although a great pilot, was more like a farmer and totally detached from Hollywood. Bert Foulds, one of the scions of Fuller Paint Company, was a test pilot and went his way far from show biz. He was an engineering pilot, and he never mixed—he was in another category in the company's hierarchy. Tommy Chastain was a fascinating man, but not social beyond the pilot hangouts where we drank. I'd relax with a few pilots in the steam rooms and then we'd go our separate ways. Many of the men were married.

My name began to appear in the entertainment columns. On the bistro scene, I was continually introduced as "Sid Luft, the test pilot," my entrée to the watering holes on the Strip and the better golf courses. People were impressed. My dream had been realized: I was a bona fide pilot. I'd endured and lived through some harrowing experiences, watched my friends leave and never come back. The glamour of the job had faded—it was no longer about smiling out of a cockpit with goggles, silk scarf, and leather jacket. I'd grown up in the air, so by now it was a bitter victory that people were enamored with me because I was a test pilot. They, too, held an idealized vision of what that meant.

Betty Hutton asked my friend publicist Kenny Morgan to place an item in Harrison Carroll's column: "Betty Hutton wants to date the test pilot Sid Luft," and in this way we started going out. Through Betty I met Buddy DeSylva, part of the songwriting team of DeSylva, Brown, and Henderson. He was a tremendous success before he became head of Paramount. He had hits on Broadway and a succession of popular show tunes. Along with Johnny Mercer and others, he formed Capitol Records. DeSylva had hoped I'd get serious with Betty: he believed in her talent and wanted to calm her down, stabilize her. He was dating Betty's friend and we often went out together. She found the business of flying exciting and pilots attractive. I buzzed her house, showing off in an A-20, blowing out a few windows. This seemed to turn her on. I liked Betty but I didn't see myself getting married again.

I had known Jeeb Halaby from the pilot scene. He'd been a test pilot at Lockheed and was now a lawyer. One day we had lunch and Jeeb expressed a desire to be fixed up with someone. I thought Betty might fill the ticket and I put them together. Jeeb was so Eastern Seaboard and so clearly on his way up. I thought Betty might trip his batteries in an unconventional way.

It didn't take, though, and they went their separate ways. When Judy was fired from *Annie Get Your Gun*, Betty would replace her. Later, Halaby was part of the Kennedy bandwagon—he became head of Pan Am Airways and subsequently the FAA. His daughter married King Hussein of Jordan. Our paths would cross again later, when Jeeb was at a pinnacle of success and I was taking a nosedive.

Around this time Minna Wallis at Warner Bros. approached me and invited me to take a screen test. I was willing, again for a joke. Sophie Rosenstein gave me three scripts to pick from. I was too self-conscious and too square to play a scene with a woman. I couldn't have pulled off a love scene. Stupidly, I kept thinking what my copilots would think of this "sissy work." Mark Stevens, a Canadian actor, did the test scene with me. The action involved my bursting into a Madison Avenue office to confront the character's brother, played by Stevens. I was dressed in typical Madison Avenue Brooks Brothers garb, with hat and briefcase. Steven's back was to the camera as I came in throwing my hat on his desk and demanding, "Where's the money?" Each take brought me closer to laughter. It began to strike me as hilarious—the makeup, the set. Somehow I carried my entrance off comically rather than with the menace I was to portray. My laughing was contagious, and now Mark was cracking up, to the exasperation of the technicians.

We threw in the towel and went out for drinks. Stevens told me he was being cuckolded by his wife, confiding he was disgusted but determined to keep his cool. Divorce was inevitable. He managed a sweet revenge by offering to take care of their house sale. According to California law the divorced couple splits the proceeds. When the sale was finalized, he was able to manipulate the escrow so that when it cleared he received all the monies, whereupon he left for Europe, never to be heard from again.

Bill Goodwin was a golfer who was the commercial announcer on the Jack Benny show, and a close friend of Jerry Colonna, a longtime feature on the show. Bill lived with his family in the Valley, in a lovely house where they gave swimming pool parties. It was at the Goodwins' home that I met Lynn Bari.

I was attracted to her right away. She had hazel eyes, a throaty voice. She was on the dreamy side with a great sense of humor. Her mother had been in and out of at least three clinics for alcoholism; her brother, John Fisher, was a navy pilot, a nice fellow—rather serious, in contrast to Lynn's personality. They were of Irish and German descent. Their father had committed suicide and Lynn rarely referred to him; I'm not sure if she ever knew him. Lynn's first husband was Walter Kane, a top agent, considerably older, and known to be a buddy of Howard Hughes. Kane and Lynn were separated when we got together.

Many of Lynn's friends were married to either directors or songwriters, several of whom were already pals of mine from the golf course. Her closest friends included Cookie Gordon, married to Mack Gordon, the songwriter. Mack was under contract at Fox, writing musicals with Harry Warren, well known for the score of *42nd Street*.

Lynn was born Marjorie Schuyler Fisher in Roanoke, Virginia. She'd been contracted as a studio player by 20th Century Fox from age thirteen. She was a successful actress on the border between the A and B films of the day. She was well qualified but had not as yet made major movie star status. Nevertheless, Lynn worked all the time and was well liked. She was tall and slim and people thought she resembled Claudette Colbert. In the B pictures she was the star; in the A pictures she'd play the other woman to Gene Tierney or Alice Faye, or even Sonja Henie, all big stars at the time. She played opposite Edward G. Robinson, who was a charming, down-to-earth person. Eddie was short and Lynn was tall, so he'd stand on boxes in the close-ups. Her biggest role was in *The Bridge of San Luis Rey*, the Thornton Wilder novel adapted to screen, after she left 20th Century Fox.

One of her friends' husbands, Bill Perlberg, introduced me to Zeppo Marx. Zeppo owned a successful theatrical agency and also had an airplane parts business. I'd watched him in the popular gin rummy clubs about town and saw how he won and lost, his approach to the gentlemen's sport of betting. I'd found my new mentor. Zeppo suggested I come work for him, that I'd make a good agent. I began to seriously consider leaving aeronautics.

For some years my heart had been in the air: I was totally immersed in flying and the world of airplanes. I was tempted by several career possibilities: a job with a commercial airline, working for a private company, returning to school for a degree in aeronautical engineering. I had responsibilities, but I decided I was not going to keep working in an industry where I could never earn the right kind of money. I was in love with a lifestyle, and I was ambitious enough to believe I could live as well as our friends.

Lynn preferred the elite sound of "aeronautic engineer," but to me it spelled little income. I couldn't see Sid Luft moving very high up in the Christian aviation hierarchy, either. Lynn believed I was too green for the entertainment industry. I didn't fit the mold and, in her opinion, didn't have a chance. I didn't belong to any mogul's tribe. I disagreed: becoming an agent seemed an excellent way to get a foothold in the business.

15

JANUARY 16, 1943, was a raw day in Los Angeles. I wore leather moccasins, gabardine army twills, and a leather flying jacket. I was looking forward to a break in the grueling schedule of test flying—working from 8:00 AM to 3:00 PM five days a week, generally testing three airplanes per day—and to a chance to be with the woman I loved, away from Los Angeles.

I was due in Washington, DC, to escort Lynn to a gala White House dinner and ball celebrating President Roosevelt's birthday. The festivities were to kick off a national bond tour. Lynn had recently completed a publicity circuit for her latest film for 20th, and now she was taking off to sell bonds. I missed her and was anxious to be with her for a few days.

I had asked Jake Moxness permission to take off early from Clover Field and had arranged a ride over to Mines Field to pick up a commercial flight to DC. I parked my gear in the adobe cottage off the runway, a hundred yards from the main hangar, where the pilots waited assignment. The pilot's cottage was not busy that day; usually there were men playing cards, studying accident reports, catching up on information about various causes of malfunctions—prop stalls, system failures—or reading about crashes throughout the world. On this particular day they were short on pilots for delivery, and Lee Bishop, the officer in charge of flight operations, asked me, as a favor, to take an A-20 up to Daggett before I left for Washington.

"Sid, we're out of pilots." It was that simple. Not only was it a request from a superior, there wasn't anything I wouldn't do for Lee. So instead of taking off for Washington at 1:30 in the afternoon, I was in the cockpit of an A-20 heading for delivery.

Earlier in the week I'd taken off in an A-20 that caught on fire, but the flames quickly burned out at a thousand feet. It seemed to be a freak situation that corrected itself, and certainly nothing structural was to blame.

I reached the Cajon Pass, where a natural phenomenon created a seventy-five-degree temperature inversion. At eight thousand feet I began to sweat, so I shed my jacket, leaving it lying against the back of my seat. I'd departed Santa Monica airport under normal conditions, but now I noticed that the fuel pressure was fluctuating from 10 to 15 pounds. I checked both motors and they were running normal. I decided to turn on the cross feed, but it didn't bring up the fuel pressure, so I just left it on and called the control tower at Daggett for landing instructions. I made three attempts to raise the tower: "This is army aircraft with a designation trying to raise the tower. Please come in. Do you read me?"

Nobody was reading me. I began to get concerned. I called the airways range station, and they advised me they would notify the control tower by telephone. I now saw that my fuel pressure on the left engine had dropped to zero. I figured maybe I was out further than I'd assessed. I changed frequencies and called again, this time anticipating trouble. I was able to communicate I was going to bring the aircraft straight in. I tried to determine the cause of the drop in fuel pressure. I attempted various procedures to build up pressure and nothing worked. The engine cell was loading up with raw gasoline. A line had broken. I hit every emergency switch and nothing was working. I was in serious trouble. By this time, I was over the airport at Daggett, three thousand feet above sea level and a thousand feet above the ground. As I proceeded to approach the field I saw blue smoke escaping from the inspection plate in the inboard side of the left engine's outer casing.

In the middle of the south boundary of the airport I extended the landing gear, and the left engine exploded into flames. I was sitting on a parachute when the fire broke out. I had to make a decision: bail out or bring the airplane in as planned. My mind raced. Was I going to die? I was determined not to panic: if I lost it, I was going to burn up. Somehow I had to stay cool. I feathered the engine and depressed the left fire extinguisher button in preparation for landing. I made a normal approach to the field on one engine, attempting to keep the craft upright. I cut the ignition switches and prepared myself for an exit. When I finally landed the airplane I was going about 125 miles an hour without brakes. I bumped along the hazardous, rocky desert mounds. The fittings were melting, and the aircraft started to cock off to the right. I was told later that I looked like a flaming rocket from hell.

The fire was burning the lines on the left side of the hydraulic system, and there were no brakes on the left. As the airplane dissipated speed the main landing gear collapsed and the plane ground-looped slowly to the left. During this roll I managed to unfasten my safety belt and throw open the hatch, holding on to the control column. As the plane zipped over the rough terrain, the nose wheel collapsed, the centrifugal force of the airplane spun fast, and I was catapulted out of the aircraft. I was hanging on to the control column in the fire and smoke, screaming, "What a fuckin' way to die." Twenty seconds felt like twenty years. I knew I was going to burn to death. I thought, if I get out of this, life is going to take on a different meaning. I grabbed the top of the deck and pulled myself onto the wing, managing to jump off it in the opposite direction of the oncoming ambulance. I saw a pickup truck, part of the rescue team, and ran across the desert to the runway to meet it. I jumped on. My cheekbone was broken, I was bleeding, my shoes were burned. The stroke of luck was the navy-issue flight jacket against the back of my seat. It had protected me from the flames; without it my back would have been embers.

I was taken to a small emergency center next to the hangar and administered an IV. Medics cut off the burned skin with scissors. I was conscious. They wrapped me in a sheet and started pumping in 900 cc of blood plasma. Finally they placed me on a stretcher and flew me back in a C-54 to Clover Field, where an ambulance waited to transport me to Santa Monica Hospital. I'd been given a few shots of morphine, and the second shot made me vomit.

Jake Moxness, Lee Bishop, and two engineering test pilots who were consultants to Douglas appeared at my bedside. I was in no condition to discuss aviation emergency precautions, but like a murder victim who lies dying, I was pumped with questions before I went under. They needed to know what happened: What were the symptoms? What was unusual before the crash? Now they revealed I'd survived circumstances that had killed other pilots. "Here's an opportunity to prevent further accident." I was told that when I ground-looped, a whole cloud of black smoke went up. The aircraft completely burned up. I knew there was a broken line in front of the fire wall, and in minutes there'd been gallons of gasoline pouring out of the hose right into the cell cavity that held the engine. I couldn't be much more help than that. The men were evaluating and analyzing the crash as the doctors attempted to sedate me. More morphine was out: they realized I was allergic. Nothing was working, and I was unable to sleep that night. My legs were treated with a spray that looked and smelled like varnish.

The very next day a pilot burned up in Oxnard. As A-20s were being delivered from Ascension Island in Brazil to Dakar in Senegal, more pilots were lost the same way.

Lynn had been notified in Washington. She called me at the hospital, relieved to hear my voice. Yes, I was alive. I didn't especially care for her to come back and see me in this condition. I encouraged her to continue on the bond tour. Meanwhile the press got hold of the story: "Movie star's pilot boyfriend in accident, caught on fire."

The second day I was still numb from the trauma. On the third day I began to experience hellish pain. I suffered first-, second-, and third-degree burns on my face and back and ass. I was able to doze for an hour here and there. My face was lopsided; my neck was swollen. I was unrecognizable.

Marylou and Gussie visited me four days after the accident. They brought me a huge basket of fruit and a bottle of champagne. Gussie left and Marylou stayed on. I was worrying that Lynn might show up while my ex-wife was in the room. I was in terrible agony, my ass was bandaged, I was leaking blood, and I could never stop feeling pain. They'd been shooting so many drugs into me I was building up tolerance. Every day I'd immerse my hand into some sort of hot saline solution, and a glass boot was attached to the leg and continued to be sprayed twice a day. I had big red sores on one side of my face, and I began to grow a beard on that side. One night, in desperation, I decided to go for the champagne. I took hold of the telephone wire and raised myself up enough to pick up the champagne with my right hand. I managed to open the bottle with the same hand and commenced to down the entire bottle. I got pissed to the eyeballs, and for the first time since the accident I felt less pain. The booze worked! It was marvelous.

When Lynn returned I prevailed upon her to bring me a bottle of bourbon. From the day Lynn came back I drank a quart of bourbon a day. I kept the bottle in my crotch. The doctors didn't approve, but I wasn't interested in pleasing the medical staff. I'd been going insane before I discovered the booze. I got up to two quarts a day before I'd pass out.

The Drs. Rooney, father and son, who took care of me were exceptionally kind. They'd reassure me and put their arms around me during rough episodes. There was a big, overweight private nurse who sat near me during the night. One night when I was delirious as a result of the booze and drugs, I imagined she was my copilot. "Fatty, get the fuckin' gear up," I commanded. The next night she came on duty and told me what I'd said. I apologized, said I was talking in my sleep. The nurse insisted, "You were drunk and you were terrible to me." I begged her to be sympathetic to my situation and not report me to the doctors. In any case, I was going to have that booze one way or another. However, I learned to put a hold on my mouth.

Four other A-20s had caught fire, and none of the pilots survived. So the A-20 was finally grounded over the United States. The problem was caused by the exhaust stacks, which had been shortened to gain more speed out of the airplane. This caused more vibration on the warm-up when the engines reached a certain temperature for takeoff. What was needed was simply to weld two rings on the pipe from the fuel pump that attaches to the hose going to the fuel gauge. For one extra clamp, all those lives had been lost.

My first day back on the golf course after the crash was blissful. I was sensitive to the environment. The fairway looked gorgeous, the grass was brilliant green, the trees were magnificent, the sky was a luminous azure—life was a valentine. I'd have been just as thrilled if it were snowing or if I were soaked through, wet and shivering. I was alive! Everything was measured by the accident, and it gave me a vantage point from which I could appreciate life with renewed respect and pleasure.

Surviving the crash left me with a long-term sense of optimism and privilege. I found out I was blessed with coordination under pressure. By not bailing out of the aircraft and bringing it in, I was able to help the engineers determine the crucial engineering defect that was killing other pilots. Both Win Sargent and Lee Bishop thought it was a good idea for me to meet Douglas himself. And so I was paraded in front of the main man.

Donald Douglas had become successful at an early age. Rumors had circulated around this rather quiet, aloof man. He lived in the Pacific Palisades, with the wife and children on one side of the house and Mr. Douglas and the mistress on the other.

Win said, "Mr. Douglas, this is Sid Luft, the pilot in the A-20. We thought you might like to say hello."

Douglas looked up. "Very nice to meet you."

I began to babble, because although he acknowledged my presence, he was cold as ice. "Well, sir, I guess the reason I'm still here is due to the ability of that airplane to stay afloat with one engine and under those conditions it's a miracle . . ."

Douglas's office was handsomely paneled, with indirect lighting. There was a striking display case filled with artifacts and objets d'art. It was daytime but the office was dark. We were not asked to sit. We remained standing, and this, too, was off-putting. I continued to talk nervously about a how I felt like a piece of straw that was driven through a telephone pole during a tornado. This went over like a ton of bricks. He was not going to say one congenial word. I let the "straw" fall, and we got out of there.

More appreciative was Vance Breese, a flier who performed mostly experimental work as a freelance pilot and was the Chuck Yeager of his day. I'd see him at QB meetings (we were both members of the Quiet Birdmen, a flying club). Years later I ran into him in a Santa Monica restaurant. I was with a friend, actress Marianna Hill, and he paid me one of the nicest compliments. He said, "You know, when we studied that accident, you became one of our heroes." I like to think he wasn't just bullshitting me because I was with a great-looking blonde.

Douglas Aircraft sent me to recuperate at a resort in Colorado Springs, south of Denver. Lynn joined me, and we decided we couldn't wait much longer to marry. Colorado Springs proved to be a place of destiny. It was there that I met Ted Law, a Texas oilman, a great sportsman, and a lover of horses, someone with whom I was to have a lifelong bond until he passed away in 1989. He was a good-looking man, married to a woman who was seriously alcoholic. I was to learn from Ted not to walk away from tough situations. Ted was enamored with the world of show business, and although he didn't make any of his homes in Los Angeles, we did become partners in Walfarms, our racing stable outside of the city. And he went on to invest in *A Star Is Born*.

16

AFTER SIXTY DAYS, I went back to work with my hands and leg bandaged. I thought it was crucial for me to return to work, yet I'd involuntarily relive the disaster. I'd change my clothes at least twice a day due to nervous sweats. I'd have nightmares, quick flashes of the scene—hanging upside down, burning up alive—and it left me a wreck, like men who survive battle scenes but can't ever pull out of it. I was sent to a psychiatrist and temporarily put on some kind of sedative.

In those days, test pilots couldn't get insurance, but I received a settlement of $7,500 through workers' compensation. Subsequently, American test pilots petitioned for insurance and won.

I wore civvies the moment I was off the field. And occasionally men would perceive me as a draft dodger. Generally the feelings of hostility came from a guy in uniform. One afternoon, I was having drinks at the Beverly Wilshire bar with Simmons, a friend recently out of the army. Simmons manufactured gas tanks for the aircraft industry. There were some girls at the bar, along with several soldiers who were working on *This Is the Army* for 20th Century Fox. They were military men playing extras. One of the men tugged at a girl's hair and fondled her. She said, "Please don't do this." This went on for some time, and finally I said, "Hey, be nice. Don't bother her."

The first line out of his mouth was "You fuckin' civilian, stay out of it."

I didn't let it alone. "Knock it off, don't cause any problems here."

He came over and pushed me, "You fucking civvy."

It was going to be trouble: two of us and six of them. "Don't push me," I ordered. I pushed his hand away and everybody stepped back.

Simmons was rougher than me—he was ruthless. He grabbed one of the soldiers by the hair and cracked him against his knee. The guy was unconscious in seconds. I hit one of them over the bar. The girls were screaming and the bartenders called the police.

The barmen told the police to arrest all the men but Simmons and me. Glass was everywhere, the bar destroyed. The press had a field day: "Simmons and Luft put away half the cast of *This Is the Army*." I used my fists but I didn't have the strength of Simmons, who weighed two hundred pounds and had a worse temper than mine.

<hr />

On May 15, 1943, the headline in Louella Parsons's *New York Journal-American* column read, LYNN BARI TO SPEED WEDDING WITH FLIER.

Hollywood

Lynn Bari is trying to arrange with 20th Century Fox to get time off to visit either Guaymas, Mexico or Las Vegas. Now it isn't fishing that is interesting the lovely Lynn in the famous fishing resort in Mexico, nor is it a vacation that may take her to Nevada. She wants to establish a residence. You have guessed it. So that she may be free from Walter Kane before November, the date her final decree comes due. She is eager to wed Sid Luft, courageous young test pilot who was so badly burned in a plane crash last January. . . .

The marriage ceremony was small, a few good friends, in the home of producer Bill Perlberg and his wife, where we were to spend a good many evenings drinking, playing cards, and enjoying ourselves.

I continued to fly for seven months after returning to Douglas. But Zeppo Marx kept on me about changing to a career as an agent. Zeppo belonged to the Hillcrest Country Club, and he would invite me to play golf with him there. The Hillcrest was drowning in folk who were important in the industry. And the members were territorial. One table would be the famous comedians' table, with Jack Benny, George Burns and company, and so on. A particular hum would invade the club when Al Jolson arrived. Jolson had a vibration to his very presence; you could feel his entrance like a rubber band spinning in your ear. I tried to avoid the excitement. It's difficult for today's generation to understand the power of the man. It was based on the public's devotion to him, like certain rock stars. In this way his fans were responsible for the tremendous position he held in Hollywood.

Zeppo influenced me in many ways, especially gambling. I learned early on if you do not have the money to pay a gambling debt, you simply don't gamble. When Zeppo told me something, I knew I could believe it. His brother Harpo, who was an extraordinary comedic actor, would get his golf ball stuck in a trap, run to the ball, remove it, and place it back on the green for all to see. Not Zeppo; he was a genuine sportsman.

He had originally opened a theatrical agency for his older brother Gummo. The agency, located on the Strip, had terrific clients like Barbara Stanwyck, Fred MacMurray—directors, writers, a host of celebrities. It was very successful. Gummo had returned to the garment business, but then gave it up to come out and help run the agency with Alan Miller. Gummo was older than Zeppo and married to Miller's sister. Miller was a lawyer and partner in the agency, so it was all in the family. When an employee named Henry Willson left the agency, a spot opened up for me. Willson went on to represent Rock Hudson and other young, good-looking men. He specialized in this field, changing their names, grooming them, and advising their careers.

Zeppo convinced me to leave Douglas and join the agency. The first person I signed was the singer Ella Mae Morse. She was a successful recording artist for a while and was in a few movies, but her acting career never took off.

Abelardo "Rod" Rodriguez was a close friend and a lead pilot whose father was the former president of Mexico. We met at American

Transport Company, and later we both flew for Douglas Aircraft. We shared an apartment briefly when I was finally divorced from Marylou. Rod owned thousands of acres of land in Mexico, and he invited me to start a development business with him. I was tempted, but I was under contract with the Marx agency and married to Lynn Bari. After the years of flying during the war, I wanted to stay near my wife.

Rod was persistent. "It's a wonderful company, we'll fertilize the land, develop it." Eventually Rod went into business with Bing Crosby, and they developed the land and became multimillionaires. Coincidentally, he married Arthur Freed's favorite actress, Lucille Bremer, who played Judy's older sister in *Meet Me in St. Louis*. She retired from films to marry Rod.

My own wife was strong minded, and Lynn's willfulness worked against her. She resisted my guiding her career and was reluctant to admit that Darryl F. Zanuck was a power in her life. Darryl had plans for her. Lynn was an excellent actress with a sultry presence on screen. And later she'd prove her ability onstage. At one dinner party, Lynn, having had a little too much to drink, made a social blunder which I believed cost her a career.

It happened just as her contract was coming up for renewal. Betty Grable, World War II's most famous pinup, was the studio's big earner, and she'd gotten pregnant before she married the trumpet-playing bandleader Harry James. This infuriated Darryl. That night he made some derogatory remarks about Grable. Lynn was not a close friend of Betty's, but she resented the remarks—she took it as a general slur on women. Zanuck could be uncouth. He angered her, and when she was in the powder room with some of the women, not holding back, she said, "That bucktooth bastard." As fate would have it, Virginia Zanuck happened to come in. "Lynn, I want you to tell that to Darryl." Virginia escorted Lynn, who was pretty high by now, to where her husband was playing cards, "Darryl, Lynn has something to tell you," she announced. Darryl looked up from his cards, took in the situation, and said, "Tell me later."

Several weeks passed and someone called from the studio. Lynn's option had not been picked up. I pleaded with her to apologize: "Your career's at stake." She refused. Now she was without a studio's protection. Our relationship suffered more strain.

———— ⊸∞∞⊸ ————

I bought one of the first Cadillac convertibles made after the war. Friends enjoyed a ride in the car, and I often gave Peter Lawford a lift. I'd known Peter since he was a kid parking cars for a living. His parents were English gentry, and Lady Lawford had pretentions. His father, an elderly man, was a general from Britain's faraway colonial past. Milt Ebbins, Peter's personal manager, told me years later that Lady Lawford dressed Peter as a little girl until he was eleven. I knew her as a stage mother determined that Peter would work in show business. Peter was charming and broke. He'd stop by our house in Westwood and have dinner with us. And he was welcome—Lynn adored him. Peter was known as "America's Guest," an appellation that stuck even though, until he became a substance abuser, he was very fair about moneys, a gentleman. He just wasn't a sport.

One afternoon, Peter invited me to drive by the Hillcrest bowling alley in Beverly Hills. Inside was a jolly group of friends enjoying themselves. Judy Garland Minnelli showed up in her bobby socks and saddle shoes looking like a teenager. Everyone wanted a ride in my convertible, but I had another agenda. I felt extremely sophisticated in comparison.

By late 1945, I had realized that agenting was not for me, and what I really wanted to do was produce pictures. After a year of going in and out of major studios, I was more intrigued by motion picture production than ever. I talked a lot with Brynie Foy at Fox, a man I respected. He had been at 20th Century Fox for years and became the head of Eagle-Lion. Fox was shooting a film about the famous racehorse Seabiscuit. I had my idea to do the story of the great thoroughbred Man o' War. Brynie told me I was barking up the wrong tree. "You can't make a picture about a winner." I told him he didn't know about the one and only time Man o' War lost a race, which was the central theme of the screenplay I had in mind.

I began to seriously research racetracks, horse owners, bloodlines, every detail related to horse racing, and I was falling in love with it, just as I'd fallen in love with aviation. Lynn was not happy with my new passion. She had enjoyed sitting at the Turf Club and playing at the races, but to her horses were an amusement, not a business. In fact, in her mind, to be serious about horses was lunatic.

Lynn was also really frightened by the idea of me moving into production. She had been disappointed at my decision not to pursue an engineering career, but she certainly recognized the futility of opposing my interest in the entertainment field. So she was not hostile to my working as an agent. But producing was another matter; in her view, no door would be opened to me.

Lynn experienced the entertainment industry as hopelessly nepotistic. She thought I'd have to start as a second assistant director—some sort of technician—which had been Eleanor Powell's idea back when. I was not talented like Arthur Freed of the famous MGM Freed unit, for whom Judy had starred in so many pictures. Freed was a gifted songwriter and a genius with screen musicals, invaluable to the studio. But I thought I saw other entry routes. Lou Schreiber, whom I admired, was a tough-minded person who ran 20th Century Fox, but he'd also been a lackey of Al Jolson's. By doing the bidding of one of the great powers in the business, Schreiber had been able to make small pictures, which led to him becoming qualified to produce big-time films for 20th. So there were ways. Lynn remained unconvinced, but we were not yet at war over the issue. As in love as I was, even devoted, I needed to pursue my field of interests—I wanted that freedom. And tension was slowly building over this factor.

One night I was on my own, going to meet Ted Law at Ciro's to discuss financing strategies for *Man o' War* and a few other movie ideas I had on the burner. I was making my way into Ciro's when I accidentally bumped into a navy captain coming out the door. He didn't speak, he just came at me with his fists. "You fuckin' civilian." Those words were coming at me again. I was already upset from a marital dispute and my anger spilled over. Two big MPs watched us brawl. Naturally, the captain had no way of knowing my background, but I challenged him on Sunset Boulevard. The doorman reported the incident to Frank Sinatra, who was apparently impressed by my actions. My reputation was building.

Lynn had an eye for the trappings of wealth. She'd make wisecracks to me about the size of the rings and brooches worn by some of the women. But I knew, underneath, she hankered after all of it. I wished she could have whatever she fancied. I certainly intended to try to make her dreams come true. She'd grown up on the lot, matured into a professional actress. She felt she'd paid her dues, having married an older man and gone through the usual starlet humiliations.

She'd experienced trauma in her life, endured the alcoholic mother, and now she was to suffer again. We found out we would be parents for the first time. Lynn was happily pregnant, eager to be a mother. This child would certainly bring us together in a profound way. Both of us anticipated the new addition. When the time came, Lynn was hospitalized at St. John's Hospital in Santa Monica. It was a natural childbirth; everything had gone well. Except the little infant girl was born with a mortally deforming disease.

"Your baby is not going to live," the doctor announced. I was in a fog.

He asked me if I wanted to see the child, and I mumbled, "No."

Then he said, "I'm sorry, but you have to."

I was crushed. It was so overwhelming, I couldn't speak. I saw our poor, tortured-looking newborn daughter. I burst out in uncontrollable tears. I felt so inadequate. I thought of bringing the tragic news to Lynn. How could I? I asked a nun to go to her.

We were in our separate hells after this. Lynn was inconsolable. We didn't sleep together for some time. We rode the tide of tragedy, and the following year she again became pregnant. This time she gave birth to Johnny, a beautiful eight-pound baby boy.

Lynn continued to be irked by my racetrack affiliations and aspirations to produce. Doug Whitney, an agent for MCA, would be having drinks with Lynn when I'd come home in the evening. He was a successful New Yorker who had anglicized his name. He'd greet me with "Here comes the boy producer!" invariably rubbing me the wrong way. If it hadn't been such a sore subject, I might not have cared. Doug had a crush on Lynn and enjoyed putting me down. They shared the opinion that I was an upstart.

Competition had accelerated in the business, as there were many movie actresses around who were no longer on studio contracts and were ready to work independently. In Lynn's case, it was a bit of a disaster. Lynn felt insecure. In her view, I was just betting on horses; I didn't have closure on any one deal. She began talking about a separation.

—————— ⌘ ——————

I continued to fly on weekends, short runs to Santa Barbara or to San Diego, to the desert. I met Jackie Coogan around the hangar at Clover Field and we became friendly. Coogan had been a glider pilot in the air force. He was currently building up time instrument flying. He mentioned he was interested in returning to the entertainment business. In 1939 the former child star had been responsible for the passage of the Coogan Act, which protected child actors; up to that point, they had been miserably exploited.

I'd also been reading about another Jackie, who mustered out of the navy: Jackie Cooper. He had been a familiar figure around town before the war. I got the notion to put the two former child actors, the two Jackies, in a film. Then it was called *exploitation*, now it's simply *commercial*. I spoke with sportswriter Dick Hyland, who agreed it was a good idea. Like all writers in Hollywood, he had a script treatment ready he thought was appropriate. *Kilroy Was Here* was an eighteen-page college story he and another writer hoped to sell to the studios.

The expression "Kilroy was here" was popular nationwide, originally a "Yank" signature during World War II. Kilroy was a cartoon drawing of a guy with a big nose, small eyes, and two hands, peeking over a wall. Wherever that was drawn, the enemy knew the US Army had been there.

When Dick Hyland and I shook hands and formed a production company, Lynn really got nervous. I put my plans for *Man o' War* on hold, and Dick and I set up a meeting with Steve Broidy, the president of Monogram Pictures.

Many independent producers got their start at Monogram—people like myself who could not step into a major studio situation. The budget was never more than $100,000 to $125,000 per film. Monogram producers included 007's Cubby Broccoli (a relative of the controversial Pat DiCicco), Walter Mirisch, the King brothers, Blake Edwards, and his partner, John Champion. Also Jack Wrather, who married child star Bonita Granville. Wrather went on to own the Wrather Corporation. Close friends of the Reagans, Jack and Bonita were the left and right arm of California Republicanism.

Jack Dietz, who financed many of producer Mike Todd's projects, also had helped finance Monogram. Jack had a deal with the mob to hold all of the films of the world champion boxing fights at Madison Square Garden. He was a good family man with a hospitable household. Todd, who was a mover and shaker, was having a tough time with his wife, Joan Blondell. They were famous for their outrageous arguments. I was not alone in my marital hell.

I thought Lynn and my basic attraction for one another would carry us through this rough domestic terrain. But Lynn did not have the confidence I could pull off the *Kilroy* deal. We temporarily separated over this issue. While apart I saw other women. I was never one to sit alone and bash my head against the wall. Although I was still very much in love with Lynn and our little family, jerking off was never in my heart. Lynn was seen about town with her drinking buddy Doug Whitney. She had flounced out of Ciro's one night when I showed up with a date, and I had quietly burned on learning that she was going out with Whitney. We were pushing all the wrong buttons in one another.

I heard there was to be a poker game at the apartment of a friend of mine, composer/arranger Axel Stordahl. Whitney was expected to be in the game. I arranged to get invited and showed up just after they started playing cards. Slightly drunk and in a jealous frame of mind, I decided to scare my estranged wife's suitor. I went up behind Whitney and stuck a gun to his head. It was empty, and it was stupidly irrational on my part, but I accomplished my mission: Whitney was terrified. I was subdued, and I left laughing.

My wild temper got me noticed by all three of Hollywood's dynamite columnists from hell: Harrison Carroll, Hedda Hopper, and Louella Parsons. If a name appeared in any of their columns, the individual became an instant celebrity-about-town. These people wrote exclusively about the industry. Carroll wrote for William Randolph Hearst's *Los Angeles Herald-Express*. Hedda Hopper wrote for the *Los Angeles Times*; her famous rivalry with Louella Parsons has been well documented. Parsons was the most powerful of the three; her column was syndicated in the Hearst newspapers and read around the world. Louella's husband, "Doc," was an older man who worked as a doctor at 20th-Fox. She probably said, "Darryl, the doc wants to practice."

Though I'd made some previous appearances in these columns thanks to my social life, it was now my brawling that garnered the most coverage. I continued to carry my marital tensions into public life. I got in a fight with Bobby Jordan, who was one of the Dead End Kids and later the Bowery Boys, when he called Lynn a hooker. We were at Ciro's on the Strip. He was piss drunk and I asked him to apologize, and he said, "Fuck you." That's all I needed to hear. I belted him. Naturally the incident was written up in the columns the next day.

I remained on edge even after Lynn and I separated. I was at the Mocambo alone when Jimmy Starr, a columnist who had a reputation for not holding his whiskey, approached me. He was short, mustachioed, and, that night, very drunk. He said something about my being the villain in my relationship with Lynn. I said, "Jimmy, don't start anything here." I warned him not to provoke me, but he invited me outside. I towered over the guy. He poked me in the face a couple of times before I broke his nose. I had to help him to the public phone in the parking lot. He called his wife and was taken to an emergency ward. The following day he apologized to me in print. The sidebar was framed by a wide black border. Years later I saw him in New York, and he said, "Sid, you know I owe you a debt of gratitude. After that fight I went on the wagon. I got Arlene pregnant. We have a great son. You did me a good thing, hitting me in the nose." I thought, what a nice twist for a nightclub brawl. It never occurred to Jimmy that *I* could have been the one to walk away.

Lynn and I reconciled, but it didn't last. She persisted in telling me I was unprepared for what I was embarking on. It came down to her judgment versus my ambition. When she asked for a divorce, I didn't fight it. I wasn't interested in divorce as a way to renegotiate our relationship; I've always considered it terminal. Once the divorce action was put in motion, as far as I was concerned, there was no turning back. I was inflexible.

Although the divorce was Lynn's idea, I came to understand that she'd acted on impulse, and that once we were legally separated she had second thoughts, while I accepted the finality of the split. Still, I was able to see our son on my terms, and Lynn was friendly to me, even seductive at times, until I fell in love with Judy Garland.

I threw all my energies into developing *Kilroy*. A deal was struck: Monogram put up 80 percent of the financing; we would put up 20 percent and own half. I signed Coogan and then approached Cooper, who also signed with us.

Hyland moved quickly from sportswriter to his idea of a Hollywood mogul. He thought he was an intellectual and behaved in an arrogant manner. The Jackies told me, "We can't stand this guy." He was always criticizing them for what appeared to be no reason, just lording it over them. I was not working for him, so he didn't bother me.

Bud Moss, one of the investors from the Monogram side, proposed that we open the film in Odessa, Texas, his hometown. I suggested a personal appearance by Hollywood star Jackie Cooper. Odessa was an oil town and Bud's family was influential. I rented a single-engine, four-passenger navy airplane from Jon Hall, the actor. Cooper, my friend Kenny Morgan, who was now married to Lucille Ball's cousin, and I flew directly to Odessa. By the time we arrived it was clear that Moss, who received associate producer credit, was the one getting the star treatment.

The theater was packed, and after the show Cooper took a bow. The audience loved it. Moss had set up a late-night party at a popular roadhouse. It was a rowdy bash; people were enjoying themselves to the hilt. I excused myself from the table and went outside to make a call from the telephone booth. I'd gotten the idea to stop off in Colorado Springs on our way back to Los Angeles to see an attractive woman I'd met while she was vacationing in California, and I had the urge to talk to her. Just as I finished our conversation and hung up the receiver, the phone booth exploded around me. Shards of glass hit the right side of my face. I didn't know what happened! It came from nowhere. I was stunned. I spun around to face a young man I recognized as the son of the rival theater owner. He was enraged: our premiere had taken away all their business. I didn't have time to see how badly cut I was. He threw himself on top of me and soon we were fighting on the ground. I rolled over and got him wedged under a parked car, his head under the bumper, when a leather boot kicked me in the side and told me to get up. My eye traveled from the ground to the boot, to the pistols, to the Texas ranger hat. Local law, no doubt about that! The man looked ominous. Red faced and with guns definitely pointed at me.

"I'm placing you under arrest."

"Hey, I want to file a complaint. I'm full of glass."

"Get in the car!" he commanded, his service pistol now pointed at my stomach.

The party was going on inside the roadhouse and I'm getting in the front seat of a cop car, picking glass out of my face and ears. "Isn't there any justice in Texas?" I complained.

"I think you better keep your mouth shut."

"I sure wish you weren't in that uniform with a gun pointed at me. I'd take you on."

"I told you to keep your mouth shut."

"You shouldn't arrest me." *Bang! Slam!* He punched me in the mouth with the back of his hand without taking an eye off the road. I thought, *This son of a bitch is going to kill me.*

We got to the jailhouse and he booked me. He took my wallet and watch, checked them with another sheriff wearing a straggly-looking beard, and together they threw me in the pokey. At four o'clock in the morning Jackie Cooper and Kenny Morgan showed up with the theater owner to bail me out for a few dollars.

Kilroy did tremendous business over the weekend. It had been my idea to bring Jackie Cooper down to Odessa, and it had paid off. *Kilroy* was booked throughout the country as the second film on the bill, like the Bowery Boys movies, also shot at Monogram. These pictures were prebooked and very popular. At Monogram, if you were lucky or a miracle happened, you might see a percentage if the project went into profit, and *Kilroy Was Here* did make some money.

As a result of *Kilroy*'s success, Monogram's New York office was interested in more deals. Cooper and Coogan got on very well, but again they told me they would not work with Dick Hyland. I had it out with Hyland, who was not willing to change his ways; in fact, he couldn't understand the problem. So I hooked up with Bobby Neal, a friend whose family owned Maxwell House Coffee. Bobby agreed to invest in the second film.

One afternoon he called me at the office. "Sid," he warned, "All I'm going to say is, beware. I can't tell you any more, but beware!"

I didn't know what he meant, but I told Bobby, "I'll heed." I appreciated the tip-off and wondered what was happening. I found out later that Bobby had attended a party where he overheard a conversation in which Bud Moss said he was going to pay each of the Jackies $20,000 as an enticement to sign with him.

A few days following Bobby's warning, Coogan came to my office. I'd had no contract with Cooper, but Coogan and I had a five-picture deal. "Sid, I'm not going to make any more pictures for you," he said. He explained that his wife didn't feel he should work for anyone. "We're going to Australia on a personal appearance tour. Please tear up our contract."

The next day I read in the trades that Coogan, with Jackie Cooper and Bud Moss, had formed a company and were working again with Monogram. Hyland had brought in Moss and I had brought in Coogan. Now Hyland had lost Moss, and I had lost Coogan.

Steve Broidy called me and explained that Monogram was forced to make the deal even though I had originated the concept. He offered 5 percent of the profits. I called Brynie Foy, who advised me not to touch the offer.

The next day, Coogan came storming into my office. "You son of a bitch." I explained that we could have settled it ourselves and that, in fact, legally he wasn't able to get out of our contract. The meeting ended on a hostile note.

Fortunately, not long afterward we shook hands. I'd discovered Moss was the culprit; he orchestrated the entire situation. So Coogan, Cooper, and I made *French Leave* at Monogram, shooting it in nine days on one stage. The writer was a good friend of Coogan's, and he wrote a funny story about two sailors and a little boy who looked like Coogan as a child.

I was looking ahead to bigger horizons. Ted Law had finally put up the money needed for the development of a script based on the life of Man o' War. I was no longer thinking Monogram.

PART IV

The Black Irish Witch

17

Dear, when you smiled at me, I heard a melody
It haunted me from the start
Something inside of me started a symphony
Zing, went the strings of my heart . . .

—James Hanley, "Zing! Went
the Strings of My Heart," 1935

IT WAS THE SORT OF affair that usually blows up, doesn't work out. Judy and I had enjoyed our short time together in New York in September 1950, but once I was back in Los Angeles I kept waiting for things to swerve in another direction or dissolve. That didn't happen.

The day I returned home from the *Man o' War* shoot in Saratoga, my lawyer friend Bob Agins called: apparently, Judy had been calling his office while I was away. She was interested in the date of my return. I remarked to Agins, "I'm back."

And he said, "That's right, you're back."

We both understood the implications behind someone like Judy Garland tracking me down. I knew I was not going to play hard to get, as I was too smitten. I couldn't help but wonder how the continued affections of someone as famous as Judy would affect me. A woman who resembled a made-up little girl, who could not go out in public without creating a traffic jam, could not drop into Schwab's for toiletries, for whom a department store was out of the question and a walk was near impossible. And it had been this way for her for many years. An ordinary life was out of the question for Judy Garland. Where would I swim in the fishbowl?

The paradox of her appearance was profound. She may have looked like a youngster, but she was not. If people treated her as though they were dealing with a little girl, Judy was hostile to them. She might employ the little-girl role with nurses, maids, accountants, but should they be taken off guard, respond too familiarly to her, Judy would quickly let them know they were out of line. She suffered strangers' familiarity. It was, "Hey, Judy you know we love you," like she was the girl next door. But she wasn't. And it was not until many years later that, like the Tennessee Williams character Blanche DuBois, Judy would be forced to rely on the kindness of strangers.

That night Judy's personal assistant Tully rang me to inquire if I was free to meet Judy. The star evidently did not want to taste the least possibility of rejection—she was not going to deal with me directly. The contact would once again have to be set up by someone else, filtered. Dottie did her hair and makeup, someone would get the gloves, the perfume, and Tully would send her out for the conquest. This time our rendezvous was to be at the Villa Nova, a café on the Sunset Strip. The bar was conveniently near Evanview, where Judy and Vincente and Liza lived in a charming three-tier house hanging off the hill.

The chauffeur dutifully delivered Judy to the dark, comfortable saloon on an evening that was heavy with night-blooming jasmine. Judy made her entrance in slacks, Capezio slippers, a fresh gardenia tucked behind her tiny ear, looking all of sixteen. I was immediately warmed by her presence. "La Vie en Rose" melted out of the jukebox. She greeted me with a solid kiss on the mouth, plus a hug.

We ordered spaghetti and a Caesar salad. She sipped a Canadian Club with ginger ale and I drank a bourbon and water. It was definitely the age of the martini, but I preferred bourbon for the long haul. Judy sipped. I drank.

Right away she asked me about Saratoga. I told her how the jockeys had argued over what horse to ride and I couldn't get it through their heads that it didn't matter, that this wasn't an actual race. The entire shoot cost $18,000. The horse representing Man o' War looked good. I was encouraged, confident that I was right about this project.

On our second meeting, I waited for her on a corner in Evanview in my black teardrop job, the Cadillac I had bought from Carlton Alsop, lightly tapping the horn to signal her. Once more we were having a wonderful lark together at the expense of Vincente. Judy would tell him, "Don't ask me where I'm going, I'm just leaving." That was her attitude: "Go fuck yourself.'"

As the days went on, our relationship blossomed; Judy and I got closer and closer. We were developing an ease of communication. Tully would reach me by phone, and then Judy would come on the line. "What are you doing?" "Where are you going, are you all right? I got a joke, a new one . . ." And she would tell me a joke, something Jack Benny had told her, or Frank Sinatra, or Ethel Merman.

Part of me didn't like myself for those secret night rendezvous. I was conventional, egotistical. In New York it had been all in the open, but now I felt I didn't need a sub rosa affair with a married woman. But they continued. My pleasure at going into dark bars with Judy Garland surprised even me. I listened to her playful, witty words, falling with expert timing over gobs of marinara sauce and cigarettes. I began to think I'd never been so amused by a woman in my life. I could hardly wait to go up the hill and honk the horn.

One night she flew out of the house into the car on the run from Vincente. He'd had a few extra martinis, and he was violent. "I can't take it anymore."

I didn't say, "Get out, come live with me." Instead, we returned to our safe, dark booth at the Villa Nova to eat, drink, and talk. A naturally exuberant personality, Judy enjoyed telling stories, comic observations. She'd tell me "safe" tales of her childhood. One of them concerned her first experience performing onstage. The anecdote has been referred to in other books, but the way she told it when she recorded the incident years later was very close to what I remembered her telling me at the Villa Nova:

> I suffered awful ear infections, one after the other from the day I was born. They didn't have any kind of medicine, miracle drugs, so they would simply take me to the hospital or the doctor's office. I'd be strapped to a table and have my ears lanced. And then I'd be smacked onto the couch at my house after being brought home the same day, and with a pair of my father's socks full of hot salt draped over both ears. I looked very much like a cocker spaniel. I couldn't hear much of anything and also I didn't have an awful lot to say, because nobody said anything to me. I was actually silent until my [maternal] grandmother put me onstage . . .
>
> [My grandmother's] black Irish side got awfully angry at my mother for some reason and decided to make a dress for this orphan called Frances who had not uttered one word, not said, "Mama," "Dada," or anything else. My grandmother got so damn mad at her daughter she made me a fancy white net dress and bought me a pair of black patent leather shoes, gave me a little bell, and without an orchestration, without anyone to sing with, she threw me onto my father's stage.
>
> I'd been sitting on my grandmother's lap in the audience, and my two sisters were on the stage performing; they were old pros by then. They'd been appearing at the New Grand for years. And, my grandmother said, "Go on baby, go up on the stage." I rushed to my mother in the pit, and she said not tonight, next week. I ignored her and went onstage [interrupting my sisters]. All I did was run around in circles with a dinner bell singing "Jingle Bells." Everybody started applauding. I liked it and I stayed there singing one chorus after the other. My mother was howling with laughter as she kept playing [piano]. My father was in the wings saying, "Come on, baby, you get off." I couldn't hear my father. I'm so

pleased that the first words from my guts and my head and my heart ["Jingle Bells"] was as big then as it is today.

I guess I fell in love with the lights, and the music and the whole thing and anyway they couldn't get me off. My father finally came out and got me over his shoulder as I rang the bell, still singing "Jingle Bells" into the wings. I was a big hit, so we became the Gumm Sisters.

It was the first communication I had ever known with people. My first communication was with an audience that approved of me—that's why I sang seventeen choruses.

At two in the morning the manager of the Villa Nova would lock the door; in this way Judy and I remained opposite one another in our private, padded world. We laughed a lot and she continued to be interested in my life, what I had to say, my bullshit. In this way she opened up to me too, and we began to share our lives near the jukebox at the Villa Nova. Judy indicated she had tax problems, but the word "broke" never entered the conversation. When she described her hospitalization it was as though she'd been making a movie, visiting crippled children and servicemen.

Judy was extremely knowledgeable about the making of films, producing, and directing, but it wasn't in her mind to take on those responsibilities. Women just didn't. There was another factor, too: Judy's notions of herself as a femme fatale, and as a woman who was dependent on men, were essential to her romantic self-image.

I'd go back to my apartment and think, do I want to get involved? Judy and Vincente's marriage was rocky. She was looking for romance. I doubted she would break away from Vincente without a replacement. As much as I was attracted to Judy, I reminded myself: here was another self-involved actress. I wanted to make love to Judy, but I was reluctant to act on the impulse. I did not want to fall in love with a married woman; it seemed chancy. Chances were for horses. I figured I could have an affair with Judy if I wasn't actually in love with her. (I'd find a way.)

Judy was excited by our assignations, and I willingly went along with the game. For people who were by nature social and extroverted, we were not experiencing any pangs of confinement at the Villa Nova, nor in the comfortable seats of my Cadillac, where we explored one another's passion without "going all the way." And that was the mood, a kind of regressive teenage hot date. Judy sneaking out of the house—shades of the Stone Canyon days, when her mother worried if she'd come home in time to be properly rested for the studio the next day. A page from one of those old MGM movies I never went to.

One night for a change of pace we drove out to Malibu. This time when I went to pick her up, I'd been surprised to find Judy waiting for me outside the house. I didn't have to signal. She was wearing a sort of mandarin-style white sharkskin jacket and pedal pushers; her hair, which was rapidly growing in, was tied up in a bandanna. Her eyes flashed more black than brown that evening. The delicate bones and face that seemed so innocent, except for the mysterious eyes, evoked a kind of overly excited response in me.

There was a bistro on the beach overlooking the ocean—nothing but one blue beam indoors and the light of the silvery moon on the sand. Here the favorite tune on the jukebox was Nat King Cole's "Mona Lisa." Judy reminisced about our introduction at the Hillcrest bowling alley in Beverly Hills.

"You were conceited, darling," she teased.

"I think it was the RCAF training, baby. Maybe I felt different from everyone. I was very sure of myself."

"You were conceited."

I thought perhaps I was meant to have made a bigger fuss over her. "Did you like me anyhow?"

"It's not good to be conceited, darling." She was not going to let it go.

I was thinking that night I would take her back to my apartment on Wilshire Boulevard. We'd been in each other's arms for nights without making love. It was time. Driving along the Pacific Coast Highway, the moonlight paving our way, the dark smooth of the ocean reflecting a diamond light here and there, we seemed once again alone on the earth, forgotten lovers.

I was to discover just how different Judy was from other women. She was uninhibited, giving herself over to her passions so completely. She said she had not been with Vincente sexually for some months, and I believed her. I was a little scared by the intensity of my reactions. If I'd been hesitant in New York, here I had my privacy, I was on home turf. Judy was not going to be stared at by the concierge at a hotel.

Still, I had my own reasons for remaining somewhat discreet. Lynn was agitating for more child care support, and she had tough lawyers. My association with Judy, especially if we lived together, would be like waving a red flag at a bull. The world, including the press, assumed Judy Garland to be very rich. Didn't she build her own home on Stone Canyon Road in Bel Air when she was only fifteen? She must be a millionaire ten times over!

So there was no romancing at the Mocambo high in the hills, no delicious dinners at La Rue's, and definitely not Romanoff's. We took a certain devilish delight in speculating on what Freddie Finklehoffe's reaction might be to our affair. Judy had a kind of repartee going with the writer throughout her years at MGM, and it was a coincidence that he and I were good friends. I said Fred was a clown. She interpreted that negatively. I reassured her he was a nice clown.

"I'm a clown," she insisted.

"No. You're a little minstrel girl."

Suddenly, Judy said, "I know who you are."

"Who?"

"The knight in shining armor, who likes to go to the racetrack."

"Wrong. I'm the mystery man."

Her eyes caught mine. "That's good."

". . . who likes to go to the track," I tagged on.

Judy spoke of David Rose, her first husband, as someone who basically wasn't focused on her needs; he preferred his hobbies. She discussed her current husband as a problem drinker who was dangerous when he drank. She would imitate Vincente, his style of smoking. He was a chain smoker. Here was this seductive, delicious woman, and her husbands were unappreciative—unaware of her emotional needs. I was sympathetic.

She talked about how Vincente was powerless to help her at MGM; he was under contract to the same studio, his career ascending as Judy's had reached its peak. According to Judy, Vincente was not capable of being a protector or a husband in the deepest sense. It was a conflict of interest. In fact, his career had already suffered when she decided she didn't want him to direct her in *Easter Parade*. He was temporarily suspended from the studio and Chuck Walters replaced him. I doubt whether Vincente ever forgave her for that. He lived to work. But he wasn't willing to let her go easily; he was in love with her.

In a sense Judy took a risk by moving out of Evanview, which she did the day after we made love so completely. Dottie Ponedel wrote in her unpublished manuscript that early in her marriage, Judy had desired a place of residence away from Vincente. She claimed pressures added up to the need for a hideaway in town. And she got a psychiatrist to back her up. Dottie said, "Kate Hepburn saw a house for rent at $1,100 a month. We went up to see it, and Judy fell in love. 'This is for me!' 10000 Sunset was a charming house, rather rustic with a large fireplace. Judy imagined candlelight, the smell of wildflowers, and 'as many highballs as I want.'"

It was a cozy, secure retreat with an unhampered view of the hills. According to Dottie, Judy had talked Vincente into allowing her to do this because in the back of her mind she had a secret yen for Frank Sinatra. She loved his voice and his jokes. And Frank admired Judy; he was a faithful friend. Dottie said, "We were there one week, no Frank, and no telephone calls." As much as Judy was relaxed in the new environment away from responsibilities, her fantasy life was yet to be satisfied. She had also looked to others to take care of her professional interests, such as Carlton Alsop, who as her manager had stood up to Louis B. Mayer. Judy came to understand a personal manager could do that better than an agency, or a company man like Vincente.

And now she was moving out of Evanview and into the Beverly Hills Hotel—for me. I was flattered that Judy was so interested, but did she think I could fulfill her personal fantasies like Frank and her career needs like Alsop? I was, in fact, a relief for her. What's more, I thought I had the qualifications to be a success in her industry, even without long-term experience. The two films I produced after my split with Lynn were unimportant ones, but they had earned a profit. I wasn't selling insurance; I was putting together another film, a more ambitious project, for more money. Still, at thirty-four I was in the middle of my second divorce. I questioned my ability to maintain a sound marriage.

The more we got into it, the more I was inwardly taken off balance. What the fuck was I doing? Judy provided a kind of edge, an excitement, but she had a reputation for instability. Then I'd reflect on the woman I was spending time with, who was so entirely loving, giving, and wholesome. I'd think about the near two decades of work that she'd been able to put out, the kind of profits she'd earned for MGM, and I'd think, how unstable could she be? Judy seemed a powerhouse.

<hr />

Hollywood was a village of stars and their satellites, and not much more. The ocean was clean and flowers bloomed year round, but there was always smog. Whenever I took a plane up I could see the dust bowl covering Los Angeles. Back on the ground it felt like living in some kind of paradise. Especially with Judy. With Judy ensconced in the Beverly Hills Hotel, we were no longer playing fugitives, but we stayed close to the Villa Nova, the beach, my apartment, and a new place, an inn at the end of Sunset Boulevard, near the ocean at the Pacific Coast Highway, where we needed a flashlight to eat.

Events were moving in an unpredictable way. I never thought I'd see Judy every night, which is what I was doing, or that I would forget all other women, which I did. Judy was busy; she had begun taking meetings with her agent Abe Lastfogel, president of the William Morris Agency. I was looking after my stable, Walfarms, managing what land

I owned, and of course working on *Man o' War*. I still didn't say "We should be together."

It was an adventure for Judy to go with me to the Tropicana Motel in Hollywood. In the early '50s the Tropicana was extremely square: the night manager was from Oklahoma and twenty-six dollars bought a very nice space, with anonymity. In the morning, Judy would call Liza and Pearl, the housekeeper. And while she put on her makeup I'd send out for breakfast. Pancakes, maple syrup, bacon, eggs, a huge container of fresh orange juice. Judy's favorite meal.

"Darling," she announced one morning over coffee, "I want to tell you why I'm a black Irish witch." She launched into an account of her heritage: her father, Frank, was French somewhere along the line, and the Irish intensity came from her mother, Ethel. "My inheritance, darling, French and Irish. You see why I'm different."

"I see someone I'm falling in love with."

We went back to sleep. By midafternoon I heard Judy's voice chime, "Wake up, Sid, it's time for your 'darling' lesson. You do not know how to say the word."

I said "darling" in an unemotional, gruff manner.

"No," Judy insisted, "say, '*Ahhh*, darling,'" In a tinkling voice she said, "Repeat after me . . ."

"Darling," I said, in a somewhat lower register.

"Oh, that's not how. Try again, please."

"Baby, I'd rather tell you about the Chickenman." This threw her completely off, but it caught her imagination.

While I was researching *Man o' War* I went to a lot of racetracks. I had the incredible luck to meet Horatio Luro, who was for many, many years one of the great racehorse trainers. A tall, blond South American, Horatio was known as "Mr. Medicine Chest," because wherever he traveled he carried an enormous portable medicine cabinet. Charlie Whittingham, his assistant, also became a leading world-class trainer. I'd won a couple of bets with Horatio and Charlie, so when my partner Ted Law came up from Texas, I introduced them. Ted liked Horatio and sent a big check from Walfarms.

Judy interrupted in counterpoint, her eyes as dark as the coffee she drank: "Darling, please end your sentences with 'darling.'"

"In those days," I continued, "every trainer was looking for someone with money to buy horses; it was the only way they could survive running a stable fold. The more horses they had, the more money they made . . . darling."

Judy echoed "darling" in a softer tone. She was teaching me.

"All horses are not qualified to compete against each other: there are claiming races, allowance races, and stake races. Different calibers of speed and breed. A claiming racehorse is entered to be bought. And it works this way, darling."

Judy smiled her approval.

I went on to explain that in this division to be eligible to buy, you had to have raced a horse once before at that particular track. And there's a limit to what a horse can be worth in each division. If a horse is worth more than $15,000 he would run in allowance races, and if the purses are bigger he can compete in stakes. I wanted to claim a horse named Bir Hakeim, so I went to the office to put up the money. Win or lose, I would own that horse. "If there's one or more buyer for that horse, all names go in a basket and the name pulled becomes the owner . . . darling."

"That's a funny gamble, darling."

I agreed. I told Judy how I claimed two horses; the second one, Bir Hakeim, cost $4,500. The horse was a wreck. He had worms, he had not been trained properly. (Judy put on a face of extreme compassion, but she didn't make me say "darling.") I claimed him because I liked his breeding. Bir Hakeim was taken to Saratoga, where he was mostly fed and brushed and pampered. Julio, the trainer I found, gave him vitamins and lots of carrots. Eventually I got to Saratoga and went directly to Julio's barn.

"Fella, you want to see your dead horse?" A gorgeous horse came out of the stall, with a magnificent coat, dapples, everything. He looked like a stake horse.

"This isn't the same horse."

"Yes, it is," Julio assured me, "and he can run."

Bir Hakeim was a beautiful bay color, a warm brown and mahogany with black legs. The next morning, we ran Bir Hakeim against a stake horse. He ran three quarters of a mile and kept up. Julio said, "We need to go to Pimlico, you'll win a big bet."

Sometime after I returned to Los Angeles Julio called me to tell me Bir Hakeim was running Pimlico Saturday and to bring money.

"What price do you think they'll pay?" I asked him.

He said, "No idea. He could be anywhere from 5:1 to 2:1."

I was elated. We could really win.

Now, the Chickenman was Julio's friend who owned a wholesale chicken distributorship, and he was a big bettor. He and Julio were partners on the track. The Chickenman would put up $10,000, and Julio would tell him what horses he was running. Naturally, they would split the money if they won. I was unaware of this partnership at the time. So I got on a train with my $15,000 and went to Baltimore. I arrived late and joined Julio at the clubhouse. It was raining cats and dogs. Julio said, "Oh boy, look at it rain." Bir Hakeim loved the mud. We got so much rain it was a gulch on the track.

"Julio, do you think this horse is gonna win?"

"Yeah," he said, "by a hundred yards." I told Julio I'd brought $5,000, and I gave that amount to him so he could bet the money. It was the last race of the day. A mile and a sixteenth. I entered the horse for $5,000. Bir Hakeim hadn't raced since March; it was now August. And he went off at 5:1 because he was a California horse. I bet the remaining $10,000 with two bookmakers in New York and two in Boston, $2,500 each. I watched the race from high up in the tower. When the gates opened up Bir Hakeim walked out on his hind legs! I couldn't believe it was true. A young South American was his jockey.

Judy was not impressed, but she feigned great interest.

As Bir Hakeim went around the turn I thought the jockey should be on the outside, because he got left at the gate and Bir Hakeim was well tuned. "The horse goes right through the pack and gets shut off. Then he goes to the outside, then he ducks in again." Now, Judy sat up as though she was watching a race, forgetting the "darling" lesson. "The horse got beat by thirty lengths. Dead last by thirty."

Judy interjected, "Is that good or bad for us, darling?"

"Bad. I lost $15,000 bucks." I went back to the barn and found the jockey. "What the fuck do you think you're doing?" I was furious. He didn't answer me because he didn't understand English.

Julio pointed to Bir Hakeim. "Look at his eye. It's blue—he got kicked to the face with a rock."

Judy was ready to cry. "Darling," I reassured her quite naturally, "it's a happy ending."

I thought Ted would have to know. Mad as hell, I boarded the train, along with the Chickenman. He was planning to get off somewhere between New York and Baltimore. We ate dinner together, and after four or five drinks I came to the conclusion Ted and I were screwed.

When I got back to New York I immediately got on the phone. "Ted, we'll get our money back. Next week Bir Hakeim will be at 30 or 40:1. All we have to do is bet $2,000 and get our money back."

Again, the track was muddy, the way the horse liked it. I went to Baltimore with $5,000 cash and found Julio saddling up Bir Hakeim. The horse was 30:1 in the racing form.

"You go and see what price he is."

I looked at the board and he's 9:1. "From 30:1 that's some fuckin' drop," I said.

"Don't worry," Julio said, "it'll go up."

By the time the horses got on the racetrack for the parade he's 8:1; five minutes to post and I haven't bet a quarter yet, he's 6:1. I go up to the window, and Bir Hakeim is 5:1. I bet $1,000, he's 4:1, I go to another window, he's 2:1. Bir Hakeim went off at 5:2. From 30:1 to 5:2.

I sat with Henry Parr, who later became the president of Pimlico. Bir Hakeim was running in the lead; when they went around the bend, he was about five lengths in front; when they hit the stretch, he's ten in front. He won by eighteen lengths. At least I won back $5,000.

"You see, when the odds are broken down like that it means Julio and the Chickenman are betting all over the country. And that's how I came to understand: you never trust anyone in racing, *darling*."

Judy cocked her head. "*Nooo*, that's not it. Much better before."

I was learning how to say "darling" in a soft and melodic way. However, as much as Judy was fascinated by the track, she never quite understood a claiming horse.

18

IT WAS VIRTUALLY IMPOSSIBLE to be cool around Judy. She was spinning a web around me, and I seemed more than willing to be caught. I did not want to feel trapped; my goal was to avoid any kind of pressure cooker, which was tough to do, since I so entirely lusted after her. I anticipated some sort of confrontation with Vincente, and this bothered me even more. Fortunately it never happened.

In January 1951, Judy was booked to perform on the popular radio program *The Bob Hope Show*. There was a comedy sketch, dialogue with Judy, singing, and orchestration. Judy asked me to attend the broadcast. She also wanted me to be present afterward at the Brown Derby, where she was to discuss her career with Abe Lastfogel and Judy's former costar Fanny Brice. Backstage I noticed Judy needed but one look at the script before she knew it. She would read it through in ordinary conversation, and the words would fall flat. Then in front of the audience she'd breathe magic into the dialogue. The audience's reaction was awesome: they tore up the studio.

We left the highly charged atmosphere to meet Abe and Fanny for dinner. The subject at hand: What should Judy Garland do next? William Morris was a powerful agency, with offices worldwide, and Lastfogel had some ideas. He suggested that Judy follow the lead of Danny Kaye, currently a giant success at the London Palladium. "Go to England, leave the country."

Fanny Brice agreed. "You need to move on with your career."

Abe had brought Fanny along to back him up. Judy admired Fanny, a brilliant, multitalented woman: she sang, painted, and wrote. (Her son, Bill Brice, inherited the gift and became a well-known West Coast painter.) Judy had made two films with her. In 1938's *Everybody Sing*, little Judy was on her way to becoming a "national asset." The *New York Times* reported, "It is, of course, only fair to admit that Judy Garland of the rhythm, writin' and 'rithmetic age is a superb vocal technician, despite her not exactly underemphasized immaturity."

Their second collaboration was the *Ziegfeld Follies* of 1946. In this all-star musical revue, Judy performed a sequence called "The Interview." Bosley Crowther in the *New York Times* described Judy as demonstrating "promise of a talent approaching that of Beatrice Lillie or Gertrude Lawrence." But the public was not accustomed to Judy in a sophisticated role, and she was quickly returned to the girl-next-door persona.

Judy was listening to Fanny and Abe, and they did a good job of persuading her. I had to agree: as much as I was reluctant to see Judy leave, the Palladium would be a marvelous career move. She was about ten pounds overweight, and on her petite physique any extra weight was magnified on the screen. In any case, there were no film offers. She would not have to worry about one pound singing in concert.

<hr />

When Judy was in front of the cameras, which she had been most of her teen and adult life, she'd been on either Benzedrine or a diet or both. It was the bane of her life. Unlike other actresses, she could not successfully camouflage extra weight, especially as she was so active, dancing and singing in revealing costumes. She could even be underweight and still appear heavy or out of proportion on screen, a tremendous cause of unhappiness for her.

Dottie Ponedel had come into Judy's life around the same time as Fanny Brice. It was on the set of *Everybody Sing* that Sydney Guilaroff, the chief hair designer at MGM, had introduced them. Dottie was famous for doing Marlene Dietrich's makeup. She was adept at creating glamorous screen images, and she changed Judy's from wholesome teen-ager to beautiful young woman. She threw away the caps Judy wore on her teeth and the rubber discs that reshaped her nose. They rapidly became pals, drinking and hanging out. Dottie, colorful and uneducated, supported Judy's antics. "Beans," Dottie's brother, was Sinatra's makeup person for years, so they provided another illusion of family for Judy.

As for her actual family, at MGM mothers were expected to report on their children to the studio, and Judy's mother had been on the pay-roll for this purpose. There'd been times, however, when Ethel begged MGM to slow down Judy's work schedule, just as decades later I was to beg her agents, Freddie Fields and David Begelman, to slow down her concert and film work (she could never work forty consecutive concerts without the use of drugs). And, like Ethel, I was frustrated in that my requests were ignored. At one point Ethel had suggested Judy quit the film industry when her weight dropped to eighty pounds during the making of *Presenting Lily Mars.*

Judy had been an effervescent teenager, and in some sense it's under-standable that she would have been mad at her mother for spying on her during those years. But Judy chose to feel permanently betrayed, much as, years later, she would feel betrayed by Hollywood when she was not awarded the Oscar for Best Actress for her performance in *A Star Is Born.*

Ethel was eventually taken off the payroll, once the studio heads were content that Dottie was keeping Judy happy and in tow. These responsibilities led to MGM paying Dottie extra, although she did not ask for it.

———————— ∞ ————————

I absorbed the conversation in our prime booth at the Brown Derby. I was trying to adjust to the idea of Judy leaving. She was not eager to go. Fanny was persuading her to say yes, "make it definite." I kept thinking of her performance at the studio, and the extraordinary ability she demonstrated in relating to a live audience. Lastfogel was pointing out, again, the tremendous success Danny Kaye had enjoyed at the Palladium. "It would be no different for you, honey."

London was an especially good choice for Judy, since the majority of her overseas fan mail came from Britain. She'd been receiving worldwide fan correspondence for years without reading any of it. Tully was in charge of doing that. The studio's publicity department answered the requests for pictures, providing a five-by-seven-inch glossy of the star on receipt of one quarter for postage. Then the letters, which ran into the thousands, would be boxed weekly and forwarded to the William Morris Agency. Tully would go in and sort it out. In those days the letters were generally of sympathy and encouragement, very much like the "Love Letter" in Billy Rose's column. Sentiments like "Go get 'em, Judy."

Judy looked to Fanny, and by the time we left the Brown Derby it was agreed that Judy would be booked at the London Palladium for April.

Vincente moved temporarily out of Evanview, and Judy returned to the house to be with her daughter, Liza, while she designed her Palladium act with Roger Edens and Oscar Levant. She had wanted me to spend time at the house, but I found it impossible to stay there. I could not sleep in another man's bed, nor was I going to hang around a rival's home. It could have been an issue between us, but Judy was understanding, and we continued to meet at my apartment.

She was diligently at work with Roger and Oscar. It was Oscar who suggested the Al Jolson hit "Rock-a-Bye Your Baby." He recognized that Judy shared with Jolson the same kind of power over audiences. "Rock-a-Bye," along with Jolson's "Swanee" and "Carolina in the Morning," subsequently became associated with Judy. Meanwhile, Roger created the vocal arrangements; together they built a dynamic forty-five-minute act.

I followed my investments. The script for *Man o' War* was about to be rewritten yet again in the hopes of pleasing the horse's owner, Sam Riddle. I was fortunate that my polo-playing silent partner, Ted Law, trusted me. He knew I enjoyed managing Walfarms, I had an eye for horses, and I raced them for a pretty good profit. There were no outstanding pressures in my life other than the ongoing battle for more money with my ex-wife. Lynn had finally divorced me in December 1950, but the decree wouldn't be final for months.

In March, Judy began her own divorce proceedings, going before a superior court judge and giving testimony as to why she desired for her marriage to Vincente Minnelli to end. At this juncture Vincente cooperated, giving custody of Liza to her mother in a legal separation.

Neither the court proceedings nor my business interests intruded in our affair. I was sure to find a way to be with Judy. I had accompanied her to several Bing Crosby broadcasts where she was the guest entertainer. Again, the audience demonstrated their exuberance and brought the house down each time. When Judy expressed insecurities about performing in London I would only have to counter, "Look how you've proved yourself these past few months onstage, in front of a live audience, darling."

Still, Freddie Finklehoffe had been calling me for weeks. I wasn't around my usual haunts, and he missed me at the track. I had managed to avoid meeting him and dealing with his double-edged curiosity. When we finally spoke, he informed me that he was aware Judy had moved out of Evanview. I quickly reassured him that she was back. This confused Freddie. "It didn't hang?" I said, "No, Vincente's out." Not knowing where to go with that, he brought the subject around to business—in this case, a horse. Freddie had known I was interested in buying a certain filly. In the interim, I had actually decided against it. I suspected the horse carried a bad infection, and I was correct. Unaware of this, Freddie went around me and bought the horse himself. He was duped, but he couldn't admit it to me. So by the time we met for lunch at the Cock'n Bull, he was on his third scotch and asking me more questions about Judy.

"I hate to admit this to you, Freddie," I said, "but I'm crazy about the girl."

His eyes hit the ceiling. "I hope you're jesting, pal."

"I think it's love." I was playing with Freddie, as I knew he must really have that sick horse on his mind. At the same time, I knew I was in love with Judy. I said, "Frankly, Freddie, it's a little nuts for me to get involved with a woman so much in the eyes of the public, every move detailed. Sure, it's been fun and games and a conquest." Freddie was turning green. I thought the truth was, I was wanted, sought after. Judy was a great boost for the ego, and it was even deeper than all that.

Freddie had named his filly Don't Tell Ella after his first wife, Ella Logan. Unfortunately, Don't Tell Ella was sick for six months after purchase. She never ran and she never became a brood mare. I attempted to explain to Freddie how the breeding of mares generally belongs to dynasties of families who have, for generations, studied bloodlines. It was an area I wouldn't touch, out of my reach. He looked bemused and ordered another double scotch.

Freddie didn't crack until years later, when he asked me to buy two of Don't Tell Ella's offspring, as if I were responsible for his grand error. He had boarded them in a broken-down barn in Northridge that he hadn't visited in two years. We went out to see them one rainy day, tramping about a quarter of a mile through mud to a paddock. There stood a creature with a big head and no legs. He looked like a funny pony. "He can't run, Freddie," I said. "It's not a racehorse." We found the other horse, just the opposite: a black stallion we couldn't get near. He was totally wild and untrainable. "You're a Harvard graduate, Freddie, but you ain't got no horse sense, baby."

19

I see America marching
led by MGM,
the other peoples of the world
avidly cheering them,
Judy out ahead.

—James Simmons, "Judy Garland and the Cold War"

THE TRIP TO ENGLAND would be the first time Judy had ever been out of the United States. As she was terrified of flying, she was going to sail aboard the *Ile de France* with Tully and Dottie. For the moment, Liza would stay behind with "Cozy," her nanny.

On the eve of Judy's departure for England, she gave me a Cartier wristwatch. The inscription read, I'M WITH YOU, BABY, a phrase she had culled from my lingo when I'd reassure her with pet phrases like, "You can do it, darling," and, "Remember, I'm with you, baby." Judy had subtly suggested I make the trip to London with her. I refused to take the hint but was unable to tell her why: I didn't wish to be trapped aboard ship with an entourage, tagged the "boyfriend."

The instant Judy left Los Angeles, I missed her. In fact, I longed for her. She sent me wires from the ship: "Darling, I love you" or "Darling, I miss you." When the ship docked in England she had Tully contact me. Would I fly over for opening night? Judy was low, and she would love to see me. "She talks about you every day. 'What's he doing? Who's he going out with?' Why don't you surprise her?"

I had anticipated Judy would call when she arrived, that I would hear directly from her. Once more she'd asked Tully to contact me. Clearly, she still didn't want to hear one iota of a rejection.

I didn't have to think twice: I flew to London, leaving my trainer Bill Sergeant in charge of Walfarms.

From the moment the *Ile de France* had docked in Plymouth there'd been an overwhelming reception for Judy Garland, and it followed her all the way to the Dorchester Hotel in London. I surprised Judy at the hotel the night before she opened. We spent a wonderfully romantic evening together: dinner in the Dorchester Grill, then on to the Savoy, the 400 Club. Judy was out to have a ball. My arrival in London in time for her opening night at the Palladium was something to celebrate, but I also was aware of a kind of suppressed anxiousness on her part. We spent the night in her suite at the Dorchester, where I remained for the run of the show.

On opening night Judy's dresser rushed into her dressing room. "The Queen Mother's coming!" She was so excited.

I said, "Are you kidding, the Queen's already here!"

Judy laughed, but it was a nervous giggle. It was not going to be easy going out onstage, and she admitted this by asking me to hold her. She craved emotional support. I was awkward, self-conscious. I held her hand a moment and then I held her until she was ready to pose her entrance, carrying a subtle message for the audience in her composure. She was swathed in a saffron-color organza concoction dreamed up by Dottie and Tully. I patted her rump and off she whooshed.

A curve of celebrities sat directly behind Judy onstage. At one point the rush of applause was so intense it actually propelled her onto one of the celebrities' laps. I stood in the wings, holding my breath as Judy opened with Roger Edens's "At Long Last Here I Am":

> *I thought it would never happen, but I finally got here.*
> *I've been all around the map an' lots of places but not here.*
> *It seemed so far away, the trip seemed silly.*

I'd always heard them say, it's a long, long way to Piccadilly.
But when Danny Kaye first told me this is where I should
*   wind up,*
I guess Danny must have sold me, I immediately signed up.
And then I knew I'd get here, even if I swam.
It's hard to believe, but here I am.
And now I admit I'm nearly overcome with delightment.
I ask you, and quite sincerely, please forgive my excitement.
I never thought I'd see what we call Buckingham.
But that's past . . .
So hold fast . . .
At long last,
Here I am!

By the time Judy got to the last line of the song, she could no longer hold back her emotions. She choked up as she sang, "Here I am!" The audience of over twenty-five hundred people began to cheer her on, shouting, "Judy you're wonderful," "Good old Judy."

Judy was sincerely moved, but she could not continue to deliver in such a halting voice. I stood there, my heart in my mouth, to see where she was going, and she made the decision on the spot. Instead of waiting to end the performance with "Somewhere Over the Rainbow," her signature number, she sang it right away. The audience was on their feet screaming for the rest of the concert.

As the performance continued, all of Judy's vaudeville savvy came into play. She spoke to the audience to make herself comfortable. Her audience was a friend whom she might like to kiss. She was chatty, seductive (her specialty), the timing right. I watched as she kicked off her four-inch heels to "get down" with the audience. They cheered. She sang a medley of songs associated with her films: "The Boy Next Door," "The Trolley Song." I heard Judy announce, "This is the greatest night of my life." More cheering.

Judy had completely captured every heart in the audience. Her strong legs had held up, but when she put her heels back on for her exit she tripped over the microphone wires. To my horror, she plummeted to the stage like a fallen sunflower.

Buddy Pepper, her pianist, got up to assist her. Judy immediately introduced him, and in a cryptic voice added, "That's probably one of the most ungraceful exits ever made."

She was answered with whistles and screams and offers of love. The audience spoke to her, responded, and she talked back. Everyone had been involved in the performance. And Judy had held nothing back. By the time the performance ended she was ringing wet. She was not concerned about maintaining a look of elegance, and the audience, too, would be drenched. It was that intense. She would get to the audience with that tear in her voice. She knew how to manipulate on a stage, and privately, in a room: when she laughed, you laughed, when she cried, you cried. (Our "special" song, "Danny Boy," was delivered in the privacy of our bedroom. Judy really never stopped singing.) The next day, Val Parnell, the manager of the Palladium, told me Judy's ovation was the biggest he'd experienced there.

The *Daily Express* was both critical and literary: "What if the final cheers are for the *Wizard of Oz* child who trod the yellow brick road for us in the darkest days of the war? It was sincere." She was a big hit, as Fanny Brice predicted. She continued to draw rave reviews and capacity audiences. It remained that way for each show, twice a night, one at 6:00 PM and one at 8:00.

I had a return ticket on TWA. I thought I'd be in London for a week. Judy, out of the States, her ties to MGM permanently severed, free at last. And then our feelings took over, and the sparks really began to fly.

In the course of the four-week tour, I didn't spend all my nights in the wings waiting for the star. I'd take care of my business during the day, very often meeting friends in the evening. Then I would go around to the Palladium after the performance, pick up Judy, and we'd go out on the town.

London had not fully recovered from Hitler's bombs, and it was eerie walking around the great city with evidence of devastation everywhere.

There were entire blocks razed to the ground. In spite of this disaster the general mood in London was one of cheerfulness; people were happy to be alive. Judy and I fit right in.

Judy, the symbol of cheerfulness through strife, America's national asset, was finally allowed to be exported. Londoners were claiming Judy for their own. This was altogether a new experience: a country relating to "Dorothy" as a political symbol. She'd been on war bond tours, entertained servicemen, visited ailing soldiers, but she had never fully understood the power of her public image. Now, she was the toast of London, cutting down the media focus on Princess Margaret, who was unconventional for a royal and currently the darling of the press. The princess's exploits had captured the world's eye and the local papers were obsessional on the subject of "Meg." But here was Dorothy in the flesh, the movie queen eclipsing the real-life princess.

We were unabashedly caught up in the vortex of her success and wallowing in it. Judy's English press had always been sensational. What was printed in the States was generally rougher in England—as much as they worshipped their idols, they could tear them asunder. Now the American profiles of Judy as an unstable mess were being disproved night after night.

The British press, however, couldn't resist commenting on the fact that she was plump. She wasn't "camera slim," and she didn't have to be. She was not the anorexic tiny teen from her film roles. But Judy was so petite every bit of flesh was exaggerated. I thought she looked simply marvelous.

A steady stream of well-wishers went backstage: Betty Bacall, Bogie, Kate Hepburn (returning from Africa, where they'd shot John Huston's *The African Queen*), Orson Welles, the Oliviers, Judy's old boyfriend Tyrone Power. Every night it was the who's who of international show business queuing up to pay their respects. Quite an impressive lot.

Judy was on the watch for her childhood crush, the distinguished actor Robert Donat. She was really looking forward to meeting him. Judy recalled:

When I was about eleven years old I worked in a movie house in Detroit where they were running *The Count of Monte Cristo*. I used to sit in the wings and watch movies. I fell madly in love with Robert Donat. I've never written a fan letter in my life, but I wrote a long letter to him in England and I cut out every picture I could find in every movie magazine and he was all over the walls of my room. He sent me a picture with a note from his secretary. I compared the signature on the picture and the note and it was the same handwriting. I wept because I knew he hadn't signed it himself. I still slept with it under my pillow for a long time. I worshipped him and it killed me to have to sing to Clark Gable, because I was in love with Robert Donat.

All these years elapsed and I went to the Palladium. I kept wondering if Robert Donat would come to see me. If I would by any chance get to meet him.

I was in my dressing room. I'd been at the Palladium for maybe a week and there was a knock on the door. I went to the door and there was a liveried chauffeur with a note for me, and a huge bouquet of roses. I took the letter and it said MISS GARLAND on the front of it and ROBERT DONAT on the back. I thought, oh, my God, I've finally heard from the man of my dreams.

I rushed into the little private room in my dressing suite and locked the door. I was sure he'd seen the show and was going to tell me he liked it, or that he wanted to come see it, or something. I opened the envelope: "Dear Miss Garland, I haven't had the pleasure of meeting you but I wanted to tell you that there's a very good psychiatrist at 212 Harley Street. And he will be available to you anytime you want him." . . . He had written in the letter that he was working on a movie.

He thought I was absolutely nuts. And had arranged for me to have help. The chauffeur said, he was waiting for an answer. I didn't know what to say so I went back in and I said, thank Mr. Donat for me very much. I didn't have the guts to write a note and say "How dare you." I was too in love with him. I went back to the hotel and about two days later, I was asleep in the morning and the phone rang. I very sleepily said hello, and I heard this voice that I'd been hypnotized by, for all of my life practically. "Miss Garland there?" I said, "Yes." The voice said, "Mr. Donat here." I went to pieces hearing his voice. I said, "Oh, hello." He said, "Well, I'm rather worried because I have to go out of town on location until Thursday. Do you think you can hold on until then?" And I said, "Well, I hope so, but I'm not sure." I didn't want to disappoint him and have him think I was sane. He was being so helpful. And so sweet, and so convinced that I was a real case that I think it would have depressed him had he realized what he'd done.

Eventually he left word at the theater, had his secretary call my man in the dressing room that he was back from location. I never talked to him after that. How to meet the man of your dreams. Later I found out at the time when he wrote me, he was really desperately sick, so actually it was very kind. It was just that it wasn't what I had pictured at the age of eleven. . . .

Although Judy recalls the incident with compassion, at the time it struck her as hilarious.

⸺∽◦∾⸺

From the moment I arrived in England Judy pushed me in the forefront. "I'd like you to know Sid Luft." At times we would be in the dressing room and she'd come over and put an arm around my waist: "This is the guy I'm in love with." She made no bones about her feelings toward me. She was precise, not ambivalent. She was also solicitous: "What would you like to do, darling?" "Would you like to go to so-and-so's for dinner, might be fun?" She did everything to make me comfortable. At the same time, she was relying on me more and more. When we were dancing or dining at a nightclub and a fan came up to ask her for an autograph, Judy got in the habit of referring them to me. "If *he* says it's OK."

The River Club was one of our favorite spots to go to after Judy's performances. A sedate, private emporium overlooking the Thames, the

River Club happened to be Princess Margaret's favorite as well. The club's owner was an American in the liquor business who was a friend of mine from Los Angeles. Very often Princess Margaret would be at the club when we were there. She'd be enjoying herself, carousing with friends, but she'd never acknowledge Judy's presence. "Very peculiar lady," Judy said. "She knows I'm here." And it was true there was no shaking of hands, no exchange of toasts.

We were aware of the English royals' genuine love for musical revue, so the princess's behavior baffled us. Maybe she was loyal to Danny? Kaye's career had been helped immeasurably by playing the Palladium. His tremendous publicity had leaked back to the States about his huge success with the royal family, how he was frequently seen in the company of Princess Margaret. Judy's audiences were not all that royal, nor were they upper class, more just regular folk who sought some escape from worldly worries, from a limited material life. A crowd that needed to be cheered and, in exchange, they cheered. That had been the deal: you lift our spirits and we'll make you a star.

For the hell of it I showed up at the theater wearing a derby and a white silk scarf and sporting a cane. For laughs . . . the dude goes to England. Judy was amused, so was I, but others thought I was foolish. We didn't care—we were so entrenched in our romance.

One night we accepted an invitation from Vivien Leigh and Laurence Olivier, the reigning king and queen of British drama. They were extoled for their performances in *Antony and Cleopatra* and *Caesar and Cleopatra*. We arrived at the Olivier house, where I was asked to wait in an antechamber while Judy was escorted to meet His and Her Highness. It was dark as though the Blitz were still on. I couldn't tell who was sitting around. People were led individually to the room where Larry and Vivien waited to receive their guests. Perhaps they'd heard Judy's beau was an ass, that I made a fool of myself dressing up like an Englishman. Years later I was introduced to Sir Laurence when I was briefly managing my daughter, Lorna Luft, on an overseas tour. She was singing at the Top of the Town. Olivier could not have been warmer, more down-to-earth.

Back at the hotel, Judy and I came to the conclusion that perhaps they'd had some loyalty to Minnelli. She managed to take my focus off the slight over a bottle of Dom Perignon and by telling me a story about the Munchkins.

The Wizard of Oz was in production for eight grueling months. The Munchkins came to Hollywood from all over the world. Club Munchkin. Some of them were foreign born. Married, single, they arrived in Oz among the palm trees in Culver City. The men were naughty. They thought they could get away with anything because they were so small. An assistant director had been specially assigned to the Munchkins, and to be sure they made their calls they had a lieutenant as boss. Apparently many of them would wind up in jail and have to be bailed out. "You couldn't lock them up for long because they were needed on the set."

With their makeup on, the Munchkins frequented Culver City bars, and after a long day of work, they drank. They were disorderly as hell, yelling and screaming. The next day, on the set, hung over, they would make Judy's life miserable by putting their hands under her dress. Judy would break herself up demonstrating the situation: she pinched her ass, laughing, "What are you doing?"

She had been sixteen playing the role of Dorothy, a child. The Munchkins, of course, were close to her size and couldn't resist teasing her, making her life a misery. The men were forty or more years old, and there was Judy with boyfriends, and feeling sophisticated at sixteen. The little girl/woman dilemma would subtly emerge in so many of Judy's stories, and as I was to experience, in her very behavior as well.

The British affiliate of the William Morris office had arranged for Judy to tour in Scotland and Ireland after the run at the Palladium. Judy was not enthusiastic about delaying her return to the screen. Bing Crosby had sent her a script with the working title *Famous*. I thought she wasn't ready for cameras. "Four weeks at the Palladium, darling—you should keep going." So I *was* expressing an opinion. In fact, I prevailed upon Judy that she wasn't ready to return to the States. She had ideas for her career that I believed were not workable. "If you don't want me to do *Famous* with Bing, and you don't think I should do this, what should I do?"

"Tour the provinces."

Now she was insisting the Morris office speak to me. I went along with it, because I seriously believed she should tour and not have to worry about her weight in front of a camera. "You're a genius at what you do with a live audience, why not develop that?"

We were immersed in our feelings for one another. Nevertheless, I thought this was going to get sticky; she was depending on me.

Judy respected Bing and she enjoyed working with him. But for a comeback film, *Famous* was awful. I told her, "Judy, this is a piece of shit. Trust me, you can't do it." I was aware she was eager to ensure her next career move, but this could not be it. I argued that there'd be more appropriate offers. Judy considered my advice.

A month passed and I was still in London, styling her hair and clothes and suggesting what career moves to make. I had other obligations, and when I discussed them with Judy she didn't want to hear about them. Soon she was saying, "Darling, if you feel I shouldn't do the film, I won't." Subsequently, it was made with Jane Wyman, an excellent actress, and released under the title *Just for You*, but it flopped anyway.

Nonetheless, Judy was determined to return to film. She brought up her interest in a remake of *A Star Is Born*. She'd acted the part of Esther/Vicki as far back as 1942 in a Lux radio drama costarring Walter Pidgeon. She went to Louis B. Mayer requesting that MGM consider a remake starring her, but Mayer was not about to take the risk of presenting Judy as a mature leading lady.

So she accepted the rest of my advice and agreed to the British stage tour. "OK, OK. I'll play the boonies." The ball was in my court.

The Empire chain, which owned the Palladium, had many theaters throughout Britain. Edinburgh was not part of the itinerary. I hankered to play golf on the greens at Gleneagles, and so I insisted she stop at Edinburgh. Abe Lastfogel called me. "Sid, what're you doing interfering with Judy's career? The boyfriend doesn't try to interfere with our management!"

She was booked one week at each theater: Edinburgh, Glasgow, Manchester, Dublin, Liverpool, Blackpool. She was alone, professionally in transition with an agency, two women as attendants, an estranged husband. Carlton Alsop was out of her life. She was needy.

I'd anticipated a more complex individual, but out on the road I discovered her to be what friends of mine would tag "a no-bullshit dame." Judy smoked mentholated cigarettes, but in moderation. She always took a sip of wine before going onstage, but she didn't need a drink to go to a party. For me, it wasn't easy to hit a room full of people sober; I'd have to throw down a few first. Judy was a hyper person with boundless energy and no doubt had been this way since childhood, but she was forthright with me, and we began to relax with one another. We were away from the crowd, and simmering down.

20

I N SCOTLAND WE HAD ten days between Glasgow and Edinburgh. We
went to Turnberry, where I taught Judy the game of golf. Sometimes
I'd back off, inwardly alarmed by the depth of my involvement. I had a
fantasy that I was a martyr, that I was the only one to save this creature,
if indeed there proved any saving to be done.

In Edinburgh the weather was dreary and we were unable to play
golf, so we visited an old castle. Then, back at the hotel, there was
some tension between us. Judy had asked me to become her personal
manager. What was I willing to give up for this woman? What was I
not willing to let go of?

"You have the experience to manage me, darling."

"I can't hang around managing you—Judy Garland's sweetheart/
pimp. Not my style." Judy was in tears by the French doors in the
sumptuous period-decorated suite. I took her in my arms. "Darling, if
I managed you, really managed you, you'd have to listen to me, you'd
have to take my advice—"

"But I would, I would . . ." she assured me through her tears, as
though she were talking to Auntie Em in *The Wizard of Oz.*

"Darling," I said, "Let's listen to music, let's make love. We can't
without a career. *Career* is so we can do all this. If I'm your lover, your
companion, and your manager, I must earn a proper living." It was late
afternoon and raining. I was looking out at a huge black cloud hanging

over a distant hill. Judy needed to be sure of me in some form. "I'm not a manager, darling. I'm trying to produce a picture."

"But you've got to stay with me, Sid. I don't want to go to Liverpool, and I don't want to go to Dublin without you."

"I don't think I've experience enough for you, darling."

"But you do, you do." And so it went.

Three people were in the audience the night Judy opened in Edinburgh. I was mortified. I'd made an ass of myself arguing with the Morris office over the booking, and Judy wanted me for her manager?

I quickly located the theater manager. "What's going on?"

He said, "Oh, Mr. Looft, you must understand—"

I interrupted him: "Don't you publicize?"

"Sir, this is the furst time the soon's been oot in the evening!" Sunshine more important than Garland?

The second show, however, proved one of the highlights of the tour. An amazing night of artistry on Judy's part, and of love from an appreciative audience. She glided onto the stage with her special gait, working her fingers dramatically through her hair, touching her face and body, extending the palm of the hand to the audience, unaware the palm is considered an erotic symbol in Indonesian dance. (Her nails were unpainted and gracefully short; studio photos of Judy with polish on her nails were rare.) The performance ended with the audience joining hands and singing "Auld Lang Syne" to Judy. There wasn't a dry eye in the house.

Freddie Finklehoffe surprised us by showing up in Glasgow along with my friend Bob Agins and an old friend of Judy's, longtime talent agent Barron Polan. Judy and I were mildly amused by their presence in Scotland. We'd grown so happy with just one another it felt like an intrusion on our privacy. Over dinner after the show Freddie revealed the purpose of their visit. He had a concept for a screenplay he believed suited Judy's filmic persona. Like Bing, he intended this to be her comeback vehicle. By now, though, Judy was more determined than ever to change her screen image, and she politely declined the opportunity.

In Dublin, I took Judy to visit a famous stud farm. We looked at many colts, and she fell in love with a little yearling with the eccentric name of Florence House. Before we left Ireland I bought Florence House especially for Judy. I arranged to have her shipped first to Long Island, where she'd be trained, and then to Walfarms in Los Angeles.

At the end of the tour, Judy longed to see her daughter. They'd spoken on the phone as much as possible; now she felt it was time to be with Liza. So she sent for her and her governess, Cozy. Liza was going to come with us to the French Riviera, where Judy was due to perform in a benefit show at Monte Carlo with her great friend Noël Coward.

If Britain was cheerful, France was a celebration. Paris, unlike London, had been untouched by bombs, left intact due to the German occupation. The buildings had not yet been cleaned up under the supervision of André Malraux, but Paris "dirty" was still the lyrical and romantic city of dreams. Couples kissed in public, the men always with an eye open so as not to miss anything. Affection was rampant. The cafés spilled over, street musicians were at every corner, lovers strolled the Seine . . . even the bums looked blissful.

Judy's relationship with Liza was so loving and filled with tenderness. I was knocked out by her gift for mothering, and they had so much fun together I was almost jealous. Before we left for the Riviera we visited the House of Balmain, where Judy bought a much-needed new wardrobe and replenished her supply of Vent Vert.

In Cannes we stayed at the Carlton. I felt distinctly out of place with the English theater crowd, the people who revolved around Noël. Judy was intent on meeting Coward and friends at the bar for drinks. I was homophobic in those days, uneasy around male couples, and declined to go with her, so Judy agreeably went her way and I went mine. I visited old haunts, tracking down the villa where Frieda Roberts and

I had our love affair all those years ago. Later that night I met up with Judy at a posh affair, throngs of people milling about. Judy asked me to join her and Noël and Sugar Ray Robinson, who were going on to another bash. I was overcome with the idea of walking Judy through the evening and apologetically bowed out.

I spent the evening talking with Genevieve, a beautiful blonde in the style of Brigitte Bardot, best described as an international playgirl. Genevieve spoke many languages and was charming. An attractive, well-dressed older woman remained in the background while we drank and chatted. I asked Genevieve if she was her guardian and she replied, "Sort of an auntie." But Auntie didn't accompany us later when we made the rounds of the Cannes nightclubs and expensive after-hours clubs, where Genevieve was always well received.

We had a wild night, winding up on the beach near the hotel, where, loaded, we fell asleep fully clothed. Around ten in the morning I awakened, spitting out sand, to see Judy and little Liza standing directly over me, backlit by the bright Riviera sun. Judy had taken a handful of sand and poured it over my face. She ignored Genevieve and in a quiet voice said, "How about a shower and a shave?" She didn't make a scene or an issue of the escapade; it was understood that it was the bachelor's last fling.

We were back in London in time for a benefit show at the Palladium, a tribute to British comedian Sid Field, who had died the previous year. I became convinced the Princess Margaret slight had been the result of Danny Kaye's influence. Conjecture, of course—but I noticed that Danny's nose got bent when Judy performed the Fields benefit. Danny dressed up as a sailor boy. He had the right people on his team—the Oliviers, the royals, et al.—and he was intended to be the star of the show. And he wasn't. Judy came out with that fantastic ability to take everyone's guts and do with them what she willed. Noël Coward remarked on that in his diary: "Took the Duchess [of Kent] to dine at the Ivy, and then on to the Palladium for the *Sid Field Benefit*—a really star-studded show. Highest spot—Judy Garland. Home about 4 a.m." Noël was to remain a friend to Judy when everyone else abandoned her.

As for me, by this point all my reservations about having a serious relationship with Judy Garland had been discarded, along with the empty champagne bottles and caviar tins in the dumbwaiters of some of Britain's most exclusive hotels.

21

WE RETURNED SEPARATELY to a sweltering July in New York City. Nearly one year had passed since I first met Judy in New York, and I was back in the soupy heat of Manhattan with life shimmering all around me, reflecting my passion for Judy and the future. I was on the telephone sweating it out in an unfortunate St. Regis Hotel with no air conditioning, talking to Abe Lastfogel, who was still talking about radio shows. I put down the telephone and said, "Fucking hell." Judy was quietly curled up smoking a cigarette. I was aggravated with Lastfogel, and I wasn't about to tell her what he'd offered.

I'd been astounded that there was no particular media welcome for Judy after her success in Britain. Understandably, she was let down. Suddenly she was insecure about her career. I was as diplomatic as possible while wondering what to do next.

Judy said, "The press are like the police: Where are they when you need 'em?" She had sailed from England aboard the *Queen Elizabeth* to a silent and empty homecoming. Later, well into her amazing success at the RKO Palace Theatre, the fact would get turned around, the papers boasting of the tremendous number of offers awaiting Judy upon her return, when in fact there were none save a few Bing Crosby radio broadcasts. Wasn't Judy the toast of London? Didn't she pack the theaters? I'd seen audiences on their feet screaming, yelling, going bananas.

"Darling, aren't they conscious of the Palladium?" Judy asked.

"Remember, they don't have a concert department . . . darling."

"Tell 'em to get one," Judy said, and then ordered up a plate of spaghetti, her favorite dish, and an iced tea. Nobody was breaking down the doors for Judy Garland except room service.

"Darling," I said, as she consumed the steaming plate of pasta with extra sauce and pepper, "remember to keep the calories down." Perspiration was dripping off her brow.

"I don't care, I'm hungry." Judy's appetite activated under duress.

"It's hot, don't eat spaghetti." But there was no way I was going to deter her from that steaming plate of pasta. She resented my comments. I watched her douse more pepper on her food. Whenever she ate anything with pepper she'd break out in a sweat. She may have been allergic to it. Curiously, she'd perspire only on her left side. Now the sweat was running off the back of her neck. She was sitting there like a lump in a white blouse and black slacks. No makeup. The windows were wide open to the muggy blanket of city air. We were both uncomfortable. "Shouldn't you be eating an apple?" I asked.

"Feel better if I ate oats and hay?"

Generally I had this jokey, paternal manner with her, and she responded deliciously. But that day I was serious. Having been with her for months, I was aware I was dealing with a supercharged instrument, but I didn't experience her as somebody I had to be careful with. Not yet. I wanted her to look her best. She had just conquered the world and now she was sweating and eating like a pig. It seemed nobody cared that Judy could have the world by its tail, including Judy.

It was now one thirty in the afternoon. Judy was distracted; she was only interested in eating, and the hell with the world. I had to get out. Unexpectedly she'd pushed the plate away like a sulky child. I knew she'd calm down; it was a ripple of annoyance. I also knew she'd resume eating.

I walked over to Broadway, where I ran into the actress Olga San Juan, Edmond O'Brien's wife, by the Winter Garden Theatre. I'd had thoughts of Judy dazzling audiences at the Winter Garden, the same as at the Palladium. But a big show was opening at the Winter Garden, so it wasn't going to be Judy Garland. I stood there chatting and thinking. Looking over Olga's shoulder, I saw in the near distance the run-down facade of the Palace Theatre, the once proud and lucrative bastion of vaudeville, now reduced to a slum. As if in a montage, the figure of Sol Schwartz superimposed itself between the Winter Garden and the Palace. I thought, *I gotta do this myself.* I had met Sol Schwartz, the president of the Palace Theatre, at the home of Jack Dietz, the friend who helped finance my two pictures at Monogram. It had been the occasion of Dietz's son's bar mitzvah.

I said good-bye to Olga and walked up Forty-Sixth Street toward the Palace. On the corner, I went into the Whelan's drugstore and called Sol.

"Sid, where are you?

"I'm downstairs in the Whelan's drugstore."

"I'll meet you in the lobby."

No sooner had I walked inside the lobby when a big rat crossed my path. Minutes later Sol rushed in, putting his arms around me. "I know what you've got in mind, Sid. I'll clean this fuckin' place. We'll reopen the Palace."

"That's just what I had in mind, Sol."

"I'll bring in the chandeliers, I'll change the seats, I'll paint the joint, and we'll open with Judy."

"Sol, did you ever see a dream walking?" I hummed.

"It's in front of us, Sid."

"You're reading my mind, Sol. Call Lastfogel, make a deal." Judy still had an agency contract with William Morris.

I walked back to the hotel in the heat. I figured Sol was already on the phone to Abe. I returned to Fifty-Fifth and Fifth, soaking wet. Judy was watching television when I entered the suite. "Darling, I've got news for you . . ."

"You look like you did something naughty."

"I engaged the Palace Theatre."

She ran up and threw her arms around me, trembling. She had so feared that nothing was going to happen. I held her in my arms. "Let's open the Palace, darling." The earlier tension was dissolving in tears.

I had left abruptly and returned victorious. Judy knew I had her well-being uppermost in my mind, and now I could prove it.

The Palace, a once noble structure, had rotted from neglect. Its heritage ignored, it had become a broken-down B-movie house with the dregs of leftover vaudeville. Entrance fee $1.00. For Judy it was one of her MGM scenarios: "We'll paint the Palace." "We'll open . . ." "Let's get Mickey . . ." An Arthur Freed production. "We're going to Broadway!"

Judy and I were still embracing when, like magic, Abe called from L.A. "I've talked to Sol. We're working out the details. He'll give us twelve musicians, a guarantee, and so on." Lastfogel was thrilled—10 percent off the top for the Morris Agency! Sol had repeated to him, "I'm gonna paint. It'll be a big opening on Broadway. I'll spend everything necessary, put in new seats, close off the third balcony, bring in the chandeliers. Sid will produce it, and Judy will open the new Palace in September."

Then came the schedule: two shows a day with Judy Garland and her company. I didn't like that. Too much work, too rough. I immediately called Sol. An old theater man, he was insisting on it. "The Palace is known for two a day."

I told him, "That's twelve shows; Judy needs to ease up."

"She can't let up, not now."

As we celebrated with dinner at Charles à la Pomme Soufflée, I said, "Darling, too much. You don't need to work that way."

"I did it at the Palladium, six and eight, six and eight in Birmingham, six and eight all over the place. Why not here?"

"It's different this time."

"I can do it, I can do it."

Judy could do it, but for how long? She was so eager, so ready. Two a day was going to translate into "Judy Garland brings back vaudeville." I had to agree. We had to go for it.

We couldn't get out of New York fast enough. We headed back to Los Angeles as quickly as you could travel with a person who didn't fly. We took the 20th Century Limited to Chicago and from there rode the

Super Chief to L.A. Meanwhile, Judy had already been on the phone with Roger Edens, who had quickly alerted Chuck Walters to announce that we'd be back in several days.

Judy had first known Walters as a dancer and as a double for Van Heflin; subsequently he became a choreographer and then a director (*Easter Parade* and *Summer Stock*). The studio moguls were homophobic, but Chuck had talent—plus manly good looks and a very deep voice, which seemed to make them feel better. The moguls had a fear of men who swished. Chuck didn't alter his lifestyle one iota. He lived with another man, a lawyer, as in a marriage. They owned property together and lived well; they also owned a liquor store in Malibu. Roger Edens was well liked too, although he didn't have the power with the studio that Chuck did. Roger was an attractive, generous man who died soon after Judy.

Judy was met in Los Angeles by Liza and her pet poodle, "John Cook." The press showed up to catch mother and daughter exchanging hugs and kisses. I sensed the attention was here to stay. Again Judy was plagued with questions about her weight, to which she replied, "I may be awfully fat, but I feel good." Actually, she was pregnant, which I wouldn't find out for another week or so.

Our relationship was more solid than ever. I had pulled off something Judy had dreamed about when she couldn't get a job in Hollywood. By the time we arrived in L.A., Roger had the opening number nearly completed. Initially, Chuck Walters wasn't available, but he too "had to go to Broadway." He wouldn't allow anybody else to take his place, saying, "You'll never open this show without me." Between Roger, Chuck, and me, the show got built. Rehearsals were held at a studio on La Cienega Boulevard. Everything, including the orchestration, was done in Los Angeles. Judy had sublet Marlene Dietrich's apartment for the stay in Hollywood. Tully was with her, as was Dottie Ponedel. Dottie had actually retired following Judy's Palladium run, but she temporarily returned to the fold. I was back in my Wilshire Boulevard apartment. But now I was completely immersed in Judy's life.

Was I going to marry her? Neither of our divorces were yet final. Judy and Vincente had married in Los Angeles on June 15, 1945, one year after she divorced her first husband, composer and musical director David Rose. Bob Agins, who had been my lawyer, was now handling Judy's divorce. She claimed that when she and Vincente were first married, she was very happy and they had many interests in common—work and friends. Abruptly, without reason, Vincente changed. He secluded himself and wouldn't explain why he left her alone so much. Tully gave the supporting testimony. Vincente, who'd recognized that Judy was intent on leaving him, denied Judy's charges of mental anguish, but he still did not contest the divorce. Liza was specifically allowed the freedom to be with whom she wanted whenever she wanted to avoid any sense of regimentation. For now, Liza lived with Cozy and Vincente at the Evanview house.

Our daily life became a hornet's nest of publicity—"Judy and Sid," "Sid and Judy." The RKO Palace was doing major publicity. I was hit with subpoenas from Lynn Bari and called "half a millionaire." The media was unrelenting. The talk was of Judy opening on Broadway, Judy and Vincente's divorce, my custody battle with Lynn.

Judy was in a rehearsal mode: silk trousers, Capezio shoes. If I looked very closely, which I did, her shoulder-length dark brown hair had tiny weavings of gray.

One evening at the Cock'n Bull on Sunset Boulevard, Judy greeted me with "Darling, I'm way past my period, haven't you noticed? I had a test and it's positive."

She was devouring her Welsh rarebit. I gulped down my bourbon, and it hit my stomach like a rock. She went on: "Darling, I'd love to have your baby."

My response was insensitive. I was thinking of the Palace. "You're what?" I yelled.

"Pregnant."

"Darling, we have contracts written, gypsies under contract, orchestrations, how could you be pregnant?" I was indignant, and she was stunned by my response. I told her I thought the pregnancy seemed inappropriate, considering the life we were attempting to set up. I thought she was purposely not cautious. I was blaming her, not commiserating. "Darling," I reminded her, "we're putting on a show at the Palace and you're coming to me with 'our' baby?" *How could she have been so foolish?*—that was my attitude. I was as unjustified as I was insensitive. And the truth was she never had a chance, which prevented her from feeling she could have a child simply because she wanted to.

Another factor: Judy's pregnancy would have engendered further scandal, as there was a strict moral code in those days. A cover-up was impossible with someone like Judy Garland. I imagined the headlines: Not Divorced, Cancel the Palace, Luft's Illegitimate Child. I handled it like a clod. I went into the legal rather than the emotional concerns. I couldn't turn it around. I was overwhelmed. I wanted to ignore the information she was laying on me.

"Obviously, you don't want my baby."

I found myself saying, "Of course I want your baby, but we've got a show to do." But if she intended to go forward with the Palace, she had to recognize the bad timing. "How the hell can you have a baby?" It didn't occur to me she was intent on marriage. I wasn't thinking in that direction as much as I was just in love, but having a baby was one way to bring the subject up.

Because of my negative reaction to the pregnancy Judy didn't confide in me where and when she was going to have the abortion, so I didn't go with her. I wasn't attentive. I didn't send flowers.

I was under stress, and one morning I awakened with an infection, a kind of ugly boil near my left eye, on the temple. It got bigger and bigger, but I tried to ignore it. That night I appeared at the rehearsal studio. Judy was not about to give me the time of day. She avoided my glances. She was very heavy into some number and I thought, well, I'll just wave good-bye and wait for her at the Ready Room, where we usually met after rehearsal. Judy didn't show up. I was well aware that when Judy rehearsed she tended to exclude the outer world to guard her concentration. But this time she went too far. I was feeling left out on the ledge. Estranged. Where was the relationship going?

The following day the cyst was worse. My doctor chose not to lance it, as it was too near the eye. Instead, he prescribed medication that knocked me out for several days. Fortunately, it began to shrink. Judy never called. This threw me off. Maybe, I thought, she couldn't tolerate any sign of weakness on my part. At the same time, I sensed that she was retaliating.

I was aggravated that I had not heard from Judy, so I decided to go over to La Cienega. I looked in. Judy was working away. Not waiting for a response, I mentioned I'd be next door at the Ready Room. Sitting at the bar I thought, what if she doesn't show up this time either? Foolishly, I threw back a few bourbons, which didn't mix well with the medication.

Earlier in the day I had called Tully inquiring how Judy was feeling. I couldn't speak to Judy directly, as she never picked up the telephone, it was either Dottie or Tully. And Judy had refused to answer my calls.

This time Judy showed up. She was cold to me, however—no warm greeting. I explained I regretted she had to go through such an ordeal. I thought she might ask after my health. In hindsight, I could see it was selfish. I was cutting myself off from her trauma of losing a child she wanted. But not hearing from her those past few days had put me on guard. "Maybe," I said, in an attempt to pull things in the open, "you can't be around illness unless it's your own."

She wasn't going to respond to the psychological approach. I told her I was going home. She sat enigmatically, across from me, still in her rehearsal clothes. It was clear she was feeling knocked out. I was not looking for sympathy, but I still felt she should have at least called to inform me how she was feeling. Obviously, she had remained angry.

It was around two in the morning, and I was beginning to feel dizzy from the booze and pills. I said good night and went to my car. I promptly pulled out onto La Cienega Boulevard and drove into a young student's car, which hit another vehicle. Luckily, nobody was hurt in the collision. The sound of the crash brought Judy running out of the Ready Room and to my side. Unfortunately, a fight ensued. Judy took my side and joined in the fisticuffs.

Dr. Larson, a dentist, had stopped at the scene of the accident. He was a Good Samaritan who, unfortunately, got in my way. I punched Dr. Larson while Judy slapped one of the boys. It was a silly melee for which I was responsible. Judy, who had been giving me a hard time in the restaurant, was now rushing to my defense, and even willing to punch out the enemy. It struck me as hilarious. If I had doubted Judy's loyalty, here she was showing her colors.

Within the hour, Judy and Bob Agins met me at the Wilshire police precinct and paid my bail of $100. In this way Judy and I were reconciled in a traffic accident melodrama.

Lynn used this incident to play up my drinking habits, to try to prove that I was an unfit father. She had Judy subpoenaed as well. The idea was to determine if my drinking would endanger our son, Johnny, in my presence.

—————— ✦ ——————

It was toward the end of the Los Angeles rehearsals that I read in one of the papers that Jock Whitney and David O. Selznick were breaking up their partnership. One of their properties had been auctioned off: *A Star Is Born*. Eddie Alperson, who was known for having sold the first talking film, *The Jazz Singer* starring Al Jolson, to the national theater owners, had bought the rights and all the prints.

The story of *A Star Is Born* was originally produced in 1932 under the title *What Price Hollywood?* The plot was based on an actual Hollywood tragedy: unknown talent marries famous alcoholic actor on the decline; their marriage enhances her career, not his. The 1937 version of *Star* with Janet Gaynor and Fredric March was written by Dorothy Parker, Alan Campbell, and Robert Carson. It ends with the female lead, "Vicki Lester," accepting an Oscar as "Mrs. Norman Maine," the name of her husband who has committed suicide. Our concept was to make a musical version of the same tragic story.

Judy had coveted the role of Esther Blodgett/Vicki Lester ever since she played the part in that 1942 *Lux Radio Theatre* broadcast, with Walter Pidgeon in the role of Norman Maine. Though Louis B. Mayer had rejected Judy's suggestion that she be cast as the star of a remake, I made a mental note: as soon as Judy was established on Broadway, as I knew she would be, I was going to hit Lastfogel with this concept.

Meanwhile, Judy traveled by train to New York with Chuck Walters, joining the ensemble and eight dancing boys. The acts continued to practice outside of the Palace, as rehearsals were not allowed inside the theater while it was being renovated.

Very quickly, though, the RKO Palace lived up to its name. The refurbished theater was transformed, as if in a fairy tale, into regal splendor fit for a princess. The crystal chandeliers sparkled with their diamond-like radiance. The Keith-Albee art collection had been returned and hung, the damask walls were trimmed with gilded moldings, and a plush red carpet was spread from the curb through the theater onto the stage. It was grand.

22

AT THE NEW GRAND . . . .

SPECIAL FOR CHRISTMAS, "Through the Back Door" with MARY PICKFORD, America's Sweetheart, in the leading role. One of the nicest pictures Miss Pickford has appeared in. You will enjoy every bit of it. A two-reel comedy "Motor Mad" will also be shown. Added attraction for Friday evening: the three Gumm girls will entertain in songs and dances featuring Baby Frances, two years old, Virginia seven and Mary Jane nine. The little girls will appear between the shows at 9 o'clock

—Grand Rapids Independent, 1924

O N OPENING NIGHT of Judy's return to the vaudeville stage, October 16, 1951, the line went around the block. All future shows were sold out. Wooden barricades had been placed outside the Palace Theatre, and police and fans alike had stood waiting night and day. Every luminary imaginable was trying to get in: Fred Allen, Sophie Tucker, Jimmy Durante, Jane Froman, Ralph Bellamy, all previous stars of old-time vaudeville, sat in the star-packed opening night audience. The atmosphere was explosive, more glorious than the Palladium. Judy was now a symbol of victorious America.

Backstage in her dressing room, Judy quietly, meditatively applied her makeup. A wall of green and white print drapes were covered with telegrams and congratulatory notes. I looked in occasionally, until she was dressed in her elegant black Irene Sharaff gown for the opening number. She was eager to know who was in the audience. I told her: everyone who existed.

There were five acts of vaudeville to go through before the star attraction would, in true vaudevillian tradition, enter onstage at the top of the second act. Time seemed interminable as we listened to the audience's robust response to each act, including comedian Max Bygraves, whom Abe Lastfogel was very much against when I suggested bringing him over from England. We had enjoyed him on our tour, and although he was English and not well known here, we thought he would be a little different and fun. It certainly was a break for Max. He returned home after the Palace and became famous in his country.

Finally it was time for Judy to make her appearance. She took a sip of white wine and, unlike at the Palladium, sailed out onstage without hesitation. The special lyrics and musical arrangements that Chuck and Roger had written would be put to the test. Hugh Martin, who wrote the score for *Meet Me in St. Louis*, was actually accompanying Judy on the piano. The show had all the appearances of a live MGM musical. When Judy slipped out from behind the eight "boyfriends" singing Edens's lyrics to Comden and Green's music for *On the Town* in a recitative: "Call the *Mirror*, call the *News*. You can say I've still got ninety pounds to lose . . ." she brought down the house, and would do so every night thereafter. The momentum never flagged for the rest of the evening, leaving the audience on their feet cheering.

As at the Palladium, Judy sang a medley of tunes from her films, including "You Made Me Love You," "The Boy Next Door," and "The Trolley Song." She went on to perform "Get Happy," the hit tune from *Summer Stock*, and, of course, Irving Berlin's "A Couple of Swells" from *Easter Parade*, with Chuck Walters assuming Fred Astaire's role. Judy sang and performed for forty minutes. Characteristically, she would toss the mike wire over her shoulder in a cavalier fashion as she sang and chatted with the audience about some of the artists who preceded her at the Palace: Fanny Brice, Eva Tanguay, Nora Bayes, Helen Morgan, and Sophie Tucker. There she was, her hair disheveled, perspiring through her Sharaff designer gowns, unaware she was wringing wet. She was not concerned with maintaining a look of elegance while she worked. Judy performed without cosmetic regard for herself.

I was never certain that the general audience understood how distinguished the cast was that Judy worked with. She would, of course, introduce them, but here was Hugh Martin playing the piano for her because he wanted to, and Chuck Walters dancing the tramp number with her because he wanted to—out of love for Judy. In the conclusion, dressed in her beloved tramp outfit, her teeth blacked out, soot rubbed on her cheeks, the little minstrel girl sat on the edge of the extended stage. Whereas the first night at the Palladium she opened with "Over the Rainbow," here she closed with it, singing without a mike. (This detail had been my suggestion.) Her eyes seemed to radiate all the emotions a person could feel as far away as the balcony.

I stood in the back of the theater, and as my eyes swept over the orchestra audience I watched Lastfogel and Sol Schwartz openly weep. They could have been crying with joy over Judy's obvious commercial success, but I prefer to think they joined the rest of us in a shared emotional reaction to an emotional and brilliant performance. This was a happening, not an opening! Judy had related to the throng intimately, as though the enormous RKO Palace was just a room full of friends. And night after night, that's what the audience became: Judy's friends. Whereas actor-singers transform themselves with different numbers, Judy's genius was that she could transform the audience by the content and sound of whatever she sang, coming from the depth of her character. They cheered themselves hoarse. The stage was blanketed with flowers before she was able to get back to her dressing room.

The Duke and Duchess of Windsor were among the opening night audience. Elizabeth Taylor, Monty Clift, Marlene Dietrich, Jack Benny, Irving Berlin, Joan Crawford, and Tallulah Bankhead were among her well-wishers and devotees in the dressing room. In the after-show crush backstage, Ethel Merman brought along the Windsors' business manager and friend Charlie Cushing, and the Windsors themselves would join us later at 21 for the opening night review party.

Ethel Merman adored Judy, and Judy loved Ethel. She was a close friend whom we saw over the years either in Los Angeles or New York. She initiated the nickname "Circles" for me, after noticing that every time we met, the shadows under my eyes got larger. I was unable to get proper rest because of Judy's insomnia. In those days I would often stay up with her. I told Ethel I felt like Vanya, the character played by Felix Bressart in the film *Comrade X* with Hedy Lamarr and Clark Gable. After struggling to escape from Stalinist Russia Vanya remarks, "I'd like to get some sleep before I die." I shared the sentiments.

It was already clear to me that Judy was a hit by the crowds fanning out over Broadway. It had been Judy's idea to leave the theater by way of the front lobby rather than taking the limo waiting in the back alley. She wanted to walk out and greet her fans. Wearing an elegant blue tulle off-the-shoulder gown, she cheerily made her way through the channel of fans (in the thousands) milling about in Duffy Square, waiting for her exit.

The gigantic letters spelling out JUDY GARLAND rose magically from the marquee. I took a big swallow, squeezed Judy's hand. It looked like New Year's Eve. We spent the night at 21 waiting for the reviews, and on arrival they proved a great victory for Judy. She was the "toast of Broadway."

We allowed ourselves to feel triumphant, and this reflected and spilled over into our personal relationship. Her happiest moments would always be performing in New York or London. Now the media was pouring out accolades: "Judy owns Broadway." The *Hollywood Reporter* wrote, "Judy came in like an atom bomb," a phrase my pal Jock McLean would confer on her as a nickname: "Little Miss Atom Bomb."

Once Judy was the "diva" of Broadway, she was a magnet for society—everyone gathered, the rich and famous. In the weeks to come she would receive statesman Bernard Baruch, General Douglas MacArthur, and many others. Some rushed to be photographed next to the *star*.

The fans were satisfied to collect and mill about Duffy Square hoping for a glimpse.

The Windsors became very much a part of our inner circle. They were an amusing couple whose fame preceded any biased thought one might have had. I certainly doubt very many Americans were aware of their sympathies, which have since been discussed as fascist. In 1951, they were lovey-dovey with one another and in all the society and gossip columns. No Eastern Seaboard party was complete without the Windsors' presence—in fact, it ensured the success of an evening. In Palm Beach, where we were to holiday after the Palace, society matrons were fighting to entertain the royal couple and, it was uncovered later, paying them to attend the social events. We were unaware of these machinations. Judy was flattered by their attention, and I was amused to be hobnobbing with a former king of England. As long as Judy continued to be in the spotlight the Windsors were our friends. It never occurred to me that the freshness of Judy's success, the very American fabric of her image, helped their image, seeding in the public mind the rare-bred royals' association with the spirit of Democracy. Their interest in us seemed genuine at the time.

Judy wasn't shy about the glory. She was the "star" in public. Judy, at least when she was sober, was the opposite in private, an easy person to be around, charming and loving. However, her secret self was well guarded. I respected her privacy. Judy's more profound psychological areas were closed off, and at the time this did not present itself as a detriment but more as a style, a personality trait.

Every newspaper in the country carried stories of the one-woman show that was breaking records on Broadway. It had made Judy the biggest show business sensation in America—and given me the opportunity to prove my own abilities. Whenever an individual showed surprise that I had produced the Palace, Ted Law would say he'd always believed in me, from the moment we formed Walfarms. In effect, the Palace was the fruition of an impulse that had begun with the pool show I organized in Ottawa way back when. Judy was the genius; I was the creative carpenter.

In our leisure hours, we picked up where we'd left off when we first met: three nights a week we ate exotic food at El Morocco, alone or with a group. New friends like the Duke or Duchess of Windsor and Charlie Cushing, or old friends like Ethel Merman, Ted Law, the Berksons (with whom we resumed our friendship), or Freddie Finklehoffe, who was in a state of awe. Nothing could diffuse what we had accomplished, so Freddie had to eat his hat. Now he was a different Fred with the greatest respect for me, and he joined a lot of people who were around kissing ass.

We went dancing at the Stork Club, appeared at the Colony, but preferred 21. Lüchow's, downtown on Fourteenth Street, was an extravagant emporium with a band that struck up "Over the Rainbow" when we walked in. The nights we didn't go clubbing and spent alone in our suite at the Carlyle Hotel, the owner of P. J. Clarke's, Danny Lavezzo, would send over chili, cheeseburgers—the dishes Judy loved and I wanted her to stay away from. Charlie Cushing also lived at the Carlyle. I found him interesting to be around. Cushing was divorced and his children were already mature. He was close to the Windsors and the Wrightsmans and other powerful names and seemed to arrange social evenings for them.

Quite often we would say our good-byes and make our way over to P.J.'s at three in the morning. Finklehoffe would be at the bar throwing down Cutty Sark, Ethel Merman would join us, and there we would sit laughing, talking, until early morning, the doors closed to the public.

For three weeks Judy had been performing to capacity audiences, standing room only, fans queued around the block. She was flourishing. She loved to go to work; she couldn't wait. We'd leave in the late afternoon for the theater, where a police escort met us for the jaunt from the back alley into her dressing room. Judy would inhale the smell of the greasepaint—more thrilling for her than making a movie. But I kept thinking: What was this unprecedented success going to bring to Judy? I was looking to the future, and my conviction was that she belonged back in film.

Word was out in Hollywood of Judy's triumph at the Palace. She was the subject of articles in the *New Yorker, Look, Life.* Media was going berserk over Garland's rebirth, how a year ago she was down and out, suicidal, and now she was miraculously back at the top of her career. I was the man of the hour. The Morris office listened; show business was opening up to me, and I was thinking about *A Star is Born.*

Lastfogel had wanted to dismiss the project. He agreed to contact Eddie Alperson about acquiring the rights, but he could hardly wait to call back with the negative news that Alperson wasn't looking to sell. "Forget about it, Sid."

I didn't believe him. Judy was internationally acclaimed. I knew Lastfogel didn't like to build things; he was an abrupt type of person. When he played golf, he'd hit the ball and immediately run after it; in business conversations if he couldn't see something concrete right away he tended to dismiss the subject. *A Star Is Born* may not have interested Abe, but it continued to interest me. I called an agent I knew, also at the Morris office. I asked him to set up a private meeting between myself and Alperson.

Alperson was eager to meet me and a date was set, to correspond with the time period when I would be staying in Los Angeles to appear in court over my custody rights. I was about to meet Alperson when I received a call from New York. "Better get back, Judy is in the hospital." Judy and I had been separated for just three days.

I booked the quickest flight back, but there was enough time to make the meeting before my departure. The Morris agent and I met with Eddie Alperson at his office in Beverly Hills. Eddie was in his midfifties, gray-haired and well dressed, a typical business executive. He could have been with a large accounting corporation. The Morris agent outlined how he'd accomplished an independent deal with Fox by bringing in outside financing. I picked up that Eddie was not really paying attention to what the man was saying. In fact, he soon turned to me and said, "Sid, I think this is wonderful that Judy made this marvelous comeback."

Eddie didn't want any part of the agent's act. At the end of the meeting we walked out of the building onto Canon Drive, where Eddie and I shook hands. I explained I was called back to New York, that Judy needed me, and then I added, "Are you coming with me?" And like magic Eddie replied, "Let's go." He went home to pack and met me at the airport. During the flight we hammered out the possibilities.

Eddie was interested in keeping the Morris office out of our deal. He was not eager to pay 10 percent commission off the top of everything. And we both agreed we didn't want Morris to package the film. Alperson was clever, even brilliant, and he was well liked in the film business world. His close friend Spyros Skouras was president of 20th Century Fox.

Eddie, of course, had his own history in Hollywood. In his twenties he was a wunderkind in charge of distribution at Warner Bros., where he made his success selling *The Jazz Singer* to theater owners around the country. Independent theater owners couldn't afford to convert their theaters to sound on their own, so Eddie's method was to take the theater operator directly to the bank, where bank officers were eager to help finance the conversion. Eddie started with one theater owner in Chicago, and the film was advertised as a "Jolson Musical." The lines went instantly around the block. It was Jolson's name that sold the film, as it was Jolson's name on a song that sold the sheet music, whether he wrote it or not, he was so powerful a draw. Eddie would go from theater to theater, and by the time he came to New York the RKO circuit was begging for it. The advent of sound was a great victory for the independent theater owner. Prior to that, the circuit got the big films and the little guy got the B movies, the westerns, the horror movies. The advent of talking pictures was like the invention of the bullet: for a moment, it made men more equal.

As we spoke, I experienced rushes of anxiety. I washed them back with bourbon and escaped into the importance of the conversation. I kept wondering what had gone wrong in New York. I wasn't thinking of Judy as a clinically ill person, or *This is an addict*. I was worried something awful had happened to the delightful, brilliant woman I loved.

When I got involved with Judy I was convinced I could change her. I had analyzed the situation. We'd had many conversations about her past. It was not out of the ordinary that a star of Judy's caliber would occasionally need to stay at a clinic. I understood the pressures. I believed Judy was intelligent, deeply in love with me, so I felt I could influence her. And actresses were usually self-absorbed by nature, so I wasn't thinking, *This is a selfish woman*. Though she needed constant devotion, it was easy, since I was head over heels in love with her.

In spite of my passion I had said to Ted and to Bob Agins, "Will I be Judy's Garland's third husband?" Meaning, once I'm married to her, I'm no longer Sid Luft, I'm Judy Garland's husband. We discussed this back and forth, and their response would come: "But are you in love with her?" And the answer was always "Yes."

Apparently on November 11, Judy performed a matinee not feeling well, then began the evening performance before being overcome with sluggishness. She managed to get off the stage only to collapse and be rushed to LeRoy Sanitarium. By the time I returned to New York, Judy was back at the Carlyle with the explanation that Marlene Dietrich had recommended a Dr. Udall Salmon, a fashionable Park Avenue diet doctor. Salmon helped women lose pounds with pills. In this case Judy had asked for other pills as well, and she was given them. With the prospect of a film she was once more worrying about her weight, or so I reasoned.

"Darling," I asked her, "do you think it's a good idea for you to take medication from a stranger, no matter how highly recommended?" My uncle Dr. Israel Rappaport had informed me, "For God's sake, that man has the worst possible reputation talking women into diet pills. Get Judy away from him." But I was soft about what happened. Judy looked in good health, and I didn't want to make too much of the situation.

Judy returned to the Palace after a four-day absence. The night of her reopening she was in her dressing room making herself up when Dr. Salmon pranced into the outer room. I blocked his entrance. He was wearing a black cape, black fedora, and muffler, dressed like the flamboyant Yiddish stage actor Boris Thomashefsky (grandfather of conductor Michael Tilson Thomas). I could hardly contain myself at the sight of this comic character. "Dr. Salmon," I said, "I'm going to ask you to leave without a scene." He was speechless. "Please don't see Miss Garland again," I pressed. With that, I dismissed him.

I had understood that this kind of experience was behind Judy, but here it was happening all over again. She had suffered a toxic reaction to whatever medication Salmon prescribed. Judy would never explain to a doctor about her sensitivity to pills, and doctors were not inquiring either. In her mind, she was never responsible for her tendency to drug herself. It was always someone else's fault. Conveniently, she overlooked the fact that her mother had fought the studio on this issue.

In my mind it was not going to be a problem. I was in charge. I would control and protect her until she was freed from the destructive habits of the past. Judy did not con me either. She did not say she would never take another pill, nor did she apologize for the inconvenience. She was, however, respectful of my approach. When I returned to her dressing room I said, "Darling, I got rid of the doctor. He has a reputation that can't do you any good."

Judy said, "OK."

"You know your career is on the line."

"But you think I'm too fat."

"I do not. I think you're fine the way you are."

That night, as it was like a mini-opening, I could see she wanted me around a bit longer. We continued to talk as she worked on her makeup. With Dottie having returned to retirement, Judy generally preferred to put her makeup on alone, a transition between home and the stage, to shore up her concentration. Eventually she would hire a makeup assistant, "little" Ernie, who was camp and very funny.

Judy responded, "What about the picture?"

"Darling, if you want to lose weight, we'll go on a diet together. You don't need any kind of medication. What you need to do is cut out the food you love."

Judy giggled at this last remark.

"Darling," I continued, "you must cut out all the luscious hot fudge sundaes you adore; no more P.J.'s cheeseburgers, blood rare with a slice of Bermuda onion and homemade relish. No more extra spicy chili with an ice cold beer. Forget heaps of mashed potatoes and gravy, and . . ." Judy was staring at me with her huge saucer eyes. ". . . no more fettucine alfredo."

By the time I was finished with the mouthwatering list of Judy favorites she was hysterical with laughter, holding me tight. "No *alfredo*," she echoed. "I may not be able to go on."

We did go on a diet, and Judy went from a size fourteen to a size six by the end of the Palace engagement—without a pill.

Judy may not have apologized to me for her dalliance with Dr. Salmon, but trouper that she was as she performed, she would intermittently apologize to her "old friends," the audience, for "not being perfect." Now the press was watching how she perspired, how she breathed, how she turned her head. The crowds were ever faithful, and I was told the night she collapsed the comedic actor Jan Murray and Vivian Blaine of the Broadway production of *Guys and Dolls* graciously entertained the audience.

On her return, she was presented with masses of bouquets and flower arrangements. It was opening night all over again. The ovation was deafening.

I renegotiated a ten-show weekly that left out Mondays and the matinees on Tuesdays and Fridays. Nobody wanted to cash in their tickets. It was the hottest show on Broadway, and that was saying something in a season that included *The King and I*. MGM had quickly rereleased two of Judy's films, *Babes in Arms* and *Meet Me in St. Louis*, along with the album *Judy Garland Sings*, to cash in on the Garland renaissance.

Judy was receiving honors and awards for reestablishing vaudeville. A luncheon was held in her honor at the Hotel Astor by the American Federation of Labor. Her stamina and virtuosity were once more likened to Jolson in the 1920s. She was given a lifelong silver card membership to the AFL.

Previous smash hits at the Palace had included Eddie Cantor and George Jessel, who had each had runs of nine weeks, standing room only; Kate Smith had played for ten weeks in 1931. Judy would go on to play for nineteen weeks to break all records. As weeks passed and I saw that she could continue indefinitely, I thought it would be a good idea to move to a nicely appointed apartment around the corner from the Hotel Carlyle. Here, our relationship became like a marriage. We had the privacy I craved, and although I still was not rushing to the altar, I was more aware of Judy's need for a formal sense of belonging.

One afternoon when we were at home before leaving for the theater, there was an unexpected knock at the front door. I had no idea who could be there, as we didn't receive people at the apartment. I called out to Judy to answer the door, but she had disappeared. It was the building manager about some minor detail. When I closed the door I looked around for Judy and found her hiding in a large walk-in closet in the bedroom. She was shaking. This was no childish game of hide-and-seek. I swept her into my arms and asked what was wrong. I was discovering that the more tender I could be with her the better we could communicate.

Judy suffered from severe premenstrual syndrome, often to the point that she felt she would never come out of the depression. Frequently, she'd ask me to be patient, "bear with me." My immediate reaction was that it must be "that time." But I knew it wasn't.

Judy explained that for an instant she'd experienced a flashback to the old studio days, when she lived in fear of the Anslinger Commission. In fact, she said that Harry J. Anslinger, US commissioner of narcotics, had once requested she be given a leave of absence from work. He wanted her to detox for one year. The man met with her personally. Judy told him a doctor had been supplying her with pills. The doctor's license was revoked, but another took his place, because MGM was all powerful and was not about to give their moneymaking star a leave of absence. Judy's reflex to hide was a holdover from this era, when actors lived in fear of being busted. And Judy in particular, an imaginative, overly sensitive young girl, envisioned herself being carted off to jail for taking pills.

She had originally been encouraged to take pills by the studio bosses, and then she began to get a buzz from the drugs, to rely upon them. She was not the only youngster to suffer: Mickey Rooney and Elizabeth Taylor, among others, were similarly caught in the studio dope traps. Uppers are sometimes recommended to people in positions of responsibility such as pilots and truck and bus drivers to deter drowsiness on the job. However, this feeding of narcotics to children was a deep, dark secret known only to those connected to the studio and the government.

Judy admitted she felt she grew inches when she took Benzedrine: the extra "bennie" gave her the courage to march ten feet tall into Louis B. Mayer's office and speak her mind. Nonetheless, drug addiction or dependency on stimulants was considered degenerate, a sin, as well as severely against the law. An individual could indeed go to prison for using drugs. In 1949, actor Robert Mitchum was sentenced to jail, where he served time for possession of one joint.

Now, helping Judy out of the closet, I comforted her as best I could. The incident was quickly forgotten.

———— ✼ ————

I began to interest Judy in short overnight trips. We would leave after the show on Saturday night and come back Monday afternoon. We'd go to our favorite inn in Connecticut, or to visit Judy's colt, Florence House, which at this point was still being trained on Long Island. One afternoon Judy accidentally got locked in the stall with Florence. She was fearless and thought it was great fun. She was familiar with horses, and in her youth she had loved to ride.

Life had achieved a certain wholesome quality in spite of our taste for nightlife. Now with the new schedule we could cut out and relax on our own, and that was wonderful. It was a heady brew; everything was experienced in an accelerated manner. The world seemed to revolve around us. Judy had lived a heightened life since childhood; she was an exotic hothouse flower. I didn't perceive her as pathological, but I was also naive about substance abuse. She was so completely seductive and entertaining—what need was there to know more?

23

M AX METH WAS Judy's conductor for the first eight weeks of her Palace run, but he could not have anticipated Judy would be performing for more than two months—already a month beyond the original contract. When other obligations forced Meth to withdraw, Judy immediately requested that her sister Susie's husband, Jack Cathcart, replace him: "He's got to conduct me." By now I had such confidence in her professional taste I was sure Judy was on the money. And Judy was absolutely correct about Jack, whom she had known since the 1934 World's Fair, where she was guest of honor and star performer on Children's Day. Jack was an attractive, charming person, a talented musician and composer. So when he said he wasn't pleased with the overture, I respected his opinion. He proceeded to rewrite it, creating a splendid new overture. He was gifted—hiring him wasn't just to do Judy's sister a favor. At the same time, it provided Judy with a nostalgic sense of family. Her life had been a succession of backstage family, blood family, and studio family, and often the families overlapped.

Roger Edens, who functioned as a creative conduit for Judy her entire professional career, bringing music to her attention, was part of her studio family. She respected Edens's taste and creative recommendations, and came to depend solely on his judgment for revue material. George and Ira Gershwin and Irving Berlin had also been integral parts of Judy's interdependent family. Judy continued to inspire these composers.

At the Palace she was able to bring the families together, the surrogate and the real. Judy's sisters, Jimmie and Susie, had long ago given up their careers when Judy became a star at MGM. Virginia—Jimmie for short—had married musician Bobby Sherwood. She allowed herself to get heavy and stayed that way. She remained outside the world of show business, living a more ordinary lifestyle in Texas with her daughter, Judaline, named for her famous aunt. But Judy did refresh her relationship with her oldest sister, Susie, whose husband, Jack, was now part of the show. Susie, who had changed her name from Mary Jane to Suzanne, was vivacious, taller than Judy, with a good figure. Sadly, like Judy, she would fall into episodes of substance abuse.

Susie's husband was a handsome man, and women were after him. This bothered Susie. In later years Jack would call our house looking for her. I'd have to tell him, "We don't know where the hell she is." His usual complaint was that she had come home and then left again without a message. One time he located her in Detroit in some funky hotel room and had to leave his work and bring her home. But for a glorious moment, at the Palace, the two sisters shared a rosy world. The RKO Palace Theatre became home.

This was Judy's "family"—Hugh, Chuck, Roger, the dancing boys from MGM, sister Susie, brother-in-law Jack, Sid the devoted lover. In addition, we had many wonderful people working with us. Vern Alves came into our lives through Ella Logan and Fred Finklehoffe. He was a terrific administrator who took over Judy's press relations, and he became the associate producer on *A Star Is Born*. Then there was Ernie the makeup assistant, who knew how to cheer Judy up. He was a small person like her, and he loved to get into drag. In the midst of one performance, as the audience broke into an appreciative applause, Ernie made an entrance onstage behind an unaware Judy. He was in a crazy pirate drag, wearing high heeled mules, with a live toy poodle on a leash. People got hysterical laughing. Judy took her bow and quickly went off into the wings asking, "Why is everyone going nuts?" Then she spotted Ernie and broke up, demanding he come out and take a bow.

It was a glorious time with one notable exception: whenever I mentioned her mother, Judy slammed a door on the subject. Eventually I dropped it.

By December my divorce was final. Lynn had managed to say extremely negative things about me to the press. She charged that I deserted her night after night on the pretext I was going to get a paper only to return home with the milkman, saying I'd been "out all night with the boys." She'd won custody of Johnny even though I had paid her considerable money in back alimony. She was not letting up, especially now that I was "half a millionaire."

I took refuge in sports and horses. Judy was not contrary to any of my activities. She was engrossed in her career and Liza. She seemed to prefer time to herself, as much as she wanted to ensure that I was there for her when she needed or desired me. My interests were in no way a threat to Judy. Rather than poison our relationship, these differences were nourishing. The poison come along much later in the marriage.

Toward the end of the Palace engagement various celebrities would try to take bows with Judy. Occasionally Judy would invite someone onstage to join her to share the tumultuous applause. Walter Winchell, devoted fan, began to show up nightly. He was stimulated by the atmosphere, having worked as a straight man in vaudeville as a kid. He took to coming up onstage for Judy's curtain calls. He'd arranged for masses of orchids to be delivered precisely at the moment when he would turn to Judy to pronounce his signature phrase, "Orchids to you." But Judy got annoyed as Winchell cut in on her ovations.

Winchell's fifteen-minute Sunday night radio broadcast was equal in popularity to today's *Sixty Minutes* on TV. He opened with the speedy announcement: "Good evening Mr. and Mrs. North and South America and all the ships at sea. This is Walter Winchell and the *Jergens Journal*, let's go to press . . ." His broadcast and his national columns made him powerful in an era when the print media could heavily influence an artist's career. Judy held off as long as she could; finally, she asked me to call Winchell on this.

I had to play the heavy, so I rang Winchell's office. I thought I might soften him up. "Walter, Sid Luft here. Remember, Mr. Olympus?" He laughed. I could tell he didn't know where the conversation was going. "What's up," he said, which for Winchell was friendly. "Walter," I said, "Judy is so exhausted. You mind not coming onstage?" There was a pause, and then his wacky voice said abruptly, "Yeah. OK." I knew he was not about to suffer a pause. I jumped in. "Thanks, Walter, and we look forward to seeing you at the Palace."

Winchell actually stopped coming around, though he was welcome, including backstage. He certainly never wrote anything negative about Judy, unlike other columnists—like Hedda Hopper, who often ripped Judy apart. Judy would not talk to Hedda. Louella Parsons had been a friend since the MGM days, when she was a pal of Louis B. Mayer. She'd never written anything scathing about Judy while she was at MGM, so Judy frequently gave Louella scoops. Judy also liked journalist Dorothy Kilgallen. She felt Dorothy understood her. Whenever we ran into Dorothy at 21, she was welcome at our table.

We were not always clubbing or going to midnight supper parties. When the smoke cleared and the laughter died down, we'd willingly return to our apartment near the Hotel Carlyle, where we were very well adjusted to one another. I'd found out Judy's taste was very feminine, preferring frills and lace, and that she was genuinely shy on an intimate level. She had a passion for antiques and carved wood, no doubt Vincente's influence. She discovered my penchant for made-to-order shirts and suits.

On February 24, 1952, Judy closed the Palace engagement, which had extended itself in triplicate. Sol had a gold plaque engraved to honor Judy:

> This was the dressing room of
> JUDY GARLAND
> who set the all-time long run record
> Oct. 16th, 1951 to Feb. 24th, 1952
> RKO PALACE THEATRE

Earl Wilson referred to the Sunday night closing as "tingling,"' and it was intense. After singing for well over an hour Judy asked the audience, "What'll I sing now?" And someone called out, "Auld Lang Syne." She quickly responded, "I'm tired. You sing it to me." It was a brilliant move. The audience eagerly stood up and sang to their favorite little minstrel girl, who sat at the edge of the stage dressed in a crazy wig, floppy shoes, and clown makeup.

I was in the first row, and behind me stood Phil Silvers, Shelley Winters, Faye Emerson, and Skitch Henderson, singing to Judy, with love. She was visibly moved; tears were falling down her sooted cheeks. Then Judy called out my name—she wanted to introduce me to the audience. I thought, *Oh Christ no.* I should have stayed in the back of the theater next to Finklehoffe, but I knew her performance would be exceptional that final night, and I wanted to be as near to her as possible. I stood up and reluctantly took a bow. I was never very good in crowds unless I was cheering a horse at the racetrack.

By this time the stage was covered with roses. James Stewart, along with the famous tenor Lauritz Melchior, who was due to follow Judy at the Palace, went onstage to join her. Melchior, with his giant arms around Judy, looked like King Kong embracing Fay Wray. He made a marvelous speech about how wonderful Judy was, and how he hoped he could achieve a small amount of her success. There wasn't a dry eye in the house. The curtain fell and I rushed backstage to congratulate and compliment Judy. I took her in my arms. "Darling, you were stunning." She held me in a warm embrace and whispered, "Thanks to you."

Judy had played 184 performances, and nearly a million people had come to see her, cheering her on in emotional and appreciative outbursts.

It was the beginning of the cult of Garland.

24

"The Silver Shoes," said the Good Witch, "have won-
derful powers. And one of the most curious things about
them is that they can carry you to any place in the world
in three steps, and each step will be made in the wink of
an eye. All you have to do is to knock the heels together
three times and command the shoes to carry you wherever
you wish to go."
—L. Frank Baum, *The Wonderful Wizard of Oz*

THE PALACE WAS a phenomenon that turned both our lives around. My goal had been to give Judy a new public image, one of stability, to overcome her MGM reputation, and we had accomplished this in a relatively short period of time. We were also able to pay Judy's $80,000 debt to the government. And we were finally on our way to starring Judy in the musical remake of *A Star Is Born*, having formed Transcona Enterprises, a company that included Judy, myself, Eddie Alperson, and Ted Law. There were considerable negotiations ahead, but I was as determined to bring this off as I had been to reopen the Palace.

While Judy played Broadway, Frank Sinatra, an adored friend, reached out to her. He was going through a period of negative career action. His show in Tahoe drew an audience of less than twenty, and further, he was in bad voice because he was depressed over his marriage to Ava Gardner. He'd been dumped by his agents, MCA. There was no recent hit Sinatra record; he'd been under contract to RCA and let go. After a brilliant career, he thought he was washed up. Frank was driving a Ford.

It was a moment in his life when no offers were coming in. And not because he had been undependable. Frank's career was simply at a nadir, and he was in need of some kind of stimulation. Hank Sanicola, Sinatra's manager, called me and asked if Judy would appear with Frank on a TV series he'd signed for. Judy would have done anything for Frank, but there was no way she could leave the Palace; her contract was legally tight, not allowing for other appearances. She wasn't happy about this. She was aware of Frank's despair. In the end, Sinatra's TV show got canceled, which made Judy feel worse about not being able to pitch in.

It was then we started to think about the possibility of Sinatra playing the male lead, Norman Maine, in *A Star Is Born*. Judy and Frank had magnificent chemistry together, and we agreed Frank had talents that were not yet tapped. Judy was so excited she wanted to call Frank right away. I calmed her down: "Darling, we haven't even got a studio. Let's wait until a deal is made. We can't offer something which is still unformed. Let the baby get born." She made a funny face as if to say *so it'll never happen.*

Then the day came when Judy's divorce from Vincente was final. We were both free at last from marital contracts. Business, however, continued. Judy had agreed to perform at the Philharmonic Auditorium in Los Angeles. The prospect of Garland, the toast of Broadway, returning to Hollywood, her hometown, was news. But first we agreed it was necessary to take a much-needed week's vacation, and we followed Charlie Cushing's suggestion to visit Palm Beach.

We arrived by train and were met by Charlie and another gentleman. The two bald gents wore Palm Beach attire: straw hats, open neck shirts, and bright-colored trousers. Invitations for every night of the week began to flood our suite at the Colony Hotel. We alternated our evenings between Henry and Ann Ford, the Wrightsmans, and the McLeans, among others.

The Duke and Duchess of Windsor were the excessive focus of Palm Beach society; still, Judy was given the celebrity treatment. The Duke adored noodling at the piano with Judy, and he knew most of her songs word for word. Judy was another small-boned, elegant, if not fragile person, like Wallis and himself. They belonged to the same world of fame and finesse. Generally Judy was not expected to sing at those soirees, although the ambiance was musical enough, the Duke spontaneously harmonizing with Judy at the piano. I preferred chatting with the Duchess, whom, I confess, I found witty and charming. I knew she'd been married to an American Jew, an Anglophile who denied his heritage, and now here she was married to the former king of England. I enjoyed her more than her husband. The Palm Beach crowd had always struck me as basically anti-Jewish. Nevertheless, I felt our hosts had to know my origins. I never covered anything up.

Igor Cassini, brother of Jacqueline Kennedy's official dress designer, Oleg Cassini, was a regular on the Palm Beach circuit. Igor wrote a popular syndicated society column in which our current hosts were prominently featured. He eventually married Charlene Wrightsman, one of four wives. Igor and Oleg presented themselves as Russian aristocracy, by way of Italy. The brothers were each smart and creative in their own way, making a splash everywhere they went.

Occasionally a hostess would come right up to Judy and ask if she would sing. Sometimes she wouldn't be up to answering requests. One night at the Fords' Ann asked Judy to sing. Judy simply wasn't in the mood. She discussed it with me privately. She said, "No, no." I was unable to dig out the reasons, and I let it drop. Just as the business of autographs had been turned over to me, it was understood the path to Judy was through me. Judy would smile and say, "Ask Sid." Everyone experienced an awkwardness except Judy.

I said, "Darling, you don't have to give me something to do."

Judy would give me her childlike seductive pout, "You really don't mind, Sid, do you?"

Eventually I thought it was neurotic: Judy's being-protected game.

———— ∞∞∞ ————

The afternoons were spent on the green with the Duke of Windsor, Henry Ford II, and Charles Wrightsman. I was briefed that you do not win in a game of golf with a king. This protocol did not easily fit my vision of the gentlemen's sport of betting. I had the impression Henry was an overgrown baby, always trying to control the situation. He had a coldness about him—an edge of arrogance. He was, of course, polite and "old boy" with me. Nevertheless, I found it difficult to relax with Henry. This, later on in our marriage, was to become a bone of contention.

On a splendid, sun-drenched day by the sparkling ocean, Wallis persuaded me to accompany her while she shopped and Judy rested at the hotel. Wallis said it would be good for me to miss an afternoon of golf. She was flirting. The Duchess threw her pugs into the back of the limo and off we went to Worth Avenue with the dogs. I found her magnetic, but I was removed from feeling anything beyond a smile. We made our way in and out of the fashionable stores, Wallis remarking, "Not like Paris but close." We returned to the limo when she exclaimed, "I forgot Saks Fifth Avenue!" The pugs hung on her every word. I said, "Should I come along?" "Noooo!" came her playful reply. "Not where I'm going—brassieres, dear." While Wallis shopped for bras, I remained in the limo.

The Duke and Duchess were the guests that season of the Wrightsmans. Peter Lawford, my old buddy, had dated one of the Wrightsman girls. The young couple was going hot and heavy when Lawford made the mistake of using Mr. Wrightsman's telephone for a long distance call without paying up. For his lack of manners, Peter was barred from the house and the daughter. This casual oversight convinced Mr. Wrightsman that Peter must only be interested in their money. I'd forgotten that Palm Beach was hardball. Neddie and Jock McLean were certainly goofy about money matters.

Judy and I were invited to the Wrightsmans' elaborate dinner party honoring the Windsors. Later everyone went to a local nightclub. That night Judy was in the mood to sing and could hardly wait to get up and join the Mary Kaye Trio. We were high, it was great fun, and our crowd couldn't have been more entertained if they'd won the Kentucky Derby.

The kid from Bronxville had jumped right into high society, no doubt inflaming my ex-wives: Why isn't he dead or in the gutter?

On our return to Los Angeles we stopped back in New York long enough for Judy to pick up something she'd earned during her Palace run. Wined and dined, tan and fit, I sat in the audience at the Waldorf Astoria watching the presentation of the Antoinette Perry Awards for Excellence in Theatre—the Tony Awards. The musical awards included Gertrude Lawrence for Best Actress (*The King and I*); Phil Silvers for Best Actor (*Top Banana*); Yul Brynner for Best Supporting Actor (*The King and I*); Richard Rodgers and Oscar Hammerstein for Best Musical (*The King and I*); and Judy Garland for "An important contribution to the revival of vaudeville."

Judy looked radiant. It was hard to believe that just the day before we had traveled rough terrain with her period. She'd been depressed, feeling awful, and she warned me, "Darling, bear with me these few days. I'll get over it." She managed to pull herself out of her discomfort, and without any apparent use of medication.

In Los Angeles, Liza joyously met her mother. Judy was thrilled to be with her daughter again. The love she had for her children was always Judy's most genuine quality. She wanted to be with her adorable, dark-eyed daughter, and the plan was for little Liza to move in with us as soon as possible.

We no longer had to duck the press, so we checked into several suites at the Hotel Bel-Air while I arranged for us to lease a pleasant house on Maple Drive in the flats of Beverly Hills. Dorothy Fields, a songwriter, owned the house and leased it, along with a couple who worked as butler and cook. Louella Parsons lived nearby. So did George Burns and Gracie

Allen; Judy's childhood friend Dr. Marcus Rabwin and his wife, Marcella; and Dr. Lee Siegel, my gambling buddy from the early years of Hollywood. What could be more perfect, surrounded by old friends, and doctors!

Marcus Rabwin was a medical student at the University of Minnesota when he entered the Gumm family life in the summer of 1920 as a traveling film salesman. Frank Gumm would rent westerns from Marcus for his theater, the New Grand. It was to be the beginning of a lifelong friendship. Ethel was unhappy at this time. She was pregnant and considering having an abortion. There was another factor, one she was never able to discuss with Judy: according to what Dr. Rabwin said years later, Frank had "transgressed" by acting on his homosexual impulses. When her husband's tendencies became apparent, heated arguments followed. But it was 1921 and not only would an abortion have been a scandal, it would undoubtedly cast a shadow of shame over the entire Gumm family.

Frank and Ethel sought out Rabwin, a friend but not yet a doctor, for consultation on this serious matter. He advised them to go home and have their third child. And so Frances Ethel Gumm was born, baptized in the local Episcopalian church, and brought to the New Grand Theater, where she slept peacefully backstage in a box. It was Rabwin's opinion that Frank sincerely believed the family was the answer to his woes. However, after ten years of marriage, in this late thirties, he became the subject of rumor and gossip. In later years, Judy became preoccupied with the memory of Frank and inquired of his friends about him. Maurice Kusell, who had trained Judy as a dancer from 1931 to 1934, knew the family well and was aware of Frank's propensity, but he, like others, could not bring himself to discuss the issue with Judy.

In 1968, the year before Judy died, she came to Rabwin and asked him if her father had been a homosexual. Rabwin did not tell her the truth: "I didn't see what sense it would have made to tell her."

While we waited to move into our new home, we were also looking for a studio to partner with the newly formed Transcona Enterprises. We wanted to make it a three-film deal, throwing in *Man o' War* (though the script was still terrible and needed work) and *Snow Covered Wagons*, a book Eddie had bought. Eddie had been skilled at making exploitation films, and he reasoned that *The Covered Wagon* had been such a great hit that some of its glory would trickle over due to the similarity of titles. *Snow Covered Wagons* was an epic written in poetic prose by a woman who was an academic, about the tragic fate of the Donner Party.

I opened an office on Canon Drive and got to work. Carlton Alsop called me one day and said he wanted me to settle the money account he'd had with Judy. I was pleased to be able to do so. When I attempted to discuss this matter with Judy she turned away; the details of business seemed to pain her, even bore her. Anything to do with the creative end of a project, the actual work, was acceptable, but not the contractual side. This aspect of our partnership was entirely up to me.

Paradoxically, it was Judy who really apprised me about the film business. She had known everyone and understood their artistic and professional value. She talked about the methods Busby Berkeley employed to get performances out of the actors. He used drugs a great deal to put in the time and energy necessary to endure and complete his concepts. As the young stars of several of Berkeley's films, Judy and Mickey Rooney were always exhausted, receiving just a few minutes to nap briefly as the crew changed light setups. By law, they had to attend school, which was an added burden in their lives, and certainly no fun. Judy experienced her life on the lot as nothing but a series of pressures: mother, the executives, "Keep your weight down," "Don't go to the commissary," "Go rest." Indeed, MGM provided a glamorous dressing room decorated in Wedgewood blue silk conducive to lounging. But Judy's energies away from the set were otherwise taken up by the choreographer, rehearsals, voice coaches, arrangements, and costumes, everything accomplished at a rapid speed. She worked eight hours at a stretch and was then shipped home or to the dressing room to sleep. And there were recordings, publicity tours, radio broadcasts . . .

Judy had aspired to play more sophisticated parts; she'd look in the mirror and see a fully grown woman. She worshipped Kate Hepburn

"One-Punch Luft," local boxing and wrestling champ.

My high school senior portrait: class of 1933
at Hun School in Princeton, New Jersey.

My college portrait: University of Pennsylvania,
circa 1934.

On the grounds of the Beverly Hills Hotel, circa 1938.

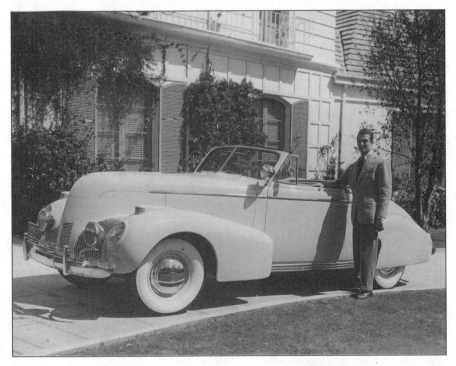

With a 1939 Cadillac Series 61 convertible coupe—conversion by my company Custom Motors Inc.

THE UNSUNG HEROES of the war in the skies over the world are these test pilots at Santa Monica Douglas plant who daily test the deadly Bostons and giant cargo ships and see to it that United Nations' fighting airmen get their planes in tip-top shape. Pictured (kneeling, left to right): C. H. Ferguson, M. E. Keyes, R. M. McIver, H. A. Johnson, L. M. Thomas and J. Paul Herman. Standing, left to right, C. Van Linge, G. W. McCracken, J. B. Chastain, P. Leaman, N. S. Luft, W. K. Scott, Bert Foulds, J. L. Harper, Doug "Wrong Way" Corrigan, F. W. Fuller Jr., F. O. Boyer Jr., Lee Bishop and Dick Richards.

With the other test pilots at Douglas Aircraft. I'm standing fifth from left, in the dark shirt.

LEFT: My second wedding, to Lynn Bari, November 28, 1943.

RIGHT: Jackie Cooper, Jackie Coogan, and me. We were filming *Kilroy Was Here*.

LEFT: Escorting Judy through the stage entrance at the Palace Theatre, New York City, November 16, 1951.

RIGHT: A rare night out at the Stork Club during Judy's residency at the Palace, 1951.

At a New Year's Eve party held at the Sherry-Netherland Hotel, New York City, 1951.

Celebrating with Judy at Romanoff's
following her concert at the
Los Angeles Philharmonic
Auditorium, April 21, 1952.

Arriving in Kentucky, where Judy headlined a pre–Kentucky Derby event in the spring of 1953.

Judy and I, circa 1954.

On the set of *A Star Is Born*, 1954.

A little romance between takes for Judy's wildly ambitious "Born in a Trunk" sequence in *A Star Is Born*.

Studio boss Jack Warner (in the dark suit next to Judy) visits the cast and crew on the set of *A Star Is Born*.

At the Pantages Theatre on Hollywood Boulevard for the premiere of *A Star Is Born*, September 29, 1954.

With Judy, Jack Warner, and columnist and broadcaster George Fisher at the premiere.

Driving a very pregnant Judy to the Look Magazine Film Awards, where she won Best Actress for *A Star Is Born* in March 1955. Joe was born several weeks later.

Judy in her "tramp" getup for the "Couple of Swells" number, here in 1955 with Frank Fontaine, who later became a popular singer-comedian on Jackie Gleason's TV series.

Judy looking radiant backstage before a concert, 1955.

At home with Judy, 1955.

With Judy in the recording studios at Capitol Tower in Hollywood,
March 26, 1956.

Judy in 1956.

Judy in the late 1950s.

At home in Chelsea, London, with Liza, Lorna, Joe, and Judy, November 1960.

With Judy, 1961.

Lorna, Judy, and Joe enjoying a day at Disneyland, 1967.

"At Home at the Palace": back in Manhattan for a four-week engagement,
July–August 1967.

and would attempt to copy her style. Nevertheless, MGM insisted on keeping Judy an ingenue.

I kept up a racing stable—no longer Walfarms, now Rainbow Farms—and other ventures: real estate, personal investments. But essentially I was managing Judy. She was my primary interest, an extremely potent enterprise.

Judy began to move some of her closets from her and Vincente's former home in Evanview. This effort would not be completed until we bought our first home. She kept everything. Judy had period costumes, a collection of old lace, coats and hats from the '40s—an accumulation that belonged in a museum. Eventually she'd build a special closet to accommodate her shoe collection. Inside were hundreds of different shapes and colors of footwear. Actually, she preferred a soft leather moccasin style to wear around the house. The moccasins were flat, unlike the near four-inch heels she wore onstage to give her the height she missed (which she would often kick off to "get down").

The shoe, of course, is a symbol of magic in fairy tales, especially in *The Wizard of Oz*. Although Judy's public persona generally is linked to Dorothy, her private life most resembled Cinderella. When the prince placed the glass slipper on Cinderella her world changed, transforming her from lowly maid to princess. In the more modern tale, Dorothy gets to wear the ruby-red, Technicolor shoes, a gift of power to transform her world.

Judy was the Cinderella of her family. Susie and Jimmie, Judy's sisters, were sympathetic but homely young girls compared to Judy. Their mother was fat and dumpy. One daughter had an outsized nose, the other an enormous behind. Judy had the face of an angel and a magic voice. All she had to do was say "hi" and sing a note, and everyone fell over.

With little Judy Garland, the studio had caught the golden butterfly. "Whatever you want, darling." "You want a house in Bel Air?" "Your mother wants money?" "Your sisters want a job?" "The studio will take care of it."

Baum's Dorothy may have longed to return from Oz—"There's no place like home . . ."—but Judy would always find a way to reject the idea. She never really longed to go home.

The magic that transformed Judy's life was not a shoe but her voice, the "love magnet" that could enchant with song. The first wizard to guard the little princess was Louis B. Mayer. She escaped from his kingdom in debt and with no security. The lion had roared and roared, chewed her up and spat her out. I was the next wizard, in the form of Prince Charming, the knight in shining armor. I saved her, worshipped her, guarded the kingdom. But this was not sufficient to happily end the story. There would be further adventures and more wizards to come as Judy, on a subconscious level, switched from Cinderella to Dorothy and back again. But Judy's life did not end "happily ever after."

<hr />

On April 21, 1952, Judy opened at the Los Angeles Philharmonic Auditorium. She played to raves: "The Comeback Kid," "Audience witness to one of Hollywood's greatest comebacks," "Garland scintillates," "Rousing ovation . . ." In the audiences sat her mentors: producer Arthur Freed, now white-haired; Louis B. Mayer, who never allowed his eyes to leave Judy. The men wept openly, watching their little lost minstrel girl make her comeback.

She had wowed them at the Palladium and brought the house down twice a day at the Palace Theatre. Now at the Philharmonic sat not only her peers but the people who had shaped her career. The old wizards were present, but here was a script they had no control over, so they simply sat in awe.

The Goldwyns, the Mayers, the Goetzes, the Coopers, Spyro Skouras, Clark Gable, Frank Sinatra, Cole Porter, Jack Warner Sr., the "crème de la crème" (a phrase journalists favored in that era)—all were Judy's devotees. And somewhere sitting ignominiously among the crowd was Ethel Gumm Gilmore, Judy's mother.

Ethel had found me in the theater one afternoon. She had not been in touch with Judy since her own divorce from her second husband, Will Gilmore, in 1948. And the last time she had seen her daughter was during the highly publicized "Garland suspended from MGM" period in 1950, when Judy nicked her throat, a scratch for attention, as she had once done with her wrists. There wasn't a scar on her neck. However, there were those fine lines around her wrists.

I was genuinely happy to meet Ethel. She was small, plump, with cute dancing eyes, younger in appearance than her fifty-eight years. Her voice, like Judy's, was a melodic singsong: "Do you think I could see Judy?" A familiar pixie quality. Inwardly my heart sank. It was the wrong time for Ethel to be here. I explained Judy was rehearsing, but I would make an exception and interrupt this sacred period of time.

I'd never understood how Judy could sweep her mother under the carpet. It bothered me. I approached her backstage. "Darling, your ma's out there. She'd love to say hello." Judy didn't answer me. I repeated, "Ethel has popped by." Judy gave her *don't interfere* look, her *this is my affair* look, her *don't try to be peacemaker* look.

She said, "Please, darling, don't disturb me. I'm rehearsing." It was clear there was no room for her mother then, or ever. In a cold, rejecting moment, Judy turned. Here things were good, everything coming up roses. I thought, *Not one ounce of forgiveness, baby?* I was in a mild state of shock.

I reported back to Ethel: "Judy is tied up in rehearsals." I wanted to make it as soft as possible by reassuring Ethel, saying that I'd work on it. "Judy is so damn busy," I echoed, offering her tickets to the show.

"All right." Ethel accepted the rejection without argument. But she walked away with tears in her eyes.

I sympathized with Ethel, regardless of the stories Judy had told me in bits and pieces: how her mother was paid by MGM to spy on her as a teenager, how Ethel had betrayed her, how Ethel's small business deals always fell through—and didn't Ethel have "Little Miss Leather Lungs" placed in the evil hands of MGM, any stage mother's dream? In Judy Garland's case, the dream surpassed itself.

Judy's later perception of events leading to her birth in many ways provided an explanation for her adamant rejection of her mother. She had this to say:

There was a great deal of time taken to convince me that from the time Mother found out she was going to have this unplanned third baby, that was sort of the beginning of the downfall, because I was not scheduled. I was really unwanted: my mother didn't want to have any more children.

From the day I was born until the last time I saw her, she always took great delight in telling rooms full of people at her house (whichever house she'd be in) how difficult it was for her. She did everything to get rid of me. She must have rolled down nineteen thousand flights of stairs, jumped off of tables, and for some reason I was a very stubborn child and was not about to be shaken loose. Eventually, when she found that out and it became too cumbersome for her to roll down any more stairs, she was eight and a half months pregnant and got a bit roly-poly, so she more or less became resolved, because she knew that she was going to have a little boy, having had two daughters. The only way she could possibly accept this ghastly thing that had happened was that she'd have a son, and when I turned out to be just another girl, after they had already named me Frank—that was my father's name—it didn't work out too well for anybody.

Whatever was roiling in Judy's psyche, I was not going to disperse it. In the end I chose to respect her wishes, reminding myself that many a parent and child do not have a lifelong relationship. It was in that frame of mind that I temporarily forgot the issue.

———— ⧉ ————

The Philharmonic was a smaller version of the Palace. The same kind of pandemonium: fans were lined up around the block. The adulation from the media was more poignant perhaps, as it was Judy's "hometown." I wanted everyone to see and meet a healthy, vibrant Judy, who but a year ago had been thrown out of Hollywood. She couldn't have performed or sung any better, and she looked fabulous.

We gave the opening night party at Romanoff's. We'd hired press agents to organize the affair, part of our hype. It was a huge after-dinner party, attended by the A-list. We invited Darryl Zanuck, L. B. Mayer, Arthur Freed, Jack Warner, Bogart, Cary Grant, Louella Parsons, and Hedda Hopper. People who hated each other filled that room at Romanoff's and danced their hearts out to the orchestra we'd hired. Everyone was there. Judy had made her comeback—and then she made her entrance.

Judy wanted everything perfect to the last detail, including having a seamstress labor over her gown for the party. It was finished seconds before she made her entrance. The party started around ten o'clock, and when Judy showed up around midnight she was greeted with a standing ovation. Judy was at her happiest; it was as though her mother didn't exist. I watched L. B. Mayer and Judy embrace, a warm, affectionate reunion. Mayer, the serious-mannered man, was beaming at Judy's success. Later, he came up to me: "Sid, I think you're the right medicine."

Jack Warner also introduced himself to me. We chatted, with Judy present, but made no mention of *A Star Is Born*. However, it was then that Eddie Alperson and I concluded: Warner was the man for us.

25

As Judy's career soared, my ex was twisting the screws tighter. Lynn continued in her attempt to deny me the visiting rights I desired. Her attorney, Sammy Hahn, was known as the "Wild West lawyer," famous for passing out gold and silver ten-dollar pieces to clerks and judges. Hahn had a lot of clout in the courts downtown. In that era there was Jerry Giesler for criminal problems and Sammy Hahn for marital problems—the show biz lawyers of their day. Hahn was a publicity hound, and he began to hover over my life.

Judy brought Liza to the Hotel Bel-Air to meet my son, Johnny. It was wonderful to watch the new playmates: Liza with her shiny black hair and Johnny, freckled and redheaded. They had so much fun playing together, I brought Johnny up to Evanview to spend time with Liza there. They were exactly the same age and got on so well, we were knocked out. However, if I wanted to see Johnny, I had first to call Sammy Hahn. The lawyer would warn, "Don't be late; if you're late she'll slam the door in your face." Or he'd say, "Be on time, and bring him back on time," as though I weren't capable.

The engagement at the Philharmonic proceeded without a hitch. Ethel had been sloughed off, and Judy was riding high. The four-week run was dancing in paradise, nothing but well wishes and good luck. Hollywood had witnessed Judy's success and saw a healthy and vital woman. It was another major triumph for Judy Garland. People were after her; "check with Sid" syndrome was heavily operative. We were escorted by the maître d's to the best tables at the best restaurants; we received invitations to dinner parties, openings, and premieres. The A-list was not complete without us. We were part of the glamour, glitz, and "in" crowd. It never occurred to us that there might be something else in life.

Judy's next engagement, at the Curran Theatre in San Francisco, was to be a bright echo of the previous appearance. The owner, Louis Lurie, a dapper, short man with steely gray hair, was a pal of Louis B. Mayer who owned many theaters, and he was a big fan of Judy. He offered to pave the streets in gold for us. Mr. Lurie outdid me in his signs of appreciation. He'd visit the theater nightly, and every day he sent masses of flowers to Judy at the Clift Hotel, where we stayed, as well as backstage.

After the show we could slip away from the crowd and actually walk around the streets of San Francisco without being harassed. We would take off for Chinatown, where Judy devoured her favorite menu. In the afternoon Judy would shop, in person, at Gump's, her favorite store. She would order outfits made out of Japanese silk, trousers, and jackets. San Francisco was so relaxed, we felt we were on a honeymoon. The bistros were low-key and romantic. Some evenings we'd walk around different sections of town with Jack and Susie. Tully stayed with Judy backstage, and Vern Alves, who had assisted up in New York, was now part of the family and dealt with the press.

One night the two of us were on our own having dinner in a favored Italian restaurant when Judy casually announced she was pregnant—this time over three months pregnant. I looked at her challenging chocolate-drop eyes shining in the candlelight, and I said, "Darling, will you marry me?"

To which Judy replied, "You and me—we're some kind of team."

I called Ted and told him we were getting married. He was happy for me and congratulated us. Then he said, "Call my brother Bob, and get married on the ranch. That way it'll be kept quiet for a while." I thought, what a good idea. Bob Law and his wife raised cattle on an impressive ten-thousand-acre ranch in Hollister, a couple hours south of San Francisco. He wasn't interested in show business, but his wife came to the Curran with a group of fans anyhow and loved the show.

We arranged for a minister to marry us on June 8, 1952. My old friend Bobby Heasley, who would be working with us on *A Star Is Born*, drove the wedding party in a large station wagon down to the ranch, where at long last Judy and I were to be pronounced man and wife. Judy gave her name as Frances Ethel Gumm, and I gave my name as Michael Sidney Luft. Judy looked beautiful, very much the bride at the lovely ceremony and homey celebratory dinner. We returned to San Francisco that evening, and minutes later the press hit. There was no respite from the media, and there never would be.

Within a month, Judy was the only woman besides Sophie Tucker to be roasted at the Friars Club in Los Angeles. For the first time in its fifty-year history, women appeared on the speaker's platform: Rosalind Russell, Olivia de Havilland, and Marie Wilson joined in the tribute to Judy Garland as the performer personally responsible for the rebirth of vaudeville. It was a formal bash. Judy's close friend Jack Benny was in London, so George Jessel replaced him as toastmaster. Other speakers included Lieutenant Governor Goodwin Knight, Ezio Pinza, George Burns, and Ronald Reagan. They traced her film career from the age of fourteen to the present moment, and she was presented with a pearl necklace along with a pearl emblem of the Friars Club.

Judy was officially titled "Little Miss Show Business." Ezio Pinza sang a parody of "Some Enchanted Evening," his hit song from the Broadway show *South Pacific*. The parody was written by Mort Greene, an ex-songwriter, currently an associate producer of Jessel's at 20th Century Fox. I kept some of the lyrics in my journal; it brought down the house:

Some enchanted evening,
You may see a stranger,
A ticket-selling stranger
Across a crowded room.
If you play your cards right and treat him just right,
You may get two tickets to Judy some night.
Some enchanted evening,
You may see a mogul,
Plead with Lastfogel
Across a crowded room.
A tear fills his eye as Abe shakes his head,
We're sold out for Garland for six months ahead . . .

And so the parody went.

The audience insisted on an encore. Pinza had to sing the number a second time. Judy concluded the evening by singing her "Palace Medley" and "Over the Rainbow."

That evening as the tributes were lavished on Judy by the most distinguished company Hollywood had to offer, her mother, Ethel Gilmore, was cooking herself dinner in a cheap room somewhere in town. She was preparing for the night shift at the Douglas Aircraft factory, where she earned sixty-one cents an hour as a purchasing clerk.

We'd checked back into the Hotel Bel-Air. One day around lunchtime I was horsing around the pool with Johnny and Liza when someone with a charming foreign accent called out my name: "Seed!" I was surprised to see Genevieve, the beautiful blonde I'd had a fling with on the Riviera. In the background stood the well-dressed woman she had referred to as "Auntie," patiently waiting. While we exchanged small talk Judy came out to the pool looking for me. I anticipated a sticky situation, but she was congenial, no hint of jealousy.

Later that year Genevieve got her exquisite throat slit, having somehow gotten caught up with a mob. She had fingered thieves who stole a bundle of cash—coincidentally, from the Jack Warner house on the Riviera. They had lifted the safe from his villa and stolen the money and jewels. For all I knew she was part of the ring. In any case, something had gone radically wrong.

We finally moved into the rental home on Maple Drive, and Judy took advantage of her pregnancy. She lolled about the pool, ate whatever she craved, played with Liza and Johnny—in general, enjoyed the good life. The house was brimming with activity.

The husband and wife team who ran the household were professionals who specialized in show business people. We perceived them as wonders, providing us with a beautifully run home. The following year we discovered that the cost for wine and whiskey had been doubled, and muffins were sixty dollars a day. They'd been ripping us off, so I let them go.

We went out to dinner and dancing at all the restaurants and clubs that had been previously restricted to us. Judy and I especially loved to watch the Will Mastin Trio at Ciro's on the strip. We thought the youngest member, Sammy Davis Jr., was a great talent. Sammy, along with his father and adopted uncle, sang and tap danced wearing straw hats, white jackets, and black trousers while twirling canes. The uncle and father were pretty ordinary, but the kid was great, with exceptional timing. Judy thought I should manage him. I wasn't thinking management, but when Sammy (a dedicated camera buff) came around to a party at Maple Drive he not only snapped pictures but also performed. And again I was knocked out by his talent. I decided to approach his uncle, who was also his manager. I said, "Will, you should retire. Just feature Sammy." Will, a short, squat fellow, wanted no part of me or what I was suggesting. Sammy's old man was sweet-tempered, but Will was a tough piece of work, like an ex-cop.

In the last trimester Judy began to suffer insomnia. She wanted me to stay up with her. I was sympathetic to Judy's late night restlessness, but I had to be at the office in the morning. I tried to do both, remain with Judy through the night and be at the office on time. This lifestyle did not work out. I was overly exhausted, the growing circles under my eyes a trademark. I hoped Judy would understand. I needed to get proper sleep to continue on with our business goals. The night came when I kissed her good night and went to sleep before two in the morning, alone. She very often would be going to sleep as I left for the office. By early afternoon, she would awake in good spirits and call me at the office to tell me jokes and inquire what I would like for dinner. "Sleep" would be my most frequent request.

Eddie Alperson, Vern Alves, Bobby Heasley, and I were busy developing *A Star Is Born*. Eddie devised a plan for nine films over a five-year period, with Judy starring in one out of three. The first three would be *Man o' War*, *A Star Is Born*, and *Snow Covered Wagons*. I was hoping to produce *Man o' War* as a starter, for the experience of making a big Technicolor film. We no longer needed Sam Riddle's approval, since the man had sadly died. There were no Riddle heirs, and his estate had been turned over to a local Pennsylvania institution.

Judy's contract with the William Morris Agency was due to expire. In this way Transcona would be clear of any contractual holds on her. By a process of elimination, we targeted Warner Bros. They were not in production, so the studio was empty; nothing but money and grips remained.

Maybe Jack Warner Sr. had let his talent go to please Washington? Jack was right wing when it was fashionable—he'd produced special projects for Hap Arnold during the Second World War—and it was now an era of paranoia in Hollywood. The House Un-American Activities Committee (HUAC) had left wounds. The McCarthy hearings had rattled the nation. At one point Judy had joined her peers and traveled to Washington to observe the hearings, but Judy, a staunch Democrat, didn't perceive either Jack Warner or L. B. Mayer as the reactionaries they were.

I had many thoughts on the subject myself, but I confess these negative aspects didn't affect our zeal when it came to striking a deal with the studio. We knew that Warner Bros. had recently divorced itself from its chain of Warner theaters. A law had been passed forbidding motion picture studios from owning theaters. The studio was now open to independent producers and had already made a deal for an independent company with John Wayne. Alperson, through Benny Kalmenson,

Warner's booker for theater chains, had received serious interest on the part of Jack and Harry Warner.

Jack Warner Sr. was head of production at Warner's. He wanted the power and was undisputedly king of his domain, but his older brother Harry controlled the money. Harry was the president of the studio and the boss of economics; he never put his foot in production until distribution decisions were about to be made. I saw little of Harry, but I was aware that he also owned horses. In those days racing stables were classified under agriculture training, and if a stable did not show a profit every five years the enterprise was a write-off. Many moneyed people ran stables for the tax break. I did not; I was devoted to the thrill and romance of the racehorse. Harry and I were both involved with films, and we both had horses, but we had nothing to say to one another.

So Jack was our in. I had already taken one meeting with him, and I was to meet him again at a lavish at-home, black tie party given by a matron who wrote a local society column. This time we did not discuss business. However, later in the evening Jack approached Judy: "You've got to make a picture with me."

I told her, "Darling, you see we're going to do it. Hollywood is interested."

Very late that night, Judy suffered a migraine headache. She was still struggling with insomnia and was irritable as a result of not sleeping. She convinced me she needed a doctor's help to get through the night, so we called Lee Siegel to give her something to ease the pain. I'd been gently excusing myself to go to bed for several weeks so I could function at the office. I could not have thought, under any circumstances, Judy would secretly bear any grudge against me, any feelings of abandonment, or that I would be held responsible for her anxieties. I thought the prospect of *A Star Is Born* must have loomed up as more of a pressure, the need to be on the lot on time, to be "camera slim." Judy was experiencing the old patterns of worry and abuse accelerated by her pregnancy.

Judy closeted herself with Lee, explaining I was not to be present, that she wanted privacy. "Darling, *nnn*, this is between myself and my doctor." She spoke in her rapid childlike speech, the seductive little girl asking for independence, a chance to be a grown-up. There was no apparent reason for me to interfere; our marriage was based on mutual considerations. I respected her privacy and I trusted Lee, so I went to sleep.

The next evening, I returned to the house and Judy greeted me from the couch, her legs folded beneath her pregnant tummy, a pair of my loafers hung over her knees, and a cigar wedged in her mouth. She spoke rat-a-tat-tat, imitating Abe Lastfogel. She knew her shtick would always break me up. And she could easily slip from a sexy presence to Chevalier to a drunken Tallulah.

Once during the earlier days of her pregnancy I had found Judy beautifully made up, waiting for me, our favorite opera *La Bohème* coursing through the rooms. She swooshed over to me for a romantic kiss before I could change clothes. We sunk into a large wingback chair, embracing. I was about to lift her into my arms and take her to our bedroom when I realized her left arm was in a sling fashioned out of fabric that matched her silk lounging pajamas. She teased me when she saw my alarm. "It's nonfunctioning, like me." I insisted she tell me what was wrong. Judy said it was some kind of temporary numbness from a pinched nerve, and she proved it by poking herself with a straight pin. I remarked, "Baby, what a strange way to treat one's body." She assured me the condition would go away. Judy was not worried; if anything she was detached. For that moment the sense of the intimacy dissolved. I brought up the subject of her arm later, after dinner. Judy quickly dismissed it, teasing, "None of your business, darling, it's all right. Don't poke in." I knew she meant it.

Benny Kalmenson had set up Transcona's first big meeting with Jack Warner. It was in the trophy room at Warner Bros. studios in Burbank. The room was on the first floor and Jack's office was not far away on the second floor. The trophy room was lined with tiers of glass shelving displaying European awards, Academy Awards, plaques, cups, a sum of all the studio's success.

I was aware of Jack's reputation as a power monger, a snob, and a practical jokester. But he also had an exuberance about him; he seemed to enjoy life. He was in and out of society. We were on a first-name basis from the outset, but I quickly realized he didn't like anyone. He drove his Rolls-Royce to the studio every morning at eleven o'clock, well groomed, wearing hand-tailored suits, a white shirt, and a high Barrymore collar and tie. Jack was dressed to kill.

Originally, I had thought it would be best for me to work with a producer from Warner's. Eddie disagreed; he believed the only way *A Star Is Born* could work was if I was the producer and Judy worked for me. I would have the entire studio at my fingertips. I was not to be an associate producer, and in those days, executive producers didn't exist. I understood his point: he wanted to show the money people that someone was there to ensure Judy's reliability, and who better than the husband of the star? Kalmenson had been to New York to see Judy at the Palace. We had spent time together, and he too insisted I was the one to produce.

When the time came for me to meet with Jack one on one, I had a two-page outline stating what we needed to agree upon, who had artistic approval and casting approval, the maximum advertising cost spent for distribution, how many prints were to be made, what Warner's responsibility was to deliver to Transcona and vice versa. I said Judy's hours on the set would be from ten to six, not beginning at six in the morning. It would be impossible for her to function otherwise, since the film was to be a tour de force of her talents: she would be on screen in virtually every frame. We even discussed Judy's extreme episodes of PMS. I needed every safety valve possible for Judy. Jack would scissor out different sections from his proposal and initial them. In this manner we fashioned the preliminary contract for *A Star Is Born*. There would be details about which I couldn't make a decision without talking to Judy.

We eventually agreed on $3 million for three films: *Man o' War* was first on the list, *A Star Is Born* was second, *Snow Covered Wagons* third. Word got around that we were busy working on a musical version of *Star*, creating a kind of cynical grapevine response from the old MGM crowd and prompting Arthur Freed to remark, "I can't believe those two alley cats are making a movie."

⟨⟨⟨⟩⟩⟩

I was more and more occupied, away from the house and not always available when Judy tried to reach me. As she came closer to giving birth, she began to exhibit a lack of enthusiasm about making a film. I noticed she was cranky, even short, especially after dinner. I automatically blamed it on her condition. At one point, feeling homebound, Judy started to work on her autobiography. She lasted about a week on the project before losing interest. She related details of her family and early childhood in a straightforward fashion. There have been considerable variations in theme since those days. Luckily, some of Judy's original work in progress has been preserved. In addition to the passages I've already shared, Judy also said:

> My grandmother was Fitzgerald, but then she got divorced and married a man named Milne. So mother was Ethel Milne. . . . She was black Irish, rather pretty, about my height, a little under five feet and dark eyes. My [maternal] grandfather was an engineer, ran a train in Duluth. And, of course, my mother hated my grandmother. She derided my grandmother, whose name was Eva, and had something like seven children. My grandfather was an absolute terror.
>
> He frightened everyone to death because he would get stoned. There was a great enormous hill, and he would get so drunk driving this train that he would get to the top of the hill and open up the whistle and everybody knew that there might be a stunning crash which would wipe out, first of all, his wife and children. He threatened every day to kill them all and my grandmother went strange about it, and my mother, I think at the ripe age of four, punched him in the nose with a metal pitcher full of water—she poured it over his head, the water first, and then hit him right smack in the face. She didn't have any trouble with him anymore, proving that she overcame that by being very brutal and then she went ahead with that same behavior pattern when she raised her own kids, one of them being me.

Mother was plump, very plump and very bad legs. I didn't look like anybody in my family. I don't know why I wound up having the features I have . . .

Father was a terribly handsome man when my mother first met him. He was so handsome it was incredible. He was so slender. Five feet eleven, slender, sensitive, he was French and a little Irish. He had a magnificent shock of beautiful dark hair. I've seen pictures in the family album that disappeared somewhere, but he was awfully attractive. He was engaged before he met my mother to the woman who finally wound up marrying the comedian and actor Joe E. Brown. And then when he met my mother, he broke his engagement and married my mother and settled down. [Francis Gumm met Ethel Milne in 1913 at the Savoy Theater in Superior, Wisconsin.] My mother had a job playing in the pit. Singers would come out in front of movie screens, where they'd show slides and sing. And she would accompany them. And then she met father and they decided to go on the stage. They'd wheel a piano onto the stage. A singing team: he sang, she played piano. He bought a theater [the Rialto] when he realized that they were going to have a family. He became rather paunchy but still attractive. Marvelous, loud laugh. Funny explosive temper.

I was afraid to ask mother if she had a middle name. At any rate, they decided to have an act and get into vaudeville. They changed their [stage] names after they were married to "Jack and Virginia Lee, Sweet Southern Singers." After all, he did come from Murfreesboro, Tennessee. Mother was born in Duluth. They traveled regionally . . . into small places where they booked themselves directly. When they discovered that Mother was going to have a baby, Father decided to go into a sensible business. So he bought the only theater in the town of Grand Rapids, Minnesota. He showed movies. The only time [the New Grand Theater] had a vaudeville act is when my two sisters became the sort of town darlings and they came out and did a sister act, a duet. They sang harmony. They were constantly singing "In a Little Spanish Town." When I got into the act, mother and father, for some unknown reason, sold the theater and we all traveled west. They were still Jack and Virginia Lee and we were the Gumm sisters.

My oldest sister's name was Mary Jane, seven years older than me; the middle girl whose name was Dorothy Virginia was five years older; and along came Frances Ethel. George Jessel, many years later, changed our last name to Garland, and my older sister suddenly decided she hated Mary Jane and she got awfully classy and chose the name Suzanne. I'd always been called "Babe," or Baby Gumm, and that's a rough rap. So I decided that if she could change her name to Suzanne, I could change mine, and I liked the song, very popular at the time, called "Judy." I chose to change mine simply so no one would call me "Baby" anymore. I wouldn't answer if they called me Babe or Baby.

I didn't return to see the small town of Grand Rapids until I was in the movies. I was about fifteen years old. An official "Judy Garland Day" had been declared in the town where I was born.

Our house was on a corner. The lawn went across the front and around the corner—a white clapboard house, two stories high; it was on a swell of ground. If I turned right again, it became a rose garden. The house was in the middle of that. I never did get to know the people [next door]. It's funny. I've always been called "the girl next door," but I never knew a girl next door. My two sisters shared the same room, and I was always put out into some room that they could sort of manage to find. Sometimes I slept with my father, sometimes I slept with my mother, sometimes I slept in an extra bedroom that was upstairs, by myself.

Sometimes in the winter, when my dad would be at the theater and my mother would be playing piano there, my older sister took care of me. We'd go out in the snow and we'd make angels. We'd lie down, do our arms like a bird, and then get up and it looked like an angel. And then we'd go into the house for hot milk and that Thompson's cocoa. I adored that. Everything about Grand Rapids had charm and gaiety. The first time anybody took any notice was my father playing the piano. I had a little girlfriend, she was just my age, and he taught us to sing "My Country 'Tis of Thee." He had an upright piano at home. He called my mother and my sisters in to listen to this little girl and me. And I was proud because they said, "She was good." Baby. Baby Gumm. . . .

⌘

The day soon arrived when Eddie and I shook hands with Jack Warner and drew up a formal contract. Jack brought a few men from the Warner legal department. Not long afterward, the contracts were hand-delivered to Canon Drive.

We had a list of possible writers and actors. Humphrey Bogart was one name. Jack, who was aware that Bogie hated his guts and couldn't wait to get out of Jack's studio several years before, said, "He's too damn old for Judy Garland." I brought up Sinatra, whom I'd met earlier in the week at the Brown Derby. Jack responded to his name with a laugh. "He's finished."

Was Jack a difficult man? I knew Errol Flynn disliked Jack, as did Bette Davis and Olivia de Havilland. But, again, there was no longer anyone under contract to Warner's. I reminded myself they have the grips, and the money. He's got to approve of someone.

26

O UR DAUGHTER, LORNA, was born November 21, 1952, by cesarean section (as were all of Judy's children). She was robust, with blonde hair and blue eyes that remained blue. Another adorable baby girl for Judy. Judy agreed to stay in the hospital for a week after she gave birth.

As fate would have it, the day she picked to leave the hospital and go home (with Vern Alves in attendance), I was in San Francisco at the Bay Meadows Racetrack watching our horse Florence House win a big race. When I returned to Los Angeles, I went immediately out to Santa Monica only to find that Judy and the baby had already left. I had let her down; I was not available for her when she needed me. Where was I? At the races. Of course, Judy knew I would be flying out there for the day. I had not purposely disappointed her, but I was aware she had decided to make a point. I went along with her game, apologizing even though she'd given me the impression it was not that critical. She seemed thrilled that Florence House had won. It was not as important, however, as watching our new little baby laugh! We had decided on the name Lorna, as my mother was Lena/Leonora, and Judy had been fascinated by the character of Lorna in Clifford Odets's play *Golden Boy*.

No sooner were mother and newborn baby daughter seemingly snug at home when Judy slipped into a postpartum depression. The familiar words before and during her period, "Darling, I'm miserable. Please bear with me," were missing. Now she didn't apologize. In fact, she was uncontrollably testy to the staff and irritable, cut off, and short tempered with me. Her eyes looked glazed. Again she battled insomnia. We were back to sleeping at different times. The nights we slept together it was clear she was on something. But what? And how? There would be no communication. She'd descend into a depressed state and, no doubt, take something to pick her up. But whatever she ingested was not working, and she became more and more depressed.

I'd come into the office and straightaway Heasley or Vern would say, "What's worrying you today?" I couldn't figure out why Judy had fallen off. Here we were, a husband-and-wife team moving steadily forward, our seed blooming every which way, and suddenly there was a frightening specter looming over our family and career: addiction. Was it only that she was intent on returning to size six, the future requiring a slim Judy, and she again resorted to pills? In the evening she barely touched her food. The not eating was a sign of speed in the system.

I was reliving that moment in New York with Dr. Salmon. Who were the suppliers? Dr. Noah Dietrich, Lorna's pediatrician and a distinguished UCLA professor, was against pills. Judy could not have been scoring any from him. Dr. Morton, her obstetrician, would not supply her. I couldn't ask her directly, as I was supposed to be ignorant of the fact that she was taking pills, and I was dealing with a person who had problems but could only kid about them or bury them.

The stakes were higher now, so I arranged with the staff to watch her more closely. I sympathized with her restlessness but was unable to reach her. And then one night Judy casually expressed the desire "to do something." I was encouraged. I came up with a personal appearance in Louisville, Kentucky, the first week in May, the day before the Kentucky Derby. Lawrence Wetherby, the governor of Kentucky, had called me. He wanted to declare the event Judy Garland Day. I was aware Governor Wetherby was probably looking for an easy way to please his constituents, but it sounded amusing, something to do, to fill in. We were at the beginning of December and Judy said, "May is months away." I said, "Darling, think about the traveling, and singing, and the Kentucky Derby." Neither of us had ever attended Churchill

Downs. "It'll be a kick." "You'll be in shape again." Something to look forward to.

—— ✥ ——

Harry Rabwin, the brother of the Gumm family friend Dr. Marcus Rabwin, was a lawyer, and he contacted me at the office on behalf of Judy's mother, Ethel. He relayed her message that she was very sad about her lack of relationship with Judy. Ethel needed financial help, she wasn't well, and she longed to see her new granddaughter. I explained to Harry that I, too, was in a quandary about Judy's total rejection of her mother. "Harry," I reassured, "Maybe one day it'll go away. Judy'll come around."

I was sympathetic, but I was seriously preoccupied with Judy's state of mind. I didn't share those concerns with Harry. Instead, I agreed to personally mail Ethel a monthly check.

Ethel was not the person Judy had described, the "demon woman" who had double-crossed her and exposed her and finked on her at Metro for a salary. Nor was she the forceful woman who purposely separated Judy from her father to go on needless trips. However, it might have very well felt like that to a little girl. She was not an aggressive monster lady who forced Judy into show business either, as from all evidence you could not keep Baby Gumm off the stage if you tried. And Ethel certainly did not propel Frank to an early death.

As in a mystery-game hunt I'd been attempting to fit the pieces of Judy's life together in the hopes of better understanding her. I knew that it was Frank, not Ethel, who delivered Judy to MGM. Judy's agent, Al Rosen, had arranged for the MGM talent chief, Jack Robbins, to listen. Judy, who was thirteen, appeared even younger, and Robbins remarked, "I'm looking for a woman singer, not a child!" Rosen prevailed, and it was Frank, not Ethel, who played the piano for his daughter, who belted out the latest hit, "Zing! Went the Strings of My Heart." Judy then sang for Ida Koverman, Louis B. Mayer's personal assistant. Koverman listened and, without voicing a reaction, rang for her boss. The short, burly Mayer joined her. This time Roger Edens was asked to play the piano; it was the start of Judy and Roger's long, close creative and personal friendship. Mayer, the essence of tough and sentimental, the great Hollywood mix, remained expressionless as he listened to the child prodigy.

In the time it took for father and daughter to return home to the L.A. suburb of Lancaster, Mayer had decided to give Judy a seven-year contract without any particular role in mind. That same month, Frank the movie exhibitor who so recently shook hands with Louis the movie mogul, fell mortally ill with an ear infection. The day after Judy announced the news of her MGM contract on the Wallace Beery *Shell Chateau* broadcast, her father died at age forty-nine. And Judy became the family breadwinner at age thirteen, earning $150 a week.

Judy's recollection of the period leading up to the MGM audition is fraught with anti-Ethel sentiments:

> I didn't know my father very well, because my mother dominated me so. . . . I was thinking that in so many cases of people who start out as children in show business there's usually a mother in the background, but you never hear about the father. Stage fathers are the most nondescript unheralded lost generation in the world.
>
> You never hear about Gypsy Rose Lee's father, just her mother. From the time we moved from Minnesota to California, there was dissention in our home between Mother and Father, and Mother always used me as a pawn with my father. They'd have a fight. I don't think anything in the world frightens a child more than their parents fighting. It's all right if there is basic love in the home, then you can have a fight and the kids don't lose their security, but if there isn't any love between the two, fighting becomes such an awful thing for a kid, because his whole life is threatened.
>
> One of the reasons they were fighting was this man that my mother was attracted to, I didn't know about it for a long time. His name was Bill Gilmore [the Gumms' next door neighbor in Lancaster]. . . . She married him after my father died. I don't know what kind of relationship they had . . . it went on for twelve years. At any rate, my parents would argue and fight and she'd come in

the middle of the night and wake me up and dress me and say we're leaving Daddy, all through my early years. And if ever I would say . . . "I don't want to leave Daddy," she'd make me feel terrible, because she'd say I didn't love her and then make me feel very guilty about loving my father. In the meantime, she left the other two girls with my father and she would put me in the backseat of the car, wrap me up, and to release her frustrations, she'd just drive hour after hour, ninety miles an hour. Hell-bent for an accident, around mountains and curves and everything. I was terrified. I don't think I ever went to bed at night without wondering whether I was going to be awakened and taken out in the night.

And then she'd take me to Los Angeles, where we'd register at a crummy hotel and we'd stay there, sometimes, about three or four months. We'd go around singing and she'd take a job as a music teacher or a singing teacher [at Maurice Kusell's Theatrical Dance Studio in Hollywood]. During that period, my sisters would periodically join us, if she got the three of us a job. . . .

We'd work little places around town. Little joints, we'd work the Star Theater in Long Beach, we always went there; the Hippodrome Theatre down on Main Street, where all the actors say they're working because they're breaking in a new act and it isn't true. It's such a terrible place, you're always saying that as an excuse. The rats backstage were so big we named them. And that's where we worked on the bill with a man who threw up for an act. Hadji Ali was his name. He'd come out with a big turban, his wife was his assistant, and he would swallow twenty-seven hazelnuts and one walnut, then he'd walk into the audience and let the audience tap his stomach and he'd come up onstage and he'd say, "Now I will bring up the hazelnuts, and when you want me to bring up the walnut just holler." He'd bring them up, then someone would say "Now." He'd bring up the walnut, and finally at the end of his act he built a great big fire and then he drank water and on top of that, kerosene . . . then he'd throw up the kerosene on it and make the fire enormous and then the water would come up and put it out, that was his finale. And God help us if he ate any lunch that day. We worked with all kinds of class acts like that. In the meantime, my father was actually a very good provider, but my mother had this maniacal streak to be completely independent of him through her kids.

The stage was the only thing I ever knew, and I remember being very happy on the stage. My feeling was that Dad must have loved the two girls more than he loved me, because he kept them and he didn't insist on keeping me. It wasn't until years and years and years afterwards when I finally asked one of my sisters why he hadn't kept me and she told me that he actually loved me more than anybody in the family but he just couldn't bear to tear me back and forth and have a screaming fight with me in the middle. Mother defeated him. But he was a very strong man, my father. Very strong—there was nothing weak about him at all. He was a fighting Irishman, you know, French Irish. But for years there was no marriage and I don't know why they decided to stay together, maybe because of the children. Daddy owned a corner theater [the Valley Theatre in Lancaster]. Very successful. . . . So during the school year when I had to stay in Lancaster, I spent my evenings at the movies. I saw every picture . . .

Clearly it was not the time to bring up the subject of Ethel to Judy. But my concern for her was deepening. She had taken to spending her nights in the den with the door closed. I braced myself: the more cut off she became, the more alert I became. There was torment in her face, and especially in the eyes. And there was nothing I could do. I realized that this was about more than getting into shape for her next project; she was impatient with the lull after giving birth, the in-between time. Her energy level was low, and she picked herself up by getting speed from someone. As always, the effect of the pills was toxic, but this time Judy's personality change was radical: her eyes were red rimmed, conversation was out, and she became more and more remote. In the past she may have kept secrets and had mysterious facets, but I knew that her general nature was vibrant, up, and fun—the opposite of the Judy I now saw before me.

I was determined to get to the source of her misery. I had enough confidence in her love for me. I viewed this as a storm, a squall that would ride itself out, but I didn't want to be stranded not knowing the cause or the cure. So I began to talk to the doctors at hand.

I contacted Marc Rabwin. He warned me, "It's the amphetamines." He explained that coming off them could be hellish. He spoke openly about MGM, those years when she'd been fed speed. We discussed the dangerous cycle of uppers and downers. He began to educate me. I went to Judy and I told her I loved her but she must be able to trust me; whatever the hell it was, "don't cut me off." Judy promised, but to no avail.

Whenever I left for work I talked individually to everyone in the house, explaining that if there was any sign of Judy disappearing, or staying in the bathroom for an undue length of time, to ring me right away at the office. "Watch her every second, man," I warned the house-man, Taylor.

The next day, he rang the office. "I'm scared, Mr. Luft. She's in the bathroom, not answering. I can't get in." I sped home. Fortunately, it was just minutes away. I raced into the bedroom, and I could see blood oozing out from under the door. I proceeded to dislocate my shoulder busting down the bathroom door. I could feel my heart in my temples. Judy was wedged in between the bath and the door. I finally got it open and picked her up. Blood, bright red in sharp contrast to the whiteness of her skin, was pouring out of her neck. I thought, she's dying, I'm losing her. Judy had cut her throat with a razor blade.

Luckily, Vern and Bobby were able to have doctors, not paramedics, at the house in minutes. These men saved Judy's life. They also ensured that the press would remain ignorant of the extreme danger Judy had inflicted on herself. I made certain this would be one Judy catastrophe that would never make the news. The doctors transfused her and stitched her up right in our bedroom.

My mind raced. This time she had not "nicked" her neck, she had actually cut her throat with a razor. What demons inhabited her soul just when life seemed so rich and productive? It was a gigantic puzzlement that she would poison herself with pills, and that the toxic reaction to whatever she swallowed would create an impulse for self-mutilation. Go write an opera about that!

Now my day's work included visits to physicians, to psychiatrists, to technicians, searching out what could be done. I came away knowing more about her emotional history at MGM rather than receiving any enlightenment on the present. There was to be one saving grace: I learned that postpartum depression often occurred, and was equally serious, in women without Judy's unique psychological history. And it was this explanation I conveniently opted for. Nevertheless, there was a tiny chime ringing in the back of my mind that, perhaps, the scratch she put on her throat when she was suspended at MGM was not, as everyone proclaimed, simply an attempt to wrest attention for herself.

The miracle was that Judy awakened from the horror show the next morning with a desire to eat: "Hi, darling, is everything all right?" The surgical bandage about her throat didn't inhibit my little darling from throwing back a trencherman's breakfast of eggs, pancakes, sausages, coffee, and toast with extra marmalade. Her first serious meal in weeks. After watching her wolf down the food I experienced the big moat Judy threw around herself in any sensitive situation. I was treated as someone apart, a fan in the audience. She did not wish to know what really happened, nor was she eager to explore the effects of her behavior, on either herself or the rest of us.

"Darling," I suggested, "you may need someone to make sense, help you figure out these mysterious depressions."

"Ah, Sid," she said. "Don't pay any attention. It's over with," Judy reassured me with her familiar pizazz. Again, I chose to believe her. A kind of relief washed over me. She quickly ordered a three-string pearl choker from Saks Fifth Avenue, and she never took it off. She wore it to bed.

With the necklace firmly clasped around her neck, she began organizing a large at-home party. It was getting into the holiday season. Judy threw herself into Christmas and the children. We were Christmas shopping on Rodeo Drive and ran into Elizabeth Taylor in a toy store. Elizabeth was married to the English actor Michael Wilding at the time. She took one look at my new black Mercedes-Benz, a postwar breakthrough in their body design, and remarked to her husband, "Why don't you drive a car like that, Michael?" Judy reveled in that moment, proud of her husband's taste. She'd regained her exuberance about life.

<hr/>

Around this time, Jack Warner appeared at the Canon Drive office for an out-of-studio lunch meeting. He said, "Sid, don't make *Man o' War*. I'll give you a movie, *The Bounty Hunter*, practically in the can. This'll replace *Man o' War* in the deal." Then he put it to me: "I'd like you to start preparing *A Star Is Born* right away." I would have preferred the experience of *Man o' War*. However, I reasoned I'd better go for it before anything else happened. So I told him I could hardly wait to begin.

I was treading water now, and I didn't want to drown. I was pleased Judy seemed to have so quickly pulled out of her trauma. I wasn't comfortable with pushing it under the carpet, but at the same time I considered it a never-to-be-repeated postpartum occurrence. We were making love again—husband and wife, lovers, business partners, Mom and Dad. I was hopeful.

Judy's party was a huge success. She sang with Sinatra, who was going to work for Capitol Records. He accepted a small part in *From Here to Eternity* for little to no money. He was feeling much better. Soon he'd be off to Spain to be with Ava Gardner, who was on the set of *The Barefoot Contessa* and rumored to be traveling with the famous bullfighter Dominguín. Frank needed to confront his estranged wife to figure out their future. I never communicated Jack's sentiment about his playing the role of Norman Maine, and Frank continued to express his enthusiasm for the part.

Jack took the opportunity to ask if we would come to New York over New Year's as his guests. Actually, he wanted Judy to sing for his daughter Barbara's coming-out party at the St. Regis Hotel in New York City.

Jack had been divorced from Jack Jr.'s mother for many years, and in the 1930s had married the actress Ann Alvarado in a celebrated Eastern

Seaboard wedding. They'd honeymooned in Europe, along with Ann's daughter Joy from her earlier marriage. Ann Warner was a stately woman with black hair and blue eyes, very much a kind of silent film beauty. She wasn't involved with the Hollywood set, as she chose to live out of state on a ranch she shared with a close female companion. Curiously, the ranch was run by her ex-husband Don Alvarado, a failed actor. This bit of information was never written up in the press.

Ann had remained Jack's trusted friend and his number-one hostess when available. She offered Judy a gift of a natural mink coat for performing at her daughter's party. The carrot of the mink coat appealed to Judy. Nevertheless, traveling to New York was going to be work. We'd be met in Chicago (changing trains from the Super Chief to the 20th Century Limited) by Warner's publicity department and the press. In New York, there'd be a limo waiting and more press, more interviews, and more work. I told Judy maybe the train ride would be good, relaxing. She'd come back with a gorgeous new coat. I reminded her how much she loved trains. Judy was never happier than on a train curled up with her books, for a brief time protected from the external world. She agreed to the gig.

Shortly after Christmas Day we picked up the Super Chief downtown and rode along with Liza and Lorna and their nanny to Pasadena, where we bade our good-byes for the week. In New York we checked into the Waldorf Astoria Towers.

Eleanor Berkson had asked Judy to participate in a big charity event at the Waldorf's Starlight Roof a day or so after the Warner bash. Judy would be joined by friends and people she enjoyed—the Palm Beach crowd, including the Duke and Duchess of Windsor. Meantime, it was all over town that Judy Garland was singing at Barbara Warner's coming-out party. The night of the event Judy wore a black velvet gown, her pearl choker, of course, and a little bejeweled Juliet cap, so called after the costume device for Shakespeare's famous female; the Elizabethan fashion caught on in the 1950s. I was seated not at the Warners' table but in the front, with C. Z. and Winston Guest, the society folk who hobnobbed with show folk. Judy had a dressing room, so she didn't sit with us; she was treated as the performer. She sang for about an hour, having rehearsed in the afternoon.

The following day the lavish ball was documented in all the appropriate columns. Judy had sung brilliantly and was appreciated accordingly, except for one peculiar element: Ann Warner reneged her mink coat offering. Instead of the golden carrot, Ann's secretary sent over a little note with two lines of thanks, accompanied by a small, square silver compact. Judy looked at it without emotion and said, "I'm going to give this to Judaline," sister Jimmie's daughter.

It was January 6, 1953. Judy was preparing to rehearse at the Starlight Roof when the tragic news reached us that Judy's mother had been found dead the previous day in the parking lot at Douglas Aircraft in Santa Monica. She had suffered a fatal heart attack as she stepped from her automobile on the way to work.

Cynically, I thought, my hothouse flower will need medication to fly back to Los Angeles for the funeral, where Susie and Jimmie awaited Baby Gumm. There wasn't time to take the train. I could only hope, whatever she took, it wouldn't trigger any episodes of depression. Judy opted for booze, and we flew home.

When it was revealed how her mother died, she felt exposed. She was not the daughter everyone thought she was, and Judy was concerned about her public image. The subject of "Mother" continued to be verboten between us. I had the job of seeding quotes to the press to diffuse the "cruel daughter" image: "It's true we did have some disagreements, but we were working out a trust fund for Mother" or "Mother didn't want to depend on me." Then came the articles: "Judy's Love for Mother Known Fact?" They said things like "What is not generally known is that Judy bought her mother a $40,000 home, in which she lived in L.A." The stories went on about how Judy sent Ethel a weekly check, how she bought her mother a new car, which her mother turned in for a secondhand jalopy. "Ethel's taking a job which she didn't need." A will was invented in which everything was left to Judy. "Judy always loved her mother."

All lies.

Susie had also tried to soften Judy on the subject of their mother. She never got anywhere. Judy may have worn dark glasses at her mother's funeral, but she did not shed a tear. I found her coldness mysterious. I was not about to trespass, but once again it struck me as severe. Inwardly, I thought, *Suppose everything Judy said about her mother was true. Is that enough to close Ethel out of her heart in such a consummate way?*

⸺ ✺ ⸺

After about a year in Beverly Hills, we were fortunate to purchase a wonderful Tudor-style house on Mapleton Drive in the Bel Air–Holmby Hills area of Los Angeles. Our neighbors were Bogie and Betty Bacall, and Lana Turner with varying husbands. At the time she was married to Lex Barker, who I thought was a big wimp.

Charlie Wick, who later became Ronald Reagan's communications expert, lived between the Bogarts and us. Bing Crosby, with his three boys, the holy terrors of Mapleton, was also our neighbor, but Crosby was very much a loner; he walked his black Labradors in the morning and the evening on schedule. Producer Aaron Spelling much later bought that property.

Joan Bennett and her husband Walter Wanger were down on the other side of Mapleton. Wanger was a fiery little guy who actually did time for shooting a man in the balls whom he suspected was after Joan. Art Linkletter and family lived opposite the Bogarts, but they rarely socialized. Some of our other neighbors were Hoagy Carmichael, Jane Withers, who had also been a child star, and the woman who owned the Broadway department stores, a large, lucrative chain in the Southwest. There was also Horace Dodge, the Chrysler heir who had married a chorus girl.

We were going to have drinks with Lana and Lex one evening when I ran into Lex in the late afternoon in the backyard. He leaned over the fence. "I understand we're coming over for cocktails?"

"Six thirty, Lex."

"I see Judy drives a Ford." He'd noticed the car in our garage. Lex went on to say how much Lana really wanted a new Cadillac. He thought a Chevy would be fine for running around the city, since he owned a custom-made Ferrari. "One expensive car is enough for the Barker family." I thought, that doesn't mesh with the Lana I know.

Later on, Lex and Lana marched over very happy. It seemed they'd recently returned from a wonderful trip to Italy and they were filled with travel stories. We were exchanging brisk small talk when I heard Lex say to Judy, "Do you like your Ford?"

"I don't drive it," Judy crisply answered.

Lana was quick to say, "Boy, I don't like Fords, I like Cadillacs." We knew what was on Lex's mind. A few days passed and we noticed Lana was driving a handsome blue four-door Seville.

Liza came to Mapleton to live with us—Judy would not request alimony—and so did my son Johnny for a brief period of time. I was "Dad" to Johnny and "Papa" to Liza. Dottie was gone, and now so was Tully; I organized outside staff to work for us instead of live-in help. Judy looked wonderful. She got her figure back and had returned to her vivacious and witty mode.

We were frequent guests now in the house that Jack built. Warner lived in a magnificent estate in the hills of Beverly Hills. Judy was Jack's star attraction at these sit-down dinners, expertly arranged by his majordomo, Richard Gully. Ann was never present at any of Jack's backstreet affairs. He always presented himself as a very married man, but the subtext was: the wife lived elsewhere.

As preparation continued on *A Star Is Born*, Judy had hoped E. Y. "Yip" Harburg, the writer of "Over the Rainbow," would write the lyrics for the film. To our dismay, he was blacklisted, and it wasn't going to be possible. This was a disappointment—Judy would have liked Yip to join the *Star* family. She settled for her old "relatives" Ira Gershwin and Harold Arlen. Judy was personally friendly with Cole Porter. She admired Cole but she didn't feel his music suited her style. She'd lean toward Ira but prefer Johnny Mercer. She adored Noël Coward and she selectively enjoyed singing his songs; she was entirely at home with Irving Berlin. She loved Berlin's lyrics, and the romance in Arlen's music, but her devotion was primarily to the song itself, rather than to the lyricist and/or the composer.

Life was full. We were invited to spend weekends with Jack and Mary Benny in Palm Springs. One weekend Jack invited golfer Ben Hogan and his wife to join us. Naturally, we spent the afternoon on the green. But Ben didn't schmooze. I was fascinated to see that he wasn't so competitive anymore, that his game had leveled off. Jack, as always, was funny and amusing. Ben held his silence. On about the sixteenth hole Jack got off his best drive. He wasn't that strong so the ball didn't go far, but it was a good shot. He looked at me and said, "What d'ya think of that?"

I said, "That's your best shot today, Jack."

He looked down the fairway and it was a long par five. He threw out his chest and said, "Ben, what'll get me home?" (Meaning, what club should I use for the shot?) We didn't expect Ben to say anything, but, speaking for the first time that day, he drawled, "Well, where d'ya live?" It was so corny both Jack and I fell down on the fairway laughing.

Judy was back at the house lounging around the pool with Mary and Gracie Allen and whomever else Mary had invited. Sometimes Claudette Colbert and her husband, who were close friends of the Bennys, would be there. Gracie was educated, politically savvy, as was Mary. Judy could always entertain them with her stories. She was an expert at certain kinds of shtick.

Judy presented herself as a very lighthearted, extroverted woman, and she did one bit better than anyone in Hollywood. She played two parts, alternating back and forth: the typical Hollywood starlet and the film producer. She'd mime, "You look like you might be another Marilyn Monroe?" and the starlet would answer, "I'm glad you think so," and the producer would say, "I hate Marilyn Monroe," and the starlet would answer, "I do too, I hate her," and the producer would say, "There are lot of other types you could be," and the starlet would say, "Yes, yes I know." And the producer would say, "I can't think of any of them," and the starlet would say, "I can't either." She'd perform this fast and furiously in different voices. She said, "That's Hollywood for you: nobody has an opinion." She loved that joke.

After our golf game with Hogan, George and Gracie, lifelong pals of the Bennys, joined us for dinner. A mere "hello" from George Burns could break Benny up. Jack told us a story about a trip they'd taken to New England with George and Gracie. The intimate group got up at the crack of dawn to see Vermont in an open touring car. The driver couldn't manage to pass a farmer driving a wagon with a load of hay— the road was a narrow one and the farmer refused to acknowledge he was blocking them. Finally, after many frustrated attempts and after trailing the wagon for what seemed like hours, the driver was able to maneuver the car out in front. The farmer looked down from his haystack just as they passed and said, "Good morning," to which George looked up and said, "Go fuck yourself."

Ed Sullivan was also a friend of the Bennys, and Jack would invite me to play golf with Ed whenever he visited California. Later Ed asked me to book Judy on his hit TV variety program. I made the decision that Judy would not appear on the show. I had a false idea about class, which may not have been professionally wise.

One sunny afternoon in Palm Springs we ran into Harold Arlen on the eighteenth tee whistling a tune he was working on for *A Star Is Born*. Judy piped up: "What's that?" As soon as we located the nearest piano Hal played the first eight bars of "The Man That Got Away." Judy knew it was right. She returned to Los Angeles really excited, and she became more and more enthusiastic about the project as we wound our way to the finish of preproduction. Moss Hart was the writer, George Cukor the director. Mary Ann Nyberg for costumes. The film was nearly cast, with the glaring exception of the male lead.

Around this time, Sinatra, absent a wife, returned to the States and to a great victory, one that turned his life around. He proved his talent by winning an Oscar for Best Supporting Actor in *From Here to Eternity*. He was reborn, and Judy and I were thrilled to see the transformation. Unfortunately, it wasn't going to change Jack Warner's mind, despite the fact that Frank had shown he wasn't "finished." In hindsight, Sinatra would have been ideal. The chemistry between Frank and Judy on camera and onstage was brilliant.

Frank wanted the part and took to bringing us gifts. One was an oil painting of a bullfighter, a beautiful rendering. I told Judy maybe it reminded him of his defunct marriage to Ava. He gifted me with a solid gold Cartier money clip.

Frank lived in the same building as his friend Swifty Lazar, the agent. These bachelors were impeccable! Their apartments were super clean. The bathrooms like operating amphitheaters, doilies everywhere. Frank hung out at our house a lot, frequently sleeping off the night on the couch. We introduced him to Bogie and Betty, and subsequently they became fast friends.

Judy envisioned Cary Grant playing the part of Norman Maine in *Star*. He was her preferred costar. Cary was as handsome offscreen as he was on. His looks were not a trick of the camera. He was a charming person who was intensely interested in the workings of the mind. He was fascinated by Judy's apparent rehabilitation. She had survived so much publicized emotional chaos. He would have liked it to be a result of psychiatry; alas, it was not. He was especially involved with modes of psychiatric therapies, especially LSD therapy, which he later discussed in articles. He read a great deal on the subject in his Benedict Canyon home, the one he lived in until his death. It must have amused Cary that when the property costs escalated in the 1970s, with his love of economy—you could say "lust" for it—he found himself sitting on millions. Cary, a mild-mannered, unpretentious person, never had to leave his nest: the birds came to him.

We earnestly began to romance Cary and his wife, Betsy Drake. We saw a great deal of one another. The four of us went out for supper several times a week. Of course, Cary knew we were wooing him. In the afternoon, Cary and I would visit the Hollywood Park racetrack. We alternated driving.

One day he merrily appeared at Mapleton in a brand-new Ford station wagon, announcing, "Henry [Ford] gave it to me for cost." He told me Henry had generously thrown in some extra chrome-plated exhausts. Cary was so ecstatic he offered to pay for the gas out to the track. I couldn't tell if he was conscious of his parsimonious nature and/ or its effect on others. In any case, he was consistently good natured. That day he also asked to pay for lunch. He was insisting. Usually I picked up the tab—but I recognized how good these two chrome-plated exhausts made him feel, somehow permitting him to be generous. Cary confided that when he was married to Barbara Hutton, the Woolworth heiress, she never allowed him to drive a station wagon—"too suburban for her tastes."

Cary, true to his character, never bet more than $10 per race. One time I bet $600 on a particular filly that was a 13:1 shot. When Cary saw that I won a lot of money, around $12,000, he was stunned. It was not real to him, almost sinful. I told him, "Cary I'm gonna bet this horse, Alleycat." It was 50:1. "You ought to place a bet." Cary, who had finished with his eight races, said, "Sid, don't bet anymore. If you bet, I won't do your picture." It was said half in jest. I laughed and went to the window to bet $50 on Alleycat. I actually won the race but told Cary I didn't bet as I pocketed the profits.

The day came when it was my turn to drive out to the racetrack and pay for the gas. At the end of the day I took Cary home. He said, "Come in Sid, have a drink, say hello to Betsy." Once inside the house, he said, "We only have tequila." I said, "Fine, I like tequila." Cary explained tequila was the only liquor besides wine that was kept in the house. I thought, *There's a story here*, and sure enough it unfolded. We were seated around their kitchen table, drinking. Cary said, "My gardener has relatives in Tijuana. When he visits he brings me back cases of tequila at thirty-six cents a case. Isn't that wonderful?" He was just too excited about saving money. I thought maybe it made him feel like a regular joe.

Was Cary going to portray Norman Maine? He never discussed the issue with me. I was hoping to catch him off the record, even postponing the time we'd say good-bye, hoping to find more opportunity to influence him. He was too busy talking about saving pennies. Now Cary was explaining how he'd invite me for dinner but . . . "Sid, Betsy ordered only two shad roe. Next time—please forgive."

We had another day at the racetrack, and it was my turn to pick up the lunch tab. I could never go wrong here. Cary was too careful an eater. He was focused on diet and longevity way before it became a national fad.

Maybe I shouldn't have lied to Cary when I bet on Alleycat, because in the end Cary did not play the part of Norman Maine. George Chasin, Cary's agent at MCA, demanded $300,000 against 10 percent of the gross. Grant was one of the few actors who worked outside of the studio system, something unheard of in Hollywood. And Cary always got what Chasin asked for. Jack Warner, who perceived actors as robots/slaves, gave his familiar laugh of contempt to Chasin's request; he agreed to raise his fee from $300,000 to $400,000, but the percentage was out of the question. Chasin insisted on the original fee arrangement. Jack would not acquiesce, and once again I entertained thoughts of Bogie, or to find a way to convince Jack about Frank.

I lost touch with Cary over the years, and then four months before he died, he came up to my table at Matteo's, a popular, long-standing Hollywood eatery on Westwood Boulevard. He was his usual polite, charming, unassuming self. He embraced me; he was warm, genuine. No mention of economies.

27

Moss Hart was in New York writing *A Star Is Born*. Judy would ring him to ask how the work was going. Writers are usually bugged by people inquiring after their work in progress, but Moss was continually gracious to Judy's nudges. "Just you wait," would be his enthusiastic response. Judy kept to her positive outlook. There was, of course, no mention of her mother's death. She immersed herself in the anticipation of *Star*, domestic affairs—the children and me.

Principal photography was scheduled for the fall of 1953. By the end of April, I'd been working nonstop. I knew it was time for a break. Governor Lawrence Wetherby's invitation was just the ticket. I was looking forward to visiting the renowned breeding farms in Kentucky's lush bluegrass country so favorable to thoroughbreds. The limestone soil provided ideal pastures, enhancing the animals' bones. Judy and I were invited to stay at the Circle M stud farm owned by Pug Moore, whose husband had died—she continued breeding the horses. As far as I was concerned, it was a horseman's dream. But we would first make a stopover in West Virginia, where, coincidentally, Charlie Cushing had invited Judy and me to join the Duke and Duchess of Windsor and friends at the posh White Sulphur Springs resort.

Once again we rode the railways in a state of benign suspension. We talked, watched the scenery, played cards, Judy still in her wholesome mode, her personality bright. We chugged along, happy to be together away from work and household. The bathroom was right in our bed-room compartment, so it was easy to monitor Judy for pills. I relaxed. Judy was playful, charming, as though the darkness had never occurred. We were traveling on a rail line owned by Robert R. Young, one of the Windsors' pals, who later stuck a double-barrel shotgun in his mouth and blew his head off when he was down to his "last $18 million." A small, charming man, Young would be among the crowd we were meeting in White Sulphur Springs. His wife was Anita O'Keefe Young, painter Georgia O'Keefe's sister. Anita styled herself after the Duchess of Windsor—the jewels, the hair, the clothes. Wallis had many imitators.

At White Sulphur Springs we stayed in an elegant suite. Judy wanted me to guide her in the fashion department. Every night we dined in formal wear. Designer Hattie Carnegie had her dress form, and Judy would order something simple in black or dark blue to show off her luminous skin. So Judy was elegantly robed, with her trusty three-string pearl choker securely fastened around her neck. I played golf daily, while Judy read or took walks with Wallis and Anita Young. The women would encourage Judy to tell anecdotes about Hollywood. These people were starstruck. And Judy was a superb storyteller. In this way she continued to be center stage. At dinner Judy held court with movie and vaudeville stories, and her preferred fans could not get enough. I'd get turned on by watching Judy exaggerate a little here, put out a bit more there. She was, in fact, giving a marvelous performance that seemed to be just a chat.

I would be seated next to Wallis while Judy was at the Duke's side. The Duchess was quite talky herself, usually about world affairs. Socially she had an extremely positive kind of personality. I was used to her dialogue, clipped and witty. The Duke in his thin voice equally enjoyed conversation. His eyes were a pale, slightly watery blue. He enjoyed cham-pagne; however, he never drank in excess. The Duke would not be caught off his guard, nor would the Duchess.

One evening at the table, Wallis wore a simple red dress and black satin low-heeled pumps. Pinned to her shoulder was one of her bejeweled tigers. The women were pale, unlike the California types. Judy fit in. We were about to be served a soufflé for dessert. So Judy dredged up a story about a soufflé. The gist of it was how producer Arthur Hornblow Jr. and his wife were invited to composer Johnny Green's house for dinner. Both men were gourmets and competitive about cooking. Hornblow was rather pretentious, wanting to appear aristocratic, while Green kept his Academy Awards lined up in the hall, hitting you in the face the moment you entered the house. Judy set the scene, how Johnny had prepared this lush chocolate soufflé for dessert, topped with an elaborate marshmallow meringue. At the appropriate moment, Green, about to serve the confection from a highly polished silver tureen, tripped. Judy got up to demonstrate how the soufflé whooshed all over Arthur Hornblow's face and shoulders.

The only person I've known who could upstage Judy was Maurice Chevalier. But he was also her devoted fan ("The Queen of Song"), so she never felt topped. She respected his work and was a master at imitating him. She'd find a bowl in the kitchen to mimic Chevalier's straw hat, shrug her shoulders in an exaggerated manner, throw out her lower lip and sing, "Every little breeze seems to whisper 'Louise' . . ." She was a very funny Maurice Chevalier. Judy knew all the vaudeville turns. She loved to drop her eyelid over an open eye and look directly at me, particularly at formal dinner parties. Judy could make ordinary events seem funny. In this sense she was never boring.

We left the bluebloods for another kind of thoroughbred, the kind I preferred. We settled in comfortably at the Circle M, and later in the afternoon Judy rehearsed with an orchestra in preparation for Judy Garland Day. The following night at the Louisville stadium, Judy performed for over an hour. The concert was a tremendous success. After the performance, Judy declined invitations to various parties. We returned to the ranch, where we had a wonderful supper and went to bed. Judy slept well. It didn't occur to me until much later there had not been a specific party to honor Judy. After all, the event was called Judy Garland Day.

The next morning was Kentucky Derby Day. I got up early to look at Pug's yearlings. When I returned to our room Judy announced, "Darling, I don't want to go out to Churchill Downs. Forgive me."

Judy convinced me she was eager to rest far from the crowd, to enjoy a bucolic day. This certainly was in character, so I didn't try to persuade her to come along.

There were twenty people aboard Pug's chartered bus. Ted Law arrived just in time. It was going to be one hell of a day. We'd made our bets in advance of arriving at the Derby. Everyone aboard the bus had their programs ready. I sat with my friend Charlie Wacker, who bred racehorses, and we talked horses and drank. I didn't think about Judy; I wasn't worried.

It was the first Saturday in May, and the Derby, an event for three-year-old thoroughbreds, was the eighth race out of ten at Churchill Downs. I noticed a horse called Witch's Brew trained by Horatio Luro in the last race. At the track I ran into a fellow from L.A. and commented, "I see the program has a horse owned by a Charles Walker. Isn't that *Wacker*?" The man said, "You discovered it!" It was actually an error. I figured it out: Charlie came down to bet on his horse. He didn't let it slip while we were riding the bus that in fact he'd shipped Witch's Brew from New York to Kentucky to run on Derby Day.

It was a simple mistake that I figured Charlie must be ecstatic over—an opportunity to pull off an enormous betting coup. I was now looking excitedly to that race rather than the actual Derby. I bet $700 on Witch's Brew.

The Derby favorite was Native Dancer, a horse owned by Al Vanderbilt. Native Dancer was a star. He had become a household name as the great TV public curiously enjoyed watching him race on television.

The design of Churchill Downs requires a horse to run through a tunnel of noise in the homestretch, and this can shatter the nerves of the most stoic horses. That day, I was to witness an upset similar to the one Man O' War lost that I'd tried to simulate in Saratoga. It was a horse called Dark Star who wore the winner's blanket of roses in this most prestigious race, and not the country's favorite, Native Dancer.

But the final race went to Witch's Brew. I returned to Circle M elated. It was my first Kentucky Derby and I'd won big. Everyone was celebrating by drinking Kentucky's famous mint juleps: eight-year-old bourbon with fresh mint picked at dawn.

The first thing Judy greeted me with was that she didn't feel like going out that evening either. Our moods were quite the opposite. I said, "Darling, not feeling so hot?"

"I'll stay here. Better."

"Baby, look, they were wrong—you deserved a party." I thought she might acknowledge Governor Wetherby's oversight—maybe let off some steam.

"I hadn't thought of that" was her cool, rather annoyed reply. I was determined not to let her off, so I continued to talk her into going out with me, and she began to weaken. Finally she said, "OK. All right" and excused herself to dress. I changed my clothes and poured myself a drink. I was beginning to relax, looking forward to the evening, when Judy made an extraordinary entrance: she'd covered her face with grotesque and crazy painted makeup. After the initial shock I realized she looked hilariously funny. Not sad. We fell down laughing until our sides ached.

"You really don't want to go out!" We laughed some more.

"Darling, go ahead," she urged, giving me permission. "Celebrate." So off I went to the party with my pals.

I got back to the farm around two in the morning. Pug was waiting for me.

"Sid, we've had a time with Judy. We had to call a doctor." Pug explained that Judy was hysterical, that the doctor sedated her. "She'd been sobbing and screaming. We didn't know what to do. We didn't know where to find you. She's sleeping now."

A chill ran through my body. I rushed to see Judy. Pug had said she was deep asleep. The term "sedated" left me no peace. I stayed at Judy's side, awake for the night, watching, guarding. I'd never experienced Judy sobbing profusely as Pug described. In fact, she had said, "uncontrollably, burying her head repeatedly in the pillow." I thought maybe it was some sort of delayed reaction to her mother's death. It couldn't be the Wetherby letdown? Then again it was hard for Judy to overcome slights. And in this case she might have felt she'd been used. It was becoming clearer, but not very encouraging.

Judy awakened the next day extremely depressed, a predictable reaction to certain medications. I decided to pack up and leave. When we arrived at the railway station Judy started to weep. I was as tender as possible. Judy admitted she didn't know what it was, and the tears continued. We were without a reservation for a compartment, and the coach was packed. We sat with everyone else in the two seats assigned to us. This proved to be disastrous. I didn't know what was going on with Judy. She continued to sob. I was bewildered. Nor was I able to see her calming down or getting a grip on herself. Now I was totally cut off, unable to reach her. I held her close, and every so often she'd emit a yell. I began to rack my brain. I thought her voice had sounded kind of raspy at the Louisville stadium. I attributed it to a slight case of laryngitis. It occurred to me she may have needed something, a boost to get out onstage, and taken something behind my back. She sang well, but there hadn't been the usual pristine clarity to her voice. How and where did she hide those pills?

I sat holding her and I thought, this is still my learning process about Judy. It was odd: she was not mad at me, she did not push me away, she just kept sobbing.

Winfrey, Al Vanderbilt's trainer's sister, happened to be on the train, in a private compartment with a friend. She came and offered us her compartment. Once we got inside, Judy said, "Get me a drink. Something. I'm so low. I've got to come out of this." Luckily, Winfrey had a flask and generously offered up her whiskey. Within an hour, Judy's condition disappeared. By nine o'clock her behavior had changed. We easily got off the train in Chicago to make the connection home.

During the ride back to California, however, the "Judy wall" was up and heavily guarded. I couldn't ask her where she hid the pills. It bothered me that I didn't see them. Judy's hidden stash must have interacted with the "sedation" given by Pug's physician, thus creating the nightmare.

Judy looked so well, her figure had come back, she was so pretty. I kept thinking, *How can this happen?* She can't be under constant surveillance, yet the situation seemed to call for it. In the back of my mind I began to feel like Mr. In Charge was not so in control. I wished so much for Judy to make it. Somewhere in Kansas, while "Dorothy" slept, lulled by the steady motion of the train, I allowed myself a tear.

As I watched the dark and light flatlands roll by under a low, starry sky, I reached back into childhood and made a wish. "Starlight, star bright, first star I see tonight, I wish I may, I wish I might, have the wish I wish tonight."

28

O UR HOUSE ON MAPLETON DRIVE was originally built by producer Hunt Stromberg Sr. The home was constructed of gray and yellow stone, a two-story, five-bath, five-bedroom palatial Tudor spread that cried out for elaborate furnishings. We didn't have the funds yet to decorate accordingly. I began building retaining walls in our 330-foot-long backyard, which disappeared over a narrow decline. The yard had to be leveled to install a swimming pool.

I often felt like a ship's captain, with a crew of thirteen plus my family: Johnny, who was frequently with us, Judy, Liza, and Lorna. Our house was a castle, fit for a princess and her consort. There were two dens; I appropriated the one in the front of the house off the large sunporch for a home office. The living room was a grand space with a vaulted ceiling and fireplaces. I had purchased a gleaming black enameled Steinway concert grand for Judy. I was told Vladimir Horowitz had played this piano in concert when he visited Los Angeles. Other than the piano, the room was near empty, with Johnny's trains in one corner on top of a Ping-Pong table, a few formal chairs, and a rug. The dining room was decorated. For our table I'd found a magnificent bronze base with turquoise patina in San Francisco and ordered a black-and-green-granite slab for the tabletop, large enough to comfortably seat twelve. The chairs were upholstered Mediterranean Italian renaissance style, and the rug was a rich gold. Venetian blackamoor statues stood at attention. We were living in a god's realm with delusions of grandeur. We'd laugh and blame it on the house: "The house cries out for opulence!" "We can't let the house down."

—————— ✥ ——————

The next significant Fred in my life was Fred Pobirs, the doctor who had ordered the shock treatments for Judy at MGM during preproduction for *Annie Get Your Gun*. At that time, Judy had been sinking into a depression as a result of her substance abuse, and unfortunately, she was perceived as having other kinds of psychological problems not necessarily related to drugs. Experimentation with electroshock was fashionable, and Judy, disturbed and deeply unhappy, had allowed herself to undergo shock therapy. I came to believe that these treatments had physiologically harmed her. She was not able to pull herself together, and in fact, they were the prelude to the Peter Bent Brigham hospitalization and Judy leaving MGM in 1950. Pobirs, nonetheless, was part of the old showbiz family. He was a familiar face, and he lived near Mapleton Drive.

After we returned from Kentucky, Judy periodically experienced intense migraine headaches. She had been prescribed the barbiturates Seconal and Nembutal, but sometimes these were not effective, in which case she'd make an emergency call around 3:00 AM to Dr. Pobirs for help. Pobirs walked in quick steps. He would arrive in his bathrobe and slippers, carrying his medical bag. He would closet himself with Judy, give her an injection, and she'd be knocked out. Judy appeared to have recovered from the depression she suffered in Louisville—but not completely. There were nights she would be unable to sleep and she'd retire alone to the bed-sitting-room. I would sleep in a guest room.

I was out of the house most of the time working on preproduction. *Star* was scheduled to start shooting in October 1953. As much as Judy wanted the film, she craved ongoing attention from me, and this devotion was tested: phone calls to the office not to exchange jokes but to challenge my punctuality—"What time will you be home?" There were no harsh words, and Judy busied herself with the children, but the occasional bouts with headaches and the PMS episodes had Pobirs in our house more than I would have desired. Fred was a small, slender man, with a pleasant face, kind eyes, and an impressive moustache, but he was basically humorless, matter of fact. In all the years he administered to Judy, he would never send a bill. Both he and his wife attended our parties and seemed to enjoy the company of celebrities. He'd enjoyed a highly successful practice for years, so he didn't need to meet anyone; he had a good time mixing with his patients. Sadly, he was to end his life by suicide.

One morning around 5:00 AM I was awakened by the smell of smoke. I ran into the master bedroom and the place was ablaze. We had not yet redecorated and the old furnishings, the chaise lounge, and the silk drapes were on fire. Flames leaped from the French windows. I pulled Judy out of bed and called the fire department. Lorna, Liza, and the nurse were quickly taken out of the house. Judy had dozed off on the chaise, allowing her cigarette to fall, then made her way to the bed, where she'd passed out. The fire raged, leaving charred furniture, peeling paint, the blackout curtain a pile of embers. For Christ's sake, our lives were in danger.

There were some absurd aspects to this crisis. Hunt Stromberg, the house's previous owner, had a habit of lighting his tobacco with wooden kitchen matches. He'd had a few incidents in which he would cavalierly throw matches onto the floor, where they'd continued to burn. Consequently, the house was equipped with a fire hose, but it turned out to be useless. Stromberg was renowned for his carelessness, having once thrown a match onto the floor of his office during a meeting with Hedy Lamarr. While they talked, Hedy's skirt caught on fire.

Judy was on bad pills. I'd been patient, hoping she'd stop on her own. The responsibility of preparing *A Star Is Born* had begun to intensify, and I needed to feel secure about Judy once we began principal photography. Now, the fire compelled me to act.

I hit on a plan. Judy loved the tango—it was one of the pleasures we shared. Whenever we walked into a club, if the orchestra didn't strike up "Over the Rainbow," the musicians played a tango. Judy would immediately say, "Come dance with me." The tango can be so easily mocked if the dancer's attitude is not exactly right, but Judy never turned it into a parody. For us it was romantic and serious. I asked Judy to dine at Romanoff's with Cary and Betsy Grant. Judy was still intent on wooing Cary for the male lead in *Star*; here was an opportunity. "Prince" Mike Romanoff knew how to cater to the Hollywood socialites, who were for the most part also his personal friends. Mike and his charming wife Gloria became part of the Mapleton gang. His fabled restaurant was neatly tucked behind the Beverly Wilshire Hotel in Beverly Hills. Romanoff adored Judy and gave her the kind of ego attention she craved. "You're some kind of dame!" was one of his best compliments.

Our dinner at Romanoff's was splendid. Judy looked wonderful, and she was on her best behavior. Afterward we visited a nightclub that featured tango music. It was a glamorous, intimate evening, and when we returned to Mapleton, instead of immediately making love, we talked. It was the one of the very few times that Judy spoke directly to me about her dependency. I explained how we must protect ourselves during the shooting of *Star*, the importance of her work, and how everything depended on her as the principal artist. Judy asked what I thought would be the best route for her to take. I loved her for that. I told her I was betting on Judy reaching into herself, discovering her weaknesses, and changing.

Judy's ancient excuse, "What can you do when you get so exhausted you can't sleep, but you know you've got to sleep to face that camera early in the morning?" had been put out to pasture when I arranged a late call for her in the contract. I'd outlined everything in her favor, and Jack had accepted our terms. However, he certainly wasn't going to be understanding if she should fuck up. I had to find a fail-safe measure. So I came up with the idea to employ Pobirs. Judy listened intently.

I suggested a wonderful woman named Margaret Gundy to be Judy's companion. Gundy was a nurse who was extremely intelligent and understanding. She had a sense of humor, and Judy had known her at MGM and respected her. "Gundy'll come aboard," I said, and I added, "So will Pobirs. Fred can oversee your medication needs, keep you on an even keel. No sleepless nights or any painful periods." I was seducing her with maintenance doses, enabling her to keep her crutches. She wouldn't have to walk on her two legs yet.

Again Judy said she wanted to do whatever was necessary to bring *Star* off. Whatever I asked, she'd cooperate. She was milk and honey. I genuinely believed I would bypass any toxic reaction if Pobirs monitored her intake. But she did add, "Darling, you know how well I want to look for you in front of the lens. I can't be fat."

"Baby, you don't need to take off that much weight. Watch your diet, you'll be fine. Trust me."

"Aw, you're an old flatfoot."

"I'm a good tango dancer, don't forget that."

Judy was admitting her shortcomings. I began to believe that this new display of self-awareness would pave the way to a sober life. She gave me a tremendous sense of optimism. Meanwhile, I would treat her as a diabetic or anyone on maintenance medication. In hindsight, I was enabling—a lesser version of what MGM had blatantly and inhumanely jammed down her throat.

———— ᐇᐇᐇ ————

When Cary Grant's agent took him out of contention for the part of Norman Maine, we turned instead to James Mason. He had to be persuaded to take the part, but unlike with Cary, the issue wasn't the money.

Mason's vivacious wife, Pamela, told me that James was not interested in remakes. He was against the practice on principle. She said, "James thought *A Star Is Born* was perfect with Janet Gaynor and Fredric March." I argued, "Remember, it wasn't a musical version."

Mason was represented by Jack Gordean, a partner at the Charles Feldman Agency. Gordean was an agent who'd been interested in representing me; he had arranged my screen test at Warner Bros. when I working for Douglas Aircraft. He knew James had a tremendous affection for Judy and her talent, so he talked Pamela into reading the script with the hope she'd persuade her husband to say yes. James adored vaudeville and musical films, and Pam had said he would have loved to have been a musical actor.

Mason, who came from a proper North England family, was educated to be an architect. Judy and I admired him, and I came to think he was one of the best film actors in cinema history. Pam had an appetite for Hollywood, unlike James, who remained detached from the general social activity of the movie colony. She would read his contracts and his scripts, cue his lines, and was in general central to his career. She told me that in England the stories running around the studios were either that she carried James's script because she was so jealous she was afraid somebody would talk to him, or that James kept her as a slave, forcing her to carry his scripts.

Finally Pam convinced James. "After all," she said, "Judy is one of the public darlings."

Judy had been determined to look like a "movie star"—she wanted to be camera slim. It was that old bugaboo. I reiterated there was no need to be any thinner. Whenever she began to drop considerable weight it was dangerous, signaling an unhealthy use of pills—though, as I was about to learn, any use of pills was unhealthy. Judy was naturally high-strung and overactive; it would seem she should not have to resort to uppers. Her excuse, of course, was the weight issue, when in fact she was dependent. And the dependency was not about losing weight, it was about keeping her spirits up, giving her an emotional boost. She confessed it was virtually impossible for her to sustain a work mode in front of the cameras without taking some kind of medication.

But I believed I had blocked out all the drops and falls and covered them. Gundy, the nurse, would arrive at 8:00 AM to help prepare Judy for the ride to the studio, at which time I would already be on the lot. I offered Pobirs two points of the film in exchange for his services, and he accepted. Both Gundy and Pobirs checked with me daily. I'd find out how she was doing: OK? Not so OK? If Judy called Pobirs, he'd contact me to help determine whether she was scoring outside medication.

Pobirs's participation did ensure the smooth work habits Judy exhibited throughout the rigors of the making of a difficult film. Also on the positive side, she was surrounded by surrogate family once again: Harold Arlen; Ira and Gershwin and his wife, Lee; Moss and Kitty Hart, who had been friends since she was married to Minnelli. James Mason was also a friend, having made his first American film, *Madame Bovary*, with Minnelli as the director. Jack Carson, who played Libby in *Star*, was an ex-vaudevillian, and Judy had played on the same bill with him when she was nine years old. The dances were created by Richard Barstow, another "relative," and it was Judy who recommended the art director, Malcolm Bert.

With her remarkable gifts, Judy was able to study a script on the ride out to the studio and have it memorized by the time she arrived. She easily learned the choreography as well. My little princess was indeed no ordinary mortal.

Away from the studio, we'd relaxed into a warm relationship with Bogie and Betty Bogart. Bogie loved to bait people when he was drinking; when we first met, he approached me and started to nudge me about being a "tough guy." I responded by picking him up and pinning his arms behind his back. He thought that was hysterically funny. He didn't weigh more than 135 pounds—a slender man with a large head on a slight frame. He was a sailor and he'd developed big forearms from working on his beloved sailboat, *Santana*. He was muscled like Popeye. His hands were expressive, and he smoked Camels like a fellow who worked the docks in Marseilles. Bogie's face was marked with lines, and he ate next to nothing; his stomach was flat as a pancake. He preferred to smoke and drink.

Bogie was in his fifties and yet still smoldered on screen. In the film *Sabrina*, from the Broadway hit *Sabrina Fair*, his character wins Audrey Hepburn's character from his young, handsome brother, played by William Holden, and you want it to end that way. Bogie was a brilliant actor but never a brilliant fighter. Occasionally his verbal jibe would backfire, but he certainly wasn't putting anyone away with his punches.

Bogie stone sober was a sweet and gentle man. Unpretentious, he liked eggs for dinner. He'd be in and out of our house: "Got a beer, Luft?"

Bogie also loved his kids. He was a warm guy who liked his whiskey and was politically keen. He hated Jack Warner. He said, "I'd rather work for a crude son of a bitch like Harry Cohn any day of the week; at least you know where you stand. Jack Warner you can't believe." By the end of the decade, Bogie would succumb to cancer. Warner, who actually admired Bogie, came to visit him at home shortly before he died.

One night Betty gave an elegant black tie affair. It was Betty's big night, with an orchestra, a tent, valet parking, the typical Hollywood-style bash. And it was a gorgeous Southern California night, silky, with lots of stars in the firmament and on the ground. Caviar and champagne were flowing. After the sit-down dinner the men gravitated inside to the Bogarts' comfortable den: Spencer Tracy, Gary Cooper, Sinatra, David Niven, Charlie Feldman, Keenan Wynn, among others. Bogie, in his cups, decided to put me on. "Sid, what makes you think you can be a producer?" He was giving it to me in front of the inner circle. The men, deadpan, smoked their cigars and sipped their cognac. Nobody cracked. I was rather soused, and it struck me as hilarious that Bogie was taking this opportunity to test my mettle. Had I not been as drunk as I was I might have figured out a more appropriate response, one fitting to the environment, but having caught on to Bogie's game I couldn't resist blurting out, "I got more fucking class than any cocksucker or motherfucker in this room." My obscene outburst left Bogie howling with laughter, along with his guests. He was amused by unconventional behavior. I got so drunk that night, I passed out in the den with my head wedged under a bookshelf. When I was discovered the next morning they were afraid I'd been decapitated.

Another time, on a September night sultry with Santa Ana winds, Bogie and Betty were entertaining Richard and Sybil Burton around their pool. Bogie had been drinking heavily and he kind of took off on me. I said, "Fuck you, I'm going home." He was too drunk, so I left. The next day he was over: "Got a beer?" It wasn't serious; I'd known that the night before.

Gossip columnist Sheilah Graham caught on to the hijinks, the "fun" gatherings of the Bogarts and the Lufts. When Bogie took Judy and me into the fold, Graham couldn't stop writing about the "Rat Pack." Judy knew Bogie and Betty from Lee and Ira Gershwin, and Bogie knew Lee Strunsky Gershwin from the Greenwich Village days in New York, when she and her sisters had open house every Sunday. It was there he had met his good friend "Prince" Mike Romanoff, a.k.a. Harry Gerguson of the Bronx, whom he hung out with and enjoyed. Connections were made and kept.

Mike and Gloria Romanoff, David and Hjordis Niven, and Swifty Lazar were part of the pack. Fringe members were Charlie Lederer and his wife, and Charlie Feldman, along with his friend Capucine, the model/actress. Betty refers to the group in her memoir, *By Myself:* "Spence [Spencer Tracy] was only an honorary rat because he lived a secluded life, but his heart was in the right place." And as Betty recalled the place was "addicted to nonconformity, staying up late, drinking and laughing, and not caring what anyone thought or said about us."

The press turned the Rat Pack into an inner sanctum more elite than the Hillcrest Country Club, where to belong you essentially only needed the cash. In actuality our group didn't care if you were rich or not. Some years later the media readopted the Rat Pack term and applied it to Sinatra and friends; the new group, largely a public relations invention, included Peter Lawford, Dean Martin, Sammy Davis Jr., Peter Falk, and Joey Bishop.

29

WE SHOT THE FIRST SEVEN DAYS of *A Star Is Born* in WarnerScope, a lens Jack Warner had hoped would compete with 20th Century Fox's successful CinemaScope. Unfortunately, the WarnerScope lens had not been perfected enough to work well. There was a distortion, a squeezing of the image. CinemaScope, technically, was far superior. We'd shot for a week at a cost of $100,000 a day, with the entire crew on salary. One look at the rushes and we agreed we had to scrap it. Alperson and I were able to convince Jack to set up a screening at 20th Century Fox of three films in CinemaScope. Jack admitted there was no comparison.

While the set was temporarily closed down we took the opportunity to change costume designers. The costumes Mary Ann Nyberg had designed for Judy were not flattering. We replaced Nyberg with Jean Louis. I also realized that our cinematographer, Winton Hoch, didn't grasp the concept of the film, so I hired Sam Leavitt, who replaced Winnie as director of photography. Leavitt had been a second assistant operator at MGM and was now an independent; he'd already had the experience of working on several of Judy's films.

We only had to reshoot one sequence: "The Man That Got Away." I convinced Moss Hart to consult with another writer on the lot about cutting down the section in which Judy (Esther/Vicki) first meets James (Norman Maine). The section was too talky, long and boring. I thought it impeded the momentum of the film. I also found a couple other sequences too static: the action of singing then moving from the night-club and through the kitchen to the parking lot when James convinces Judy to quit the band, and the audition at the studio.

Meanwhile, Louis B. Mayer contacted me regarding a property he believed was perfect for Judy. He thought I might be interested in buying the rights to a play, *The Painted Wagon*. Mendel Silberberg, a lawyer we had in common, set up a breakfast meeting so we could talk it over. Louis greeted me with the now-familiar "Sid, you've created a miracle. The one we couldn't." He continued, "We never should have let Judy go. We believed the three psychiatrists who didn't think she'd make it through the year."

I was not about to confess to Mayer I'd already been on shaky ground regarding Judy's pill dependency. I was confident we were going to ride these destructive habits out to pasture. I knew she'd kick them forever. I thought of the three beautiful children gracing our lives, a gorgeous home, a public who heaped accolades on my wife, a great film before the cameras. Hadn't Judy acknowledged her dependency and expressed a desire to conquer the demons? What was there to worry about?

I knew enough about Louis B. Mayer that he didn't have to fill me in on much. His first wife, Margaret, had been in and out of Austen Riggs Center in Stockbridge, Massachusetts. She was a victim of dieting, desiring to stay skinny to compete with the young women Mayer was around all the time. When Margaret was away Louis would show up at the popular Trocadero supper club to dance away the evening: "Dancing is an excellent cure for insomnia." Eventually Louis met Lorena Danker. He sold his racehorses to make a divorce settlement with Margaret and then married Lorena.

Louis, who began as a humble immigrant from Russia, had an intense patriotism that earned MGM millions in the 1940s. His assistant Ida Koverman had once been Herbert Hoover's secretary. Mayer was entrenched in Republican politics. He was a snob who admired the

English upper classes, the very stratum of society that is traditionally anti-Semitic.

There's no question that MGM was the grand studio, with the best commissary in town, the most powerful police force (its chief was Mayer's best man when he married Lorena). Mayer was king—and Judy had been his court pet. Her deference to paternal figures had given him an aura of stern authority. And I'm told that he behaved no differently with Lorena's daughter from another marriage. L.B. was a strict stepfather, and his moral code paid off, as the young girl became a nun. His own two daughters were amazing women: Irene and Edith (Edie) both lived distinguished lives. Edie was considered the greatest hostess in Hollywood.

I told Mayer I would read the play and discuss it with Judy. Judy said, "Not *The Painted Wagon*, Sid." I had to agree.

———— ✵ ————

The original concept for *Star* included twenty-five minutes of music. By Cukor's admission he was not a director of musicals—he was not a Vincente Minnelli. And so Judy's production numbers were directed by the choreographer, Richard Barstow. Cukor was happy with Judy's work; he thought she was a revelation in her emotional scenes. He said, "She manages to get the same thrilling quality . . . that she does when she's singing a song." And it was a tour de force for Judy, as she appeared in every scene.

George Cukor's directorial style often involved milking a scene. This didn't intrude until about halfway through the film. Everything was going wonderfully; everyone was working hard. It never occurred to me that it could be a problem. Alperson loved the rushes, as did both Jack and Harry. Then Judy, Alperson, Cukor, and I looked at the booth scene. We all agreed it was monotonous. There were four pages, primarily dialogue between Judy's character, Esther/Vicki, and James's Norman Maine, at the Downbeat Club, and it dragged on. I called Moss. "Judy and Mason are in the goddamn booth talking and talking. I'm starting to yawn."

Moss said, "Cut the goddamn thing, then. It's too long."

"George won't cut it." Cukor didn't want to step on Moss's toes—he thought everything Moss wrote was a jewel. He didn't want Moss Hart saying one day, "You cut my scene."

"*You* cut it," Moss suggested.

"I'm not a writer. How about a guy I know on the lot? He's capable."

"Good, get him."

The one other disagreement I had with Cukor was over the color of the walls in a scene. He wanted red to match Judy's outfit, and I had to say that I never saw studio walls painted red. I overruled that detail.

I didn't make it a habit of hanging around the set when Judy was working. To be honest, I didn't want to see my wife in a love scene with another man. I was childish. Husbands of other actresses sometimes enjoy watching their wives kissed by other men; it turns them on. Somehow my possessive streak got irrationally kindled. Judy knew that about me, so it was more comfortable for her if I didn't show up.

The maintenance medication was a success. Judy was cooperative, working without letup. There were long stretches of time when she didn't take any pills at all. I was proud of her. It looked like we were going to pull it off. Judy had said to Gundy, "I love my husband so—I'm such a weakling," and Gundy had encouraged her to try AA. A hairdresser suggested Narcotics Anonymous, then in its infancy. I had every reason now to believe that Judy was anxious to kick her habits forever.

When Judy schmoozed with Kay Thompson, Lee Gershwin, or any one of her friends, she could easily disclose sensitive information. I realized I had to be mindful about what I told Judy, especially regarding business. She'd confide in a friend or even a stranger and then forget what she'd said. She'd talk to everyone but not her husband. Judy played out a yarn about how much patience I'd had with her: "I don't know how he puts up with me." And it got back to me. It was complimentary but out of character.

I had to be particularly careful when I discovered a big hole in Moss's script. The score encompassed standards—"When My Sugar Walks Down the Street," "I'll Get By," etc.—ingeniously put together to tell a story, but there was no musical number to transform Vicki within the storyline. The audience needed to see why she became a star. The gap occurred when Vicky Lester and her husband/mentor Norman Maine attend the premiere of Vicky's first starring film. There's a shout of elation from the audience, and suddenly the couple are seen leaving the theater without witnessing any of Vicky Lester's talent. I privately came to the conclusion I'd better find someone other than Moss Hart to write a musical number linking these two scenes.

I went directly to Roger Edens without saying a word to Judy, for fear my concerns would leak out before I was able to put together a solution. Judy would be informed at the appropriate time. Within the week Roger called me. "I think I've got something. Can you drive over to my house in the Palisades?"

He had outlined the song called "Born in a Trunk." He played the first eight bars. It was a bookend for a miniature bio of an artist going from unknown to discovery to stardom. It was, in fact, the story of Judy's life.

He wrote the big musical number with his companion, Lenny Gershe, an aspiring writer. But Roger was making three other films at the time, under contract to MGM. It was fine for him to write the opening for Judy at the Palace, but to write a piece of material for a competing film company was legally not possible. I went along with Roger's request to have Lenny receive sole credit, so the sequence known as "Born in a Trunk" was attributed to Gershe. Lenny went on to write the film *Funny Face* starring Fred Astaire, produced by Roger. He also wrote the hit Broadway play *Butterflies Are Free*. We agreed that I would pay Lenny $10,000 in cash; Roger requested an elaborately hand-carved chest of drawers belonging to Judy, who'd never liked the piece. The chest, a present from Vincente when they were married, no doubt brought back memories, so it was stationed out in the hall. In this way it was I, not Warner, who bought what would become the "Born in a Trunk" segment outright.

Ira Gershwin and Harold Arlen were not composers and writers of special revue material. Roger Edens was the master of the form. Ira and Harold had each been paid $40,000 by Transcona out of the film's budget to write songs for the film. Since I couldn't hire Roger I shot craps and paid Lenny. He signed a "quit claim" giving me all the rights, and I became the legal owner. Lenny was gifted and he may have made a contribution; however, Roger had years of experience: he'd been Ethel Merman's accompanist, and he'd created Judy's "Dear Mr. Gable" lead-in for "You Made Me Love You," originally written by Al Jolson. He tailored everything to the individual artist. As far as we were concerned it was the "Edens touch." Roger had written in less than a month a brilliant minibiography told through music that didn't take away from the screenplay.

He was eager for Judy to hear what he'd done, so he came over to the house. Roger explained how I'd come to him, and then he swore Judy to secrecy. I thought, *Good luck!* Then he sat down at the Steinway and began to play what he'd put together.

Judy's reaction was explosive. She was as excited as she'd been on the golf course when she heard Hal Arlen whistle "The Man That Got Away." She knew it was great. Roger went back to work and completed the sequence. For once Judy kept her word and didn't utter a sound about the project. A month later Roger returned with a shooting script.

Per my anticipation, when the rough cut was run, the collective response was "we need a big musical number." Fortunately, I had "Born in a Trunk" ready to go. We were dependent on Warner's financially, though, and this segment would cost somewhere between $200,000 and $300,000 to produce. Transcona was not part of this budget. We brought Jack down to one of the sound stages, along with Barstow, and he loved the sequence. Jack brought in Steve Trilling and other executives twice, and they agreed to go ahead. Roger had accompanied her on the piano. It was a marvelous performance—perhaps better, if that's possible, than what we ultimately shot. Warner's wanted to buy the rights to "Born in a Trunk," but we wouldn't sell. It was our souvenir.

———— ∞ ————

I called Jack Warner by his first name from the outset of our relationship. My place in the green room, his private dining room, was on his left, and this space was kept reserved for me at all times. We'd meet daily at the stroke of 1:00 PM. Mervyn LeRoy, who had produced *The Wizard of Oz* so long ago, was among Jack's inner circle and frequently joined us at the table. I listened and learned.

Jack and I seemed to share similar appetites. We were both social and had a taste for practical jokes and the high life and wealth—a life-style to which he was accustomed and to which I aspired. At lunch Jack held court, openly using me as a sounding board. He could clown and tell jokes. Sometimes Bill Orr, head of Warner Bros. television, would join us in the green room, but never Jack Warner Jr., my old pal from when I'd first arrived in Beverly Hills. Jack Jr. worked as the liaison between Transcona Enterprises and the studio.

Jack Sr. rewrote history in his memoir, *My First Hundred Years in Hollywood*. For example, he referred to Elsa Maxwell as a "hustler," when in fact he depended on Elsa to organize his parties. In Europe he called her every day, for guests, introductions, dinners, whether his wife Ann was present or not (generally, she was not). As for me, I became a rogue and a criminal to his recollection.

Jack would refer to his wife as "my loving Ann," but I rarely saw them together. There were mistresses, one in particular whom he dumped when he aged. She had been on call for years and then he just stopped taking care of her.

Jack's aspirations were about power and class. He'd even been made an honorary colonel and occasionally he wore his uniform, until one day a professional army colonel visited the studio. Jack held out his hand to shake the colonel's and announced, "I'm a colonel too." The authentic one said, "You are? Then you should have saluted me."

Jack never wore the uniform again.

Twice a week when Jack called me to his office, we previewed rough cuts. One day he said, "I want you to read this wire from Sam Gold-wyn." The wire stated that seeing the latest cut was one of the great moments in Goldwyn's life and that he was certain the picture would make millions. "Jack, you could make $25 million."

Jack said, "Sid, you're going to make a lot of money."

I said, "Great."

Jack continued, "Now, I want you and Judy to join me for a holiday in the south of France." I thought, not much of a holiday for Judy. She'd be expected to deal with the European press, promote the film. Nevertheless, I ran it by her. Per my expectations she was less than enthusiastic about going to Europe on a junket for Jack. Further, we decided we couldn't afford such a trip. Our personal expenses were astronomical: the children, the staff, our lifestyle—all costly. We lived well, but we were not rich. Not yet.

The subject of traveling to France came up again at lunch one day. I explained to Jack how Judy hated to fly and that she preferred to relax at home. She had no desire to publicize the film as yet, or to be photographed. "It's a lot of money anyway."

Jack chimed, "Sid, it'll cost you exactly $25,000. I'll advance you the money." To which I replied, "If *Star* is going to make $25 million as you say, I'd be happy to borrow the money. If I can get Judy to go."

"Of course it's going to be a big hit. You'll make personally $5 or $6 million. It's the biggest hit since *Gone with the Wind*."

I asked Judy again, and this time it was "yes" and "no." Later on in the week she said, "Darling, do you think we'd have some fun?" I told her we'd enjoy ourselves. We could take a train from Paris down to the south of France, where we hadn't been in three years.

The next day Jack called: "So what does Judy want to do?"

"She's weakening," I reported.

"Let me know, I'll write you a check."

That night Judy surprised me. She said, "Let's go." She'd been talking with the photographer Richard Avedon, who was going to be in Paris. Dick had fed her ideas: the Tour Eiffel, the Champs-Élysées, going up the Seine, Dior, Café de Flore, supper with Chevalier.

Whatever he said appealed to her romantic nature. And his previous photos of her were stunning. Judy was eager for new sessions. What better setting than France? Summer in Paris. I rang Jack up and told him Judy had changed her mind. Within an hour he sent a $25,000 check to the house along with a note for me to sign. He called me and said, "When you get your share from the picture, you'll pay me back." He was casual. He then added, "Oh, Sid, I've got some buried francs in Paris. I'll have $5,000 delivered to your hotel."

Jack agreed to make all the necessary reservations in Paris. He assured me it would be wonderful, and added, "I've taken care of the champagne and caviar aboard the plane." No mention of either his wife or a girlfriend. I had one problem: prepping Judy for the flight. She would have to be bombed to get aboard. "Darling, you know I'm terrified; get a case of whiskey for me."

"We do have the plane to ourselves, darling, so you could relax just a little." Howard Hughes was loaning Jack a plane for the flight over and back. I had met Hughes about town, and the one time we'd held a conversation at a party, at producer Sam Spiegel's house, we'd discussed our respective airplane accidents as pilots. He wasn't a talkative guy; he presented himself in a detached and unavailable manner, although he was on the party circuit for years.

The passengers included only Jack and his white-haired valet, our associate producer Vern Alves, Judy, and me. Vern was wonderful with Judy and the press. It was a large plane, with just a pilot, copilot, and hostess, a luxurious and comfortable flight. But Judy was still scared to death, and nothing I could do helped.

Fortunately, Jack was not exactly aware of the drama being played out. He had the plane stuffed with Greek delicacies—plus, we were given the superstar treatment from the hand of Jack Warner himself. But the calming effect of this privacy and luxury quickly wore off. The pills and the booze kicked in and Judy became more and more panicked as the stimuli triggered phobic responses. She stopped eating and clutched my hand all the way to Paris Orly Airport. As soon as we landed, the first person she rang up from the airport was a friend who was married to a doctor. Judy was hysterical. She had probably taken uppers and was unable to relax or fall asleep aboard the plane.

When we arrived at the Hotel Raphael, a stone's throw from the Arc de Triomphe, the good doctor knocked her out and she slept through the night till one o'clock the following afternoon, thereby missing her session with Avedon. Once again, the pattern of the star: she got sick, recovered, and everyone else was left for dead. And we had departed Hollywood with such high hopes. Word was out that *A Star Is Born* was a great film, being compared to *Gone with the Wind.*

Happily, for the rest of our time in Paris, Judy was fine. We spent a few days saying hello to friends, dined and danced, absorbed the Parisian atmosphere. We boarded the overnight for Cannes with a minimum of press dates behind us. Vern did an excellent job of fending everyone off. We enjoyed our privacy.

Once we were comfortably installed in our suite at the hotel Cap d'Antibes, Jack kept repeating the theme: "Sid, you're going to make so much money." It was his song. Unrequested. I began to believe him, and so did Judy. Meanwhile, he had called on Elsa Maxwell to arrange his dinner parties in Judy's honor. There were extravagant evenings at Cap d'Antibes with the visiting dignitaries, cocktail parties and sit-down dinners expertly organized by Elsa.

Several nights Jack and I dined by ourselves at a favored restaurant, La Bonne Auberge in Antibes. There he'd take me in his confidence over bottles of superb wines and cognacs. In this setting I learned that he hated his daughter Barbara's fiancé, having discovered he was a homosexual. Warner boasted how he arranged to have him busted in bed with another man, thus ending his daughter's romance. I learned he hated Charlie Chaplin but liked his brother, Syd. Of course, Syd did not help form United Artists; Warner didn't approve of competition. During these dinners, Jack professed a love for gambling, presenting himself as a true sportsman. I withheld my thoughts on this subject, as my one sporting experience with him was over a horse, and Jack seemed utterly naive about the racetrack.

A few weeks earlier Jack had given me $200 to put on my horse, Sienna II. (In his memoir he wrote that he'd given me $500—he upped the ante by $300—but by then he was looking for a scapegoat.) Eddie Alperson and I bought Sienna II from trainer Paddy Prendergast in Ireland. I'd bought horses in the past from Paddy, so when he'd called and said he was working with John Dewar, the whiskey mogul, and had a very nice filly to sell, I was tempted. "Sid, you should buy the horse," Paddy said. Dewar was selling his stock to make a fresh start. The horse was beautifully bred and would cost $18,000. I was not about to pay that amount, but I thought Alperson might buy half. So Eddie and I became Sienna II's owners. The horse was well cared for at Rainbow Farms by my trainer Bill Sergeant.

Jack had known I was going to the racetrack to watch my horse run, and he'd asked me if he could make a bet. Sienna II lost that race. When she ran again and I told Jack he should make another bet, this time he said, "I don't bet on horses." And this time Sienna II won. It was a huge win. I stopped at La Rue's, one of my favorite restaurants, after the racetrack to celebrate by downing a couple of martinis. I was feeling real good. Bill Sergeant normally received 10 percent of the win, but this time he requested a car instead. I bought him a Cadillac Coupe de Ville, not a Chevy. I was immediately criticized for this gesture. Word got back to Jack, who was unable to understand my largesse.

Rainbow Farms was doing fine. I was lucky to know trainer Charlie Whittingham and to have had Charlie train several of my horses. Judy enjoyed Whittingham and his wife, Peg. They would visit us at Mapleton for parties and spend the night. Willie Shoemaker, the phenomenal jockey (and our one treasured friend shorter than Judy) who was already up to a thousand wins by 1953, would also visit us with his first wife, Babe. "Shoe" rode a number of my horses over the years. This was another world of royalty, and Judy was as flattered by Charlie and Peg and Shoe and Babe as she was by the Duke and Duchess of Windsor.

On this particular night Judy had been feeling lousy and said she'd remain at the hotel. She knew I was available: if she was in any kind of trouble, without question, I'd come to her aid. As Jack and I dined at La Bonne Auberge, the balmy Riviera evening blasted the scent of gardenias and jasmine. The intense charm of the local eau-de-vie and a delicious dinner obscured any possible negative thought or impulse, including my observation that Jack dyed his hair and moustache and was wearing makeup. I'd assumed it was an attempt to look younger.

Jack finished unloading his last confession and we left La Bonne Auberge for the Palm Beach Casino in Cannes, where Jack played chemin de fer. Jack told me he'd loaned Darryl Zanuck $100,000 the other night at the casino. Stakes were always high at the Palm Beach Casino. Apparently Jack could win or lose up to $400,000 in one night. He loved to show off his money in this manner.

The casino was an extravagant environment where the guests were catered to, very much the sort of gambling establishment pictured in James Bond films. Jack had invited me to gamble, and I agreed to take 10 percent of his action, win or lose. That night he got lucky and won $300,000. I smiled, "Congratulations, you own me $30,000." Jack's reply: "That's too much money for you." I thought he was kidding. "Jack, we made a bet. I was prepared to win or lose." He peeled off bills, "How about if I give you $3,000?" I thought, *Christ, it was a typical bet and he's refusing to honor it.* I said, "I'll take it on account."

Jack didn't know anything about the world of betting or the rules of sportsmanship. If he bet on a golf course he wouldn't pay off—*Because I'm Jack Warner,* that's how his mind worked. He dabbled where it suited him while presenting himself as a sportsman. He wasn't in any sense an authentic gambler, someone who bets on baseball, football, horses, everything and anything. He preferred a casino surrounded by many people who would watch Jack Warner and Darryl Zanuck exhibit their finesse with "shimmy." Should he lose, it would be a sizable sum, $200,000 or $300,000, enough to bring oohs and aahs from the spectators.

Jack was a gambler when everybody was looking; he never sat down and played poker with the boys. It was part of his aspiration to greatness and the upper classes. A gentleman who gambles and loses has the obligation to pay up before he pays his rent. The rules of the game. For Jack gambling was publicity, not sport.

There was a wonderful energy to the Côte d'Azur that season. Just enough tourists, a sensual atmosphere of relaxation and comfort, the smell of orange blossoms wafting through the night air off our patio. Our rooms opened out onto the Mediterranean. I looked forward to slipping into bed beside a dreaming wife, quietly sleeping. Instead I returned to an empty suite of rooms. I knocked on Vern's door. He said they'd been playing gin, and over the course of the evening Judy had periodically expressed feelings of loneliness and would start to weep. The crying increased. Vern said she began to complain that she couldn't move her head. "I've got a migraine. Please get a doctor." Vern found a doctor who refused to sedate Judy unless she was admitted to the local clinic, where she was presently spending the night.

I was angry, not sympathetic. I felt she had let me down. After the initial wave of anger washed over me, I began to feel disappointed by her. It was as though she couldn't survive a minute of stress—someone needed to be called in to knock her out. I couldn't shake my unhappiness. We still had the additional "Born in a Trunk" sequence to shoot; she'd have to pull herself together. I kept thinking about the fact that she was asleep with assistance from yet another drug. Speed made her nuts, so why didn't she use calming medication? I reminded myself that barbiturates zonked her out and could grant that temporary illusion of courage that speed seemed to provide. I wondered how this high/low pattern, too wired to eat or sleep, was ever going to disappear. I didn't rush over to the clinic. In the morning I asked Vern to bring Judy back to the hotel.

30

But it's all in a game and the way you play it
And you've gotta play the game you know
When you're born in a trunk at the Princess Theatre
In Pocatello, Idaho.

—"Born in a Trunk," *A Star Is Born*

JUDY SURPRISED ME by telling me after we got back from France, "Darling, I'm kind of exhausted and I feel I really want to get off everything." I was encouraged: she wasn't ducking what happened. She was eager to be in the best shape possible for "Born in a Trunk." We went up to Ojai for a long weekend. Judy rested and detoxed from all medication. She expressed a desire to investigate AA as soon as the film wrapped. I'd been so confident about her during the making of *Star.* I reasoned that flying had always presented obstacles, and there were many people who had a fear of flying and got besotted before they boarded a plane.

In Ojai, Judy told me she couldn't have made this film without me. "You're responsible for all of this, darling." She was loving, sincere, and appreciative. Again I was committed to doing whatever was needed to bring permanent stability to her life. Judy went on: "I've worked for rather important producers, and I think you're the best."

"Come on, Judy."

She said, "No, it's true, your taste and ability to work with a script in all areas is perfect. You've come a long way, darling, and I'm proud of you." I allowed myself to be flattered, even if it was from my wife. It was a hell of a seduction.

Since shooting on *Star* was supposed to be finished, the sound-stages had been shut down. We hired a new crew to shoot "Born in a Trunk." Irene Sharaff came out from New York and did the costumes. The sequence took five days to shoot and would lengthen the film by fifteen minutes. On its completion we threw an enormous party at our home for everyone connected to *Star* and friends. The inside and outside of the house were lit by rows of pink and white candlelight; pink and white flowers were arranged in large masses everywhere. Champagne and music were flowing. We were confident *Star* was a big hit.

Judy, in spectacular form, looked sixteen. She was greeting the guests at the door when Lucille Ball and Desi Arnaz arrived. Someone remarked to Judy, "You know Lucy?" Judy perversely answered, "Boy, I hate this woman!" She was sardonic, as she adored and respected Lucy. After fifteen minutes or so she was informed that Lucy was weeping in one of the upstairs bathrooms and refused to come out. Judy raced upstairs to Lucy, who admitted she'd taken Judy's riposte to heart. Judy was astonished. She apologized and kissed Lucy, explaining it was nothing more than a tease. Incidents such as this never deterred Judy's sense of humor or her style.

The buzz surrounding *Star* had continued to build. There was so much hullabaloo over Judy's performance—all the congratulations justified the extra work and expense. Harry Warner shook my hand. Benny Kalmenson thought it was tremendous. He was hoping to book the film simultaneously in two New York theaters, one on Broadway that would run *Star* from eleven in the morning until two at night, and the other a smaller house that would play the film on a two-a-day basis with an intermission. *Star* was going to be a blockbuster! One of the most talked-about films in history.

The L.A. premiere was considered the last of the Hollywood-style premieres. The footage from the TV coverage shows movie icons, along with those who would later become household names, streaming en masse into the Pantages Theatre on Hollywood Boulevard. I was quite drunk during all the ballyhoo. Spotlights had been arranged to form a large, glistening high star over the theater. An estimated twenty thousand fans jammed the vicinity. Much ado about Baby Gumm/Cinderella/Dorothy.

We took off for the New York premiere with a sense of victory. Judy was very up—and pregnant with our second child. She was eating what she wanted, rested, and back to her wholesome mode. We stayed at the Waldorf Towers, where we celebrated my birthday along with the premiere of our film. Judy gifted me with diamond cuff links shaped in a clover cluster and diamond tear-shaped studs. She wrote on the hotel's stationary, "Happy Birthday, I'm so in love with you darling—Judy."

The actual premiere was held in the smaller house without an intermission. The response was incredible. Judy was at the center of social activities. The Duke and Duchess of Windsor were in town; Babe Paley hosted a dinner. Other friends were on the scene, including Peter Lawford and his new wife, Patricia Kennedy, with Pat's brother Jack Kennedy, the junior senator from Massachusetts.

JFK was young, lanky, and extremely outgoing. He'd asked Peter and Pat to introduce him to "Dorothy" in the flesh. With Kennedy's gift for oratory and Judy's talent for telling stories, it was the start of a fun-loving, comfortable friendship. Judy and I shared the same perception—that brother and sister alike were still suffering the loss of their older brother Joe.

Prince Aly Khan was also staying at the Waldorf Towers. Aly had known Judy since MGM; he'd visited her on the set many times. He was involved with the glamorous Gene Tierney, who adored titles, having already been married to "Count" Oleg Cassini. Gene was a great beauty with slanted, turquoise eyes, a flawless complexion, and a gorgeous figure. She was one of the great beauties off screen as well as on.

It seemed at the time that she would be Aly's next princess, but that unfortunately was not to be.

Aly and I had been together socially in Hollywood, and we shared a passion for horses, women, and fast cars. While he could easily afford each category, I was in the audience. I was a faithful husband. I drove fast, but I didn't race cars. Aly took risks. I once accompanied him on a hair-raising ride to Normandy at 130 miles per hour to look at horses. Along the route he'd stashed three different women in various hotels and villas. The idea of fidelity was foreign to him. He was famous for his sexual endurance, supposedly practicing an ancient Muslim technique that prolonged the sexual act indefinitely. We never discussed our personal lives, however. He was impossible to keep up with in every department. Aly gave Judy and me extravagant gifts, including an exquisite diamond and emerald brooch in the shape of a tortoise. One Christmas I received sapphire and diamond cufflinks. He was generous, at times embarrassingly so.

The reviews of *Star* made the front pages of *Variety* and the *Reporter*, the two trade bibles. (Films are normally reviewed on the second page.) Column after column was written. The movie had ended up costing $5 million, which was an astronomical cost in 1954. At the same time, it added to the movie's glamour. Everyone seemed to think Judy would get an Academy Award and the film would gross "at least $25 million," to quote Sam Goldwyn.

Professionally, I was flying high, but personally, it had been a hell of a year. Just months earlier, my father had died suddenly. Had it been so long since we last saw each other? It seemed like we'd just been strolling down Columbus Avenue in New York after a leisurely dinner, father and son. We talked about my sister, Peri, what a talented painter she was. I admitted I was a dilettante by comparison. Norbert confided he'd suffered minor heart problems—translated, he meant attacks. His wife was concerned but he was not. He assured me there was nothing to worry about. We exchanged exotic information: I confessed I was going to marry Judy Garland, and he told me he was taking nitroglycerin.

I thought he'd successfully underplayed his condition, then left me the very moment in our lives when we were appreciating one another. As his death weighed on me, I began to show signs of stress. I ran into Pam and James Mason at a fundraiser, and Pam, noticing the deep circles and shadows under my eyes, jokingly asked, "Is there a panda in your past?"

Then the professional difficulties began. When *Star* premiered, it clocked in at just over three hours. It was long, and I suggested an intermission. Jack agreed with me, but the regional theater owners didn't go for it. Ominously, they started to complain that three showings a day would not be enough; they demanded a cut short enough to fit in five daily screenings. As intermission was rejected, so was raising the admission price to compensate.

In matters of distribution, Harry Warner ruled the studio with an iron fist. Though he and his brother Jack hated each other, Jack could not go to banks and borrow money on film production without Harry's approval. So Jack had no choice but to agree when Harry said, "We need a bigger turnover in grosses. We'll cut the film."

Cukor was in India, so he left it up to Folmar Blangsted, the editor, to make the key decisions regarding how to cut down the picture. Folmar's second wife, Else, said he was distressed. He wired the director in India but was left hanging. The cuts were eventually arrived at over the telephone. Two musical numbers were cut, both vintage Garland: "Lose That Long Face" and the great "Here's What I'm Here For." I'd begged Cukor to make the cuts himself, but he had refused to alter anything before he left. Folmar never spoke with Cukor again.

In the end, the studio butchered the film to benefit Harry's projected cash flow, cutting it down from three hours to 154 minutes. Harry anticipated an astronomical profit, but overnight *Star* was transformed from a sure winner into a loser. The film could not work, in my opinion, except in its entirety.

I said to Alperson, "The distribution is fucking up this film, Eddie." He said to consider it out of our hands.

We were committed to promotional tours in the four major cities—New York, Detroit, Chicago, and Los Angeles—and were both obligated to attend all regional openings. Judy lost interest in the tour. Her pregnancy, already in its fifth month, furthered her discomfort and disinterest. She wanted out. I was firm: we must do everything possible to promote it. After all, it was still our film.

The film's grosses fell off as word circulated about the nearly half hour of deleted material. Judy and I took the brunt of this disappointment. We were heartbroken. People came up to me: "Sid, have you seen what they've done to your movie?"

There'd been a convention of theater owners in Pennsylvania. The Paramount theater chain offered Warner's a 90/10 deal. It was a chain of fifteen hundred theaters, having nothing to do with Paramount Pictures. Ninety percent of the box office gross would go to Warner's and 10 percent to them, but the film had to be shortened further. It was an offer Warner's couldn't refuse. Judy and I pleaded, "Don't do it."

Not only did Harry have the power over Jack, but he was getting old and a little dingy too. Now he complained Jack had spent too much money on the film to begin with. Harry's spiel was "Money isn't coming in fast enough." The new cuts—down to 100 minutes—would enable two matinees. The Paramount theater owners began to show the cut version, and this time the critics took note of it. Bosley Crowther of the *New York Times* called it "A Star Is Shorn," and the pun echoed through Hollywood. The grosses fell off by half. We went from heroes to failures. I said to Judy, "Jesus, baby, this picture is not going to make any money!" We couldn't believe what was happening.

Thirty years later Ron Haver, head of the department of film at the L.A. County Museum of Art, went through hundreds of pieces of film to recover most of the lost celluloid. The original cut was put back together, reopened at Radio City Music Hall in New York, and proclaimed a "classic." In the August 1983 issue of *American Film*, Haver chronicled his efforts. Referencing the premieres of the restored print in New York, San Francisco, Chicago, and Dallas, he assured the reader that they "will serve to give audiences the chance to experience hundreds of 'those little jabs of pleasure.'" Pleasure he'd apparently reveled in as a teenager when he first saw the film. In the last paragraph of the article he wrote of the achievements of George Cukor, Judy, James Mason, Moss Hart, Harold Arlen, Ira Gershwin, musical director Ray Heindorf, and cinematographer Sam Leavitt. But he failed to mention me as the film's producer.

An even more lethal blow to the ego awaited me at the Academy of Motion Picture Arts and Sciences in Los Angeles. It was a benefit celebrating the restoration of *Star*. Acting president Fay Kanin introduced the film to the audience and, like Haver, forgot I was the producer. I sat separated from those who had the illusion they had not only recovered lost footage but had produced the film. It was eerie, as though I never existed. I was in a twilight zone where a guy who fought for the film, busted his ass to get it to function, got it to work, was totally forgotten. Sammy Leavitt approached me after the screening: "Sid, this is the most disgraceful thing I've ever attended."

The restored version of *Star* went on to sell to television and on videocassette. The film would earn back every penny, plus an ongoing profit.

But back in 1954, I felt destroyed as a producer, and Judy was devastated. Film critics were all-powerful and influenced the box office results. *Star* lost money in the first eighteen months, the grosses falling from almost $500,000 a week to $200,000. The film actually grossed about $18 million, but it needed to gross about $20 million to break even. I was personally blamed for the film's financial failure.

There were offers for Judy to star in other films—the screen adaptation of John O'Hara's bestseller *Butterfield 8*—but she was not able to be so quickly back in front of the cameras. Elizabeth Taylor starred instead and won the Academy Award for Best Actress. MGM asked Judy to headline the film version of *South Pacific* and *The Three Faces of Eve*. In the case of the latter, I thought it too close to home, though it ended up winning Joanne Woodward an Oscar. We were exhausted from our efforts of nearly three years to bring off *Star*. The decimation of the film left us burnt out. We would have to pick ourselves up from the ashes.

❦

Judy went into labor at Cedars of Lebanon hospital on March 28, 1955, two days before the Academy Awards dinner was to be held at the Pantages Theatre. Dr. Morton, Judy's obstetrician, tied off her fallopian tubes at her request during the cesarean operation. I waited in the room with Frank Sinatra and Betty Bacall Bogart, who were keeping me company.

What seemed like eons passed and still no word. It was early the morning of March 29 when the three doctors, Morton, Dietrich, and Rabwin, appeared to tell me Judy had given birth to a premature baby boy whose one lung had not yet opened. Suddenly we were in the midst of a personal melodrama wondering if our baby was going to survive.

Judy was very brave and kept her anguish to herself, as though she was holding her breath until she heard one way or the other. Fortunately, our son Joseph Wiley made it. Judy wept openly when Joey was finally placed in his mother's arms.

What followed on March 30 certainly didn't equal the drama she'd been through. With Judy being the presumptive Academy Award winner, she was miked up in her hospital bed, prepared to tell the TV public her feelings on receiving the Oscar for Best Actress. *Look* magazine had already given Judy its award for best female performance of the year; we'd considered that a pretty good indicator. The competition for Best Actress included Jane Wyman, Dorothy Dandridge, Grace Kelly, and Audrey Hepburn. Betty Bacall was at the theater ready to run onstage and accept the Oscar on Judy's behalf.

I held Judy's hand as the TV technicians wired her up for the win. John Royal, an old friend, was with us along with Gundy that night. *Star* received six nominations: Best Actress, Best Actor, Best Art Direction, Best Song, Best Score, and Best Costume Design. But *A Star Is Born* did not receive one award.

Grace Kelly won Best Actress for her performance in *The Country Girl*. Judy was funny about it; she certainly didn't flip out. She'd had so many acclaims, so many awards. Groucho Marx sent her the now-famous telegram, "Greatest robbery since Brinks," which pretty much echoed our sentiments. Vern was so deflated. He arrived long after the awards had been announced, expecting to find us in mourning.

I was told the count was very close. The Academy members from Metro and Paramount voted for Grace to win. She was on a loan-out to Paramount from Metro, where she was under contract. I liked Grace, but I thought she gave a cockamamie performance in an old sweater and a funny voice. We'd felt helpless, as Warner had not publicized *Star* in the trades, and at the time Jack was in personal conflict with the Academy.

Cukor believed that Academy members were influenced by the cuts to the film. Its very rhythm had been disrupted. Without moments of relief, the performances tended to look exaggerated. Cukor thought this cost Judy the Oscar.

A salvage clause had been written into the agreement between Warner Bros. and Transcona that allowed for any of the partners to purchase whatever was bought or rented from the studio at the end of the production, for ten cents on the dollar. The partners had first choice, the studio second. There were objects, furniture, and paintings we liked, and we took advantage of the salvage clause. Jack recalls this episode in his memoir unfairly; he writes that I came to him with a story that we didn't have furniture for a party, and he loaned everything to me on the condition I bring it back at the end of the weekend. In fact I bought the merchandise for the agreed sum, $4,000. When I sued Jack for libel, I won my suit.

I would continue to become more and more acquainted with Jack's ruthless tendencies. I had never questioned why Jack Jr. didn't join us for lunch in the green room. It was later that an ugly scene unfolded. Jack Sr. fired Jack Jr. in front of other people, then had his son escorted off the lot by the police. He was tough on Jack Jr. and humiliated him. He didn't wish to recognize him as a professional. The younger Warner was born to wealth, an upbringing that was the opposite of his father's, who grew up struggling and scuffling economically, from shoe repair to butcher shop to mogul, the story of the American Dream. Jack Sr. couldn't forget his humble beginnings, and he was bitter.

Jack also sabotaged his relationship with his brother Harry. Both agreed to sell their shares in Warner Bros., but Jack later reneged and watched his share rise. By 1958, shortly before Harry died, the brothers were not speaking. In 1967 Jack sold his holdings and earned a 33 percent profit.

It wasn't his family alone who suffered the slings and arrows of Jack's wrath. His blistering typhoon desecrated other lifelong relationships. When he sold the studio, Jack told Bill Orr to fire his partner in a successful TV series. "Fire Benson, he's finished" (one of Warner's favorite edicts). "And when you're through firing Benson, fire yourself. I'm closing out." Then he called in David DePatie, his comptroller. Warner announced, "I'm going to Palm Springs. I want you to fire Steve Trilling." One of the most respected men in the industry, Trilling was head of the studio, a decent, well-liked person who had worked for Jack for more than thirty years. Mrs. DePatie told me that he then repeated the litany, "After you get Trilling off the lot, you can wind up your business, and fire yourself, too." That's how lifetimes of allegiance ended. Everyone was treated as an inferior. People he had depended on like Richard Gully and Elsa Maxwell were servants to him, and he could snap them out of his life like blowing out a flame.

⁂

I could have continued developing projects at Warner's, but my impetus to produce turned sour. I certainly wasn't going to waste any time making conventional movies. I'd come a long way from exploitation films, but I now had an unrealistic approach to the business. My new point of view was that film had to be creatively worthy. This was bullshit, as box office most often buys ordinary concepts.

We broke our contract with Warner's. Jack, of course, said anything to vindicate himself. He was a powerhouse with the press, and the disinformation was that I didn't know what I was doing, and Judy had caused the film to go over budget.

I'm told Warner fell in love with the film later on.

31

THE CONTRACTORS ROLLED in daily to fill in the backyard. This work would take two years to complete. I'd oversee the comings and goings when I had the time. The kids were on the trampoline; Judy was lolling about the house. Johnny and I would watch the trucks roll in and dump the dirt. I had a strong sense of family and property in those moments. By 1955, the retaining wall was up, an eighteen-foot-high wall of concrete block and steel.

I was constantly working on the house as a kind of hobby. I hired Miro Korsik, who alternated between helping me rebuild the house and working as our cook and butler. We rebuilt Judy's wardrobe room, installing glass doors. I custom designed my bathroom in the spirit of my love affair with lifestyle. Jokingly, when *A Star Is Born* went under I commented to Judy that I could always work on renovations and probably make more than in the film business. But I didn't really believe that. *Star* was not the success we'd anticipated, but we were not about to disappear off the scene no matter how dejected we were. We continued to entertain and go out while I conjured up business.

One night we were at Romanoff's and Nick "the Greek" Dandolos sent over a bottle of expensive champagne. Nick lived right around the corner from Romanoff's at the Beverly Wilshire Hotel, and he was famous for sending over champagne and picking up checks. Judy didn't know about him and I explained: Nick gambled for a living, shuttling between Las Vegas and Beverly Hills. He was proud of his lifestyle; his attitude was what intrigued everyone. Judy was amused.

The parties thrown by Edie and William Goetz were without a doubt the pinnacle of the A-list in Hollywood. Edie was Louis B. Mayer's daughter, famous worldwide as a hostess; cynics found it hard to believe that Mayer, an immigrant, could produce such a social leader. The Goetzes were sophisticated people who lived in great style. Their art collection was famous for its masterworks. Everyone who was invited came to their black tie affairs without fail. Invariably, one hour after dinner, the men smoking cigars and bullshitting, Edie would ask, "Judy, one song?" And depending on how Judy was feeling she'd sing two or three songs. It would also depend on who was there, how formal the occasion. And there was applause. In those years as one was led into the main salon by the butler you could pretty much count on the same scene in the huge room where everybody gathered. You'd find Gable in one corner with his group, and in another corner was Gary Cooper and his group. Kirk Douglas, the one guest who was not in formal attire, the Goldwyns, the Zanucks, and Jack Warner. That would be the list. Judy was there because she sang and was witty.

Later I discovered Judy and Edie had a telephone pal relationship and shared speed connections. Pills were popular—diet pills, Dexedrine, Seconal. Like today, people relied on stimulants, and some got hooked. Many of the women were taking Dexamyl, no longer on the market. Dexamyl was a mild combination of upper and downer, very popular. Someone who was not a substance abuser could take Dexamyl and not be threatened. Judy would merely add it to her list, and if she mixed it with alcohol she could fall into an irreversible mood, so any pill was a threat.

Fortunately Judy hadn't suffered from postpartum depression after Joey was born—she was in good health. And she continued to express a vague interest in attending AA meetings. It was the one and only stretch in our long relationship when she acknowledged her dependency. She would, in the future, ask for help when she was desperate, even check herself into a clinic for a week's detoxification, but she would never admit she was a substance abuser. I had psyched myself out to think of Judy's addictive nature as a sort of chronic disease. Nevertheless, I looked forward to the day she would mature and leave these habits behind. I believed it was possible. But now that our lives had been turned around by the financial failure of *Star*, things were off track.

Because she wasn't working, she stayed up through the night sometimes, not going to sleep until midmorning. She was not aggressive; she would often leave me a note of apology:

Honey—
It's about time for me to try to sleep   10 A.M.—
So good night my darling—
See you later
I love you,
Judy

I'd hear her laughing in her bathroom as she listened to Bob and Ray on the radio. She'd have spent the night in her rooms while I slept or stayed in the den wondering, was she on pills, and if so how did she get them? Judy would go through these periods and then come around and we'd be back to normal. Her mood could shift with a "goofball," the mix of upper and downer. But our life had extremely wholesome aspects which I was intent on maintaining.

We made it to one AA meeting in Pasadena, way the hell out in a big old house where she was not recognized. We were offered coffee and cake. Everyone was saying in chorus, "I'm an alcoholic." Before the meeting ended we took one look at one another and said, "Let's get out of here," and we left, laughing.

I said to Judy, "Are we going to the second meeting?" Judy avoided the subject. The Pasadena evening was like a church social compared to our experience with Narcotics Anonymous. The fledgling group met somewhere in the San Fernando Valley, in a room lit by spooky blue lights—everyone was in silhouette, faces hidden; it had the atmosphere of an opium den. Judy remarked, "It's enough to make a person wanna stay bombed forever."

Judy did have a sort of support group: her telephone pals like Edie Goetz. Judy's friendships were limited to people we knew in common. She was not one to have close relationships with women, but when she wasn't working and up at night, she was often on the telephone with other women who were insomniacs. They were on pills and had no place to go. They'd encourage each other, try to buck up their spirits. Most of all, they'd gossip. The conversations were meant to be confidential, but Judy, who by nature had a hard time keeping anything but her personal feelings to herself, would relay the gist of the schmooze the next day. From Jean Peters, after she separated from Howard Hughes: "He's a brilliant guy, awkward to be married to, doesn't like sex." Jean was fascinated by Judy's talent—and her problems, which at this stage of her life perversely intrigued many people rather than turning them away.

Who's doing what to whom was the general theme. Judy would communicate what she considered the juiciest gossip. I'd wonder what in hell she was telling the girls about her own problems. Judy would find a way to make the information funny—she'd be laughing so hard she couldn't finish the story. I was happy Judy was getting through the night without me, as I needed about five years of sleep.

Lee Gershwin, Ira's wife, was an aggressive, intelligent woman and another of Judy's phone pals and speed connections. So was Gary Cooper's wife, Rocky. Marilyn Monroe, who visited the house, was another late night telephone buddy.

Marilyn would also visit us at the house. She'd sit by the fire, not talking much; she was a quiet presence. It was work bringing her out, but of course she may have been on some pill. Marilyn was sweet and very unhappy. She'd chat with Judy and play with the children, hang out. She was separated from one of her husbands, whom she complained was a nice person but, sadly, didn't know how to make love to a woman. She'd been forced to go down on him as the one means of getting him aroused to orgasm. She'd hoped this pattern would change when they married. She was frustrated and disappointed.

We did not give a lot of formal parties. Friends were in the den, about the house, or around Judy at the piano. Dean was there, Frank, Marilyn, the Bogarts, Charlie and Peggy Whittingham, my pal Charlie Wacker, Freddie Finklehoffe . . .

One day Judy's relatives on her father's side arrived in our circular drive unannounced. They were obese people, about six of them. I was amazed they fit in one car. They were short and fat with huge behinds, wide-ettes all the way from Oklahoma. And the cousins were eager to see Judy. I went upstairs to Judy's private bath and sitting room, where she was closeted. Judy told me to tell them to go away. There were many relatives on both sides of the family, and she never felt like seeing any of them. She'd reach out to her sisters every so often and they'd respond to their baby sister, as they adored her, but Judy wasn't interested in what they thought; neither sister could influence her.

I cooked up a mild performance schedule for Judy, a West Coast tour of seven cities, two concerts a week over a three-week period. We'd travel by train; Judy could relax. Initially, Judy's enthusiasm was high: "Let's have some fun, put on a show, darling." I was happy—she was in great physical shape and she was excited about performing. So I arranged the Seven City Tour beginning with San Diego. We'd wend our way up the coast. When Judy sang at the Long Beach Auditorium, Sinatra came down with friends: Bogie and Betty, Sammy Davis, and others. She was surrounded by loving, supportive peers. Judy was "at home."

Eugene, Oregon, found Judy performing in a gymnasium with a bunch of college kids in the audience. I'd sent out PR people to set up the promotion, and I saw nothing demeaning in the grassroots approach. I didn't suspect Judy would resist regional audiences. I thought of this tour as a regeneration of her concert skills, much like the tour in the British provinces. But Judy had come to think of the Seven City Tour as a comedown. In Portland, she announced out of the blue, "I can't work today. My throat's scratchy." It was Sunday and I tried to reason with her, explaining that although the show was not sold out, I'd hoped she'd be a good sport; otherwise we'd have to return everyone's ticket money. I was counting on her as a trouper. Judy's reaction was "Forget about it. Tell 'em they'll get their money back."

Judy was never concerned about losing money. She didn't care. She was not to be bothered about business; she wasn't interested in investments, costs, payments, income. Like royalty, she didn't carry an amount of money on her person, maybe just five dollars or so. I was unable to discuss financial matters of any sort with her. She simply refused.

I dreaded facing the Portland audience with the news "Miss Garland is ill." I pulled out every diplomatic move I knew: "Look, don't sing, people want to see you. Tell a funny story, whistle, say hi, a song will come to your mind, your throat'll get better. Tell a joke." But nothing worked, so we had to cancel Portland.

However, Vancouver, British Columbia, was wonderful. Judy was in great voice. My old pal Simmons from my knock-em-down Beverly Wilshire Hotel days had been living in Vancouver and attended the show. We went out afterward, and Judy had a marvelous time.

Seattle was the last city, and it too was a smash hit. She'd long forgotten Portland. I was paying attention: my little diva was not content with small cities. I'd have to come up with exceptional bookings. Loving fans were not enough.

The scales tipped when we returned from the tour. Judy went on a bender.

I couldn't figure out where the pills were coming from or what it was she was swallowing, but it left her aggressive, often telling me to "get the fuck out" of the room and not to butt into her business. She was calling Dr. Pobirs to come out in the middle of the night and give her something to stop the migraine. And the nighttime distress was genuine: she wasn't eating and she couldn't sleep. She'd caught herself by the tail. Fred recommended she get in the car and go to an anonymous clinic in Orange County for three or four days to get back on schedule.

But meanwhile we'd RSVP'd for one of Edie and Bill Goetz's dinner parties. Again it was a black tie affair. Judy looked gorgeous. She was wearing a spectacular outfit, and I was in a dinner jacket and black tie. We got into the Mercedes, and I observed Judy's eyes were more chocolate than usual. They were heavily glazed, and when I brought it up she resisted answering me. We got through the evening, although Judy didn't sing that night. We left the party in a crashing downpour. She asked me if we could go for a ride. I laughed at her. "Darling, it's not a night for tooling around in a car, for Christ's sake."

"*Hnnn*, it's a perfect night, darling." I was annoyed with her but relieved she was talking to me, so I drove from Beverly Hills out toward Venice in the heavy rain. The world looked emptied. We drove through abandoned streets, sped down the Harbor Freeway, and came out in Venice. Now Judy wanted a nosh. That too was a good sign. I found an all-night taco place. Judy remained in the car while I went in to buy some food. There wasn't an umbrella in the car, so I threw my dinner jacket over my head and ran into the dive. I waited for the double order of burritos, listening to the rain crash down in steel sheets. With the steaming burritos in hand, I ran out. Neither the car nor Judy were anywhere in sight.

I returned indoors, furious. Five minutes went by and still no sign of Judy. I ate both burritos and ordered a coffee in the hopes the rain would slack off and my wife would return for me. There was no way I could get a taxi, and I couldn't think of bringing anyone out in this night; it was far too late for a favor. I began to worry about how she'd handle the gears, which I had rigged in a special way. I realized I'd have to walk back to Holmby Hills. It took a long time to get home. I prepared myself for disaster as I dragged myself through the dark, wet streets. When I arrived at the house, the first thing I saw was that the Mercedes was perfectly parked in the garage. I looked in the bedroom, and Judy was sound asleep. I laughed—somehow she'd managed those gears.

The trick was so rotten I was not going to address it. Late in the day, Judy said, "Hi, darling," all smiles and giggles. "How'd you get home?"

Judy and I spent many an evening at Peter and Pat Kennedy Lawford's beach house in Santa Monica. The house was once owned by Louis

B. Mayer. Peter Lawford may have inherited his mother's penurious mantle, as a young man never buying a girl dinner, but he married someone who didn't need to have dinners bought for her, nor did she seem to care. Peter was handsome, witty, a delightful presence to be around. Lots of charm. If no cookies were distributed in Lady Lawford's house, Peter and Pat Kennedy Lawford were the opposite: wonderfully hospitable.

Along with the cheap gene, Peter also had a sense of honor. He had bought Pat a beautiful, costly engagement ring, which took him a long time to pay off. But when they divorced, Peter would not accept anything. It was later when he became an addict that he'd look for money from anyone, including strangers.

It was at the Lawfords' beach house that I was introduced to grass. I was hoping Judy might enjoy a joint; it would have been much better for her. She refused to smoke, having tried it some years ago at MGM. She said it made her sick. I wasn't a smoker either, but it wasn't as though I didn't try to be, since it was all around.

As long as JFK was alive and Pat had the beach house where both her brothers, Jack and Bobby, relaxed and played when they were on the West Coast, Peter was important. He was important when he had a production company. There were films—*Ocean's 11* and *Salt and Pepper*, with Sinatra and Sammy Davis Jr. The greatest impediment to his growth as a human being was the destruction of his brother-in-law, JFK, his most revered and intimate friend.

The scenes at the Lawfords' were heady—at times Jack was there or Teddy or some other member of the Kennedy clan. I was never quite sure why they so enjoyed show business, why they felt the need to hang around movie stars. Nevertheless, there they were. Peter knew damn well if he brought girls around, Jack would take over. He'd steal any girl in sight.

Anyone Judy was fond of—the Edenses, Cukor, the Lawfords—she'd welcome with a warm embrace and a kiss on the mouth. An affectionate hug from Judy and you knew you were accepted by this rare creature; you felt as though you'd never been appreciated before. When she was introduced it was a real handshake, and she was polite, courteous. Judy was aware of her fame. And Jack Kennedy responded to Judy's warmth and vivaciousness. He looked quite different from the skinny guy we'd had dinner with in New York, when he'd seemed just a preppie freshman until he spoke. And Judy brought out his wit and charm. Judy even said, "You're going to be president!" Over the years she'd say this about Jack to different people, always getting the reaction "Impossible. A Catholic?" As time passed, and we'd run into one another at the Lawford home, Judy became even more convinced.

Jack was in constant pain—he was unable to sit through a movie, even if it was good. He could never sit longer than twenty minutes; he'd have to get up from the rocking chair. Maybe he just felt better lying down. I generally saw him kibitzing horizontally from the Lawfords' pool, afloat.

—∞∞∞—

Eventually Judy did make a short trip to a clinic, and she returned feeling well. She lolled about the house while I concocted business deals.

She liked to keep books piled up on the table next to the chaise lounge in her sitting room. She'd read one book halfway through, put it aside, and pick up another; in this fashion she'd alternate two or three books until she'd read them all. She was a rapid reader and remembered the text easily, just as she could commit to memory scripts, lyrics, poems, after one reading. Her mind did work differently from the rest of us mortals. I was especially impressed by her ability to write backward as easily as forward. Such abilities may easily have befuddled her mother rather than bewitched her as Judy had done to me.

Our neighbor Horace Dodge invited us to dinner, and this time we couldn't refuse. Judy wasn't eager—she found him a boring drunk, as opposed to a "stimulating lush." I thought he was nice. Though Horace was the Chrysler heir, his chorus girl wife unfortunately didn't help him cut the mustard on the party circuit. Horace was a pleasant dullard but his wife was considered uninteresting; when Horace died she married a policeman and found happiness. Judy didn't last the evening and made an early exit. I decided to finish the night at Bogie's, where the talk was about Frank. Sinatra was playing at the Sands Hotel in Las Vegas. He'd invited friends to attend, always a splendid host, creating a festive and luxurious environment. Frank also owned an interest in the Sands at the time.

Later Sinatra organized a posse to attend Noël Coward's opening night at the Desert Inn. We flew up with Charlie Feldman and Capucine, the Bogarts, the Romanoffs, David and Hjordis Niven, and Swifty Lazar, who was with actress Martha Hyer. I had asked the Lawfords to join us. As most of our mutual friends were going, it seemed silly they were not invited, but Frank would periodically be mad at Peter for one reason or another, and for the moment they were not speaking. I thought Frank might suck it up and be civil to Peter in Vegas, but it didn't happen. JFK's nomination and subsequent presidency would bring them closer, but that didn't last either. Peter suffered Frank's rejection until he died.

At the table, Peter and Judy got caught up in an exclusive conversation about the late Robert Walker, whom I'd also known when he was married to Jennifer Jones. Peter and Judy were speaking lovingly about Bobby. He'd costarred with Judy in *The Clock*, and Peter hung out with him in those days; they were close friends. Walker was a pill-taker like Judy, and he mixed it with booze. Friends would have to call the police to break down his door to see if he was OK, and in the end he wasn't.

After the show Judy partied with Noël and friends; she was adored, and her acerbic wit was encouraged. For my part, I was not that relaxed; I was eager to return to Los Angeles. Everybody we were with loved Noël; but he was not going to attract an audience in Vegas. It was altogether the wrong environment for his talents. A mistake.

Back in Los Angeles, the Bogarts threw a bountiful western barbeque for the very British Coward; there was much mayhem and fun. Little did we suspect that within two years, Bogie, my magnanimous host, would be dead at age fifty-seven.

32

J UDY BECAME EXCITED by a new offer. In fact, she set her heart on it: a thirty-three-city train tour MCA was going to book for her. MCA had sent Jerry Lewis and Dean Martin out the year before, and though their tour lost money, everyone believed it would be different with Judy Garland. The notion of her on a private train, barreling through America à la Sarah Bernhardt with her "family," was like celebrating Christmas every day.

Unfortunately, the thirty-three-city tour by train fell through, and we were contractually obligated to either perform for film or television or suffer a lawsuit. MCA had secured only eight contracts from St. Louis to Cleveland, and we needed twenty-five plus a specified minimum of money in advance to go forward. Judy was disappointed, and I had to get out of the canceled contract debt.

MCA came up with a ninety-minute TV special, *Ford Star Jubilee*, CBS's first color telecast, and they wanted Judy Garland. Judy was nervous—she was not camera slim, and hadn't even thought about cameras since *Star*. Now I was suddenly under unexpected stress: Judy's anxiety about her appearance in front of cameras and my concern about her state of mind. She would want to reduce, and she wasn't going to accomplish this by diet alone. What's more, CBS put up an insufficient amount of money to pull off such an extravaganza. I immediately told the network it was impossible to bring the show together on what they were willing to put up. We argued and I held my breath, as there wasn't an out clause in our contract. We had a forty-five-day period to decide. I had to tough CBS out. I was sweating. On the forty-first day I heard from CBS: they agreed to a larger budget. I met with their writers, who were a conscientious team but inexperienced in putting across a talent like Judy Garland. The script was bad and Judy hated it. I was desperate. I told my Riviera golfing buddy Charlie Lederer my problems, whereupon he offered to redo the entire show with his writing partner, Ben Hecht. Their fee was a new kitchen stove for Charlie and a small sailboat for Ben.

Charlie Lederer was the nephew of Marion Davies. A congenial man, Charlie inherited Marion's estate when she died. At one point, he owned the Cartier Building on Fifth Avenue. I knew Charlie from card games and golf courses. His house was open, he wasn't a snob, and he was very funny. Charlie's second wife was actress Anne Shirley. However, his first wife had been married to Orson Welles, and she and Charlie used to fight like cats and dogs. One of their fights was a famous Hollywood inside story. His wife said she was moving out of the house, and she asked him for some money. Charlie wrote her a check. That night she moved into the Beverly Wilshire Hotel. She gave the check to the night manager with the request that it be cashed in the morning. She proceeded to the elevators when the manager called after her, "Mrs. Lederer, do you mind identifying the signature on the check?"

"Of course, it's my husband's."

"Oh? Can I show you the signature?"

She returned to the desk, where she read the check. It was signed "Peter Rabbit."

Charlie and I played golf regularly at the Riviera. His golfing togs were unconventional: white pants, a blue sleeveless shirt, and an inverted sailor cap on his head. He was not fashionable. There were ongoing gin games at Charlie's house; more often than not he'd be out while his friends played. Charlie begged the card players to dump their ashes in ashtrays, but his request went unheeded and the ashes piled up on the rugs. So Charlie got ten large helium balloons and attached ashtrays to them. He suspended the balloons and ashtrays throughout the house. The carpets were still covered with ashes.

Curiously, the Lederer home was the very house where I'd spent so many days and nights in my early Hollywood years as the guest of Eleanor Powell: 727 North Bedford Drive, Beverly Hills. Eleanor had originally rented the house from Charlie's mother.

There was a camaraderie at Charlie's you couldn't find anywhere else in Hollywood. His holiday parties were famous—five hundred people, all feeling good.

Out of friendship, Charlie and Ben wrote a great show. There was, however, one more hurdle to overcome: Judy. She'd lost some pounds by taking pills. Her behavior had been normal, and I was unconcerned until the morning of the first day of shooting, when I couldn't rouse her from sleep. I'd been occupied with work and had hired an assistant to be at Judy's side when I wasn't available. Judy was to be up at 6:00 AM in time for the dress rehearsal at the studio. I tried to wake her but she was in a semiconscious state. I was stunned. I went to the kitchen, where the companion told me she'd come down to make a cup of tea. I said, "She's virtually unconscious!" And the woman said, "Oh, she's sound asleep."

"Sound asleep?" I repeated, "She's unconscious!" I sat on the edge of the bed. "Judy, can you hear me?" There was a groan and saliva coming out of her mouth. She was punchy. I got her into a cold shower, dressed, and moving.

"*Hnnn,* I'm depressed," she said. She wasn't secure about her looks or how she would perform in front of the camera. Her speech was thick tongued. There was no time for me to speculate on what she'd taken. I thought, *Judy can't be left for an instant.* Then I worried that her voice was off. At the studio I ordered in Chinese food, her favorite, in the hopes of sobering her up, to give her strength—let the soy sauce absorb the chemicals! When she went out on the sound stage I heard her announce, "I can't sing. I'm saving my throat for tonight." I thought, *Brilliant.*

The night of the show, Judy was hurriedly dressed in a costume from *Star* to save funds. She knew she looked ridiculous, and we began to laugh, and soon we were doubled up. I began to think, *Que sera, sera,* whatever came out of her mouth. But Judy had sobered up. By the time she got to "Over the Rainbow," the grips, ushers, audience, everybody present—myself included—was magnetized by her performance.

We had a big party back at the house to celebrate. Surrounded by her peers and close friends, she was effervescent, happy, the perfect hostess. Any attempt I made to communicate with Judy about her earlier behavior was rejected. Once again I was not permitted to cross over the invisible line. If I became her psychiatrist, I could never function as her husband/lover/producer. The morning's incident was forgotten.

———— ✎ ————

Freddie Finklehoffe was the sort of guy who had always been hovering. At our home, on the set of *A Star Is Born*, wherever it was, he was on the scene in his rumpled fedora, creased Ivy League drag, and shades—primarily in the hope of picking up a betting tip. He must have lost a half a million dollars in bogus tips. He was a racetrack freak who traveled the horse world from Aqueduct to Belmont to Hollywood Park and back. He'd listen to everyone and everybody, which is how he lost his money. Though around this time, when I advised him to bet on one of my horses, Ozbeg, Freddie struck pay dirt.

Freddie had delusions of grandeur more than most of us. A colorful aspect of his character, it was also his downfall. At one point he bought a secondhand Rolls-Royce, which ran for about two months and wound up a landmark permanently parked in front of his farm in Bucks County, Pennsylvania. He respected me because I was close to the world of racehorses but was not a compulsive bettor. This mystified Freddie. Fred's marriage to Ella Logan had ended due to his obsessive gambling. For some reason Freddie considered himself a ladies' man, and while he was married to Ella he met a young, pretty woman, Carolyn. He dumped his other tootsies and took up exclusively with Carolyn. Their relationship was serious, and after he and Ella divorced, Freddie was looking to marry her, but he didn't have the money.

Freddie came to think of our house as a castle of magic where anything was possible—Carl Reiner breaking up everyone with his humor, Judy, of course, singing and cracking jokes, Sinatra, Peter and Pat, Charlie and Peg Whittingham, our crazy staff, Harry, Miro, Marvin-Schmarvin. Freddie loved the circus and knew he'd never be turned away.

I'd bought Freddie's lucky horse, Ozbeg, from Aly Khan. Aly and I'd had an ongoing correspondence, essentially about horses, but once in a while he'd inquire if I'd heard anything of Gene Tierney. Judy and I had believed Aly was going to marry Gene, but their relationship had fizzled out. Aly's inquiries as to Gene's whereabouts were tacked onto the horse business but held a plaintive air. Judy and I thought Aly had cared more for Gene than he'd been willing to admit.

Aly wrote me that his horse Poona had run "a wonderful race" in the 2000 Guineas Stakes, finishing third. He was pleased, as Poona was now worth three times his original cost. He was selling Poona and two other horses, Ozbeg and Nechao. I bought Ozbeg. He advised in one letter to run Ozbeg in blinkers for best results, as he was a tremendously fast horse. He suggested Ozbeg be jumped out of the gate to make his way for home. There were several recommendations in that letter on certain horses good to bet on. Ozbeg, in his opinion, should be allowed to win a small race in "good style" and then be passed on at a profit. According to Aly there were more horses of equal caliber at the right price. Ozbeg was not a partnership; he belonged to me, unlike Sienna II, the successful stake horse I'd bought with Eddie Alperson.

Freddie was a close friend of Kentucky Derby jockey Conn McCreary. Conn was an educated, literate man. He was racing in Florida and he rang Freddie to fly out. "You might win a bet or two during the week." Conn enjoyed Freddie's company, and Freddie, dreaming of the big win, boarded a plane for Florida right away and proceeded to bet a huge amount of money. It was Finklehoffe's luck that the horse ran off the track. Freddie blew his money and was absolutely furious. He rushed into the jockey's room and angrily stared at Conn as though he were personally responsible, "What in hell happened?"

Conn stared him back. "It's a good thing we weren't betting fingers."

Ozbeg ran under Rainbow Farm colors. Our colors had been black with slashes of red, green, blue, and pink. Then we switched to a white background—not that it seemed to affect our chances for winning; it was more an aesthetic change.

Ozbeg had won several races, but he had a bad ankle and I was finally going to sell him. We decided to bring jockey Basil James back to win one more race. Nobody would bet on James, who'd long retired into the restaurant business. I knew he could pull it off, especially after shedding thirty pounds. I told Freddie he'd better get his hands on some money, as we were going to win a bet. Freddie complained he was busted; when I encouraged him to borrow, he knew I was serious. "Call your mother, call your brother, call somebody."

The first day Ozbeg ran I recommended Freddie not bet. It was an easy race. I didn't want Ozbeg to run. Freddie bet anyway, and he lost. The horse was beaten by seven lengths and ran fourth. Basil insisted, "I could've been right there at the wire, if I let him run!" When we did cut Ozbeg loose, Freddie won enough to buy a Mercedes-Benz, marry Carolyn in our house on Mapleton, and disappear into Mexico for a long time.

———— ∞∞∞ ————

Easter 1956 came and we threw a lovely party. Judy was grateful but not entirely sober. She left me a note with great flourishes of script, especially the *y*s and *j*s:

> Darling,
> You were so sound asleep, I was afraid to kiss you for fear of waking you. But I kiss you with my heart.
> Thank you for giving your family such a lovely Easter. Your love surrounded each of us, and made us feel so warm and wanted and secure.
> God bless your big fat heart.
>
> I really adore you,
> Judy

Judy's flowing script, well punctuated and girlish, never failed to touch me. I imagined her at MGM putting in the obligatory hours with the tutor honing her writing skills.

MCA contacted me and told me they could get me $100,000 for a half-hour TV show with Judy for General Electric; did I have any ideas? Ronald Reagan would be the host. I came up with a concert-style show: *Garland and Bernstein*. Leonard Bernstein, or "Lenny," as friends spoke of him, had been at the same New York parties as us, and he had played for Judy at the piano. I knew Judy loved being around him, as did many women, including Betty Bacall, who seemed to have an equally intense crush on Adlai Stevenson. It was the time before Bernstein became a household name, before his morning sessions with children or his conducting the New York Philharmonic, and before *West Side Story*. We knew he was a genius, but the country was not yet informed. In *Garland and Bernstein*, I proposed, Judy would sing eight songs with Lenny conducting a sixty-piece orchestra, and there would be a poster. Judy was ecstatic. This was no Seven City Tour! MCA was enthralled, said it was a great idea, as they also represented Lenny. Then a week passed and MCA notified us that General Electric didn't want Leonard Bernstein. I had to go back to Judy with the news. "Why?" she demanded. We tried to get to the bottom of the rejection. Lenny was talented, he was handsome, and he was a charming presence. How could GE say no without an explanation? Lenny was known to be a liberal, outspoken, and he was Jewish. We analyzed the situation and came to the conclusion that GE was acting on some kind of extreme conservatism, which we detested. Judy wasn't interested in working with anyone else, but MCA had trapped me and I had trapped her. I'd made the decision I'd never present anything to Judy that I didn't believe in. Work for work's sake was out of the question. Now the show was turning out to be another job, and in Judy's view, one to be avoided.

I came up with another concept that, fortunately, she agreed to: a Richard Avedon photographic session set to music in black and white. We'd hired a hot, young pianist who'd been praised, won a big award. Judy OK'd Avedon and the pianist, but it wasn't easy: there were still roadblocks. At rehearsal Judy would complain about the pianist, "This guy's putting me to sleep." And he wasn't right, as nice and cooperative as he was. Then I'd come home and it was clear Judy was back on pills. The original concept that had excited her so much just wasn't happening. It wasn't Lenny Bernstein, it was making do. I remembered another pianist Judy liked, Joey Bushkin. Since a piano player was not the star as Lenny would have been, along with his orchestra, I figured GE couldn't object to the name Bushkin. I located Joey in Santa Barbara, where he was living. He must have roller-skated down to L.A. that night, because he was there bright and early the next day.

Judy was slim as a result of her dope intake. She worked twenty minutes out of the half-hour slot in costumes designed by James Galanos. He created a new version of her tramp costume. It was hilarious: she wore trousers, a cutoff jacket, a white hat, and spats. She looked like Mickey Mouse. She was bleary eyed. Avedon was great with his camera, but Joey turned out to be completely inappropriate and Judy's voice was way off due to pills. She got through it.

—————— ◆ ——————

Now Judy had a yen to play Las Vegas. I put out feelers. There were new hotels going up every day; I'd contacted a fellow regarding the opening of a big new hotel and he disappeared on me. Eventually the New Frontier Hotel called me and said they wanted Judy. I made a deal and booked Judy for two weeks, and the date was extended to a month.

Once again, Judy was off pills and booze. She was joyous on and off the stage. It was her nightclub debut, and she was the highest-paid performer to date in Vegas. We stayed in a private cottage with Liza, Lorna, and Joey, and the nurse. My son Johnny was spending less and less time with us. Judy's sister Susie was there, with her husband, Jack Cathcart. My sister, Peri, came up to lend a hand and assist Judy in the dressing room, hang out, and join the family.

A terrible blow had been dealt my sister. Not that much time had gone by since Peri called me from Florida to tell me her husband, Lou Fleishman, who was a doctor, had terminal leukemia. I caught a plane and arrived in Miami late in the afternoon. I went directly to the hospital. Lou had taken his own blood smear and diagnosed himself. My head was reeling: the diagnostician discovers his incurable disease! Lou's cheerful demeanor belied his fate. Sitting up in his hospital bed he tried not to upset his family. "Hi, Sid." He looked all right too, until he reached out and I saw his upper arms were discolored.

Lou lasted five days. He called his lawyer, his accountant, his insurance broker. By Friday he'd methodically taken care of all his business on earth. Saturday around noon he said, "Sid, do me a favor and take Peri for a ride. We'll visit later."

Peri and I drove up the coast to Fort Lauderdale and grabbed a sandwich along the way. It was a nadir for Peri, an awful wound. She'd found her niche in Florida, with a family she loved. They were happy. Two children—a son, Peter, an adopted daughter, Jane—and now she was losing her young husband. We talked about a medicine rumored to be available in Canada that had been effective on advanced leukemia patients. We both knew it was wishful thinking, but it filled up the sad silences. By midafternoon we returned to the hospital and were informed Lou had suffered a stroke. He died at one o'clock the next morning.

Lou never cracked. He'd say, "I'm going to have lunch now," meaning he wanted to be left alone. By the time he died he was a very dark color, nearly black. It was hard just to be there. As much as I was inwardly shaken, I was also overwhelmed by this man's courage. In the future I'd return over and over again to Lou's courage as a reference.

My mother, who'd been living with my sister in Florida, also came to Los Angeles and was back in our lives. She fell in love with L.A., took her own apartment on Beverly Glen, and found work in Beverly Hills in a dress shop.

While Judy played the New Frontier, her "family" was extended and as cozy as ever. The club was packed night after night. Judy had no interest in craps, and twenty-one held her attention for five minutes, but poker was a great relaxation for her. She could hold her own; she knew how to bluff. On our return to Los Angeles, we would begin to play poker with the Lawfords and the Gershwins on a regular basis. Judy loved poker, she loved to kibitz, and she loved to win, although she was a poor loser. She had no stomach for rejection in games or work—the least slight from someone important threw her into a panic. She experienced working only as the "star"; anything less was in fact a crisis. In this sense she was no longer a journeyman performer, like she'd been as a child.

Every night at the New Frontier was a Saturday night audience, and I thought Judy gave too much of herself. She received nightly standing ovations. "Darling, you're bustin' your chops. Hold back, conserve energy." But she wanted to give her all. Judy couldn't hold back; she was secure and she wanted to perform. Judy missed only two nights due to a raw throat during the entire six-week engagement at the New Frontier. Dr. Lester Coleman, an ear, nose, and throat doctor from New York who was vacationing with his wife, Felicia, treated Judy. We all fell in love with one another and subsequently became very close friends.

One of the nights when Judy lost her voice, I asked Jerry Lewis to sub for her. I thought she could go out onstage with Jerry and kibitz with the crowd. And so she came out dressed in her beloved at-home Chinese silk jacket, trousers, and slippers. The crowd went crazy. The emcee explained to the audience that Judy's voice was gone temporarily, but she was with a friend, and then Jerry walked out. The audience yelled, "We want Judy." Very quickly they calmed down. Judy apologized for not being able to sing but promised to make it up to them, and she did. Jerry and Judy told jokes and cavorted; Judy whispered the lyrics to her songs in his ear while Jerry sang. It turned out to be a great show, and later Jerry recorded her arrangement of "Rock-a-Bye Your Baby" and it was a big hit.

The last night at the New Frontier I noticed a crowd around one of the gambling tables. The young man with the dice was a good-looking kid who was rolling the dice for an oilman, a big gambler who later got blown up in a car. That night he had the entire front of the table lined with black chips. I started out with two hundred dollars. The kid held the dice for nearly twenty minutes. I was never a Vegas-style gambler, favoring the horses; I felt relatively in control betting on a horse I ran, or if a trainer I knew convinced me the horse had a shot to win. But that night my money was on the longest ride it would ever take at a craps table: I won $18,000.

When we got back to Los Angeles I had a diamond bracelet designed for Judy's birthday. It was delicate yet opulent. We celebrated with the Bogarts at Romanoff's with supper, cake, and champagne. Judy placed a note on my bedside table. It was written on her monogrammed JLG stationery:

> My wonderfully attractive Sid—
> Thank you for giving me the happiest birthday of my whole life.
> To coin a phrase, "I'm with you," Thank God.

Judy had approved of the New Frontier, and she was equally ecstatic when I signed with Sol Schwartz for a second engagement at the Palace Theatre. Judy back on Broadway! There was a problem, though: Judy was on another bender.

Judy sober, in her natural state of mind, was not combative. But one pill could send her off in the wrong direction. "I have stomach flu" or "My throat is sore" were sure signs that she was taking pills. I was patient with her, and I understood her complaints of extreme tension and uneasiness before her period. Ordinarily the moment would pass, but if it escalated into "I'm bleeding profusely," "I'm depressed as hell," and "Jesus, either give me a drink or bring me up," then I knew there was a crisis at hand. If it was the middle of the night and Fred Pobirs needed to be summoned, it was Judy who would do the telephoning.

I could never interfere. I had to prepare myself that she might get too high and come down too low.

As these patterns seemed to intensify, affecting our quality of life, I was concerned that Judy was scoring dope from not just her doctors or her girlfriends but someone in the house, the staff. Judy detested my questioning her and my careful scrutiny of her quarters. I couldn't be casual when it was clear she was out of it most of the day and night, and we were virtually living separate lives, Judy roaming about the house during the night and sleeping through the day. If I were to show concern she'd abruptly tell me to "fuck off." She was on speed and probably drinking as well. She wasn't eating.

She kept her desk locked; the poems she'd written for her mother as a teenager and her privately bound letters were off limits. The mirrored wardrobe room, built specially to accommodate her growing collection of clothing, was treated with respect: Judy's vaults. My attempt to keep her from herself, to seek out the hidden stashes of pills, the culprits who were aiding and abetting my wife's dependencies, were, most of the time, futile. Judy would eventually break down and ask to go to a clinic, or sober up as a result of sleeping off whatever she'd been ingesting. After an enormous breakfast, I'd be seduced into believing nothing was wrong—with a dreamy, "Hi, darling."

But as the Palace engagement approached, I knew something had to be done about her condition. I confronted her: "Baby, you're always looking for pills."

"You're always acting like a flatfoot."

"I love you. I'd like to see you around."

"Well, you don't trust me. And that's not fair. I'm not Marylou with society credentials, and I'm not Lynn Bari, Queen of the Bs. I've worked every waking moment of my life, and I do what I want to do. I wasn't born with, *hnnn*, a sliver spoon in my mouth. Custom-made shirts, custom-made shoes." She was on a roll, and there was something comedic in her doped-up misery. "Don't fuck with it, Sidney"—she lowered her voice as far down as possible. I'd have to laugh.

The next morning, she left me a note:

Darling,

Let me tell you again—what an angel you were last night. Your patience and kindness and deep understanding meant so much to me, that I'll never forget them. Those things make a great human being—and you're a great man. I'm a helluva lucky woman to be married to you—the only thing I can give in return is my ever-lasting love.

God bless you,
Judy

33

I miss the East Side, the West Side,
The North Side, and the South Side.
So, take me back to Manhattan,
That dear old dirty town.

—Cole Porter

JUDY'S NEW SHOW at the Palace Theatre followed the same program as her Vegas run, with a few minor changes. Instead of the "tramp" number, Roger Edens wrote a clown number. There was a new opening number, a medley of "New York" tunes, but after a few weeks Judy would replace it with "This Is a Party" by Roger Edens and Leonard Gershe, which she had performed in Vegas to great success. Roger continued to write special material and vocal arrangements for Judy. He'd written "This Is the Time of the Evening" with Leonard Gershe for *Ford Star Jubilee* and the Seven City Tour. The "This Is a Party" production included sparkle and glitter on outsized placards that spelled out J*U*D*Y G*A*R*L*A*N*D. The audience would burst into thunderous applause each time.

Judy and I had attended a huge benefit at the Biltmore in downtown Los Angeles; Tony Martin was one of the entertainers, and he had introduced a young comedian, Alan King. I thought Alan was hilarious, more a monologist than a mimic. So I remembered him a few years later when I was booking the second Palace show. I called his agent in New York, who was also a friend of Sol Schwartz, and I made the deal over the telephone without having met him. Alan was placed in the first act, but he wanted to close the show. I'd booked Kovach & Rabovsky, a dance team that was receiving publicity for having been aboard the *Andrea Doria*, to close the first half of the show. Alan appeared before K&R, and he was not pleased. I explained I was booking the show my way! There was also a family of Spanish clowns, a wonderful act, and of course the superb dancing boys.

Alan did his "suburban" routine in front of the urban Manhattan audience. He was filled with trepidation but it worked out, because of his innate gift with monologue. Judy was fascinated by the young comedian and watched from the wings in her backstage funky terry cloth robe, the collar smeared with makeup. She thought he had something. Alan came off the stage angry. He had not played in the spot he desired. He walked up the stairs to his dressing room in Siberia thinking he'd like to quit. Just before Judy was due onstage, she climbed up the three flights of stairs, beautifully attired in her Norman Norell gown, knocked on his door, and said, "You can close my fucking show anytime." It was the start of a marvelous relationship.

Alan broke Judy up on and off stage. However, he remained at the Palace in the spot we originally agreed upon; in later productions he would perform before Judy closed. After King finished his act he'd immediately go into the audience, find an aisle seat (like Judy, he was claustrophobic), and watch Judy work. Eventually she taught Alan the Fred Astaire part in the "Couple of Swells" routine.

I'd tell Alan I thought he was a "charming rogue," a "rough and tumble guy from the streets of New York." This would get a certain reaction.

"Sid, I'll take your head off," he'd challenge. Alan began to hang out and drink with us. He'd be around during the backstage squabbles, and the good times as well.

Judy couldn't breathe in the outfits designed for her show—the Norells and other fantastic gowns were restrictive suits of armor. Judy was best in a short, handsome silk jacket and tapered pants, which would become her 1960s uniform. She'd gained a little weight, and I watched her like a hawk, because if the weight gain was the reason she was so uncomfortable in those gowns, she'd have to lose some pounds. And once again this presented a big obstacle: the personality changes, the mood shifts.

She tried to cut back on her appetite, and this left her irritable. She'd lock herself in her dressing room and not come out. I'd reason with her and she'd complain, "Nobody wants to listen to me." At times she'd smash a glass in anger at the thought of getting into those outfits. It was too late to redesign the show. If I suggested she cut back on her appetite, we'd argue. "It's too late to change anything." She'd sneak a pill and a drink and then suddenly not want to go out onstage, overcome with fear. I'd have to hold her, give her a swat on her ass to get her out onstage. Then she'd glide out there, take a breath, and bring the house down. Every night there were celebrities in the audience, and this motivated Judy to get into her uncomfortable clothes. Alan would prep Judy by listing the stars in the crowd: Julie Andrews, Cary Grant, Lana Turner with Johnny Stompanato, neighbors from Mapleton, and so on.

The eight-week run was extended to seventeen weeks, and we brought the children to New York. My mother had been staying with the children on Mapleton before they came east. She ran the house and looked after our domestic affairs.

Judy was capable of handling everything. She was performing one show a night, eight shows per week, so she wasn't overworked. The children were with us, and she was very attentive to them. We were living our lives, together in the same apartment; there was no separation. I'd take Lorna and Joey to Lindy's deli. It didn't feel like a delicate balance.

Offers were coming in, as Judy had proved herself yet again. She was asked to do *Funny Girl*, among other prime projects, but she wasn't ready to take on another major film. Judy was getting tired as she wound down the last weeks at the Palace. One night Sonny Werblin, a man I respected who worked at MCA, New York, came backstage and said he wanted to talk to me. We spoke on the telephone the following day.

Sonny asked if I thought Judy would be able to do a show sponsored by Buick. We were under contract to CBS to deliver one special a year. I was interested, but I needed to discuss it with Judy. And I was not eager to disturb her at the moment, because I knew she was exhausted—and touchy to deal with. However, I told Sonny it might be possible. Sonny rang me again to announce, "Sid, you're on! We want the show delivered six weeks from the closing date of the Palace." Just weeks to produce a special with Judy!

We needed to go back to Los Angeles. We'd received news that Bogie had died, and this upset both of us and depressed the hell out of Judy. Before we left, Sonny came over to see us at the Carlyle Hotel with Freddie Fields, a young agent I'd not met before. When Judy announced to them she was not prepared to do a show right away, Freddie piped up, "How about a show with five bands?" He was thinking about his brother, Shep Fields, and a few other bandleaders. Judy softened and said, "It's not a bad idea." But it wasn't a yes, and Judy wasn't really ready.

After Judy had owned Broadway for the second time, the journalist Marie Torre came out with a piece that said a CBS executive told her Judy's special was not going forward because Judy was overweight, which was untrue. Judy was incensed; the issue of her weight was an open wound. She'd been working night after night to great acclaim, offers were coming in, and now a major New York columnist was telling the world she was fat and not getting work because of it. Judy made up her mind that she was not going to be attacked, and she went to her lawyer, who agreed it was libel. I thought it was frivolous, but Judy didn't agree, and I wasn't going to interfere. To Judy a few extra pounds meant the difference between getting a part or not. It was a sensitive issue, and this time the report was totally inaccurate. Judy was adamant. "What the fuck is going on, seventeen weeks at the Palace. I look the best I've ever looked and this dame is putting me down to the public."

Torre could have written an apology but she did not, and the case went forward after we returned to Los Angeles. Torre would not reveal her source, and the judge held her in contempt.

The strenuous run at the Palace and the Torre/CBS incident irked Judy and gave her some cause to fall back on pills. We had a few run-ins at the house. Then Judy was booked to perform at the Riviera in Detroit, and she was insistent that I approach Henry Ford II about putting up preproduction money for the adaptation of a novel we owned, *Born in Wedlock*. I wasn't racing to talk to Henry about the movie business. I thought I understood Ford's character: he was a hard-driving business-man who was not about to gamble change on a Hollywood film. After the performance at the Riviera we met Henry and a young, good-looking man who was his assistant at the popular restaurant the London Chop House in downtown Detroit. Judy was in good form, telling anecdotes about old Hollywood. She told Henry about the making of the 1946 film *Till the Clouds Roll By*, the life story of composer Jerome Kern (my mother's old customer from Bronxville). Judy had appeared as Broadway star Marilyn Miller; Robert Walker portrayed Kern opposite Lucille Bremer (who later married Rod Rodriguez, my old buddy from Douglas Aircraft) as Mrs. Kern. Lucille, who was Arthur Freed's mistress at the time, had her eyes on the prize—she aspired to stardom but had never quite made it. The movie was a series of production numbers; Sinatra starred in the finale singing "Ol' Man River." Judy explained to Henry how Sinatra wasn't convinced he could give the song the proper interpretation. To his surprise Kern said to Frank, "Sing it your way," and it was a smash. When Kern died, Sinatra asked to sing "Ol' Man River" at his funeral. Henry was captivated by the story. When Judy mentioned *Born in Wedlock*, explaining it was a story about a turn-of-the-century traveling vaudeville family, Henry smiled and ordered another round of cocktails.

Back in Los Angeles, I was having breakfast at the Riviera golf club with Neddie and Jock McLean and Dan Topping, co-owner of the New York Yankees. I mentioned to Jock that Judy was hot and heavy about Henry putting up preproduction money for *Born in Wedlock*. Neddie was also after him—for an oil deal in Oklahoma that Ford did eventually support. Jock thought it unlikely Henry would put money in film.

Jock had a nervous tic that took some getting used to when he spoke. His jaw would drop in a nervous spasm for a few seconds and then he'd resume speaking. He was recalling the time when his mother, Evalyn, was financing the reward for the return of the Lindberg baby and he got stuck on the first syllable of "reward." Jock was basically a warmhearted person himself, and he indulged Judy and loved her for herself.

We'd been invited to Henry's birthday party in Southampton, New York. Anne, Henry's wife, had asked if Judy would sing at the birthday party, and I mentioned to Topping, "Judy doesn't sing at birthday parties. She sings when she feels like it." He thought I was foolish to take that position at the moment. So we changed our minds about that and Judy agreed to sing at the event, even though I was convinced it was a waste of time.

Neddie and Jock and I frequently played golf together, but our lunches and breakfasts were taken up with conversations about how to get Henry to invest. Generally I had nothing in mind for him, but the McLeans had lists. They were close friends with Henry, and Jock would find women to introduce to him. I was amazed when he later married his second wife, Cristina, a warm, earthy woman, not his type. He must have suffered a lapse.

Henry's current wife sent a limo to the Carlyle Hotel to take Judy and me out to Southampton, where we were put up in a suite at the charming Southampton Colgate, a small, elegant hotel. Anne Ford was docile, sweet, and accommodating. She never countered Henry in public. The night before his birthday party, the four of us were having dinner at their house. Henry, who was a drinker, enjoyed brawling and fooling around like a big kid. We were having cocktails in the living room before dinner was served. Our host was boisterous, and as we were talking about boxing he asked if I would show him how to throw a punch. He got so worked up his face turned beet red. I managed to change the subject and took him up on an earlier offer to show me his custom-made dune buggy, painted pink and green. We scooped up our martinis and off we went to the beach for a predinner ride in the sunset. At the beach I gave Henry a few pointers on how to spar.

At dinner he said, "Anne, I want to show you something." He turned to me, "Sid, can I throw a punch at you?" I said, "Of course." He was a difficult person to spar with, because he was so overweight. I didn't want to cripple him, either. He made a motion of throwing a punch, and I caught his arm, sparred a little and encouraged him to try again. Fortunately, there was something in my reflexes that cracked through his martini miasma and brought everything to an abrupt stop. We happily returned to our turtle soup.

The next afternoon, we had drinks with Anne's sister, who was married to a VP at Grace Shipping. She was a lovely woman, recently recuperated from an illness. Judy spoke to her about the possibility of Henry backing a film for us. The woman's immediate reaction was "Don't trust him—he won't come through. He's a blowhard." Apparently she hated her brother-in-law, but we never knew precisely why. I'd long ago put to bed the idea Henry would be financing *Born in Wedlock*, but I would go through the motions for Judy.

Henry was a control freak, a master puppeteer, and he had been brutal with his brother. He was a stern ruler, and now his sister-in-law was telling us he had a vicious and selfish nature. At Hollywood parties I'd noticed Anne seemed frightened of him when he was drunk. He could be abusive and insulting, with a reputation of *beware*.

The day came when I met Henry at his posh, elegant apartment at the Hotel Pierre. He was very different from the Henry around the dinner table or the Henry having drinks at the Riviera golf club. He was a cool stranger, all business: "Sid, I want you to meet my board." I knew how to play hunches, and I agreed with Jock that Henry never appeared to be someone interested in the film business. I was, however, curious to meet this board of movers and shakers, the industrial heads dictating the play of the national economy, dealing the life and death of workers—creating American lifestyle, making millions in profit to put behind the politician of choice. I still wasn't betting, but it would be interesting.

The meeting was arranged for the following day. I arrived at a building on Madison Avenue in the Fifties. I made my way to the conference room, where I was faced with a dozen executives sitting at a round table with Henry at the head. A scene right out of Paddy Chayefsky's *Network*. It was chilling, each man a more frightening mask of Anglo-Saxon business acumen than the last. I made my speech, step one, two, three, etc., how much a film costs, how to make distribution, how much is needed to finance. I completed my pitch to an unearthly hush. Not one fellow had interrupted or asked me a question. Henry finally broke the silence: "Thanks, Sid. We'll talk soon."

I felt foolish. I was angry. I couldn't get to the humor of it. I had to let my humility cool on the flight back to Los Angeles. Why, it wasn't even a long shot.

34

BOGIE WAS GONE, and the high spirit of the neighborhood had left with him. But we were still living an extravagant lifestyle that I had to keep balancing. I needed to devise original schemes to make money; consequently I was immersed in promoting and financing Judy's performances. Judy's irritability about where she worked presented severe problems. She was uninsurable, and we had to put up our own money in advance.

If Judy was stoned and didn't feel like performing, one of her popular ruses was to complain of a "stomach flu." Generally the migraines and the laryngitis were real, due to the ingesting of certain pills. Sorting out what was authentic and what was bullshit was tricky. Now Judy gradually descended into a diet of uppers and downers, which left her malnourished, and she'd scream out in agony with intense migraine headaches.

As Judy never permitted me to call Fred Pobirs, I'd wait out her episodes feeling uneasy and hoping she'd call him. He might come by on his way home after work to take a blood count, give her a vitamin shot—and the "vitamin B" shots could well have been Dr. Feelgood shots. She'd feel better . . . but it wasn't going to last. Pobirs would force himself out of his bed at three or four in the morning to give her a shot—sometimes it was Thorazine, sometimes a placebo, depending on what he thought was needed. I had to trust his judgment. "The Needle in the Night" was there for her.

Judy's protocol regarding the doctor's visits never flagged. I wasn't permitted in the room with Pobirs. I'd wait downstairs to thank him. In the beginning I'd say, "How do you cure her, stop the pain?" And Pobirs, who could be cocky, would answer "There's no cure." Other times he'd say, "Try AA" or "Take her away" or "Total abstinence." Other nights I'd express myself: "Jesus Christ, when is this going to end!"—more an exclamation than a question. Fred would reply laconically, "She's your wife, you have to take care of her." Which was precisely my thought, and once I said to Fred, "You must love her, just like I do." He didn't respond.

One night I escorted Pobirs out of the house around daybreak, and as I thanked him I said, "I don't know how long I can keep this up."

Pobirs countered, "Did you ever ask yourself why you married someone like this?" Adrenalin shot through me, and I considered maybe this *was* going nowhere, a dead end—maybe Judy would never make it, that there was no hope. Then I'd go up to see her in the bedroom and she'd be sleeping at last, all tension out of her face, and once again, the alluring, devilish child was at peace. I'd lie next to her, exhausted, fully clothed, and go to sleep. There was definitely hope.

As the current bender progressed, however, it presented the possibility of self-mutilation, as in her postpartum depression after Lorna's birth. Judy, stoned on pills, was not only an indication of the need to escape but something darker, a hidden vein of depression so deep and private no one was permitted entry. I had to concern myself with her impulses to harm herself physically when the pills locked in.

My worry was the exact intake of pills, what she was putting in her system, for by now I understood that some pills were more toxic than others, and the combining of certain drugs was next to deadly. Judy might have resisted the effects of one particular drug, but not in combination with others. I became rather proficient in detecting what mood was the result of what drug or drugs. Mind altering drugs left her paranoid, imperious, and without humor. When she challenged and weighed every word I spoke, I called it her neurotic jeweler's loupe syndrome: she was coming off speed. I wasn't living on guard, exactly, just testing the waters. There'd be evenings when I'd say, "Darling, what've you been doing?" And the response would be "*Hnnn*, nothing." I'd notice her chocolate glazed eyes, dulled by something. Sober, her eyes were like clear candy drops. If I tried getting tough with her she'd withdraw until there'd be an argument: "Mind your own fucking business."

But my monitoring would very often save her life, and our marriage. During these bouts she had contact with the children for only short periods of time. And the children were pacified, they were going to school, they had two nurses. We weren't sleeping together, but if I wasn't in the den I'd be in another room not far from the master bedroom.

She'd be locked in, either sleeping or watching television, cut off. Several days of sheer hell would pass. I'd be waiting for the moment when she'd admit to Pobirs, "Christ, I'm so sick," and he'd tell her it was time to withdraw. I knew she'd have to hit bottom, holding her head in her hands before she was compelled to give in. She'd go for seventy-two hours with no food, suffering intolerable migraines.

Pleading never worked. "You're killing yourself."

"So, *hnnn*, I'm going to kill myself."

I was desperate to bring her out of her misery. "We're miles and miles apart, darling. You've got to get back on the track."

"We'll get back on the track."

More time would pass and she'd be unbearably ill. "*Hnnn*, I'm sick, baby, help me."

There was no communication in her twilight state. And when she came down, detoxed, it was forgotten. "Hi, darling."

As this cycle repeated, Judy was building up a tremendous tolerance to pills. One sleeping pill wasn't going to put her to sleep. She'd have to take three. One Dexedrine wasn't enough of a lift—she needed four. If I'd taken ten I might have died; Judy would take twenty and fall asleep for hours and not die. Her collection mounted, three from here and three from there.

Though I was concerned about how and where she was accumulating them, there wasn't time for me to play sleuth. I had to tend to business, and my business wasn't in working order. Judy's voice, of course, was at issue. Chemicals dried out her larynx. Sober, her speaking voice was lilting; under the influence, she sounded husky and raspy, impeding the singing voice.

Once, she'd been on pills that found her easy but up all night in her private room, drawing pictures and reading. I could put my arms around her, and sometimes she'd say, "Hold me, baby."

The next day I found a note, the familiar circles dotting the *is*, her apology:

Darling,
I was really sick all goddamn night—It's now 7:20 and I'm going to take a crack at lying down and try to sleep.—Anyway don't wake me for "nuttin."

In spite of all my pukiness—I loved you all through the night. Not an attractive thing to tell you—but when you adore your husband—what are you gonna do. God bless you my Sid for having so much *class*. See you sometime today. All my devoted love, forever—Judy

---

By the summer of 1957 Judy was touring, and we had bigger plans for our return to L.A. The Greek Theatre in Los Angeles was in a class of its own. It was home turf, and Judy was looking forward to working in front of her supportive peers. We'd begun working on the opening night party guest list on the road in Dallas. Our assistant Vern Alves had already received many acceptances:

DEAN MARTIN	ROGER EDENS
ALAN KING	LENNY GERSHE
AMIN BROS.	GEORGE BURNS
IRA GERSHWINS	COLE PORTER

JIMMY McHUGH

LOUELLA PARSONS

GEORGE CUKORS

BETTY BOGART

FRED FINKLEHOFFE

GEORGE RAFT

ARTHUR LOEW AND DATE

BETTY FURNESS

DON LOPER

JEAN NEGULESCOS

JACK WARNER

ART LINKLETTERS

GEO AXELRODS

DR. AND MRS. POBIRS

MIKE CONNOLLY AND DATE

JERRY WALD

SAMMY CAHNS

GENE BYRAMS

BILL GOETZS

OSCAR LEVANTS

RAY STARKS

CHUCK NORTHROP

MONA FREEMAN

LEE SIEGELS

JACK CATHCARTS

ARMY ARCHERDS

VERN ALVES

JOHNNY DUGANS

BOB MITCHUMS

MR. AND MRS. LUNN

HAROLD HECHTS

HENRY GINSBERG AND DATE

GORDON JENKINS

MRS. ROCK HUDSON

MINNA WALLIS

PANDRO BERMAN AND DATE

LOU SCHREIBERS

DESI AND LUCY

GEORGE ROSENBERGS

Opening night at the Greek, Judy made up a story for the press: she told them in the last chorus of "Over the Rainbow" a moth flew into her mouth, and she had to keep it there until the end, when it was able to fly out. This amused the columnists, and we got a lot of free PR. We had several parties, one at the house and one at Romanoff's. Ronald and Nancy Reagan were having a good time at Romanoff's, where most men wore dark blue suits. I was bemused by Ronnie's sartorial choice of color: Who wears brown suits? President Reagan does.

35

Now that *Born in Wedlock* was out of the question, Judy's focus turned to England. One day, Judy came to me: "I'd like to play the Palladium." I thought, terrific! She was so edgy around the house, in and out of benders, Pobirs arriving in the middle of the night to knock her out. She had anxiety about her career; she didn't have the confidence in herself that I had in her. I found out the Palladium wasn't available, but I flew to London and arranged to have her play the Dominion, one of the Rank theaters. A month's engagement. Judy was thrilled. "We'll open the Dominion like we opened the Palace!"

Now that we'd been booked in London, we had to get there. Judy was insisting on taking twelve dancing boys, Liza, Lorna, Joey, a nanny, a stage manager, a hairdresser. It was the one time I persuaded our business manager, Morgan Maree, to come to the house and explain to Judy why it was not feasible without her going on the road beforehand to raise some cash. I was counting on Morgan's straightforward approach, the fact that he was bona fide and there weren't any personal tugs of war. Judy, of course, laughed and threw her seductive gaze in Morgan's face, not budging from the theme of performing, *en troupe*, in England. Finally, Morgan laid it out: perform here first for the money to take the show abroad. But Judy didn't want to just work, she wanted to perform. She longed to recapture the Palladium, to be the artiste playing to adoring audiences, especially her supportive peers, and nothing less. I said, "Be a sport, darling. What happened to the trouper in you?"

The economics were unimportant; the significant factor, to Judy, was the applause. But because she longed for the British audiences, she did agree to work. I booked her for Washington, DC, and Philadelphia; the fees would just cover our expenses for the English tour. Her attitude on the road was evident: *I want to get this over with, to get to London with my troupe, to see those people standing and cheering. I need to see the rave reviews of my performances, and I want to keep reliving New York and Los Angeles.* Now she had a reason to indulge in a sequence of pill-taking to get her through something she didn't want to do.

Her disdain was not mitigated by her trademark wit. Judy could laugh at herself—but not about present miseries. Episodes and anecdotes from the past were given a theatrical treatment, satirical, comic. She'd make fun of herself, but it was always past history.

Judy arrived in Washington complaining of a sore throat. She found a doctor to "treat" her. The result of that private consultation was twenty Seconal instead of three. She also needed Dexamyl to get going the next day, ten instead of two. She had to fortify herself against the drudgery of playing Washington and Philadelphia.

She played four nights in DC. On the fifth morning her breakfast sat waiting for her to come out of the bathroom, where she'd been lingering. When Judy came out in her short white lace negligee, her arms were in front of her and she said, "Look, darling, what I've done!" Her wrists had been slashed and she was bleeding profusely. Within minutes, I managed to put tourniquets on both arms and call the house doctor. We got her to a doctor's office without the press's knowledge. She awakened from the anesthetic: "Darling, what time is it?"

"It's five o'clock."

"I've got to get to the theater."

"Darling, we had to cancel the show."

"Oh, goodness!"

We drove directly to Philadelphia from the wrist stitching. Judy wore a collection of pearl bracelets on her arms.

In Philadelphia Judy fell and twisted her ankle and had to perform with her ankle strapped. Now we were canceling two shows in Philadelphia.

Instead of making $100,000 as anticipated, the available cash was dispensed for living expenses and salaries. The writing was on the wall: there wasn't going to be sufficient money for the English tour. I racked my brain as to how to raise funds. Judy was counting on leaving the country, whereas I was in the frame of mind where I felt it would be better if she checked into a clinic.

Judy had hated Washington and Philadelphia. It was the living moment she couldn't get through, and she got back at me by showing me her bleeding wrists. She had to live and perform in an exalted manner, otherwise there'd be hell to pay. At the time, after two weeks of failure, I didn't have the luxury to think about the psychological aspect of Judy's behavior. There were twelve dancing boys, the children, the nurse, a stage manager, and a hotel bill that was running up. I left Philadelphia early and went to New York to raise money for the Judy Garland traveling circus.

I checked into the Hotel Pierre and started to work on raising funds. The McLeans refused to loan me a cent; they told me, "That's the way the cookie crumbles." Peter Lawford wired me money, and so did Charlie Whittingham. I was also forced to sell my share in the racehorse Sienna II. I didn't want to lose her. She was a bay mare, with black legs. I'd paid $18,000 for her, and I won the biggest bet of my life when she was a four-year-old. Sienna II beat Bubbly and King's Mistake, mares of the year. I sold her to Mrs. Touron, Nicky Du Pont's cousin, who owned Sienna II's half brother. It was painful, but the show had to go on!

I'd thrown all my personal cash into Judy's shows and lost. As I was cursing my situation, in sailed Freddie Finklehoffe from out of the blue. "Just like Mary Poppins, Freddie." He sashayed over to one of the Pierre's well-upholstered lounge chairs and sunk down while picking up a telephone to order himself a big double martini. "You might like one. Do you own a horse called Roman II?"

"Yep."

"He broke his leg."

Freddie was right: I wanted a double martini. I had $30,000 coming to me from Roman II's insurance.

Then Norman Weiss, an agent at MCA, rang to tell me that Judy could play Ben Maksik's Town and Country nightclub in Brooklyn, and that the chances were Maksik would advance money against a future appearance in March after England. This sounded marvelous.

Early in the evening, Judy arrived wearing a big straw hat, with a trillion pearl bracelets covering her wounds. "Hi darling, how ya doin'?"

I had four martinis in me by now, Roman II had left me a legacy, and close friends had come through. "I'm doin' fine, baby."

I thought the deal was nearly finalized with Maksik. Judy/Cinderella was in her princess mode, wearing an exquisite fur collar and looking terribly continental. I'd written checks all over the place, to Cunard Line, to the dancing boys. I'd sent money to the house. Later in a cubbyhole downstairs in the bar I met with Maksik and Weiss and a deal was struck. We were going to have nine days in England before Judy opened at the Dominion. Time to promote, and time to rest.

The day of departure was scary. We were aboard the *United States* and her whistles were blowing, and there was no sign of Maksik aboard with the cash I needed to cover the checks. Judy was casually buffing her nails in a corner while I sweated out Maksik's arrival and waited for the chauffeur who was going to deposit the funds. (The insurance money from Roman II would be sent to London.) I took a deep breath of relief when, in a flurry, everyone came aboard at the last minute. Norman Weiss was holding the contracts, Judy was ignoring the reporters, and Maksik was waving a brown paper bag filled with cash.

The ocean crossing was like going to heaven. Judy didn't take so much as a motion sickness pill. It was all shuffleboard, Ping-Pong, captain's table, and romance.

***

Alan King had taken his wife, Jeanette, to Europe for a holiday. I knew he wasn't interested in working but I needed him. He was a wonderful entertainer, and Judy loved to work with him. I'd called Alan in Rome and awakened him in the middle of the night. I was convinced Alan had to work with Judy in London. I asked him to meet with the J. Arthur Rank people who owned the Dominion while in London. "Let me know what you think of them." I was counting on him seeing his name in lights, something I'd arranged to change his mind. He couldn't say no. Forgive me, Alan! In the end he agreed. I took some heat for booking him, as he was still unknown over there. I always came back with "This is Judy's preference."

Judy live with an audience was unsurpassable. It's tragic that not one of these extraordinary performances was ever filmed or recorded. There were problems miking a pit orchestra; rarely was anything set up acoustically for live recording as it is today. The state of the art didn't advance until 1962, when mobile units were brought in.

During the Dominion engagement Judy performed at the Palladium as part of the Royal Variety Gala—it was a command performance. The singer Mario Lanza was also featured in the program. He was managed by the Mills Music Co. Mills was an older man who happened to be staying at the Dorchester, where we were living. He approached me, concerned about Mario's place in the revue. Judy had asked to perform her tramp number. Val Parnell, who organized the gala, thought there wasn't enough time. However, Judy insisted, and Lanza had to follow her act, which had brought the house down. Lanza sang well enough, but the audience cruelly laughed at him. It was a turn of events nobody could have anticipated. He suffered every performer's nightmare, and we were horrified. Immediately after he finished onstage Mario made a getaway straight to the toilet, where he vomited his guts out. He couldn't take it. It was a vivid example of the obverse of adulation: the crowd can love you and the crowd can kill you! Judy respected Mario, and in 1960 she asked me to manage him. I declined. I really never cared about managing any performer other than Judy.

Godfrey Winn, a popular London journalist, invited us to his house for an interview. I persuaded Judy to keep the appointment, as I felt it would be helpful. Judy was negative: "Don't tell me what to do." I was able to convince her it would be good PR. For the interview Judy wore a classic black dress and coat, and a little Juliet hat decorated with brilliants and pearls, Judy's tiara.

Winn asked Judy about my impact on her career, and as always she answered that she depended totally on my taste and my sense of "show": "Sid has entire control." Little did Winn suspect the fiasco that had preceded our arrival at the White Cliffs of Dover!

In general Judy found American audiences enthusiastic but insecure as to how to react to the performer, while the English audience was more at home with variety and revues. One of the most requested medleys was the "Born in a Trunk" sequence from *A Star Is Born*. We never thought of the production number as a live performance and we'd not brought any orchestrations with us, but the audiences were interested in the thirty-two bars. We eventually adapted it to the stage for Judy's Metropolitan Opera House tour. Meanwhile, Gordon Jenkins, Judy's musical conductor, had written a special number for her, "The Letter," which didn't compete with Roger Edens's material.

Judy would invariably tell an interviewer that "Over the Rainbow" was her favorite song. Judy had many favorites, and there'd be times when she'd resist singing "Rainbow." Professionally, of course, she wouldn't give it up, as "Rainbow" closed the show and never failed to bring down the house. Judy would confess that more often than not she'd force herself into it, and then find herself genuinely crying by the end of the number.

Our children, Joey and Lorna, were natural born troupers; they fit right into our London adventure. They had a wonderful time seeing the sights and meeting other children. They were outgoing children with a lot of energy. Judy never spoke down to them. She enjoyed relating how Joey at age two ran across the room holding not a toy but his favorite record of his mother, insisting she play it. The press ate this up. Judy would talk about the children's interest in words, how their new vocabulary would be rhyming words from songs: rice, ice, nice. Lorna would call Judy from the connecting suite and beg her to come in and listen to some new word she'd taught Joe. Judy was very family minded in these interviews, even referring to Johnny as "our" child: "We have an eight-year-old and an eleven-year-old." Johnny and Liza were both in private schools.

All of Judy's children were born in a trunk. Liza was motivated to perform early on. She worked hard at becoming an artist. Lorna, who sang, and Joe, who played the drums and sang, were around Judy's performances from birth. Lorna understood the word "recording" when she was just a tot.

Gordon Jenkins's orchestration, his use of strings, matched Judy's emotional pitch in texture and sheer strength of voice. He understood her phrasing and distinct sound. It was a wonderful marriage of talent. Jenkins also had a wacky sense of humor. After the command performance, he arrived bombed at the gala. The party had been in progress for some time, and it was jumping. A footman announced the arrival of each guest. When Gordon was asked to give his name he said, "Mr. and Mrs. Men's Room," and so the couple was presented.

While we were in the UK, Aly Khan asked me to go to Newmarket and bid on a filly. I was away for a few days and Judy swallowed a few uppers, which gave her insomnia. She persuaded Alan King to stay up with her and take her to look at the hookers in Petticoat Lane. She kept him up all night, sending him back to his wife exhausted. Fortunately, her behavior did not escalate into a bender.

I purchased a filly for forty thousand pounds, a very good price for the horse. On my return Judy cooled down, and our life proceeded without a crisis.

In the old days, Walfarms had been a good racing stable. Within one week we'd won four races with three horses: Bir Hakeim, La Franza, and the Driller, who won twice. The papers thought it was newsworthy and wrote us up, which was unusual in those days. We were to sell Bir Hakeim in Florida, but we won considerable money with the Driller, which was a claiming horse and raced for eleven years, becoming a great winner for us. I'd claimed La Franza for $7,500; he was a winner as well. Once I ran the Driller in a stake race. Nelson Bunker Hunt, the tycoon who owned a thousand race horses, was shocked. "Sid, what are you doing running a claiming horse in a stake race?" The Driller was on the board 20:1, but as the day went by he was 7:2. Bunker was astounded. We made a bet: Bunker's horse, a stake horse, would lose to the Driller. Bunker's horse ran last, and the Driller, God bless him, was next to last, so I won the bet!

Rainbow Farms was equal to Walfarms, but I was not certain how long I could sustain the operation. Gone were the halcyon days when I'd take Liza, Johnny, and Bill Sergeant's little boy to the stable and to the racetrack to see the horses. The children had been in love with the barns and the horses. Liza and Johnny were growing too old to play with little Lorna and Joe. A sense of leisure was going out of my life.

36

No matter how creative, how imaginative I was in coming up with ideas for concerts and tours, they couldn't all equal the Palace, a Broadway appearance, London. I knew by now that Judy lived to perform, but I had learned to be on guard whenever we toured a city she perceived was not of her class. Just when I thought I'd appeal to her reason, she'd pull something—if it wasn't a sore throat, it would be news of the death of a performer she'd once worked with. We began to have fights in the dressing room. I'd shake her up: "Baby, you've got to get out there." And more often than not, I was taking her by the hand, leading her onstage to explain Judy Garland had laryngitis. I wanted the audience to see that she wasn't falling down drunk. Sometimes the audience would chant "Judy, Judy, Judy" and she'd begin to sing, in her robe, and she'd get into it and give a bravura performance. But I couldn't rely on it.

For all of Judy's success at the Dominion, the run had not earned us a profit. Financial responsibilities were mounting. At home, Judy's days were occupied with Lorna and Joe, but I sensed an uneasiness about her and I was on guard. It was a bad time for my ex-wife Lynn to ask for more money for Johnny, who was in boarding school.

It occurred to me that we live in a huge house, so why not have Johnny move in with us? Lynn was married to a psychiatrist, Dr. Nathan Rickles, and they lived in an apartment in Beverly Hills. I thought rather than pay out more child support, my son could join our family. This required going to court. And the judge did award Johnny to me. Lynn made a scene in court, exclaiming, "No, no. He's my life." The judge said he believed it would be better for the boy to live with a family.

I'd won, but I knew that winning was not a victory. I wasn't able to be at home; I couldn't oversee the children. I had to depend on Judy and the servants, and Judy was not her normal self. Sure enough, in ten days' time, Johnny was back with his mother, where he remained until some years later, when he went off to college.

Lynn would continue to use Johnny to subtly express her ambivalence toward me. One minute she'd be pleased he spent time with me, the next instant she'd be sabotaging the father/son relationship. And she'd find new cause to bring me into court over one thing or another. I never knew when she'd attack. She was in the business of cooking up causes: lifelong support for the boy, schooling, college—in and out of court, she never let up. During Johnny's teenage years, he'd have little contact with me or my family.

Then from out of nowhere in 1972 Lynn called me and asked if Johnny could come to live with me. "You take care of your son," was her command. The boy was now a young man of twenty, who had somehow survived the 1960s but clearly not without scars and habits. I felt introduced to a stranger. Nonetheless Johnny joined my new family—Lorna, Joey, and my fourth wife, Patti Potts. He was with us for one year and left without a word to anyone. I didn't hear from Johnny again until the day after Lynn died, in November 1989. A period of sixteen years had passed.

Judy faced her own child-rearing issues with her ex, though hers were not as severe. Vincente had agreed to send $500 a month for Liza, but his accountant argued that as Vincente legally was to have Liza six months of the year, he owed but half. However, Liza lived with us year round. Money was never an issue in our relationship with Vincente, which was friendly. I wasn't going to argue the point.

Liza as a child adored her mother. She was an amazing dark-haired little girl with incredible black eyes and an energy and cheerfulness that never flagged. She was a few years older than my son Johnny, who by contrast had fiery red hair. By 1957 Liza was a preadolescent who spent her days at school, and this time around she did not have time for a kid brother; in fact, they tended to scrap.

I was still working hard to stabilize our income. Judy was in and out. I now relied entirely on the staff to run the household. Judy would be up all night, cut off from me, sometimes not going to bed until noon.

The contractual obligation to Ben Maksik was coming due, and Judy was not eager to play the Town and Country nightclub in Brooklyn. Every time I discussed Maksik with her she was negative. I was always encouraged when she came to me saying, "Darling, I think I should go to a clinic for a few days." She'd have to shape up for Maksik's, but it didn't look as though it was going in that direction.

We played a few engagements, including a return to Las Vegas, where Judy performed at the Flamingo Hotel. We arrived the day after Christmas for a three-week commitment. New Year's Eve found Judy performing in front of an irreverent Vegas booze crowd. No one paid attention to my diva. I realized too late that I shouldn't have booked her there in the first place. It was my fault. She was embarrassed. Women were walking up onstage high and dancing with each other. Judy was furious there wasn't any security in front. So Judy left the stage and the job. She returned to our room and switched on the television set, not speaking, furious. Vern, who traveled with us, attempted to distract her, offering to play gin, anything. Nothing worked. In the morning she opened her mouth to express herself: "How could you book me here?"

There were two weeks left to work, and Judy wasn't interested in my answer. I was responsible for her misery, for the audience's stupidity. As she yelled she took off her four-inch stiletto-heeled shoe and hurled it in my direction, catching me in the forehead as I turned to leave the room. The show was canceled. We returned home, where the atmosphere was chilly. She wasn't speaking with me. I was concerned now that the Maksik Town and Country engagement could be aborted, throwing us into debt.

One evening her behavior was so peculiar I wondered if she'd been doing booze and pills. She'd left half-filled glasses around the house as though she'd been only sipping. She wasn't responding to my questions, and her coordination was off. Judy wasn't hostile, because she wasn't there. I frantically searched the bottles in our fancy mirrored bar. They were filled. That didn't make sense either; people came to the house and there was considerable social drinking, our lifestyle. Why would all these bottles be full? On closer scrutiny I uncovered the mystery: they were filled with water. This was serious. MCA was going to dump us. She couldn't be insured. She'd fucked up at the Flamingo, and Maksik's was light years from her idea of where she should be performing. And now Judy was combining her pill habit with heavy drinking.

The day arrived when I had to take a closer look our staff, at the people I'd trusted and enjoyed working with. Vern Alves confessed to me he'd supplied her once. Miro, the all-purpose carpenter, had a big truck with all of his paraphernalia parked in back of the house. Judy had enjoyed everyone I'd hired. Naturally, they were her connections.

"Marvin-Schmarvin" was a high-class gofer. He dressed in blue suits and liked to gamble. He kept a nifty little pad on Doheny, where he'd sit down and roll himself "the world's perfect joint," smoke it, and drink "the world's perfect martini." Moderation was Marvin-Schmarvin's bible. I suppose he interested me by his use of the word *moderation*, a concept I longed to have in our vocabulary.

Harry Rubin, who'd been on our house staff through most of the 1950s, was an electrical contractor, but when he worked for us he was just someone around the house helping. He'd be a butler, a cook, or do some wiring. Harry was bright and he could banter with Judy. He was young, red-faced, black-haired, and Jewish, and we got along. Harry said Judy had hit on him many times, and he'd gone through a period when he was also dependent on pills. Harry was a loveable guy, but he turned out to be another of Judy's connections.

I chewed out the staff and fired a few of them. I let Harry go: "I know it's you." Harry returned to the electrical business and real estate. The last time I talked to him, he'd bought his tenth house.

I found a note while Judy was sleeping; she'd left it on her writing table in her dressing room. Judy was not religious, but this was an indication she'd acknowledged a higher power, an echo perhaps from the AA meeting. I could only guess; she wasn't going to discuss the note with me.

Dear God—
I am asking for help. I need help. I need strength and some kind of courage that has left me. My soul needs healing. My needs are many. Give me the strength to crush my fear and cowardice. Let me face life and the fun it must hold. Help with my bad nerves and illness until the whiskey is out of my body. Let me see the loveliness awaiting me. Help me find you. Help me make the most of my splendid life. I have lost my way—please God—let me find it. Let me find dignity and health—

Judy hadn't slept in a few days. She was becoming more and more irritable and aggressive. It was obvious she was also extremely uncomfortable. Once again she saw me as an obstacle, preventing her from destroying herself, or in her terms preventing her from doing what she "wanted to do." She'd assail me: "You're defying me!" Her language had a comic edge, and combined with her petite size, the picture often held an air of absurdity. But, of course, it was more complex: to have to confront the very person I was in love with, who possessed the kind of authority Judy manifested, was like climbing Everest in high heels.

37

DESPITE MY CRACKDOWN on the staff, someone was still supplying Judy with pills. I was in a quandary most of the time trying to figure out who it was. She turned my concern into a game: I was the "cop," the "narc," the "flatfoot." On the road she could score from anyone—a chorus boy, a musician, a hairdresser, a friend—but at home the avenues were limited. I'd searched every nook and cranny and could find nothing. Infuriated, I blocked off the house. Nobody could come in or go out without my approval, as if I were a security guard at the White House.

One morning a package arrived from Saks Fifth Avenue. I took the liberty of opening it and found a spanking new white terry cloth robe, brightly lined with red-and-blue Tuinal capsules. A friend had bought the robe and sewed the Tuinal into the lining, returned it to Saks, and asked them to deliver it. Judy had unwittingly tipped me off by telling me she was expecting a package. That night Pobirs had knocked her out, and at four in the morning the two of us were on an Easter egg hunt looking for her hidden stash. We went through Judy's closets, overturned the rugs, examined the drapes. And this time we scored. Pills were hidden in packages of cigarettes; her Jean Patou Joy bath powder was loaded with Seconals; the clothes hamper was filled with beer bottles and a vodka bottle, all empty.

In the past Vern Alves and I would wait for her to wake up from a bender so we could get down to business. With her tenacity, she would usually come out of it, asking for a steak, loving and warm as though nothing had happened. In this instance, she wasn't coming out of it. I tried to figure out what was pulsating deep within her. I thought, people take pills, people drink, but they don't always damage themselves. Her mind was swift, and her intelligence near genius—what was it that she couldn't juggle, that weighed so heavily? I, the watchdog, pondered the one pill too many, the accumulation of multiple prescriptions. Something burned in her psyche, but it was still a mystery. Judy just didn't momentarily get out of her skin; if she tipped the scale she was most likely to be in a life-and-death race. I'd been getting in her hair; I was the villain. "I can't answer why I took that first pill," she told me. "*Hnn*, I can't sleep," and she'd refer to me as "the foolish ass upstairs." The hostility was snowballing.

Shortly after we moved into Mapleton, I had installed a safe in my bathroom behind the designer towel rack. Judy never mentioned it. Now, aware I'd won a big bet, she confronted me: "I want that combination. It's half my money." She wanted to get into that "goddamned safe," she yelled. "I must have the combination. *Hnnn*, suppose you die?"

"I forgot it."

"You did not."

"It's written down in the office."

It was strange, as money had never been a subject that concerned her. I figured she wanted the money for more pills.

Two days later she'd forgotten about the safe and the money. Her attention was focused on how much she didn't want to work in Brooklyn, at Maksik's. We were embroiled in fierce arguments. I found myself threatening to walk out. I tried every trick in the book—I'd make myself scarce, then I'd attempt to reason with her. This was a tough wave, and I wasn't rolling with it. Nothing was working, and her isolation was escalating. She'd ring Pobirs, "Come over here." Fuck you and your family, just get here. And he'd come.

Even Pobirs was mad at Judy. One night on his way out he told me, "Goddam it, you're kidding yourself if you think she's going to be cured." It was five in the morning and he was tired and disgusted. And I was kidding myself. But I liked to do that. Pobirs was a disgruntled uncle; he wasn't going to abandon her either. He was as much of an enabler as I was.

I enjoyed drinking but I was not a drunk, and I respected sobriety. I knew how much Judy loved me, and it was that love I'd been betting on. She'd come out of it. She had been on uppers and was coming off barbiturates, and she had taken the unknown quantity plus a mystery drug. The mix had transformed her into a raging pixie. But these periods of irrational behavior were dangerous to her and to the family.

The children stayed in one wing of the house. Judy would pay them visits wearing her lounging outfit or a robe, and they'd sing and talk for a while. They wouldn't realize she was stoned. If she was immobile, the children were told Mother wasn't available, and as they were used to their mother rehearsing or reading in her rooms, her absence didn't seem unnatural.

Rather recently Judy had packed up the kids and the nurse to go off to Ojai. It was her reaction to my pressuring her to sober up in time for Maksik's. We were not arguing; we were very compatible, and close. In Ojai, she slept off what she'd ingested and came home. "Hi, darling, I'm back." Her sobriety lasted twenty-four hours.

Now Judy had cut me off to such a degree that I thought I'd better shake her up. I decided to go through the charade of leaving the house, hoping to bring her around, wake her up. Not only was my action futile, but it triggered a new kind of desperate behavior on her part.

I told Judy she was giving me command performances, and I didn't think I'd be up to it much longer. Time was running out. One night I packed two bags and walked into the master bedroom, where Judy was sitting in bed. I was overwrought. "I'm leaving," I announced, hoping she'd sober up for a moment.

A look of recognition passed over her face. She stared at me. "You want to walk out on your children? Walk out, you son of a bitch."

"Why can't you stop?"

"None of your business."

"OK, darling, this is what you want, I'm going."

There was no reaching her, but she got out of bed, angry. She wanted to make contact by hitting me. She was spinning with Dexedrine, Seconal, and booze, unreasonable, obstinate. She came at me with hooded eyes and wagging tail, the way a caged animal who once licked a trainer's hand in appreciation turns one day for no reason. As she came for me I caught her by the leg, taking her off balance. Gripping her by the leg and arm, I gracefully twirled her, like a figure skater with his partner. I tossed my bundle gently back onto our enormous bed. Judy, stunned, landed on her side, like a befuddled Raggedy Ann doll. I had to suppress a laugh. "You've just been thrown through the air, baby. You landed good and now I'm leaving." There were tears in my eyes. I felt like Willy Loman with a suitcase.

She didn't show any care and she didn't say "Call me." She said, "I don't give a fuck. Get lost. I dare you to leave."

I checked into a small hotel on Wilshire Boulevard, and the next morning I read in the newspapers that Judy and I were divorcing. She'd contacted Jerry Giesler, the famous criminal defense lawyer. Judy knew exactly where I was, and I stayed in touch with the staff at the house. I rang Giesler and explained Judy was dramatizing a family argument. She was on an extended bender and eventually she'd come around, she'd sober up. Meanwhile, Giesler hired Fred Otash, a private detective, to guard the house. I knew Otash rather well, so I went over to Mapleton with Clyde Duber, a friend who was also a private detective, to check. I told Otash to watch Judy, as she could do something naughty. She was smoking too many cigarettes. Otash assured me, "Don't worry about it, Sid." I was worried for her and the children.

Sure enough, there was a fire. Judy burned her elbow. Fire engines were clanging in and around Mapleton, which didn't go over well with the neighbors.

I had a meeting with Giesler. I explained we'd had intense arguments about pills, which Judy liked to call "medicine"—no doubt a euphemism inherited from MGM. Her contacting Giesler was a new wrinkle: divorce was a word she'd never used. I considered her angle. She was trying "divorce" on for size. She'd asked Giesler to file papers—the reason: I'd "attempted to strangle her." She'd also tell Giesler, "Sid poisoned the dog" or "Sid hit me" or "Sid threatened me," all untruths. I knew she'd sober up—it was taking longer this time, but she'd sober up. I explained that this was the pattern when she was on a bender, only this time she tried on a new shoe. Giesler said, "Sid, here's an opportunity for you to get out of the marriage, to start another life." He didn't understand I was in love with Judy and had no intention of leaving her.

Judy left for New York without me, semisober. I followed her there and checked into the Warwick Hotel. It was nasty March weather, cold, gray, and dirty snow piling up everywhere. I knew Judy was sick. In Brooklyn, she was presenting herself as someone in need of a manager, and she was fucking up. The supportive peers were not driving out to Brooklyn. Maksik had notions of taking over as Judy's manager. She was playing everyone against one another, furious that she had to perform in Brooklyn. Bobby Van, who worked as her opening act, called me daily at the hotel to tell me what was going on. Van's most typical remark: "It ain't good."

I learned that Aly Khan had gone out to see her, the lone prince in the back of Ben Maksik's Town and Country! There was one supportive peer who was loyal. Judy had the children with her, Lorna and Joey, and the nurse. She still wasn't taking my calls, but I knew she'd contact me sooner or later.

I ran into Doug Ornstein as I was coming down in the hotel's elevator. He had been my first flight instructor in my Clover Field days. We hit the lobby and stood looking at the newsstand, where the headlines for March 23, 1958, blasted, MIKE TODD DIES IN NEW MEXICO AIR CRASH! We turned to one another and both said, "That fucking dummy, he iced up and spun in." Todd had recently produced the Academy Award winner *Around the World in 80 Days* and was married to Elizabeth Taylor. I was saddened for Mike and for Liz.

I had little time to meditate the consequences of Todd's untimely death, as that night Judy walked off the stage at Maksik's, refusing to perform. She rang me at the hotel: "Hi, darling, come and get us. I'm all packed." Then she commanded me to call the police, saying Maksik had "attacked" her.

She'd worked ten days out of her three-week contract and couldn't continue; she was really ill. I went out to Brooklyn in a limo, collected my family, and brought them back to the Drake Hotel. Judy, in one of her rare moments of communication, asked to go to a clinic to detox: "Take care of me, baby." She was, at that moment, the reasonable little girl.

38

Extra Special
Lancaster Theater
Sunday and Monday, May 22–23
Mr. and Mrs. Frank Gumm and Daughters will present
a cycle of songs and dances between shows each evening
at 9 o'clock and also at the Sunday Matinee.
Having purchased the theater, I am taking this method
of introducing the family to the good people of Lan-
caster and Antelope Valley. It is my intention to con-
tinue presenting the high class picture program as given
by Mr. Claman and I cordially ask the support of the
public in keeping the entertainment up to the highest
possible standard. Your cooperation will be appreciated.
Respectfully, Frank A. Gumm
—Antelope Valley Ledger Gazette, 1927

IN JULY 1958, I BOOKED Judy at the Cocoanut Grove, a haunt from
our respective glorious pasts. I was intending to ignite some forgotten sparks, inspire enthusiasm. The Grove, situated in the Ambassador
Hotel in Los Angeles, was an exotic environment of monkeys, parrots,
and lush tropical palms. Impressive and costly shops lined the arcades.
It was altogether a fantasy of superabundance, notoriety, and history:

the young Norma Jeane Mortenson, a.k.a. Marilyn Monroe, hung out at the hotel's swimming pool whenever she was in town, and later Robert Kennedy was to meet his death on the premises.

Judy played for two weeks to star-studded audiences—the "right" crowd, her supportive peers. She'd made a few appearances plus some recording dates before the Grove. She hadn't thrown any command performances in the dressing room or walked offstage, nor was she rejecting me or isolating herself. In fact, she'd sloughed off her defiant, hostile stance with me since Pobirs prescribed a newer drug: Ritalin, a medication used primarily for hyperactive children. The effect of the pill was to render Judy zombie-like.

The Grove, however, was one of Judy's "homes," a place where she was relaxed and comfortable performing. Sinatra was there, Brando was there, and she'd schmooze with the audience: "A long time ago I came down to the Grove with my mother, and she talked the orchestra leader into letting me sing a song . . ."

Judy was bringing her mother into the act every night. She seemed to be in the grip of some kind of intense nostalgia, commenting on how she was shuttled from stage to stage as a child. And Judy had worked the Cocoanut Grove as early as 1932. I thought, *She'll talk about her mother to the audiences but she'll hold back from me.* And she wasn't letting up on the subject. In a rare emotional recollection, Judy said:

We visited California, some of mother's friends by the name of Devine. And then we came back to Grand Rapids. My parents decided to move to California, so my father sold the Rialto. We got in the car. The family had an awful time with me, because I got carsick. It was stopping every hour. I'd upchuck and we'd go on. It was such a bore, but we worked our way to California.

My mother and father went back to their original Vaudeville life—"Jack and Virginia Lee, Sweet Southern Singers" and they booked us as the "Gumm Sisters," because two acts made more money than a family. We played funny little theaters all across the country. . . . We'd work one month, get some money, and then we'd travel a little more, and had some fun. We wanted to work again, Dad said no, we had enough money.

We would go up to a town we thought looked good and thought we'd enjoy and my dad would go to the manager of the theater and say, "Look, I'm a theater owner too." We'd work in the stage show. And the three of us would go out and watch my mother and father.

We'd applaud my mother and father; then when we'd go on, they'd go out and applaud us. My mother used to sing a song that I've always wanted to record. She'd come out, play the piano, and sing, "I've Been Saving for a Rainy Day." And she sang it so well. It was a very sad kind of song.

Every time I'd sit out in the audience and watch her, I'd just cry.

When she told this story to the audience, people would be wiping tears from their eyes by this point, and she hadn't even sung "Rainbow" yet. She certainly caught me off guard with a catch in my throat. And then there'd come the audience's requests to sing "I've Been Saving for a Rainy Day." I'd think wistfully, Judy *is* sad, but there's nothing I can do. Some nights she'd tell them, "You may not believe I was a little, little girl . . ." and she'd proceed to chat them up about how the family finally arrived in Los Angeles. Judy said:

We drove through Lancaster. My father did mention that it would be a good place for a theater, because there weren't any around to buy. We lived around Glendale and we had a little turquoise stucco house. We were still very happy. And, for a while we lived not far from Melrose Avenue. Across the street from the Devines. We had a little bungalow. That's where my sisters taught me to play jacks.

The audience would go wild. I always knew they'd be thrilled just to hear Judy talk. I'd personally given up on her confiding to me. I really wasn't as focused on Judy's withholding of feelings or thoughts anymore. Our marriage's tantalizing passage had delivered us to a point in time where, for once, *I* was concerned about her weight. My femme fatale had been ballooning up, mysteriously filling with air, her eyes on the way to becoming slits. It would be some time before I'd come to understand that her physical condition was actually a sign of the cumulative effect of toxins in her system.

After the Grove, Judy gave a superb concert at Orchestra Hall in Chicago along with Nelson Riddle and his orchestra. She sang Jack Cathcart's overture from the Palace Theatre, and she was in great voice. The program included such tunes as "When You're Smiling," "Day In, Day Out," "I Can't Give You Anything but Love," "Zing! Went the Strings of My Heart," and "Purple People Eater," a song that was popular in the 1950s. Roger Edens did the vocal arrangement for "Purple"—it was funny, kind of a throwaway. Alan King joined her for the "Couple of Swells" number. At the end of her performance, the Riddle Orchestra sang "Auld Lang Syne" to Judy. Orchestra Hall was a wonderful night.

We went immediately from there to the Sands Hotel in Vegas. It was an intimate room and she loved playing there. I'd booked Judy at Sinatra's request. He'd told me Judy had promised him she'd work there, and I struck a deal with both Frank and the manager of the Sands, Jack Entratter. Judy and Frank and Dean performed to an audience of supportive peers and those lucky enough to have a table reserved. It was dynamite; the improvisation between them was a joy, almost a once-in-a-lifetime performance. Frank brought up his friends, nobody commented on Judy's weight, and everybody had a ball. I began to acquaint myself with the ins and outs of Vegas, and this time I made friends. These connections were to serve me well in a few years' time when I'd be persona non grata, an outsider in my own home.

The new helium-faced Judy hadn't diminished in style, but something was terribly wrong with her body. By now I was certain she was suffering a toxic reaction to the Ritalin, which seemed to calm her down but left her without energy. I wondered how many she took daily.

After the Sands we went to Thousand Oaks in the Valley and stayed at the Come and See Us Ranch with the intention of helping Judy lose some weight. It was a rest for the entire family. Judy didn't lose an ounce, although the diet was strictly celery and carrots and low-calorie dishes. Her face returned to normal, but not her body. I was happy to see her enticing, saucer eyes wide open again.

At the end of the month the Masquers, a famous L.A. social club, was going to salute Judy. On the evening of the affair, about halfway through the ceremony, one of the men on the dais keeled over and died of a heart attack. It was an eerie and sad event. Judy had prepared for a jolly evening of insider show business, but of course the death put a damper on the proceedings. Then Judy performed at a benefit in San Bernardino, staged by Sammy Davis out of gratitude for the local hospital that had been so attentive to him after he lost his eye in an auto accident. Other than these few appearances, she wasn't working.

At Mapleton, music would float from one room to another. My collection of records was minimal compared to Judy's. I tended to listen to favorites over and over again. I'd grown up with well-worn Caruso records and the opera *La Bohème*—super romantic, impassioned music. The famous duet toward the end of *La Bohème* fascinated me as a boy. It was a revelation that love between a man and a woman could be at once so beautiful and so sad. I was forever gripped by the melodic strains of the particular melody in which the heroine is confessing. I'd play this part over and over again. It secretly turned me on, the play of voices locked in an eternal longing that somehow can never be fulfilled.

Here and there Judy would join me when I played Italian opera; she favored classical violin if she played classical music at all. Judy loved Gordon Jenkins's popular arrangements, which were always rich in strings. However, Judy's tastes were eclectic—she appreciated jazz and, in general, held a far greater technical understanding of music than I did.

But Judy agreed with me it might be pleasant to get away from the popular to the classic, so she accepted my invitation to see the Swedish tenor Jussi Björling sing *La Bohème* at the Shrine. Björling, offstage, had a drinking problem. One night during the run of the opera, Björling, who was a short man weighing over 250 pounds, got bombed. My friend Lee Siegel was the doctor on call. In the middle of the night, I received an emergency call from Lee to come to the hotel and help him with Björling. "I can't handle this big moose!"

Björling was so pissed he wanted to box with me as we attempted to get him to bed. *Va va voom!* It was a tense struggle. Finally we had to knock him cold with a barbiturate before we were able to haul him up to bed. The next morning he was fine, and that evening he performed beautifully. Björling was so grateful afterward that he called me up and apologized.

Sometime later at a small birthday celebration at the 21 Club in New York, Judy arranged for Björling to come all the way from Sweden to sing "Happy Birthday" to me. He was still thanking me for putting him to bed that night.

There were minor distractions but nothing exceptional on the professional horizon for Judy. I had several concepts in mind, but I was beginning to wonder if she could pull them off. I decided if it was important enough, she'd come through.

Around this time, one of Jack Warner's lawyers called me up and said that Jack wanted to "write off the $25,000." At first, I had no idea what he was referring to. I'd suppressed memories of Warner and *A Star is Born*. I realized he was talking about the note I'd signed back in 1954 when Jack was convincing me to go to France, telling me I'd be a millionaire several times over and not to worry about the advance.

I said, "I don't owe Jack a quarter."

"Well, we have to sue you in order to write it off."

"Sue me."

"What would you settle for?"

"Nothing."

"OK, give me $500 and I'll tear up the note."

Again I emphasized that I'd give Jack nothing—and, further, if they continued to press me for that note, I'd sue them.

"Fine," the lawyer replied, "Sue me, but sue me without publicity."
I figured out that for their purposes they needed to show a suit before

they could write it off. The conversation left me numb, then a wave of nausea washed over me. I was left in a rerun of despair; submerged feelings of disappointment and failure returned. I didn't file the suit, and I never heard from them again.

Judy had been sitting at home. She'd listen to her own recordings as though another artist were singing. And she began to have an "I don't give a fuck" attitude. She wasn't hostile, just listless, out of gas. I suggested she might check out her increasing weight gain with one of the doctors, and for the first time in our marriage, she declined to see a doctor. The Ritalin had calmed her down but left me unhinged as to what was physiologically going on with her.

Somehow, it didn't seem to impair her ability to work. "Baby, your voice is so great you belong at the Metropolitan Opera House."

Judy came up to me and put her strong arms around my neck, "Stop it Sid." She was childlike. "Don't tease me."

"I'm dead serious."

She giggled. "You mean it?" It was as though Dorothy were on her way to Oz. Her dark eyes turned to me with a shine. "Darling, I do need to look forward to something."

Roger Edens had sent over tickets for Maria Callas at the Shrine Auditorium. Judy, who admired Callas, bowed out. I went to the show without her, curious to see the great diva. And Callas proved magnetic, displaying her genius of acting and singing—not unlike Judy. I thought about Fred Schrang, an expert in booking classical concerts and operas, whom we'd met in Cannes. He adored Judy. I rang him up regarding my notion of Judy at the Met.

Fred explained that a commercial tour was not allowed at the opera house; however, a nonprofit or charity event was permitted. This seemed silly—the proceeds would go to charity while the bills came to me—but I'd go along. I discovered unexpected complications. The Met's unions were afraid of servicing just one performer, a small chorus, and an orchestra numbering thirty-five. They insisted on enough stagehands to accommodate the Bolshoi Ballet.

We solicited the charity City of Hope for sponsorship, and were flabbergasted when the organization asked for $50,000 under the table to lend their name to Judy's performance. Judy was ill but uncomplaining. It was, after all, the Metropolitan Opera House. We ultimately enlisted the Children's Asthma Research Institute and Hospital in Denver instead.

Not since the Scottish comic actor and singer Sir Harry Lauder made an appearance at the Metropolitan Opera House in the 1920s had a popular performer been featured. (Keeping it all in the family, years later Liza would appear for one season at the Met in a ballet, *The Owl and the Pussycat*, choreographed for her by the Martha Graham dance company.)

On May 11, 1959, Judy made her Met debut. Alan King was the monologist, and John Bubbles the dancer. Judy made her appearance in the first act following King's and Bubbles's routines, which were designed to interact with the full all-male chorus. She backed onto the stage wearing a luxurious white fox stole over her gown, graciously acknowledging the audience's reception before the chorus continued: "Are you the new Wagnerian soprano? / A new Mimi for *La Bohème*? . . ."

Judy replied: "My name is Judy . . . But my children call me 'Mama!'"

Roger Edens proved once again that he was a master at writing for Judy, creating new numbers in the recitative, aria style that she projected, so similar to that of opera singers. Edens's material was laced throughout with operatic themes from *La Bohème*, *Pagliacci*, etc. Judy also performed a version of Edens's "Born in a Trunk" designed especially for the venue.

In another set she sang "I Happen to Like New York" by Cole Porter. She continued with Lerner and Loewe and a Rodgers and Hart medley opened by Bubbles dancing to "Me and My Shadow." Judy would come out in a tux and join him as the shadow. It was sensational. Alan closed the first half with the all-male chorus tapping their behinds off. Judy performed Gordon Jenkins's special material from Judy's album *The Letter* and danced "A Couple of Swells" with Alan taking Astaire's part. She gave them the "Minstrel Girl" medley: "For almost twenty years, I've been a minstrel girl / Singing for my supper in the throngs / And in that time my world has been a minstrel world / And the history of my life is in my songs."

She'd sit on the prompter's box dressed in her tramp clothes and bring the house down with "Rainbow." Judy told the audiences, "I'll sing 'em all and we'll stay all night." Standees were lined up three deep along the aisles. Judy turned in a performance of bravura proportions.

The newspapers echoed the audience's response, the *New York Times* writing, "From the roars and bravos that echoed through the house it was evident that long hair or short the Metropolitan still was the haven of good company." Jim O'Connor wrote in the *New York Journal-American*, "Her full, thrilling, throbbing voice welled up in the vast cathedral of vocal culture, filling every bit of space above the orchestra, the boxes, and family circle."

Judy performed one week at the Met to standing ovations, cheering throngs, and as many bravos as an opera singer would dream of. But her weight was an issue, and there were nights when she was not well. She was a trouper and gave her best. With two more grand opera houses on the tour, the Civic Opera House in Chicago and the War Memorial Opera House in San Francisco, I was still asking her to see a doctor, and Judy was still refusing.

I came up with a seemingly casual situation: a doctor friend, someone Judy didn't know, came backstage to chat while taking the opportunity to observe her. He took one look and subsequently proclaimed my wife "bloated," not fat. He'd managed to "accidentally" touch her shoulder near the neck, and he explained she was filled with fluids—a sign that one of her organs was not functioning, either the spleen, pancreas, or liver. It was clear she needed tests. We had to finish the opera tour, and then I'd need a miracle to get Judy to a diagnostician.

The rest of the tour went well; it was the kind of show Judy believed she deserved. But it didn't provide the kind of money we'd have earned in Vegas. By the time she made an appearance at the Friars roast for Dean Martin, she was a zombie. She gave a mechanical performance without any spirit. I was now deeply worried over the state of her health.

I contacted my uncle Israel in New York and made a plan. I told Judy I was going east on business and that I'd wind up in New York, where there was to be a big bash for my pal Charlie Wacker that we were all invited to attend. I mentioned that Freddie Finklehoffe was already at the Waldorf Astoria.

Charlie was going to escort Judy to the fictitious party directly from Los Angeles. Freddie was prepared to help me in any way possible. And he certainly stood by me. He'd been privy to some of Judy's escapades and dramas, and he'd ask, "How the fuck do you take this shit?" Now, Judy had hit bottom and was barely functioning. She was eager to go, but she was reluctant to fly. We persuaded her to knock herself out and get on the airplane. So Charlie delivered Judy, stoned, to the Waldorf Astoria. We had a suite at the Towers (which we really couldn't afford), and Israel was waiting for me to confirm that Judy was in town. I had set up a consultation with my uncle and his daughter, now a practicing physician herself, for the following morning. I wasn't wasting a minute.

———— ∞ ————

In the morning, the ride uptown from the Waldorf was nightmarish. Judy was insisting we have a cocktail. I said, "Certainly, darling, let's take our martinis with us in the taxi." I'd agree to anything.

In his office Israel told Judy her life was in danger, that her liver was four times its normal size. The cause of the liver imbalance was obvious: liquor and pills. She'd have to be hospitalized immediately, and he told me he didn't know if they could save her. "Your wife is critically ill."

Judy was checked into Doctors Hospital in Manhattan for treatment. I rented a small, cell-like room next to Judy. I couldn't watch television, I was too anxious. I listened to music, the only thing that kept me calm. It was a day-to-day hardship.

"Is she going to make it?"

"We don't know."

It continued this way for three months! Meanwhile, the children were home with the nurse while I watched and waited.

Judy received a line of visitors at the hospital—Aly Khan and Elsa Maxwell, the Berksons, Bennett Cerf. Our good friends Dr. Lester and Felicia Coleman were in touch daily. Whoever was in New York came by to see Judy when it was OK for her to see people. They'd wish her the very best, encourage her. She was surrounded by flowers, gifts, and supportive peers. Later Bennett arranged a contract with his publishing company, Random House, for her autobiography.

It was on the twelfth day of our three-month sojourn at Doctors Hospital that Judy was pronounced out of danger. It was the very day the children had viewed *The Wizard of Oz* for the first time. That night Joey and Lorna were on the phone to Judy crying, as they'd been frightened by the movie. They were terrified of the wicked witch, whom they thought was responsible for their mother being gone. Judy succeeded in pacifying them and assuring them she'd be home as soon as she was completely well. We found the best way to keep the children's anxiety down was to speak with them every day. The stronger Judy became, the more intense was her desire to be with the children.

Joyously, Judy was released from the hospital sometime in February 1960. On the train back to Los Angeles she genuinely relaxed for the first time in months. She seemed content. We sat up and watched the lights go by, slept easily and comfortably, and experienced a wonderful closeness. Once more we were happily on the Super Chief, which Judy loved. When we transferred in Chicago, Doris Day and her husband picked up the train. We had a delightful time all the way to California, playing cards and talking, the two all-American songbirds with their Jewish husbands/managers. Everything was good, but I wondered just how tough it would be on Judy not performing.

The doctors had advised me Judy would be "semi-invalid" for the rest of her life. After we returned home, Judy was indeed partially bedridden, with nurses around the clock. For the time being, there could be no work, no pressures, no socializing. How was I going to support a famous wife and three children in the lifestyle they were habituated to? There was no income and no health insurance. Doctor bills had to be paid. I was dejected, mad as hell. I was running out of money.

Luckily, Rainbow Farms owned a gray mare, Queen of All; I'd bought her from the razor blade king of Ireland. She was cow hocked, and she was rushed on the track. Queen of All injured her hind legs, but I knew she'd make a superb brood mare. A trainer who understood bloodlines offered to buy her for breeding. I sold her on the spot. Not too long afterward Queen of All threw a great racehorse, Papa's All.

I'd prepared myself during those long days and nights at Doctors Hospital for the realization that Judy was not going to have a future career. My uncle's words would ring in my ear: "semi-invalid." Judy was in a wheelchair, then she was moved to a regular chair. After several months she was walking about the house and asking to go out. She'd progressed to the point where she was functioning, not with full stamina but certainly not a "semi-invalid." In my mind I switched the phrase to "semi-retired"—that sounded more hopeful, not a death knell. However, I was certain if she were to fall back on the crutch of chemical abuse that it would be disastrous for her. Nonetheless, the truth was Judy was not going to be the megastar she'd once been; she was simply my wife, and that was fine.

———— ✧ ————

An acquaintance of mine had come to see me at the hospital with an invention: a little box about twelve inches square and ten inches high. He put the attached plug into the wall socket, then he took a small plastic cylinder and shoved it into the slot. It was an early tape deck. The box was made by Viking and played music but did not record. (Ampex was the only company for recording purposes in those days.) This struck me as the beginning of a new era. I remembered that when Judy worked with Bing Crosby in 1951 his agent, Rosie Rosenberg, had given Judy a present of the first tape deck I'd ever seen, made by the Lake company.

I was inspired by the device, because I immediately thought of hardware that could play on airplanes, soundtracks that would distract and entertain the passengers. Such devices could especially help individuals like Judy who were fearful of flying. I knew Howard Hughes had developed inflight movies for his company, TWA, but at the time there were no headsets for audio programs, no music-player-in-the-air for each passenger.

I contacted my old partner, Eddie Alperson. My skills as a producer and a pilot, along with Alperson's experience introducing sound to independent theater owners, could make us a viable team again. And Eddie fell madly in love with the project. We formed a company: Aerophonics Electronics Corporation.

I believed I was on to something. Judy was slowly feeling better; her stamina was returning. I'd asked if she would perform a lead-in for an Aerophonics tape I was producing for the premiere program when she felt able. She balked at the suggestion, but she came around.

In the early 1960s everything was monaural, but Sony had developed a stereophonic machine that played out of two speakers. I wanted our box to feature stereo sound as well. For that to be possible, we'd need to build dual amplifiers and other new hardware. I located a man named Rudy Stoklos who made these heads for professional machines that were not yet recording in stereo. I found Rudy in Santa Monica and I asked him if it was possible to build a tape deck and change the configuration; he said yes, he could do it. The stereo sound would come from a Möbius strip, a single-sided, continuous loop. The technology wasn't patented, so various people were manufacturing these cassettes.

I went next to Capitol Records and presented the box. "I think this is going to be the future of selling music." They looked at me like I was an extraterrestrial. I decided that the continuous loop had many disadvantages and that the prototype should be redesigned. A contact I knew at American Airlines introduced us to a father-and-son team, "Davis Engineering," in Coral Gables, Florida. When they came to California, Judy and Eddie and I discussed the project with them. It seemed feasible that Davis could build precisely what I had in mind.

As I built the foundation of Aerophonics, I kept an eye on my wife. Judy was the healthiest she'd been since we married. It was a rerun of when we'd first met in Manhattan. She looked wholesome, and her behavior was that of the normal, beautiful woman I'd fallen in love with. But I was wary of her newfound verve and energy. I didn't trust that her recovery would last. I spoke with Uncle Israel, and he said to take it very slowly.

Though Judy was feeling fine, she was now without a career. She did make an appearance at a Democratic fundraiser on July 10, a banquet for Jack Kennedy as he faced off against Richard Nixon in the presidential campaign. For the dinner at the Hilton Hotel, Judy sat with Jack on the dais. I was at a table between Rose and Joan Kennedy. Judy sang "Rock-a-Bye" for Jack, and she was in great voice. I was struck by her stamina and vivacity. She'd have to give a full performance sooner or later.

Liza was very friendly with a little girl whose family manufactured hearing aids. They were affluent and lived well, and their daughter spent her summers in a private school on the French side of Lake Geneva. Her uncle, a young rabbi, began to visit us along with her parents while Judy was recuperating at home. He adored Judy and they got on, spending hours at the piano noodling away, making up crazy lyrics, and exchanging a nutty kind of repartee: Judy would say, "Tony Bennett," and the rabbi would proclaim, "Barber!"; he'd say, "Frank Sinatra," and with a flourish on the piano keys Judy would answer, "Maître d'"; and so it went. Judy was perky, her wit as fine as a razor's edge. It was clear in her present nontoxic state that nothing had dulled.

The mother of Liza's friend encouraged us to send Liza along to Annecy with her daughter—she'd learn French, and it'd be a different kind of summer holiday. Liza was so excited by the idea that we had to agree. And so we arranged Liza's summer.

Perhaps Liza going off to France gave Judy the idea to travel abroad herself. Or maybe she'd been inspired by correspondence with friends such as the distinguished British actor and writer Dirk Bogarde. In any event, Judy came to me and said she'd like to take a vacation on her own. She'd gone from being an invalid to being well, and she wanted a change of scenery, to travel. This in itself was an unusual request from someone who was, in general, phobic about getting in a car, let alone boarding an airplane. I was thrilled. We didn't have the money for her to travel in the style she'd been accustomed to, so I said I'd sell a piece of art that we owned by the French painter Maurice de Vlaminck. It was a painting that we both loved, but I thought it was important that she go.

Judy left for New York, where she stayed with Eleanor Lambert Berkson and visited friends. Then she traveled with socialite Sharman Douglas to London. Our relationship was smooth. We were more in love than ever.

PART V

On and Off the Road

39

We stand today on the edge of a new frontier—the frontier of the 1960s, the frontier of unknown opportunities and perils, the frontier of unfilled hopes and unfilled threats.

—John F. Kennedy, July 1960

Judy's hallucinatory circles dotting the *i*s floated on the Savoy Hotel stationery. The perpetual schoolgirl script and the content of her letter—someone busy, full of life—were reassuring to me:

Darling—

How I miss you—London is not the same without you. Had a good trip over—after a lovely party at Roddy's and arrived on time to find beautiful weather. Had a hectic press conference with the usual newspaper bastards. The result—the usual—"fat," "matronly, but happy." Fuck 'em! How are my babies! Tell them that I'm thinking of them every minute and how I love them. I talked to Liza and she will either come to London for a couple of days or I shall go to see her in France. The recordings had been put off 'til Aug. 2 so I shall go to Rome on Wed. the 20th and come back here to record. Had dinner last night with J. Clayton and Pat. We dined in my room as I was exhausted and wanted to get to bed early which I did. Worked with Soily Pratt this morning and have new arrangements set. I'm going to Dirk [Bogarde]'s in the country today at 5:30. There's a party Sunday and I'll be back here on Monday.

They've passed a law taking all of the whores off the streets. It's a little like taking the trolleys out of San Francisco. Some of the color has gone. But the girls still advertise on bulletin boards outside the pubs. It's either French lessons or massage. Both interesting but underground. Am thrilled about Kennedy. Everyone here thinks he's great. Tell Lenny I've called Joyce Grenfell and will see her when I return from Rome. She's busy Sunday and can't make Dirk's party.

Well that's all for now. Write me and tell me everything. But mostly that you love me and miss me and I do you—

Judy

P.S. To Joe and Lorna
X X X X X X X X X X X X X X X X X X

On her trip to Rome, Judy also visited the island of Capri, where she called me frequently from the hotel. She was rested and tan, and very excited about John F. Kennedy's progress in the race to the White House. The hotel was owned by a retired British vaudeville star. This gave Judy an idea: "Darling, something for me to consider?" I told her I couldn't see her flouncing into the salon in the evening to sing one or two favorites. "First, we'd have to buy a hotel, darling, and we ain't got no money, not yet." As usual, money was the least of her considerations.

Ten days passed and I yearned to be with her. Judy was lonely as well, so we arranged to meet in London. We reunited at the Westbury Hotel, where we were nestled in a garishly posh suite. It was sort of a high-class whorehouse effect, with deep red velour and lacquer, which added to our mood of celebration. We were unrepentantly nostalgic and romantic. Judy sustained the warm, marvelous persona she'd left home with. We went out dining and dancing, both happy to be back in London, our home away from home.

One night Judy said, "Darling, maybe we could live in London? Bring the whole family over. I'd really love that." At this stage in the development of Aerophonics I could be stationed as easily in London as in New York or Los Angeles. And Liza was in Annecy, already in Europe, so why not bring the rest of the family over? I thought that might be the best therapy in the world for Judy. The next day, I found a real estate broker, and in a matter of days there was a house available in Chelsea, owned by director Carol Reed. I quickly managed a second mortgage on our Mapleton home, and within three weeks we were tucked into the Chelsea house, the children settled into private school. I was immersed in Aerophonics, monitoring Davis Engineering in Coral Gables, while Judy planned a trip to Annecy to visit Liza.

Freddie Finklehoffe arrived in London with his wife, Carolyn. Judy had tried to work with Freddie back in Los Angeles on the book Bennett Cerf contracted her to write. Freddie was a screenwriter but knew little about writing books, and they'd accomplished very little. The time had been spent casually, Freddie throwing back the Cutty Sark and Judy telling funny stories. Nothing came from it except a few laughs and a friend around to amuse Judy while I took meetings, and by the time we moved abroad the project had been dropped. But, absurdly, Freddie decided Judy had let him down, and here he was in London expecting us to support him. It was another one of his fantasies.

Freddie and Carolyn were merry bohemians. Freddie would pixie me to death. He was amusing, disarming, but I had one pixie in my life and that was enough.

He would lament, "Sid, I've gotta have $500, I've gotta, Sid."

"Freddie, you owe me already," I'd reply.

"But, Sid, if I don't get it, there'll be hell to pay. You gotta."

Freddie had sent me glowing letters in the past thanking me for my generosity, but I never got any of the money back. His ongoing attachment to Judy from the Metro days was genuine, but once the funds dried up Freddie would take a powder and not be responsible. At the moment I was anticipating severe financial setbacks. I'd cooled it on the horses; in fact, Rainbow Farms was history. So I told Freddie, not only did I not have to "gotta," I wasn't going to "gotta." So the Finklehoffes took off.

Generally our life was homespun, close to the hearth—Judy in the kitchen working with the Spanish cook, afternoons in the park with the children. She was conscious of Aerophonics having already recorded a demo tape for us, and she was interested in its potential. At the same time, I was indeed running out of funds. The cash flow was down to nothing, and there was the question of how to keep up the mortgage payments on Mapleton, the children's schooling, and the doctor bills from the past six months, not to mention our lifestyle. Paradoxically, I was never more content in my marriage. I wasn't desperate. I was confident of the future; even though I was having a rough time, I knew it would pass.

Other friends were in and out of our life. Ted Law had remarried and spent the greater part of his honeymoon in London with us. I was very happy for Ted; I thought he'd paid his dues with his previous wife. We had a lot of empathy for one another. Ted was thrilled to see Judy so well. He knew it was a kind of triumph, one I'd worked hard for. There were Judy's old pals—Dirk Bogarde, who lived with a gentleman who'd been married at one time to the actress Glynis Johns. Judy was "Darling Judy" and Dirk was concerned about her. He was devoted and eager to be her friend. Whenever she was invited to their country home I was absolutely pleased to see her go there. I knew that most likely Noël Coward would also be a guest and that Judy would perch on top of the piano while Noël played, and she'd sing his songs, one after the other. So whenever she came to me and said, "Just to get out of town, darling, I know you're busy. If you'd like to come please do, but I'd like to visit Dirk over the weekend," I'd encourage her to go. There were no drugs and she was very straight. She'd receive attention from the supportive peers, and she could dish and relax.

Occasionally I'd join Judy in the country home of Fleur Cowles and Tom Montague Meyer, and composer Lionel Bart frequently spent the evening at our house. Elizabeth Taylor and Eddie Fisher would come over whenever Elizabeth was in town from Rome, where she was filming

Cleopatra. The four of us enjoyed a pleasant tea at our house, and it struck us funny that here we were, four Americans, meeting for tea, not drinks. The English press had lambasted Fisher for leaving Debbie Reynolds for Elizabeth; now there was a bigger scandal brewing.

That afternoon, Eddie took me aside and asked if I would meet him, alone, the following day at the Dorchester Hotel, where he and Elizabeth were staying. He appeared anxious and unhappy. The press was pouring out a lot of heat and steam. Eddie felt he was getting the shit kicked out of him. I commented that the circles under his eyes were worse than mine! I told him when we met at the Dorchester that he should get an agent and go to work. He was essentially sitting around and holding Elizabeth's hand. "Let her hold your hand for a while," was my advice to Fisher. I tried to explain that women like Elizabeth and Judy were self-centered, and that he might try to take a stand. "Don't sit by and get wasted." I'd no idea what he actually wanted to hear from me, but I had the impression he was ignoring my suggestions even as I spoke. In fact, he may have intended to tell me something else entirely. It was, of course, only later that we learned from the press exactly what was causing his depression: Elizabeth had fallen in love with her costar Richard Burton.

I was facing my own personal issues: for the first time in my life I was struggling with an excess of weight. I'd started gaining while Judy was in the hospital, and continued as I wrestled with the burden of our growing financial responsibilities. The larger the debts, the bigger I got. Drinking relaxed me, but it was a sensitive area, as Judy was completely sober. We were happy together, yet I was alone on the heath with the bottle. I'd always considered myself a social drinker, but I was aware my drinking had accelerated.

I wasn't a drunkard, but I was close to it at times. My drinking didn't interfere with my marriage. I wasn't out of control. I suffered no personality change, only the occasional hangover. However, a few years later when Judy and I were temporarily estranged, she'd bring up my "drinking in London" as a weak and negative action on my part. Since that was a period when she was clear of intoxicants, she had to call me on it. In hindsight this criticism of me was the tip of a bigger iceberg, one in which she felt inwardly diminished by her chemical dependencies and I, in her view, was so free of them as to make her envious, even hostile. The fact that I was assiduously fighting to keep her sober and alive was not, in her toxic states, experienced as a loving and positive action but rather as a show of superiority: she was "weak," and I was "strong." In her sober mode I was, of course, never able to question or discuss these deep-rooted dysfunctions, which Judy would neither admit to nor take responsibility for.

✷✷✷

I'd admired Douglas Fairbanks Jr., and I was aware he was involved in every conceivable kind of entrepreneurial action—real estate, manufacturing, little pieces of many business schemes. He was a consultant for British business opportunity, and he became fascinated by the Aerophonics prototype. Subsequently, he introduced me to a fellow who had been with Rolls-Royce and was currently managing director of British Overseas Airways Corporation.

Doug and his wife, Mary Lee, socialized with the Queen of England and Prince Philip. Their personally inscribed photographs were prominently displayed in the Fairbanks living room. I was under the impression that Doug aspired to be appointed ambassador to England. Although the treasured appointment never came about, their friendship with the royals continued. To his credit, Fairbanks never aped an upper-class British accent.

When we'd have dinner at Les Ambassadeurs, Doug would decline the menu, sighing, "Every time I have to eat these dinners, it's troublesome." The food was too heavy for his pristine tastes. He watched his diet religiously. A physically handsome man, he took exceptional care of himself, believing in high colonics and pretty young girls whose photographs were filed in one of his desk drawers.

During one of our dinners out with Fairbanks, Judy held everyone in thrall with old Hollywood stories, which Doug certainly could relate to. That night she told about how the MGM commissary had entertained the MGM/Loews theater distributors with a dinner featuring all the studio's big stars. Judy had been asked to sing, and a new comic on the lot was elected to perform. It was quite an opportunity for the unknown comedian. When his time came to entertain he walked about the tables, jauntily exhibiting confidence. As he approached Louis B. Mayer's table, not knowing with whom he was kibitzing, he greeted the mogul with "Hiya, nosy!" En masse, everyone drew a deep breath; a blanket of silence covered the MGM commissary as the naive comic continued, "Are you havin' a *parfate?*" Judy could barely finish the story she was laughing so hard. "That was the last anyone *ever* saw him again."

Eventually I shared Fairbanks's offices on St. James's Place. He introduced me to a doctor who dispensed injections of pregnant women's urine, a new regimen which helped patients lose weight. The diet was extremely effective, and within a relatively short time I returned to my normal weight and physique.

40

Liza was dressed like a French schoolgirl. She looked happy. The landscape was serene, far from the hustle and bustle of cities, a tranquil combination of lake and mountains. Clearly, Annecy agreed with Liza, and she was speaking French beautifully for so short an exposure. I was impressed, and so was Judy, who couldn't stop hugging her daughter. I asked Liza what she thought was the best restaurant in town and she said, "Pop, there *is* the best restaurant in the world on the other side of the lake, called Père Bise." I told Liza to invite a friend—that we'd be eating at Auberge du Père Bise that very night.

We hired a driver to pick up Liza and her friend, and we met at the restaurant around eight. It was a magnificent evening—the air was pure and the sky mixed with soft grays and streaks of violet, high like a vaulted church ceiling. We walked into Père Bise like an ascension.

Someone called out, breaking my reverie, "Hey Sid!" I turned and recognized Dick Lassiter, whom I'd flown with during the war. He was with a group at a large round table. We embraced and he explained he'd borrowed an airplane and flown it out of Cincinnati to Switzerland for the week. I'd known Dick when I worked for ATC as a civilian; he was part of the Army Air Forces, their youngest colonel. He'd enjoyed the excitement and the glamour of Beverly Hills, to which I had introduced him. Dick and other fliers would come up from Long Beach to have dinner and look for starlets.

As it turned out Lassiter was sitting at Père Bise with the Lear family: Bill Lear, his wife Moya, their daughter Shanda, and Bill Jr. The Lears had left California and were living outside Geneva, where they'd built a California ranch–style house. Bill was in the process of building the Lear jet, one of the reasons Lassiter was there. Mrs. Lear's father had been a famous vaudevillian whom Judy knew as a child. He was part of a Greek comedy team that would jump in the orchestra with an ax and beat up all the musicians. Apparently audiences at the time found this excruciatingly funny.

Liza had been correct: we were served superb food. Throughout the meal we exchanged tastes with Dick and the Lears. After dinner we sat together, and they invited me to play golf the next day. Bill explained that he'd established an office in Switzerland to facilitate the manufacture of certain aeronautics parts. He was, in fact, still raising monies. He'd built a fuselage and designed the wing, but there wasn't an airplane as yet. It began to feel like the early years of my relationship with Judy—creative, evolving, a constructive momentum.

The following morning, we were arming up on the green to play on the practice range. In the distance a couple was walking on the eighteenth tee about eighty yards from where we stood. Suddenly, I saw the woman fall to the ground, and the man tried to lift her up. Then I heard her scream. I ran across the green to help, and as I turned her over I saw her eye was a mess. Her husband was an older, slight person, so I picked her up and brought her into the clubhouse. She was in excruciating pain. An ambulance was called, and she was quickly taken to the hospital where, tragically, she lost her eye. One of us must have hooked a deadly golf ball.

Instead of the gay evening we'd anticipated, we were a dour gathering around the dinner table of the Lear home. We'd look at one another, wondering just whose golf ball was responsible for the tragedy. I was a good golfer, and Bill Jr. was pretty good, but Bill Sr. was erratic.

Bill complained to me that the mountains were too quiet for him. In a wooded area in the back of their house, he had installed eight speakers in the trees. His tapes played bird sounds and cricket noise to fill up the silence. I told Bill I'd had a Lear radio in my Monocoupe, so I'd been aware of him for some time. When I described Aerophonics to Bill he immediately expressed an interest in the hardware.

The following week in London we met over lunch, along with several men from Lockheed. I brought them back to the house, where I demonstrated my four-channel cartridge. I later remarked to Judy that I didn't think Bill was likely to invest, as he was in the process of moving his operation from Switzerland to Wichita, Kansas. There it would be cheaper and easier to perfect his Lear jet, which he was very close to doing.

I was to discover that Bill was a person with outstanding vigor. He had two mistresses that I knew of, one who lived in Los Angeles in a luxurious high rise, another in New York. So here were three different establishments on the Lear payroll. Bill not only successfully manufactured the Lear jet, but he also went to Japan and developed an eight-track cartridge for use in the automobile.

―――――――― ⚬≋⚬ ――――――――

During our stay in Europe we were not exempt from the American media, which was periodically upon us: Were we going to remain in London? Were we returning to Los Angeles? In general, what were our plans? The truth was, we didn't know. Around this time Pat Lawford called Judy and asked if she would entertain the troops on American bases in England and Germany to promote the absentee vote for Jack. Judy, of course, wasn't working, but she would do anything for Jack. She was gung-ho to perform on his behalf. Hadn't she predicted he'd be in the White House one day? She desired nothing more than to feel she'd contributed something toward that end.

I was supportive of Judy's desire to work, but certainly more as a hobby than a career. I'd effectively ruled career out, having taken Uncle Israel's words literally. I had prepared myself for the professional demise of my partner, Judy Garland. When Judy earlier had indicated she was going to do some recording and work at some minor studio gigs, I considered this nothing more than a distraction. Now she was asking if she could do just a little live performing. "Darling, I'd like to do a concert somewhere. Nothing heavy."

"You really think you're up to it?"

"Yes, I'd love to. I'd really love to, darling."

I was cautious, and Judy agreed she would first have another complete physical checkup with our doctor, Phil Lebon, a young physician who'd deftly removed Lorna's appendix recently in an emergency operation. I had a lot of confidence in Lebon, and when he issued Judy a clean bill of health, I arranged through Val Parnell at the London Palladium for a Sunday night concert.

Judy sang very well. So she performed another concert at the Palladium. The month of October found Judy begging for work. She asked if I could book her in Paris.

I arranged two venues with some difficulty, largely due to our lack of cash flow. Of the two appearances, the one at the Olympia was the more successful. The audiences for the shows at the Palais de Chaillot were not at capacity. Judy basically wasn't at home performing in front of the French. It wasn't her turf. She adored the British, and she was secure with them. She knew she could always pull them out of their seats. Nevertheless, the first night audience at the Olympia was filled with supportive peers, and the rooting section was headed by Chevalier in the first row. And she sang her heart out for them.

While we were in Paris, Gloria Guinness gave Judy a marvelous party at her penthouse. *Tout-Paris* was there, including our old pals the Duke and Duchess of Windsor, who were now living outside the city in the Bois de Boulogne. I thought Gloria, a socialite and fashion icon, was wildly intelligent and extremely beautiful that night. She made us feel wonderful.

The following evening Wallis and the Duke arranged a sit-down affair for ten couples. Judy and I sat at the hosts' table. Judy was next to the Duke, and I was to the right of Wallis. Like old times, Wallis could relax with me. We were in formal attire, and the Duchess, of course, wore her famous jewelry. Perhaps it was my absence of funds that inspired me to focus on the jewels that night. Her diamond ring was large enough to choke a cow, and the previous night she'd worn an elaborate emerald necklace with earrings to match. The emerald choker was accented with ravishing diamonds, and I couldn't help laughing inwardly and thinking someone could live well for the rest of his life off her neck and earlobes.

Judy also looked up Deanna Durbin, her old costar, who lived with her French doctor husband and family in a semirural setting near Paris. Judy returned after the visit with a soft, melancholy glint to her eye. She related how happy Deanna appeared, so unpretentious, slightly overweight. We thought maybe we'd missed the boat somewhere.

I wanted to test the waters and Judy's stamina, so in between the Paris shows, I booked a night in Leeds and one night in Birmingham. Judy came up smiling, healthy and vigorous, but I was still skeptical. I wasn't about to send her on the road or look for time-consuming engagements. I was immersed in Aerophonics; on the side I was booking Judy. We also flew to Wiesbaden, Germany, where Judy performed a "Koncert for Kennedy" for the absentee vote.

Whenever we had played regional concerts, even with Judy sober, it was dicey. I walked on eggshells just in case Judy might decide it was beneath her, or in case she'd pick a fight with me for booking her "down." Nothing erupted this time around.

I booked Judy for one night in Manchester, and we decided to hire a limo and drive there for the concert. We drove up in the early evening, the night before the event. It was again romantic. Eventually the chauffeur got tired and I took the wheel. We drove all night. It was the first time I'd driven up north, and I was tired myself. Around five in the morning I was approaching Manchester; Judy was sound asleep, and so was the chauffeur. There was a wide fork in the road with three different paths; a truck was coming toward me on one road, and a motorcycle was coming toward me on another. The two vehicles seemed to converge on me. I nearly went off the road. Judy felt the swerve of the limo and awakened, anxious. "What happened?" Fortunately, the cycle and the truck avoided us, and I said, "A rabbit in the road, baby, nothing happened."

Actually, I was terrified. I'd thought I was going to hit both vehicles. A few miles outside of Manchester I gave the limo over to the chauffeur. Judy had gone right back to sleep, indicative of the profound change in her behavior. She was less phobic, more robust, not as fragile, not as changeable. It was indeed a stunning transformation.

We stopped somewhere and had a bite to eat. I experienced a tremendous sense of love and freedom. I was convinced I'd returned this creature to the world, this wisp of a hummingbird whose fragility was to be honored and protected. My devotion had taken the form of a pledge. I was going to be the hero, and for all appearances it looked like we'd been to Lourdes and the miracle had happened: Judy was cured.

On our return to London we were greeted by a hefty leprechaun by the name of O'Brien who wore a derby and represented the Kennedys. He asked if Judy would make an appearance on Jack's behalf in Frankfurt. We flew there and back, and I was impressed by Judy's apparent lack of phobias while flying. Here was the born-again Judy boarding airplanes without the help of a pill or a drink, striding on and off, sober—the dependencies conquered along with the symptoms: no claustrophobia, no insomnia. She'd come a long way. And everything about her behavior was the living realization of my belief in her. She was proving herself capable of living her life sober, which was enough for me despite her reluctance to acknowledge that she'd ever had a problem.

———— ⚭ ————

Judy's liver had miraculously healed, and now she was expressing the desire to officially go back to work. I was leery. I still believed what my uncle had told me regarding the fragility of her health and the profoundly toxic effect of chemicals on her system. I also recognized the twinges of restlessness and her need to be busy. I thought perhaps the bucolic days were over, but that it would not be destructive if Judy had the proper kind of bookings, the right kind of booking agent who would suit her and not destroy her health. I certainly did not have the funds available to develop shows for her. Soon I'd be traveling, doing demonstrations for Aerophonics. Meanwhile, I learned British Overseas

Airways was not interested in our hardware. They'd developed a rather primitive device using an earplug. It was not stereophonic like our product, but they were satisfied.

Judy and I finished our travels for the absentee vote, and I had to go to Los Angeles to head off foreclosure on Mapleton and raise some cash. I immediately borrowed money for Judy from my sister, Peri, and had it wired directly to London. While I was in L.A., Arthur Jacobs came over with Freddie Fields. Arthur was a PR person before he became a producer at 20th. He'd contacted me in London and mentioned that Freddie had left MCA and was in the process of establishing his own talent agency in New York. Apparently Fields was only going to handle a few clients, and he was interested in Judy. I remembered Freddie from Judy's second Palace engagement, when he'd come to us with Sonny Werblin and suggested multiple bands as a background for a Judy Garland TV special on CBS. Freddie had been a junior VP and had sold his shares in MCA for $300,000 when the agency broke up. My impression of him at the time was that he was a typical New Yorker: quick on his feet, cunning, and driven by ambition. He was wiry, well dressed, and sported a mustache. Freddie spoke in a rapid, nasal voice, the kind I associated with some New Yorkers.

I thought it might not be a bad idea. After all, Freddie was trained by the best, Jules Stein. Always immaculately dressed, Stein would listen in a meeting as though you had the key to eternal life, while writing copious notes on his Cartier pad. Artie explained that Freddie had tried to shop his little company around with people at the Charles Feldman Agency. Nobody seemed to be interested. On the good side, he had few clients—Hank Fonda, currently on Broadway, and Phil Silvers. He'd be able to give Judy a great deal of attention. This appealed to me. If she seriously wanted to perform again, this might be an excellent representation for her.

But when I'd told Judy in London that Artie Jacobs had inquired if she was interested in meeting Fields, her reaction was *absolutely not*. "What do I want to do that for?" Now Artie was bringing Freddie over to the Mapleton house to meet me again. This time I saw a streetwise, calm, and in-control Freddie who wanted to be the best manager the business had ever known. The one unusual characteristic in the otherwise impressive package was that his hands struck me as unusually small and gnarled for someone so young.

———— ∞∞ ————

On November 8, 1960, Jack Kennedy, age forty-three, became president-elect John F. Kennedy, ushering in the "New Frontier." What was banned in print in the early 1960s would be featured everywhere by the end of the decade. While Judy and I tangoed, people would be twisting at the Peppermint Lounge. An explosive, dangerous decade lay ahead of us on many different levels. However, Judy and I were stuck in the cocoon of our relationship and our economic pressures, not thinking much of the country's future.

Judy did several more concerts in England; she performed for the Royal Variety Gala and was presented to the Queen for the third time. Once I returned to London, Freddie Fields popped up in town and rang the house asking to meet Judy for lunch. I explained to Judy that in the next few months the Aerophonics hardware would be finished and I'd have to be on the road. Lately, she'd been talking about returning to the States. I said I thought it might be a good idea to get a manager. To which she replied, "I don't like Freddie Fields. Leave it alone. I don't want anybody. We'll be fine."

But I persuaded her to accept the invitation to lunch, and when she did she came home having made a one hundred percent switch: "He's bright, very bright, and he's got some wonderful ideas. He kinda sold me a bill of goods, darling. I think it'd be good for me." And so Judy was to sign a management agreement with Freddie Fields Associates, 410 Park Avenue, New York, New York.

I had not been successful in raising enough money to pay the mortgage. It was not a huge amount of money, but it was difficult finding the cash. We decided to give up our lease on the Chelsea house and return to New York, where Judy could work more directly with her new agent and I would be nearer to Florida and important business contacts.

We arrived in New York close to New Year's Eve. The family checked into the Stanhope Hotel near the Metropolitan Museum of Art on Fifth Avenue. It was one of those winters that hadn't kicked in yet and I could move around Manhattan without a coat.

The following day, we went over to Freddie's apartment. In the course of the evening Freddie's wife, the actress/singer Polly Bergen, filed and polished her nails. I thought it odd: she's polishing her nails and Freddie is asking Judy what she'd like to do. So casual. The new decade, the new style. It seemed kind of goofy. I had intended to impart necessary information, my professional knowledge of Judy to Fields. It was crucial he understand that she didn't read contracts and that she was unable to work a demanding schedule. However, Freddie wasn't allowing any gaps in his attention to Judy. I sat there uncomfortably while they spoke, taking a backseat. I was used to MCA, as I had been used to the William Morris Agency, and I expected to work with Fields regarding Judy's new career. I rationalized that perhaps it wasn't the right time. We said our good-byes with Freddie's voice ringing in my ears: "Whatever you want Judy, you've got it."

As I had to come up with the mortgage payment by early January, I went to Fields and asked him to loan us the money. I was surprised to find him very cold, a turnabout from the last time we'd met. He said, "Sid, I'll sign if you put the house in Judy's name." I told him I was not willing to do that. I'd find the money elsewhere.

I left Freddie's two-room offices on Park Avenue and walked slowly back up Fifth Avenue to the Stanhope, past the zoo, the old Brokaw mansion, every once in a while looking at the barren trees in Central Park, their branches and trunks like inky brush strokes against a peculiarly warm evening sky.

There was no doubt we were temporarily trapped by low finances, and it may have appeared that this was the way we generally lived.

And I wondered what in the hell Fields really thought of me . . .

PART VI

Leopold and Loeb

41

"WITH FREDDIE SOMETHING CLICKED," Judy told *Life* magazine. "He seemed to know how to do exactly what I could not do: channel my work." Although Freddie ran the office, he needed someone to do the legwork with the clients coming aboard, especially Judy Garland. He needed a "runner," a high-powered go-getter with a mouth, and that mouth was David Begelman. Begelman's career began as an insurance agent in New York. Freddie got him a job at MCA in the mail office, and then, with his knack for bullshit, Begelman became an agent there. Together the two would take Freddie Fields Associates to the next level and form CMA, Creative Management Associates.

Fields and Begelman were both smart dressers, but Begelman was the more elegant and sophisticated of the two. He was always impeccably outfitted in an expensive tailor-made suit, and he was known to wear a pale blue shirt every day then change into a white shirt each evening. Both men were witty, vivacious, and full of energy. "Leopold and Loeb." That's the name Judy came up with for them. She had a name for everybody. Well, almost everybody. I didn't have a nickname that I know of. I was just "darling" or "that bastard."

Fields and Begelman wasted no time in laying out their game plan for Judy's career. They set out to prove to the industry that she was reliable, eager, and willing to work. They would begin her concert tour in smaller markets and later graduate to major cities, then make her the most important act in the Vegas and Tahoe nightclub circuits. Finally they planned to reestablish her as an important actress in motion pictures.

In January 1961, following a seven-year hiatus from making movies, it was announced that Judy would return to the screen in Stanley Kramer's upcoming film *Judgment at Nuremberg*. Kramer had originally considered Julie Harris for the part and agonized over the decision for some time before Freddie Fields convinced him to give it to Judy. She was to be paid $50,000 to play the small but important role of a German hausfrau named Irene Hoffman Wallner.

The first confrontation I had with Judy relating to Fields and Begelman occurred when the three of them formed a corporation called Kingsrow Enterprises. "Darling, isn't it great?" Judy said to me. "I'm gonna have my own little corporation."

"Who are the officers?" I asked her.

"Well, I'm the president," she said. She was the president of this company, but there were no officers. They issued all the stock, but the only stockholder was Judy. It was comical!

I made a suggestion. "You know, what we *should* do is have this company be between us."

She wouldn't consider it. "Oh no, darling, just let me have this little thing by myself."

"It's not a very good idea in a family," I told her. "It'll raise hell with us eventually."

"Well, let's try it."

So naive. All I saw was doom. What we later learned was that they formed a company that would double-tax Judy, meaning Kingsrow would be taxed and Judy Garland would be taxed. Field and Begelman didn't care, though. They took theirs off the top—and the bottom!

Judy and I couldn't agree on anything. It was around this time that she took the children and checked out of the suite at the Stanhope where we'd been staying, and moved into the legendary Dakota Hotel on Central Park West. That split began a series of separations and reconciliations between us that went on for most of that year. I went back to California with Eddie Alperson and stayed busy with Aerophonics. I tried to keep my sanity while dealing with huge corporations like American Airlines, Pan Am, and so on.

Judy was on her own, with her career and with the children, but I was gung-ho to turn over control of her career to someone else. Begelman was assigned to work exclusively with her. As it turned out, he was Johnny-on-the-spot on tour. He was the new troubleshooter, so I could finally release those reins, and I did so without giving it a second thought. Even though we were apart, I was relieved knowing that Judy was in good hands. Or so I thought.

Judy's concert tour officially kicked off with her playing the State Fair in Dallas on February 21, then moving on to Houston. She paused for a couple of weeks to film *Judgment at Nuremberg* in Hollywood, and we reconnected and reconciled on Joey's sixth birthday. I was with her for the next show in Buffalo, and then we were off to Washington, DC, where Judy sang at Constitution Hall on April 8. While in DC, we accepted an invitation to the White House, having the privilege of visiting with Jack Kennedy during his first few months in office.

In the coming years, JFK would ring Judy from either the White House or Camp David and ask her to sing to him over the telephone. He'd request "Over the Rainbow," by then a tune beloved by the world—and least appreciated by Judy, probably because she had to sing it so many times. But the fans never knew, and President Kennedy was a fan. Milt Ebbins, Peter Lawford's personal manager and partner, was at Camp David one weekend with Peter and his brother-in-law the president. Kennedy loved showbiz stories, and after a round had been exchanged, he expressed a desire to reach Judy and have her sing to him. Judy was located somewhere in New York and obliged the president with several renditions of his favorite melodies.

Milt Ebbins subsequently became a personal friend of Jack's, much to the Kennedy clan's consternation. Peter rarely traveled without Milt. Peter, whose life was also to end as the result of his addiction to narcotics, loved Judy and remained a loyal friend. Years later the jazz singer Mel Tormé wrote a book around his brief relationship with Judy in the 1960s when he came to work for her on her CBS TV specials. Mel was not understanding of her condition—he'd gone into it thinking he was working with a normal person—and he denigrated her in his book. Peter never spoke to Mel again; in fact, when Peter and Milt happened to be passengers on the same airplane, Peter ignored him.

———— ✿ ————

Sunday, April 23, 1961, was a night that went down in history. It was the highlight of the tour when Judy played New York's Carnegie Hall. I was backstage with Judy when Fields and Begelman showed up. Were they surprised to find me in her dressing room! Judy suffered one of her anxiety attacks just before the show. She was standing over a toilet and vomiting and I thought, *This girl isn't going to make it. We'll have to cancel the show.* Outside, thousands jammed the streets surrounding Seventh Avenue and Fifty-Seventh Street. The doors were held until just minutes before showtime, leaving the crowd to nervously speculate that Judy might not take the stage. She was really unsteady on her feet, even a few seconds before the curtain opened, but she pulled herself together. She insisted upon performing that night, and she went out there and just killed them!

A who's who of show biz assembled that night at Carnegie: Julie Andrews, Leonard Bernstein, Richard Burton, Carol Channing, Henry Fonda, Rock Hudson, Spencer Tracy. The list goes on. Roger Edens was there, too. "Good, solid, raw talent creates excitement . . . that was the charm of the Carnegie Hall concert," Judy's longtime musical mentor explained to *Show Business Illustrated*, describing the magic he and the rest of the audience experienced that night. "I had never seen her on the concert stage before. I still don't believe anything like this could happen. She practically burnt the house down. She said, 'Let's do it,' as though she had never done it before. It's there and when she touches it, it emerges. It's alchemy."

The night before Carnegie Hall, Judy had told me, "I want to get away from everything and get a good night's sleep for tomorrow. I've had a rough tour and I need the rest." I checked us into a suite at the

Sherry-Netherland Hotel overlooking Central Park, where we played gin until about three o'clock in the morning until she finally fell asleep. She promised to not take any pills, but I stayed up all night just to be sure that she didn't. Not so much as an aspirin! She didn't. Not one pill. She was clean as a whistle for Carnegie. And that's still one of the great albums of all time. *Judy at Carnegie Hall* sold over a hundred thousand copies in just the first few months of release and went on to win five Grammys, including Album of the Year.

Shortly after Carnegie Hall, Judy told me she had good news. She had met with Fields and Begelman, and they agreed to put me on payroll of Kingsrow as an associate producer at $400 a week. "Let's go out and celebrate!" she said. I played along. We went to P. J. Clarke's, where the owner sat down with us and talked about racehorses and breeding until we closed the place down at 4:00 AM.

"That was some goddamn celebration," Judy said coldly when we ducked into the limo and headed for the Dakota.

"Well, the guy kept the place open for us," I told her. "He loves to talk about bloodlines."

"I'm not interested in bloodlines!" she snapped. "I'm interested in what you thought of what I did for you."

"You mean that $400 a week?" I said, knowing where this was headed. "Why, that's a two-bit tip for a groom compared to what I've given and done for you. You don't know a fucking thing about finances. If you think that $400 a week is anything, when you're making $100,000 a week, you're misinformed."

With that, she slapped me in the face. It was the first time she'd ever done that. She was angry at me for not paying attention to her after she had ordered Freddie to put me on the payroll. But that $400 a week was an insult and she didn't even know it! I said to Judy, "Shove it! I don't need your $400." We continued on to the Dakota in silence.

Freddie called me up the next day and said, "What happened last night?"

"What happened? You opened up an account for me, that's what happened."

"Wasn't that something?"

I said, "Why don't you shove it up your ass, Freddie," and hung up. Fields and Begelman were just busting my balls! They were controlling Judy's every move, and I was being treated like some kind of butler or servant. What did they think it cost to take Judy Garland out for the night? To go out to dinner and go dancing, it was easily $200 or $300. She was earning $100,000 to $200,000 a week and I got $400. It was a slap in the face. Literally.

For Judy, that summer was filled with concerts all up and down the East Coast: Atlantic City, Miami Beach, Hartford, White Plains, Newark, Pittsburgh, Rochester, and so on. Out on the West Coast she played Hollywood and San Francisco. Although we were separated much of the time, Judy and I were usually in good fettle. I felt as though we were trying to hold on to the relationship and make contact with each other. We always seemed to like the idea of her doing these concerts and me being away from her. It was a job to her. There was no cocking around when it was just a job to earn money. She knew I was busy with Aerophonics. I was going my way, she was going hers, and then we'd connect with each other when we could.

I received a letter from her explaining that she was moving to a summer house in Hyannis Port, adjacent to the Kennedy compound. "Have peace of mind—we'll all be fine," she wrote. "I couldn't do anything to hurt them—and I know you feel the same. Goodbye for a while. —Judy." She seemed distant.

I continued to live at the house on Mapleton Drive for a few months while she was touring, but I was so deep in debt that I was eventually forced to sell it. I never wanted to, of course. I later said to Judy, "Let's fix it up and go back and live there," but she associated that house with some dark days. I was able to sell it for $225,000, but after all the debts had been paid, just $10,000 remained. The sad commentary is that the property has since been sold in the neighborhood of $6 million.

Within a day or two I read in the news that Judy had been hospitalized in Hyannis Port for a "kidney attack." This sort of news in the past had been a cover for another overdose, and I called the hospital right away. I tracked down Judy's doctor to inquire about her condition and let him know her history of abusing medications. Judy was furious. "How dare you start probing into my personal life?" she shouted into the phone at me. "Calling my doctor behind my back!"

"I was concerned about you."

"Well, don't be concerned."

One of the next times I saw Judy, she casually told me, "You know, Sid, I'm going to divorce you."

For some reason, this time I believed her. I wasn't quite sure how to respond but said, "Well, if that's the way you want it—but think it over carefully."

We didn't see each other for some time after that. I went back on the road, traveling the country for work.

That fall, Judy and the kids settled into a rented house at 1 Cornell Street in Scarsdale, an affluent New York suburb, and Fields and Begelman secured a part for Judy alongside Bobby Goulet in *Gay Purr-ee*, a full-length musical cartoon feature. She spent several weeks in Hollywood recording the singing and speaking voice for the lead cat, named Mewsette.

Judy and I reconnected in November, and I moved into the house in Scarsdale with her. As the year wound down, she just kept right on going. She played Toronto's O'Keefe Centre before finishing out the tour with a show at the Armory in Washington, DC.

Judy flew to Berlin for the world premiere of *Judgment at Nuremberg*, the film that soon earned her an Oscar nomination for Best Supporting Actress. She then returned home to Scarsdale in time for the holidays, which we spent together with the children. It was an unusually blissful time for our family.

The year 1961 signaled the rebirth of Judy Garland. It was a new incarnation, a new Judy for the 1960s. Just take a look at what she did from January through December. It's incredible! Around this time, Shana Alexander profiled her for *Life* magazine, saying, "Judy Garland today is not only the most electrifying entertainer to watch on the stage since Al Jolson. She has moved beyond talent and beyond fame to become the rarest phenomenon in all show business: part bluebird, part phoenix, she is a legend in her own time."

That story followed Judy from one venue to another. Word was starting to get out that she was really healthy and in great form again. If you look at that rundown of 1961, there were forty-four concerts. It was a real ball-buster! For the first time in a long time, Judy was alert and fit and in very good physical shape. "This is the best year of my life," she told the *American Weekly*. "I'm well again—can you believe it?"

From the Catskills to the Boston Garden, when Judy and Fields and Begelman were on a roll, it was one successful concert after another. Judy was flattered by all the attention, and there was no denying her. Leopold and Loeb gave her whatever she wanted. "It's not like the usual artist-manager contract," Judy told James Goode in *Show Business Illustrated*. "We're partners; they see that the lights work and the curtain goes up."

I have to give those guys credit. They were clever enough to see her potential, and they tried their best to keep her going. It's just like a vintage automobile. It might overheat or blow a tire, but you get a guy to fix it up. You fix the water pump, fix the radiator, fix the ignition, change the spark plugs, crank it up, turn the key, and see if you can get up the hill. That was Judy. All she needed was some electricity, some speakers, a piano player, a drummer, a spotlight, and some people to applaud her.

Judy lived on applause. That was her life, that was her gift, and she knew how good she was. She knew she was the best. She might not have given anybody that impression, because she was a great actress, but I knew her better. Judy was more than just a voice. She was more like a three-act drama. She was a *force*. As Moss Hart said, Judy had "that little something extra." Judy knew what she could do to an audience, and she knew when she would be a failure. The applause was her food. Those people who came to see her and applaud her were hungry, too, and ready to eat her alive. They needed her. But she needed them.

"A really great reception makes me feel like I have a great big warm heating pad all over me," she told *Life*. "People en masse have always been wonderful to me. I truly have a great love for an audience, and I used to want to prove it to them by giving them blood. But I have a funny new thing now, a real determination to *make* people enjoy the show. I want to give them two hours of just *pow!*"

Judy's audiences applauded her if she coughed! But she coughed better than anybody I knew. And they applauded when she asked for a drink of water. She'd turn her back to the audience, talk to her piano player, and then she'd say to the audience, "Talk to yourselves for a few minutes and give me a breather and I'll be right back with you," and they went hysterical. Nobody ever did that to an audience!

42

JUDY WENT TO CALIFORNIA for work at the start of 1962, leaving me to close the Scarsdale house. Once I joined her on the West Coast, we lived together in a rented house at 924 Bel Air Road. She was doing a special with Dean Martin and Frank Sinatra for CBS, and I was working on Aerophonics business. Judy was so proud of me when I brought the Aerophonics music hardware back home to show her. She said, "What did my Sid do?" She showed it to Fields and Begelman, but they didn't give a fuck. They couldn't afford for me to be successful. Not at that point. They still needed Judy to pay their rent.

Then came *A Child Is Waiting* for Stanley Kramer, a picture I never saw. I do know it was a story about mentally disabled children, and Judy played the part of their music teacher. She really loved working with them, but that picture was very trying for her. By the end of production, she had started taking medication again. I don't know what she was on then, but I am certain she was on something.

I thought things would surely improve once she finished making the picture, but Fields and Begelman committed her to go to England to make another movie, *The Lonely Stage*, which would later become *I Could Go On Singing*. I thought to myself, *These guys are nuts to do this to her*. I fussed and fumed about it. It was bad enough that she'd just done all those concerts, but now she was doing two major motion pictures back to back. How could she do it? I knew Judy well enough to know that she had to have a breather. She needed at least a month to recover in between pictures. In the past, she might be all right for the first week or so, but when things got going and she wasn't getting enough rest, she would most certainly resort to more pills.

"Don't worry," Judy assured me, "I can handle it. Freddie and David can handle it." Of course they were telling her, "Sid's going to try to get in your way. He's going to be jealous." They were much subtler, I'm sure, but because of my objections, they had a clandestine meeting without letting me in on their activities. I couldn't even bring myself to talk to her about it, I was so frustrated at the time. Helpless. The modus operandi for her new lifestyle was that Sid should not be included. I wasn't invited to any of their meetings. "Keep Sid out of it," she had told them, which I only learned years later. I felt like an outsider.

For whatever reason, as soon as she completed *A Child Is Waiting*, Judy moved into the Beverly Hills Hotel. She said it was because of the pressure of making the movie, so I didn't question her. Liza was with her, but Lorna and Joey were with me at the house in Bel Air. She wasn't at the hotel for more than a couple of weeks when she packed up and said, "I've gotta get out of this atmosphere." I told her OK, and that I would make preparations. "I want to go to New York alone, ahead of you," she said. "You close up the house and bring the children to New York."

It took me several weeks to close the Bel Air house. During that time, I received a call from Grant Cooper, a prominent Los Angeles trial lawyer, telling me that Judy wanted me to sign documents for a legal separation. I refused. "It'll blow over," I told him. "Judy always acts this way. That's the way she takes out her frustrations and fears on me. She's done it before."

It seems Judy considered herself separated. I found out later that she was going out with Eddie Fisher while in New York. He mentioned it in his autobiography—what an utter asshole. He was still married to Elizabeth Taylor. Years earlier, when he was with Debbie Reynolds, they got lost while looking for a house on Mapleton Drive and stopped by our place. They knocked on our door, came in for a drink, and I remember Eddie was so shocked to meet Judy Garland.

When we got to New York and checked in at the Stanhope, I learned that Judy had reserved a suite for the children and me on a floor separate from hers. She knew I was in the hotel but, for whatever reason, she wouldn't see me. She was really off from the pills and booze, and she just stayed locked in her room. Our friend Dr. Lester Coleman went up to her room. Judy really liked this guy and she'd called him over. Lester told me there were martini glasses everywhere and the place was in disarray. He said, "She is a very sick woman, Sid. She's not capable of taking care of kids."

With that information, I made up my mind that, for their own safety, the children would stay with me. On the morning of April 28, I still hadn't seen Judy, but I was on the phone with her from one floor to the other. We were screaming at each other and she was saying she wanted the children. She didn't want to *see* them; she just wanted to take them. Judy wanted the children to get on a plane with her and Liza and go to Europe, but I told her I didn't think it was right of her to take the kids to England at this time. I didn't think she was well enough. "Leave the children here with me," I suggested. "I'll bring them over."

"I want the kids to go with me!" she screamed.

I knew it was not right. Liza did not want to go, either. I'd met Liza in Central Park that day and she pleaded with me not to go to England and explained how she could stay in New York and study. Liza had a boyfriend who was an actor. "I can stay with him at his house," she said. She was only sixteen and I think the boy was probably twenty. I told her that as much as I wished she could, I was not capable of making such a decision. "That decision has to be made by your mother."

A while later, just when I thought Judy had finished battling me about taking the children to Europe, there came a loud knock at the door to my suite. "Sid?"

"Who is it?" I said cautiously.

"It's me," Judy said.

"Are you alone?"

"Yes, Sid."

"I don't believe you." Why would I?

"No, no, please," she said. "I just want to talk to you. Maybe you were right, Sid. Maybe they should stay."

"Are you alone?" I asked a second time. She swore she was.

I opened the door, let her in, and as the door started to close, Judy started screaming, "He's hitting me, he's hitting me!" Just then, a private detective and a cop busted in. The two men forced their way into my suite and held me down. It was all very dramatic. One had me by the neck, the other by the arms. While I was restrained, Judy grabbed Lorna and Joey and ran out of the suite. They left the hotel, went immediately to Idlewild Airport, and flew to England.

Judy and the children arrived in London to headlines reading Judy Flees Country and "I'll Guard My Children with My Life" Says Judy and Judy Flies In as Husband Storms. She had Lorna and Joey under twenty-four-hour guard and told the press that I'd threatened to have her declared an unfit mother and take away the children. "I don't know why Sid says I'm an unfit mother," she said. "The children love me. I hear he may be coming over to take them away from me. He will never do that. There is no chance of reconciliation. My marriage is finished. We have tried reconciliations, but they were hopeless."

David Begelman, the man who arranged the kidnaping fiasco, interrupted to tell the press, "The studio will make sure that no unauthorized person—even Mr. Luft—will be allowed to see the children at this stage."

I flew over to England about a week later, and things were still very chaotic. Judy had convinced the High Court to make Lorna and Joey temporary wards of the court so neither she nor I could take them out of the country. I didn't see Judy, because she was shooting *I Could Go On Singing*. She was living in a rented house at 33 Hyde Park Gate while making the picture. I rented an apartment about six blocks down the road from her and was finally able to see the children.

While in London, I received an unexpected call from Judy one day. "Would you like to come to a prerecording?" she asked. I'd seen the kids, but that was the first time I'd seen her in a couple of weeks or maybe a month. I was apprehensive, but also I was curious and concerned. She sang, not badly, but not well. After seeing her, I was sure she was on tons of Ritalin. Sometimes she was in and out, but she was very affectionate that night. "Take me home, darling," she said afterward. I don't think she knew if I was Sid Luft or David Begelman. I really don't! That's how strong that drug was. I went home with her and she said, "Why don't you stay with me?" I agreed. After all, she was my wife. She was tired and we went right to bed.

"What are you doing here?" Judy shouted at me the next morning. "Get out of my house!"

"I thought we were trying to reconcile," I said.

"Forget it. And when we get back to the States I'm gonna divorce you!"

The medication changed Judy's whole psyche. I didn't know her half the time. From what I gathered, she was on Ritalin or something else throughout the whole film. Later, when I met Jack Klugman, one of Judy's costars, he said to me, "Sid, I just wish you two were together when we made that movie, 'cause it was so difficult making that with her. She was trying to cooperate, but I know that she was on some kind of medication. But she got through it." Even so, the shoot did mark the end of her friendship with another of her costars, her old friend Dirk Bogarde.

I Could Go On Singing was finally finished, and in August, after we attended a court custody hearing, Judy prepared to return to America with the children. I tried to defuse things with the British press. "I'd naturally like everything to work out the best possible way for both of us—and the children," I told them. "I shall be seeing them before they go. I have been able to see them here. It's all been very amicable—there haven't been any problems. After all, we're civilized people."

———— ✆✆✆ ————

News of the untimely death of Marilyn Monroe on August 5, 1962, came as a shock to the world. This was especially troubling to Judy, since Marilyn had been one of Judy's telephone pals during her years of insomnia. Judy remembered her relationship with Marilyn in a 1967 piece for *Ladies' Home Journal*:

> I knew Marilyn Monroe and loved her dearly. She asked me for help. Me! I didn't know what to tell her. One night, at a party at Clifton Webb's house, Marilyn followed me from room to room. "I don't want to get too far away from you," she said. "I'm scared!"
>
> I told her, "We're all scared. I'm scared, too!"
>
> "If we could just talk," she said. "I know you'd understand."
>
> I said, "Maybe I would. If you're scared, call me and come on over. We'll talk about it."
>
> That beautiful girl was frightened of aloneness—the same thing I've been afraid of. Like me, she was just trying to do her job—to garnish some delightful whipped cream onto some people's lives. But Marilyn and I never got the chance to talk. I had to leave for England, and I never saw that sweet, dear girl again. I wish I had been able to talk to her the night she died.
>
> I don't think Marilyn really meant to harm herself. It was partly because she had too many pills available, then was deserted by her friends. You shouldn't be told you're completely irresponsible and be left alone with too much medication. It's too easy to forget. You take a couple of sleeping pills, and you wake up in 20 minutes and forget you've taken them. So you take a couple more, and the next thing you know you've taken too many. It's happened to all of us; it happened to me. Luckily, someone found me and saved my life.

The death of a friend was always tough. One time when were in Texas on tour, somebody had called Judy up at the hotel to let her know that Bob Alton had died. He was a choreographer and friend at MGM. Well, I noticed that night that Judy's eyes were dilated. I could always tell when she had taken Dexedrine or Benzedrine. Then, without warning, she walked out onstage and told the audience, "I'm awfully sorry, I can't sing tonight. Go to the box office and get your money back. Hopefully I'll come back, but I can't sing because a very good friend of mine has died." That was the only time she did that, but she was certainly capable of the bizarre.

One time Judy had decided to kick her pill habit cold turkey, which is always a painful and dangerous way to withdraw. She said to me, "No doctors, no phone calls," and she locked herself up and screamed her way out of it. I went through it with her and could only watch and hold her as she buried her head in a pillow and screamed. Eighteen hours later she came out of it. That was one of the most terrifying and most courageous goddamn things I'd ever seen.

But Judy was a pill-taker and nobody could stop her. She couldn't think straight when she was taking them, and she certainly wouldn't listen to me. I watched my friend Dean Martin squander his talent and drink himself to death. I couldn't stop Dino, and I couldn't stop Judy. But I tried. The fact is that she was married to the drugs before she met me, and she never really got divorced.

You can feel great compassion for someone who is ill or in pain, but when a person is drunk, using profanity, and you can't deal with them, or if someone is just out of control, your compassion disappears. You take on another personality. A stronger personality. You have to keep saying, "Hey, don't do this" or "Don't do that." You constantly ask, "Where are the pills? Let's find them. Let's get to the bottom of this."

They say the pill-taker is probably the most difficult person to deal with, or to keep clean. Heroin has a substitute, methadone, but there is nothing but total abstinence for the pill-taker. There is no methadone. There is no cure. There was no cure for Marilyn Monroe, and there was no cure for Judy Garland. Only abstinence. Total abstinence.

Back in the States, Judy headed for Las Vegas, where she began a run at the Sahara on September 18, 1962. She wasted no time filing for residency in Nevada. I knew her next order of business would be to file for divorce, but there would be a waiting period. She wanted to get jurisdiction in the state of Nevada, but I wasn't going to go for that. So I beat her to the punch, filing for divorce in Santa Monica. They located Judy about four o'clock in the morning in Vegas and served her. That meant I had jurisdiction in the state of California.

The story going around then was that Judy was going to divorce me and marry David Begelman. Apparently Begelman was going to divorce his wife, Lee Reynolds, so that he and Judy could be together. At least that was the rumble. The papers reported on Judy's dependency on him and how he had rushed to her side in London after the ordeal at the Stanhope. His wife wasn't pleased and took a trip of her own to Puerto Rico. According to the gossip columns, "The amount of 'babysitting' and attention required by a star of Judy's talent and temperament sometimes gets to be more than a manager's wife can bear."

I later learned that Begelman visited Judy frequently when she was in London making *I Could Go On Singing*, and letters and telegrams revealed they'd had a physical relationship. "No one will ever receive my love, my mind—my body—my breathing again," she once wrote to him. "I gave you all I had to give."

Foolishly, I hadn't even suspected that Begelman might be having an affair with my wife. Maybe I just didn't want to believe it. I was the dumb husband. In hindsight, there was definitely evidence of it. And it would've been just like Begelman to take advantage of his station. With a guy like that, the obvious next step was to start fucking the star.

I started watching these guys, especially Begelman, like a detective. I wanted to know what was going on with them, so I flew up to Vegas and got in touch with Clyde Duber, my private investigator friend. I knew my way around Vegas, but Clyde was a friend of a Jack Cherry, a district attorney there, so it was very easy for him to get around. We found out Judy was going to be in the audience at one of Tony Bennett's shows. The maître d' arranged for us to sit just where we could see Judy, holding us a table right behind hers. As the lights dimmed and the overture began, Judy walked into the room. She was right in front of me, sitting with Stevie Dumler, Freddie Fields's secretary. Stevie spotted me during applause, and Judy soon turned around and grabbed my hand. We held hands, and she was trembling that famous tremble. The minute the show was over, in walks David Begelman wearing a new brown suit and one of his new custom-made shirts. He brushed right by me, grabbed Judy, pulled her through, pushed her in front of him, and waltzed her out. Like *he* was Mr. Luft! I had been replaced.

43

WITH THE NEW YEAR 1963 came the news that Judy had signed the biggest deal of her career, a four-season, $24 million contract with CBS for a weekly variety series to be called *The Judy Garland Show*. "It was a big decision, but a wonderful decision," Judy would tell the press. "I don't think of it as so formidable. I'm going to be a female Perry Como."

A few days after the announcement, I was staying at the Beverly Rodeo Hotel and sound asleep when a call came in at 4:00 AM. No one should have known my whereabouts, but Judy had used her black Irish witchcraft again to track me down. "Hi, darling," she said. "Do you think we'll ever have a chance?"

"Judy, we'll always have a chance," I told her. "Where are you?"

She was in Miami. "Do you think we can sit down and talk—that there's any chance after what we've gone through?"

"We always will. You know as well as I do, we love each other."

We decided then to meet halfway. I splashed some cold water on my face and headed to New Orleans, wondering what I was getting myself into.

Judy was waiting for me at the airport with confetti and a bottle of champagne. As we danced in a nightclub on the French Quarter, she kept whispering in my ear, "This is it, baby! This is it!" But when we went back to the Prince Conti Hotel, she said to me, "Darling, you go to your room and I'll see you in the morning. Good night." I was puzzled to learn she had reserved two separate rooms for us on separate floors. "Good night, Mrs. This-Is-It," I told her, and headed for my room.

We stayed in New Orleans for a couple of days, saw the sights, and tried to come to some sort of understanding, but we both agreed that something was missing. "Perhaps we're both too scarred up," I told her. Early the next morning, Judy had already checked out of the hotel when I discovered an envelope left under my door. The note inside, written on my Aerophonics stationery, read:

> Dearest Sid:
> No matter what way or what manner you handle what's ahead for us in our divorce—your children need, love, and want you. You're their father and always will be! Our marriage failed—but I'll be your friend forever.
>
> > With deep sincerity,
> > —From J.

We'd reconciled again by Valentine's Day, spent some time together at the Fairmont in San Francisco, and then Judy took off to London for the opening of *I Could Go On Singing*. In March, we met with lawyers in New York while staying at the St. Regis. They were all set to take our depositions for the divorce proceedings, but Judy told them it was off. "I'd rather reconcile with this guy!" she said.

From there the children joined us for a two-week vacation on the Cat Cay islands in the Bahamas. There was to be no more talk about divorce. I thought that portion of our lives was behind us.

What I didn't realize at the time was that the real reason for the reconciliation was that Fields and Begelman thought it would be better to get me back in the picture now that Judy was doing this television series. It was a ploy; we made up because she was told to make up. CBS didn't need any heat. They felt it was important for their star to have a husband, and they probably knew she'd go bananas without one. Their thought was *If she and her husband start fighting and divorce, she won't have the energy to do the show. So let's make up with Sid so he can get you through!*

Judy was certainly optimistic about *The Judy Garland Show*. As she told the press, working on a series would allow her to remain close to her family and home, and also promised financial stability. "You know how I look on this series?" she said. "As a secure way of living. I can get up in the morning and go to work and come home at night to things that are familiar and mine. I'm so tired of being on the road. The concerts have been marvelous for me, but I've been living in hotels now for the last three years and I've had it."

Fields and Begelman were certain that this television series was going to be the most important thing in Judy's career and life. They were promising her she would be rich. She thought those shows were going to be worth $1 million apiece and that after their first airings they'd be shown all over the world. As she explained to the media, "David Begelman told me there was no reason I shouldn't have a steady home with my children, be very rich, and do a weekly show—that I should have been very rich a long time ago, like Bob Hope or Perry Como."

It was almost like brainwashing. They said, "Think of it Judy, if you do the first thirteen shows and the next thirteen, that's twenty-six shows. They'll be worth $1 million apiece. We've done our homework. You'll have freedom, because you'll own twenty-six of your own shows. That's like owning twenty-six of your own movies. And you know who will be in your first one? Mickey Rooney, just like the good old days."

I was concerned about Judy's finances, though, and how Fields and Begelman were handing the hundreds of thousands of dollars coming into Kingsrow Enterprises. I was especially upset when I learned she'd given them power of attorney. I never took financial power of attorney from my wife, nor would I unless it were absolutely necessary. I don't believe in that. I don't think it's right to think for somebody else. But, as I told Judy, I do think a husband has power of attorney *morally* with his wife.

I was getting reports of Begelman's gambling in Vegas. He made enemies, and some people began to spread rumors that he was wasting

Judy's money at the racetrack and other places. Sure, I was gambling, too, but I was a successful gambler. I *made* money, I didn't lose it. And I wasn't gambling with Judy's money—I had my own, and I had Ted Law backing me. My best day at the track was $56,000. My worst day at the track: $2,000, maybe. But Judy had always had a business manager. You couldn't gamble if you had a business manager. You couldn't ask him for money to go to the racetrack!

Judy assured me through all this that she was in very capable hands financially. She met with Herb Allen, a very successful investment banker, at the Four Seasons Hotel. That's a powerhouse place to have lunch. The plan was that CMA was going to turn over some of Judy's earnings to Herb to invest. She was very happy about that, and it seemed to be a successful meeting. But it turned out to be just another one of their tricks. Fields and Begelman convinced her that was how her money was being dealt with, but that wasn't the case.

I was sure Fields and Begelman were pocketing money from her, or at the very least mismanaging it, but I needed to be able to prove it. After much pressure from me, Judy finally agreed to let Guy Ward, my lawyer, look over her financial records. Guy passed them on to Oscar Steinberg, a Beverly Hills accountant who was hired to audit the books, which were dated January 1961 to April 1963.

Tensions were high when Judy arranged a meeting at the Beverly Hills Hotel with Fields, Begelman, and me so that we could try to mend some of our fences, so to speak. They were telling me they were going to cooperate in every way, how they respected that Judy and I were together as husband and wife again. After the meeting was over I said, "The jury's out right now." What I meant was that I was waiting for Steinberg to do his thing. I wanted to buy some time until I could get my hands on that report telling me what the hell went on in 1961 and 1962.

When production for *The Judy Garland Show* moved from New York to Los Angeles, our family rented a house in Malibu for several weeks. In June 1963 I found us a house at 129 South Rockingham Avenue in Brentwood. Judy borrowed the down payment from a bank somewhere and bought the house in her name only, which pissed me off, but I couldn't say much. Ours wasn't what you'd call a solid reconciliation yet.

A couple of weeks before the first taping for her show, Judy and I hosted a lavish housewarming party at the new house on Rockingham. This seemed to solidify our relationship and signal to everyone that our marriage was back on track and we were stronger than ever.

It was the end of June and they were rehearsing the first episode of Judy's show, the one with Mickey Rooney, when I finally got the five-page report from Oscar Steinberg. I met with Judy's lawyer, Grant Cooper, as well as Guy and Oscar, and we read over the report together and started discovering all the discrepancies. It was worse than I could have imagined. As it turned out, David Begelman had embezzled funds from her on multiple occasions, totaling $200,000 to $300,000. Of that, $78,967.20 had already been documented. They were taking double commissions, making deposits into their own accounts, and in some cases they were paying Judy what should have been *their* commissions and keeping the rest of the money themselves.

"I wish to advise you of certain items requiring additional explanation," Steinberg wrote. These included thirteen checks, totaling $35,714, written by Begelman to "cash" on Judy's Kingsrow account. The checks, drafted between May and October 1962, ranged from $500 to $6,000 each, and Begelman cashed them himself at either the Sahara or the Dunes Hotel in Vegas. The total was listed in Kingsrow's bookkeeping as part of Judy's salary for "protection."

Additionally, a $50,000 bank transfer was made from one of Judy's accounts at the Chase Manhattan Bank in Berkeley Square, London, to the Chase Manhattan Park Avenue branch in December 1962. A letter Judy signed before a notary was included, instructing the bank to deposit $24,355 of the $50,000 to the "Executive Producer Account, Special, for David Begelman," which was an account to which only Begelman had access. The letter also instructed that $3,245 of the $50,000 be deposited into an account labeled "201 East 62nd Street Building Company, Inc." Interestingly enough, Begelman and his wife, Lee Reynolds, had

moved into a cooperative apartment building that was being built at
201 East 62nd Street.

A check in the amount of $10,000, written on the Kingsrow account
to the Chase Manhattan Bank, was listed on the Kingsrow ledger as
a bank transfer. "I was advised by an officer of the Chase Manhattan
Bank," Oscar reported, "that such check was deposited to an account in
the name of David Begelman, in trust for Judy Garland. Subsequently,
the account was changed or transferred to an account in the name of
David Begelman and the funds were withdrawn."

Looking through the files Oscar used in making his report, I discovered that when Judy appeared on *The Jack Paar Program* back in 1962,
part of her recompense was supposed to be a new 1963 Cadillac convertible. Judy's signature was even on the letter about the car from Jack
Paar's production company, but she never knew anything about it. Just
a few months after she appeared on Paar's show, Judy and I moved to
California and had to buy two new cars. She didn't even know about
the Cadillac. She said to me, "I don't have a car."

After reading the first couple of pages of the report, I said to Grant,
"These guys must be crazy!"

"Crazy? My foot!" he said. "This is all criminal!"

When a lawyer like Grant Cooper says this is all criminal, you take
heed. This was criminal! But how do you deal with it? In cases of fraud,
the government's not going to play bill collector for you. You've got to
get the money back from these guys yourself. I guess Grant and Guy were
looking for Fields and Begelman to just confess and say, "Look, we want
to make it up to you somehow." But of course they were ducking it.

It was all fraud. For example, in all these concerts that Judy did,
there were souvenir program sales. On the ledger it said that "program
sales" totaled $274 for forty-four concerts. You sell a program to one
out of every four or five people in attendance. If you've got two thousand people in a theater, that means you sell five hundred programs. At
$4.00 each, sales of five hundred programs would generate $2,000. Do
that for just a week's worth of shows and that's a lot more than $274.
It's $16,000 a week. Cash! They were pocketing all of that money, too.

The unfortunate beauty of Judy having Kingsrow and giving power of attorney to Fields and Begelman was that they were allowed to pay themselves. That's such a huge conflict of interest on their part. That kind of relationship was absolutely idiotic. They claimed it was necessary to meet her needs as a person and as a performer. Perhaps, but it was completely unprofessional.

If the IRS had looked into the situation, they would have found the fraud. Just look at the books and you can tell they were conscious of the possibility of being audited. All those amounts of cash were in Judy's ledger as "protection." They tried to say, "This is a high-security lady!" Those were amounts of money that went into *their* pockets for protection, in the amount of $115,000. Freddie knew all of this was going on. He was as guilty as Begelman, but Begelman was fucking the star, so Freddie went along with it.

Judy was at CBS when she heard the Steinberg report was ready. She asked Oscar to bring the report with him to the studio, but Guy told Oscar *not* to take her a copy, because we didn't want Fields and Begelman to see it. I waited until Judy took a week off from taping the show and finally confronted her with the news. I harassed my wife as little as I could during the making of those shows. I felt that it would be better for me to not be around and possibly interfere with the television responsibilities that she had, but I couldn't help it this time. I was under the influence of this report.

If Judy had wanted to, we could have buried Begelman. She was devastated to learn she was being robbed, but she didn't want to face up to it. These men were deeply involved in the production of her television show, and she was anxious of spoiling anything. Deep down, she knew these guys should have been fired, but they were written into every detail of her agreement with CBS. They were to be her provider, her agents of record, and they were going to act as assistants to the producer to get the show together. CMA was putting together the package of stars and musicians for *The Judy Garland Show*. Firing them right then would have presented a legal hassle. There would have been a lawsuit and a real mess for everybody.

Needless to say, Judy and I started fighting again. "Look, suppose he did steal $200,000 to $300,000," Judy told me. "Sweep it under the rug now. I'm going to make $20 million on these television shows. What is $300,000?"

Judy didn't know what she was doing. I'm a businessman, and I know the implications of unreported income. I wasn't going to be a part of fraud—*her* fraud—no matter how much money she was supposed to make. If you make $20 million you cannot sweep it under the rug, and knowing that a fraud was committed means you must expose it. I told Judy that I was the husband and I had to expose it. If I didn't, I'd be a party to the fraud as well.

Fields and Begelman had Judy running interference for them. It was the strategic planning of two con artists, and she didn't get it. I tried to warn her, but she wouldn't listen to me. As long as they gave her some money when she needed it, everything was fine. They didn't steal *all* her money, but they certainly stole enough to gamble and buy shirts. They were keeping her career alive, though, so Judy didn't care. All she cared about was being onstage.

And so began another war. Accusations, arguments, and unrest at home. It was a nightmare. Everything was so convoluted and in disarray. Fields and Begelman wanted it that way, though, so they could control everything. They were controlling Judy, she was trying to control me, and we were all fighting each other. That's a perfect thing for Leopold and Loeb. If Judy's on pills, doesn't trust Sid, is fighting Sid, and is not letting Sid in on anything, then those two can operate unseen, freely in the background.

It was as if her guards robbed the bank, undetected, and were looting until she was totally wiped out. They were supposed to be watching the icon and guarding the treasure, but there was nobody there to watch them. They just took all the treasures, moved them out quietly, and nobody said anything until it was too late. *Unscrupulous* is a good word to describe those two. There was no moral integrity whatsoever. They were absolutely fucking ruthless!

The *Hollywood Reporter* soon announced that Judy and her Kingsrow Enterprises had signed a new three-year agreement with CMA. A telegram was sent to me and several others saying that we should not go looking into Judy's past. It was too painful for Judy, they said. We were to look forward to the future or get off the team. Then Judy fired Guy Ward and Grant Cooper. I knew the moment that happened that she was in grave danger. As soon as they were gone, Fields and Begelman thought they were out of the woods. Guy and I could have saved Judy, but when she was being totally controlled by these guys, she was mincemeat. I knew she was a fucking goner, because she was getting along just fine and she was in love with the world. That meant she was on whoop-de-doo pills!

I became so uncomfortable with what was happening and the way we were living that I just couldn't do it anymore. I took a long, peaceful drive down to Newport Beach and checked into a hotel for the weekend. I just needed some time to cool off. I left a message for Judy saying where I was, but when I came back to the house the following Monday, all of my belongings were gone. The family had quietly moved me out of Rockingham. I was out of the house, and Judy was out of control.

I settled into a little apartment on Manning Avenue. There was a sense of relief, but at the same time there was no relief whatsoever. The relief was that I didn't have to deal with the responsibility anymore. I could let somebody else do it. When I left, I thought it was going to be smoother sailing, but that never happened. I still had two young children who needed their father.

———— ⚭ ————

Freddie Fields and David Begelman interloped in my family. As Judy's agents and managers, they were supposed to merely guide her career. That's all. This was my bone of contention from the time we started out with Freddie. We should have had a much closer understanding. Judy didn't mistrust me before them, but then Begelman became Judy's hero when he said to her, "You know, Sid hasn't done his 1958–1959 tax returns, but I stopped the IRS agent." She blamed me for not paying taxes, of course, and now Begelman was the hero. It was then that I knew I was in serious trouble with these guys.

I arranged a meeting with Fields and Begelman on August 22, 1963, at a Sunset Boulevard office building, where we argued and fussed for more than three hours. What they didn't know was that my cigarette pack in my shirt pocket was actually a microphone in disguise. Our voices were transmitted to a reel-to-reel tape recorder in a car outside being monitored by a private detective I'd hired.

I told them both, "Look, I'm out and you're in now." We acknowledged there was a three-way cold war going on. There was a war between Freddie Fields and me, one between David Begelman and me, and yet another between Judy Garland and me. The one thing we could all agree on was that there had been two and a half years of unrest for everyone involved. "I think we should get some of the things out that are bugging me," I said. "And I've got a lot of things that are swirling around in my mind." There should have been a consensus between all parties from the start. Ground rules should have been established and boundaries defined.

The problem was this, I explained: I really felt that for two and a half years there was a lack of intimacy in our marriage. An intimacy that a man should have with his wife. I wasn't talking about sex. I was talking about the intimacy of a man with his wife to know her business, to protect her, to protect her children, to look after their welfare. I had been the father, the sweetheart, the lover, everything. And now I was being relieved. I was being replaced.

"I think that you and Dave should have come to me as the husband," I said to them. "You should have come to me and told me certain things after Judy and I reconciled."

According to Freddie, though, Judy had told them early on to keep me out of her finances and other business-related issues. "Keep Sid the fuck out," she apparently said. "I don't want him to have anything to do with this. Don't show him the accounts. Don't let him see the contracts. I want to help Sid keep his dignity, and I never want to hurt him, but one thing you must never do is talk to him about my financial affairs."

I told Freddie he should have walked away right then. He tried to argue that "Judy had that human right," but I told him nobody has that right when they're married to someone.

I brought up the audit that Oscar Steinberg had done. I wanted some explanations as to where all this money went. "You want to know where the money went?" Begelman said. "You know how much money was paid to get cops into the Stanhope? Uniformed policemen broke in on you at the Stanhope and took your children away from your arms and it was illegal."

"Of course it was illegal!" I said.

"How do you think they did that?"

"I don't know."

"Cash, you shmuck! The only weapon she had against you in the last two years was cash. . . . You had the children under your arm asleep and all of a sudden thirty-nine uniformed policemen broke in and ran you over like Red Grange ran over the line. You were left with the phone in your hand, calling for a lawyer. It was like a bad comedy sketch!"

That wasn't exactly how it had happened, of course, but the memory still stung. "Who rigged that one?" I asked.

"Cash rigged that one, pal. Cash. She bought the fucking precinct."

Another expenditure requiring explanation was the $50,000 London bank transfer that Oscar had uncovered. Several days before this meeting, I'd spoken with Begelman on the phone and asked him about it. He told me it had been used to bribe someone who had taken a picture of Judy in a British hospital. I didn't believe that story for a second. When I asked him about that in the meeting, with Freddie present, he was trapped.

"I'll tell you, that was the most disturbing phone call that I had with you about that $50,000 thing," I said. "That photo negative . . . $50,000."

"I didn't tell you that . . . did I?" Begelman said. "Because I swear on my life . . . on my child's life."

"You said it on the phone. You said to me, 'The nurse took a picture with a camera.'"

"I told you this on the phone?"

"Yeah . . . Judy said, 'Yes, I saw the negative.'"

"But I told you this?"

"Be quiet," Fields said to Begelman.

"And I said to you, 'Dave . . . what happened to that $50,000 from England?'"

"Do you want me to tell you the truth?" Begelman said. "Apparently she was taken to the hospital; they were pumping her stomach and she was disrobed down to here and somebody took a picture of her. But, I mean, this kind of picture."

"You saw the picture?"

"Oh yeah, oh yeah, oh yeah, oh yeah."

They tried to convince me that all this money went to blackmailers or hoodlums and that a lawyer was involved. I asked them who the lawyer was, but they never answered the question. They couldn't answer it. There was no lawyer. It was a made-up figment of Begelman's imagination. This was all bullshit. This was a hoax. That someone would take a picture in a hospital, I just couldn't buy that. No newspaper in the world would dare to print it.

I asked them the whereabouts of the negative and prints. They said everything was in a safety deposit vault in New York. "Get rid of it," I told them. "But I want to see it first."

"That's not the issue now," David said.

Our conversation went on for hours until David finally asked me, "What do you want from us? Believe me, Sid, I wish you were sitting in my chair and I was sitting in your chair."

"Well, I'd like to have peace of mind. And a peaceful reconciliation with my wife and family."

"How can we do that?" Freddie asked.

"God, I don't know."

My Aerophonics work had started to dwindle by this time. I'd demonstrated our in-flight music player for Pan Am and they said, "It's a wonderful idea," but they didn't want to get into show business. American Airlines said, "We want it!" Then I foolishly revealed who had made the device for me. Marion Sadler, the president of American

Airlines said, "Mr. Luft, if we like this form of entertainment and decide we want it, we'll pay you for it." Nothing could have been further from the truth. They should have said, "We're gonna steal it from you!" That's what they did.

I told Freddie and David that I was busted. "I can't borrow any more," I said. "I'm having a rough go of it. I've got no dough, I'm living in a hotel, and it isn't easy. I need a job. Don't I need a job? Don't I deserve one? And where was that job at CBS, really?" They had previously promised to bring me on board with the production of the show.

"It was more than a job," Begelman said.

"It was the best fucking opportunity you ever had in your life," Fields chimed in.

"Well, get it back again," I told them. "I'm a pretty intelligent fellow and I've had a lot of experience. I've produced some of the best things that Judy ever did in her life! You can't deny it. I've done it . . . *A Star is Born.* She was up for an Academy Award! What about the Palace? You can't deny those things and neither can Judy. If she wants to, that's her business, but I know the truth. I've got to get on my feet, because I'm frustrated."

Later in the conversation, we tried to come to some sort of an agreement. "I think that Judy cannot stand this harassment any longer," I told them, "and I don't think that she'll function properly unless we have an understanding."

"Freddie, I would like for you to draw a check to Sid for, like, $1,000," Begelman said. "Here's what I'd like to propose . . . that we give Sid $1,000 for each episode of Judy's new television series. You follow me? I mean give him the $1,000 now because he needs it tomorrow."

"Or yesterday and the day before," I uttered.

"But give him $1,000 a week," Begelman continued, "subject only to a relationship between us—you know what I mean. That's certainly not a buy-off or a payoff. This is the only way we can make our handshake a little more realistic with you . . . it'll take the pressure off of you to try to come up with a plan . . . because when you're under pressure . . .

when you're desperate, then you obviously—you translate your desperation to her. Will that relieve some of that pressure?"

"Of course it will."

"Well let's start with that. Sid, you know, look, we're playing such a fucking dangerous game with you and I don't care, so I'll go all the way with you. All right."

"And I'll only tell you this," Fields interrupted. "If you—in anger, in an emotional, weak moment, or for any other reason—ever really divulge all of this, then I'll laugh. Then I'll just . . . I'll never talk to you again, but I'll laugh, you know, because you're a schmuck."

"Deny it," I told him.

"No, I won't deny it," he said. "I'll just laugh because I think it'll all work against you in the end. You know?"

"Yeah."

"You know?"

"Yeah."

Freddie and David were only talking to me in their own self-defense. They were trying their best to appease me, and at the same time intimidate me, after the Steinberg report came in and we'd all been made aware of the hundreds of thousands of dollars in unreported income. I took that one check for $1,000, but that was it.

The tragedy was that this great artist should have fallen into the hands of three guys like Freddie, David, and me. I'm to blame. I'm to blame because I shouldn't have let myself get carried away with Aerophonics. I should've continued handling Judy's career. I could have done both.

On September 5, 1963, the courts granted Judy custody of the children and gave me visitation rights. The next night, I went to the Rockingham house and had dinner with Lorna and Joey. I was about to leave around eight o'clock when Judy suddenly appeared in the living room. "Would you like a drink?" she asked.

"A scotch, please."

She made herself a vodka martini, which was unusual since she was a sipper and liked long drinks. There were four or five glasses around the house at any given time. She'd sip on one, put it down, then get another drink. "I know you're in bad shape financially while I'm making a lot of money," she said.

"I'm busted," I told her, "but I'll get by."

Judy told me she was going to give me anything I wanted. "You'll never be broke," she said. "I want to see you get that job at CBS and we'll start off and I'll give you $10,000 or $20,000 or $30,000. Whatever you need." With that, Judy wrote me a check for $10,000. "Now put this in your pocket," she instructed me, "and pay off some of your debts. You've helped me, now I'm going to help you."

So far so good.

She began to compliment me, telling me, "You're the best producer," this, that, and the other. "You know how to do things. You can build houses, you can make pictures, you can do *anything!*" She was very sweet, very nice, and very affectionate.

She went around the bar, got another drink—not a long one, but a quick martini—which she tossed down almost in one gulp. Then, without any warning, Judy turned on me. "I'm so fucking mad at you!" she began. "To think that we could be so good, so right together, but you're insisting on digging up all our past financial troubles. I want to forget it, darling."

"Judy, I don't think I can get to you," I said. "I'm confused about us. We get along momentarily, and then we don't. You never want to hear about your tax problems. You have them, Judy, and I'm going to level with you. Things that happened in the past will catch up with both you and me when the government does an audit."

"Sid, I don't want to hear what's going to catch up with me," she said.

"What I'm trying to tell you is—and you won't accept this, but in the very near future I have either to join you or disown you as a husband, as far as our taxes are concerned."

"But, Sid, why didn't you take care of those things then?"

I tried to explain the complexities of the tax returns, but she snapped, "You just do the goddamn income tax! Do it, and I don't want to hear about it. I'll do my shows, and don't interfere. Don't bother me or else I'll be so upset I'll blow the whole thing."

She started to berate me. I didn't say one thing. I just listened. I finally spoke up and asked, "Is this the way you really feel now?"

"Yes, that's it," she said.

"Oh, fuck, Judy!" I shouted. "Here, take your check. I cannot accept it this way. I could if we were on a friendly basis, but there's too much hostility between you and me and I don't need your money. You just aren't going to make it. These programs aren't right for you."

I tore up the check and said, "I can't take your $10,000 like this. I won't. I'm not being dramatic about this, and I will accept it when you want to give me a check with affection, and you want to do something like a husband and wife should do. Then I'll accept it." And I said good night.

I wasn't about to settle for anyone else's terms. Not unless I was going to be treated fairly. I was forty-seven years old. I'd given half a million to a million dollars to my marriage and I could prove it. Judy just needed to be fair with me. Be nice. Don't give me $10,000 and then tell me what a villain and bastard I am. I'm not. And she knew better than to say "Here's $10,000" like she was giving it to some actor.

I went out to the car and started to drive away, but Judy closed the gate on me. I walked back in again and she was in the kitchen making a peanut butter sandwich. I said, "Judy, let me go home. I'm tired." She continued making her sandwich. "This is too goddamn serious now," I told her. "I can't live this way, in this house or out of it. . . . This is a walkout, Judy. As far as I'm concerned. I'm going to walk out of this house and I'm going to walk out of your life."

I went back to the car, drove to the gate, and, again, it closed right in front of me. I went back in and said, "Judy, I'm exhausted. Open the gate. . . . Darling, this is no good. No fights." She was smiling a kind of naughty child's smile, but I wasn't falling for it. "Judy, I've got to get out of here. Now, for Christ's sake, let me out!" This time the gate remained open for me to drive through, and I headed back to my place. It was about 2:30 or 3:00 in the morning when I finally got into bed. Then at about 4:00 AM the phone rang. "Judy?" I asked. Who else would it be?

"There're prowlers about!" she said in hysterics. "Come back here, you son of a bitch, and guard your family!"

"Call the police, Judy," I told her. "There are no prowlers. Just keep the gate closed." I hung up. The phone rang again and again; each time it was Judy. "You son of a bitch, you're no husband, you don't love me, you don't love your children," and so on. I finally told the switchboard to just cut off all my calls.

The Judy Garland Show premiered on September 29, 1963. The cavalcade of guest stars appearing over the course of the series was unrivaled: Tony Bennett, Vic Damone, Lena Horne, Peggy Lee, Ethel Merman, Barbra Streisand, and even Miss Liza Minnelli, who was becoming a star in her own right. Judy gave a party when the first show aired, and I was invited. "Where have you been?" she asked. It was becoming predictable. "What are you doing? I miss you! What chance do we have?" She seemed to not remember what had gone down between us. She was on something then, too, though. If you watch her on the show, she was very good—phenomenal, even—but you can tell she was constantly under the influence of some form of medication.

There was a void in Judy's life now that I was out of it, but she sure didn't waste much time filling it. During the making of her shows, Judy was telling everybody how much in love she was with Canadian actor Glenn Ford. Glenn had known Judy for many years, all the way back to the time when he was eighteen and she was still a member of the Gumm Sisters. Soon, word around town was that Glenn was hanging around the set and that he and Judy were seen holding hands. They had a history together, and this seemed to initiate a fling that lasted for several months. I didn't pay too much attention to it. I knew this guy well, and I knew that this was the blind leading the blind. Talk about a sick man. He was an irritable drunk! I just felt sorry for Judy that Glenn Ford was the best she could do. My conclusion then was that I would not interfere or cause any trouble. I would just go away quietly.

Unfortunately, *The Judy Garland Show* never really had much of a chance. There was trouble brewing from the very beginning, probably because CBS never laid out a clear plan. There was a chain of three different executive producers, but the biggest obstacle Judy faced was the show's time slot, opposite *Bonanza*. CBS president Jim Aubrey and the network brass refused to move it to another night or time. By the time they started to get their act together, the series was set for cancellation after its twenty-sixth episode.

"I wasn't disappointed that we didn't get higher ratings," Judy said in the papers. "I don't think we deserved them. The time slot was impossible. After four or five years of loyalty to *Bonanza*, I can understand why viewers did not switch to my show. . . . But I did prove to everybody that I was reliable. They said I'd never answer the bell for the second round. But we turned out 26 shows. And some of them were damned good, too. Especially the last five we did."

PART VII

End of the Rainbow

44

BY SPRING 1964, Judy was traipsing around the world with her new beau, a young actor named Mark Herron. The two had met at a party on New Year's Eve; he was a gay fan of hers. CMA booked Judy for shows in Australia—two in Sydney and one in Melbourne. Neither Freddie nor David was along with her for the journey, just this young Mark fella. I was worried about Judy. She was like a zombie at this time. I'd never seen her in such a state. The shows in Sydney came off OK, but Melbourne was a disaster. She arrived onstage more than an hour late, was off-key, and kept forgetting her lines. The audience booed her. Many walked out on her, and others demanded their money back. The headlines were brutal: JUDY STONED, JUDY DRUNK, and JUDY DRUGGED.

Judy was not feeling well when she and Mark headed next for Hong Kong. When asked what she was suffering from, she replied, "Australia!" Arriving at their suite on the twenty-second floor of the Mandarin Hotel, they were met by Typhoon Viola, the worst such storm in that country's history. During the typhoon, Judy overdosed and fell into a coma. She was admitted to the hospital, her stomach was pumped—unsuccessfully—and she had to be placed in an oxygen tent. At one point, a nurse informed Mark that Judy was dead! Reports began to flash around the world, but it was just a false alarm.

What wasn't false was that Judy's sister Susie had died in Las Vegas around this same time. It was announced that she'd died of cancer, but it was actually an overdose of pills. She was forty-eight years old. In fact, none of the women in Judy's family were to enjoy long lives. Judy herself would live to be forty-seven, while her mother, Ethel, died at fifty-five. Judy's niece Judaline died at an early age of emphysema, while her mother, Judy's sister Jimmie, was fifty-nine when she died of a heart attack, having lived the longest of any of them.

For now, however, Judy left the hospital, and when they returned to their hotel, Mark hired a private nurse named Snowda Wu. She was Chinese but spoke fluent English, and she was able to care for Judy round the clock. Once Judy recovered, she and Mark were "married" by a Buddhist priest in a Chinese wedding ceremony. Headlines reading Judy Garland Marries Mark Herron in Ceremony Outside Hong Kong Harbor began to surface, and I started getting phone calls from friends all over. I just laughed it off. How could they get married? Judy and I weren't even divorced yet! Her lawyer quickly denied the marriage headlines to the press. Someone from *Newsweek* called me and said, "We understand you're still married to Miss Garland." I told them, "If you ask me, they got married on the Good Ship Lollipop. It's a fairy tale. I'm sure Judy and Mark are aware of their legal status. She and I are still married."

The couple came back to America, and Judy moved back into the Rockingham house with Mark sometime that December. The private nurse, Snowda Wu, came with them and lived in the pool house. The children called her "Snowy" and were awfully fond of her. I was not impressed. Snowda Wu changed Judy's whole life. She was giving her all kinds of daily injections, and I don't even know what the material was. I don't think it was heroin, but I hold her responsible for the state of mind Judy was in at that time. She had many raging, screaming outbursts, and the children were often frightened of their mother.

I obtained a child custody hearing in Santa Monica that fall. Judy had full custody at the time, meaning I could see Lorna and Joey just two Wednesdays and two weekends a month. But she was nowhere to be found, and I was angry! My children were being raised by the help at the Rockingham house when they should have been with me. My lawyer argued on my behalf that Judy was mentally unbalanced and emotionally disturbed. We didn't hold back this time. "On at least three occasions during 1963 and no less than 20 occasions in previous years, she has taken overdoses of barbiturates. On six occasions she has attempted suicide by slashing herself on her wrists, elbows or throat." After that Judy and I had joint custody.

I'm not a doctor, of course, but to be honest, I truly think Judy had become very mentally disturbed. She had a history of so many illnesses. How much of this could the children take? I felt the children needed to be with me. That Christmas, Judy told everyone I'd kidnapped them, but they *wanted* to be with me. On Christmas Eve, a bench warrant was issued for my arrest for not having returned the kids. I had a wonderful time with my children. I would rather have gone to jail than miss my first Christmas with them in three years. It was a happy and delightful holiday.

Once I went over to Rockingham to take the children out for the afternoon when the phone rang. Judy said, "Oh, darling." It was Mark Herron. She said to me, "I'd just love for you to talk to Mark."

So I got on the phone. "Hello, Mark."

"Hello, Mr. Luft." I called him Mark, he called me Mr. Luft. He said to me, "You know, I'm very much in love with Judy and we're getting married. I love the children, too, and I'll be a very good father."

"Listen," I said, "why don't you just play husband and *I'll* be the father." That was the only time I ever talked to Mark Herron.

Our divorce was finalized in May 1965, and Judy and Mark got married in Vegas the following November. She was just totally out of it for the occasion, so wobbly that she could hardly stand up. It was pathetic. Snowda Wu was along for the trip, so that explains it. The nurse wasn't around for long, though. Judy turned on her, and Snowy packed her bags and headed back to Hong Kong.

Mark Herron didn't stick around long either. He and Judy separated within six months after their wedding ceremony. To hear her tell it,

Mark simply went away and didn't bother to leave a forwarding address. "He just walked into my life like most people have as if I'm some kind of terminal," Judy later said.

> Like Grand Central Station, people just walk in and out, or right straight through. Some stay around until the building closes. After I married Mark, I practically couldn't find him. He actually left right after the wedding ceremony; he said he had to be back in Los Angeles to work with some little theater group. It hadn't been too bad to fight with Sid Luft. He could fight back. But I never knew where Mark was. I used to hear from him once in a while. I think he called from a phone booth on casters.

So Judy and Mark split up. Godfrey Isaac, Judy's new lawyer, later asked for an annulment, citing that Judy "entered into the marriage as a result of fraud" and that the marriage had never been consummated. That's unsurprising, as Mark was gay; he went back to living with his longtime lover, actor Henry Brandon, who was sixteen years his senior.

———— ◅◦▻ ————

From 1961 to 1966, Judy's gross income was between $12 million and $15 million. But no matter how much she worked, no matter how many concerts she performed or television shows she did, she was always in debt. By the fall of 1966, Judy realized how serious her financial difficulties were. There was no money coming in, debts were piling up, and her house was threatened with foreclosure. "It's because of the people I've known most of my life," Judy tried to explain to a reporter. "They get into the Judy Garland business. They take all the money and I find myself with nothing left but bills."

Judy had been advised to file for bankruptcy, but she refused. She was more than $100,000 in debt and owed more than $400,000 to the government. There was a sign placed on Judy's house on Rockingham saying it was to be sold within ninety days because she hadn't made any arrangements with the IRS whatsoever. The government had also put a lien on Capitol Records and any people who owed her any money. My thought was always that the American government should have paid Judy—as a national treasure!

Judy was also recognizing that those she'd considered to be her real friends were no longer her friends at all. They'd all disappeared, including Fields and Begelman, who wouldn't talk to her. She couldn't even get them on the phone anymore. Judy was desperate. That's when I was called back into the picture. It was September 1966 when Judy phoned me to say she was penniless and didn't have any food in the house. "I want to see you, Sid," she said. "I'm broke!" This was after twenty-six episodes of *The Judy Garland Show*, fifty or more successful concerts, three stints in Vegas, and the Carnegie Hall album. She'd earned over $10 million, and now she was broke. And I had known she would be.

"What about the television shows?" I asked.

"The television shows are gone," she said. "I'm selling my house, and I have no money."

I hadn't seen Judy for many months. She no longer made herself available when I visited the children. I went over that afternoon and was shocked when I saw her. She couldn't have weighed more than ninety pounds. "I don't know where to begin," she said, pacing back and forth. I kissed her on the cheek. "I don't know what to do," she continued. "I'm broke. I have no money. I have no resources. I'm too sick to work. We're going to be on the street, Sid."

Who was going to take on Judy Garland, though? Are you nuts? Are you crazy? She had a track record six miles long of hysteria, attempted suicide, and walking off of movie sets. She needed my help, and the children needed my help. As always, I assured Judy that everything would be OK.

First, I convinced her to leave CMA. Then I agitated her enough that we both joined forces in a multimillion-dollar lawsuit against CMA, Fields, and Begelman in New York. The suit asked for $2.5 million in damages and argued that Fields and Begelman had "improperly and unlawfully paid to and retained for themselves from the gross earnings of Judy Garland and Kingsrow Enterprises property and monies

substantially in excess of the commission to which they were enti-
tled. . . .They deliberately and systematically misused their position of
trust so as to cheat, embezzle, extort, defraud and withhold over $1 mil-
lion for their personal use, which rightfully belonged to Judy Garland."

We took the evidence we had—the material from Guy Ward and
Oscar Steinberg's audit, my taped conversation with Fields and Begelman, the Kingsrow ledger, the canceled checks, the whole nine yards—
and we built this case. How could a woman who worked as hard as
Judy did in from 1961 to 1965 be broke now in 1966? How in the
hell does that happen?

After the suit was filed, I received a phone call from a man who said
his name was Frank Sacco. He told me he was with David Begelman
in Begelman's Madison Avenue office and that he wanted to be the
middleman who could straighten things out. I felt he was threatening
me, so I told Sacco that the only place the suit would be straightened
out would be in court. I never heard from him again, but it turned out
that he was part of the East Coast Mafia.

———— ✿ ————

Film producer David Weisbart wanted Judy for the role of fictional
Broadway musical comedy star Helen Lawson in *Valley of the Dolls*, an
upcoming film for 20th Century Fox based on the novel by Jacqueline
Susann. I proposed the idea to Judy and she said, "I've got to do it,
because I need the money." So I hired an agent named John Dugan
to negotiate on our behalf. "I want $100,000 a week for her," we told
them, but we settled for $75,000 for eight weeks' work, then $25,000
for any additional weeks she was needed.

Judy headed to New York to be a mystery guest on the *What's
My Line?* television show. They paid for her stay, and it was around
this same time that Barbara Walters did an interview with her. On
March 2, 1967, Judy joined Jacqueline Susann for a press conference
at the St. Regis, where it was officially announced that she would have
a starring role in *Valley of the Dolls*. Given Judy's history with pills,
the reporters didn't miss the chance to ask her about the film's subject

matter. "The book deals with pills, to some extent," one said. "Have you found that prevalent around show business people?"

"Well, I find it prevalent around newspaper people, too," Judy replied with a sly smile. They asked why she was she taking on a role like this. "There are bills to be paid, groceries to be bought, and children to feed," she said. "I'm delighted to be in *Valley of the Dolls*, although my slanderous press already has me walking off the set! Mind you, the set hasn't even been built, but already they have me walking off it!"

The next day, we all gathered for Liza's wedding to Peter Allen at the apartment of Stevie Dumler, who was now Liza's agent. Peter Allen was a singer and dancer Judy had discovered during her stay in Hong Kong a few years earlier. She had brought him and his performing partner Chris—they were collectively known as the Allen Brothers—along to be her opening act in London. Judy played matchmaker, and in no time Peter and Liza were engaged. It later turned out he was gay. I thought he was gay all during the marriage. I suspected it, anyway. I remember going up to their apartment and Liza made a pasta for us. Over the fireplace was a portrait, a painting of a guy, and I said, "Who's that in the picture?" She said, "That's a friend of Peter's."

———

A call came in to Judy during her stay at the St. Regis informing her that she was about to lose the Rockingham house. It seemed as though things always crept up on her and caught her off guard. "People are always keeping reality away from me," she explained to a reporter. "It's perfectly awful! It's awful finding out about things after the wolf is at the door. I don't understand it at all."

I got the government to back off the sale of the house, which bought Judy a few more months. "Well, if worse comes to worse," she told the reporter, "I can always pitch a tent in front of the Beverly Hilton and Lorna can sing gospel hymns! That should see us through, somehow."

Filming for *Valley of the Dolls* began in mid-April in Los Angeles, and I was called to the set the second day of shooting when Judy wouldn't come out of the dressing room. She was dressed, with makeup on, and she'd tell them, "Be right out." But she didn't come out, and they'd had to stop shooting to wait for her. I got there and she said, "I'm a little rusty, Sid. But I'll make it all right. Tell them out there not to worry—I'll get it." I knew she was terrified and had been stoking herself with pills. Finally, after several days like this, Judy said, "I cannot read these lines. I just can't." And they fired her. Judy cried a little in her dressing room and was driven home in a studio limousine. She called me in tears. "They fired me! They fired me! I don't know why they wouldn't give me a chance."

I went by Rockingham when I knew she was home and comforted her as best I could. She was still upset. "See if you can get me that job back," she said. "Sid, get it back for me!" I went in to see Richard Zanuck, who was running the studio at the time. As her ex-husband and the guy she was known to listen to, I said to Dick, "Give her one more chance, please." I begged him, but he said he couldn't do it. He was very firm: "Listen Sid, we gave her all the chances we could. We can't disrupt this film like this. We have to replace her."

I came back to Judy and said, "Fuck 'em! The hell with the goddamn thing. That part wasn't for you anyway. Listen, if you can't read those lines, it was a mistake in the beginning. The whole world is not gonna come to an end. You're gonna be all right." This was one of the toughest things I ever had to do to Judy. "You didn't come out so badly," I told her. They did give her half of her promised fee, although the IRS took most of the money. And that was that. That was the end of the *Valley of the Dolls*.

Judy finally lost the house not long after. It was put up for sale and sold, and Judy Garland was officially homeless. The IRS didn't get a hell of a lot of money from the sale, but I was lucky: I got Judy some of her money that had been held in escrow. We put everything she owned in storage, and I started organizing the next tour for her.

Judy was philosophical about the whole thing. "In a way I'm glad they're taking the house," she'd told that reporter in New York. "It's too big, too impractical. Besides, the man who lived there before didn't love his wife. That sort of put a pall on it from the beginning! There are acres of gardens, and a swimming pool, and the place needs at least four servants and four gardeners to keep it in shape. I never really liked it. It looks like a Gloria Swanson reject. I say good riddance!"

45

Judy's new tour began at the Westbury Music Fair on Long Island, and soon we were headed back to the Palace in New York City. Judy opened there on July 31, 1967, and played for a phenomenal four weeks. We called it "Judy Garland at Home at the Palace." It was her third time there, and she even brought Lorna and Joey onstage as part of her act each night. I negotiated a new recording contract with ABC/Paramount, and they released a live album with selections from the Palace shows.

Judy tried for a reconciliation with me around this time. I knew she'd been on and off again with Tom Green, a young publicist she'd been seeing. They were even engaged at one point. Needless to say, I was surprised when she called me to her suite and said, "You know how I feel about you, Sid, and I always will feel."

"Well, I feel the same way," I said, "but I'm not ready for that, Judy."

"Sid, has something happened to you?"

"Yes," I told her. I was emotionally confused, and that made her angry.

"Don't tell me you've switched and become a fag!" she shouted. Who can blame her for wondering? Look at the cast she attracted! The likes of Vincente Minnelli, and then Mark Herron.

One reason I wasn't in a hurry to get back together was that I'd been seeing a pretty girl named Marianna Hill since Judy and I split.

She was a very young actress, early twenties, and was making a Howard Hawks picture at Paramount at the time we met. She thought I was very attractive but much too old for her. And I agreed! I didn't fall in love with her, but she was great company. She was the first woman I slept with after Judy. It was not the same, though. It was a sex thing more than a love thing. She was interesting and a nice girl, but I didn't want to get married. I really broke her heart, so I'm told.

After the Palace run, Judy did a tour I'd set up for her of ten major cities, including Boston, where she gave a free-to-the-public, open air concert on the Boston Common. They built a twenty-four-foot platform especially for her; she loved a runway like that so she could move about. It was her largest audience ever, more than a hundred thousand people. God, it was packed! John Collins, the mayor of Boston, presented her with a silver souvenir Paul Revere bowl and said, "Judy, we've taken you into our hearts; I think that is the sentiment of all of us. God bless you."

I got Judy a gig opening November 30 at the brand-new Caesars Palace in Vegas. It was one show a night, $30,000 a week, plus other incentives. It was one of a very limited number of shows Judy performed in 1968. A few were triumphs, and a few were tragedies due to medication issues. I'd never seen Judy in this condition. I was convinced that she was suicidal and figured she'd never live out the year. If she made it through the year, she'd never make another movie. I was also sure that her voice would wear out from amphetamines and abuse. She just didn't care anymore.

Judy was totally burned out. Wiped out. Destroyed. I couldn't save her. If anybody had a chance to save her, it would've been me. But I'm a survivor type of guy—it's just my nature—and I wasn't going to be dragged down by anybody. I warned Judy. I *begged* her. She said "Get out!" And I got out.

Finally, by the middle of 1968, I couldn't go any further with Judy. I couldn't get to her after this period. I went back to California with Joey, and then Lorna soon followed. When I left Judy for the last time, Lorna left her mother, too. She had been Judy's caregiver for far too long—and at, what, fourteen or fifteen years old? She called me up and said, "Daddy, I can't live with her anymore. I want to come and live with you."

Judy was always fearful and obsessed that I would kidnap the children one day, but now she was sending them to live with me—with her blessings and regrets. She just couldn't care for them anymore.

———— ✥ ————

CMA showed up around this time and dangled an $8,000 check for accrued royalties in front of Judy. In return for the funds, she agreed to drop the lawsuit against them, and she signed a new contract with Fields and Begelman. How could she? That lawsuit was the only thing she'd had going for her. They'd used her and made themselves rich, busted the two of us, and now she was penniless. This is still a sore wound with me. She never should have dropped that suit and gone back with those crooks.

Soon, I filed a motion of intervention that would allow me to take over the suit, and in December 1968 the New York Supreme Court granted my motion. A few days after Christmas, Fields asked me to meet him at Frascati's restaurant. "Sid, I know what you want," he said to me, "and I have $100,000 in my pocket. But before I give it to you, you have to take an ad out in *Variety* and the *Hollywood Reporter*. The gist of the ad will be that the things you have said about Freddie Fields and David Begelman are a figment of your imagination."

All I could do was laugh. "I don't want your $100,000. The only thing I want from you is to get you in the goddamned courthouse." But I'd never see my day in court; the suit dragged on for a decade before being dismissed in 1978 for taking too long make it to trial.

———— ✥ ————

In the years after we separated, I'd always had some kind of a handle on Judy. I always had an idea where she was—in Vegas, in New York, or wherever—or who she was with, and she knew how to get in touch with me. But now I felt awful, because there wasn't anybody to look out for her. In the back of my mind I was always conscious of her.

I remained concerned, especially when rumors would get back to me that she wasn't well. I think it was a great struggle for her too, being without me. I tried to ignore it, but I really couldn't, because I knew better. I just knew that without me, she was really doomed. Somebody would fuck up.

Judy stayed in New York and got mixed up with a guy called John Meyer, who claimed to be—or imagined himself to be—a songwriter. She was living with him in his parents' apartment on Park Avenue and singing in a gay and lesbian bar where he played piano. Just like the others, this guy thought he could save Judy. He did succeed in getting her on *The Merv Griffin Show* and several other national shows, and I believe he was the one who originally lined up a five-week engagement for Judy at London's Talk of the Town.

I had a chance meeting with Judy in December 1968. I was on my way into the dentist office on West Fifty-Seventh Street for a root canal and she was there with John Meyer visiting another dentist office in the same building. "Hey, you, hey, fella!" she called to me. She looked terrible. She was so thin. That was the last time I ever saw Judy.

I really didn't know what happened to Judy after that. I later learned that when John Meyer was flat on his back with a debilitating case of the flu, Judy made a leap from him to a man called Mickey Deans. Deans was twelve years Judy's junior and the night manager of a popular New York discotheque called Arthur. Looking back, Judy meeting him was bad news. I knew it and I hadn't even met the guy! But I knew of the circle of people, who they were and what they were. Deans picked up where John Meyer left off and headed to London to accompany Judy to the Talk of the Town engagement, where she received mostly rave reviews.

Two months later, on March 15, 1969, Judy married Mickey Deans at the Chelsea Register Office. The wedding reception was held at Quaglino's, a popular West End restaurant. Word was that it was to be a star-studded event with everybody from Bette Davis to James Mason in attendance, but very few of her old friends showed up. The next day's headline read, JUDY WEDS BUT STARS STAY AWAY.

Judy and her opening act, Johnnie Ray, set off on a four-city tour with stops in Stockholm, Gothenburg, and Malmö, Sweden, finishing up in Copenhagen, Denmark. Her concert at Copenhagen's Falkoner Centret on March 25, 1969, would be her final performance. "The air was thick with rumors that the star was no longer a star, that she had not only lost her voice, but that she could no longer even get through her program," wrote a critic for the *Politiken*.

> Suddenly she stood on the enormous stage and disproved all the rumors in the world. . . . After a large number of curtain calls, she finally gave in to the deepest wish of the audience. She sat down on the stage floor and began to sing "Over the Rainbow." It was as though she sang it for the first time, with fervent innocence and sweetness. Tears came to one's eyes. All the spectators arose and cheered Judy Garland. She had a great triumph.

June 22, 1969. Judy was living in London with her then-husband Mickey Deans, and he had allowed a doctor to give her a prescription of Seconal because she couldn't sleep. She would pop those things like candy, so you'd have to watch her. Judy would tell me, "Don't put more than three Seconal by my bed," and I'm sure she told him, too. I have to believe that Deans did it purposely. They say Judy had thirty or forty Seconal next to her bed, and Deans was nowhere to be found. He disappeared, this fuck! He was known for taking late night walks in a nearby park, so who knows where he'd been or who he was with. He came back the next morning from wherever the hell he'd been, and there was a phone call for Judy. It was the singer/pianist Charlie Cochran calling. Deans saw Judy wasn't in the bed, so he called to her, but there was no answer. She was in the bathroom, he figured, so he knocked on the door, but there was just silence. He had to get into the bathroom through a window from the roof. It was then that he discovered her. Judy was dead.

The coroner ruled it an accidental overdose. Judy didn't commit suicide, which was what a lot of the public assumed at first. But it seems as though Judy had awakened in the middle of the night, went to the john, and her head just dropped. She swallowed her tongue and suffocated. Ordinarily, if she took that amount of Seconal, she would have vomited some of it up. That, or her head would be up and she would have just gone to sleep. But when her head dropped, she suffocated. That's what happened to her.

The doctor who prescribed this medication should have known something about Judy Garland and her history with pills. You don't put thirty sleeping pills by her bedside. You might recommend three or four Seconal, but not enough to kill her! She wasn't taking the normal dosage of any of these things. She'd take handfuls a day. She would treat that stuff like it was popcorn. You might say the Seconal killed her, but it could have been any number of things, too. Maybe she was doomed. Her death was a kind of assisted suicide, in a way. A lot of people took advantage of her and made a bad situation worse.

I consider Freddie Fields and David Begelman responsible for Judy's death as well. It's an interesting study of Hollywood behavior when you think of this: Freddie Fields became the president of MGM, and David Begelman the president of Columbia Pictures. Columbia chose Begelman to head the studio in 1973, but just a few years later, in 1977, it was revealed that he was under some sort of investigation. It came as no surprise to me when, after seven weeks of looking into Begelman's files, Price Waterhouse came back with a report that he'd been caught stealing from the studio. David had obviously cut his teeth on this kind of scam with Judy. He was just stepping it up when he did it at Columbia. He went from stealing hundreds of thousands from Judy to millions from Columbia.

Surprisingly, the Columbia board of directors decided they could live with that, and they launched a plan to cover Begelman's tracks. They covered up for him just like Fields did in Judy's case. In fact, there was a list a mile long of people who'd covered up for Begelman. He was finally let go from Columbia anyway. Begelman ran amok, and he finally ran out of gas. He couldn't live with himself. Eventually he blew his brains out. When a friend called me and said that the bastard had shot himself, I said, "Well, he sure as hell shot the right guy."

Our family never recovered from what Freddie Fields and David Begelman did to us. My life and the lives of Lorna and Joey were never the same. The only person who recovered financially was Liza. Emotionally, none of us ever overcame it. It wasn't just an accidental overdose; Freddie Fields killed Judy Garland, and David Begelman was his accomplice that did the shooting.

Leopold and Loeb may have gotten away with it, but Freddie still had to live with it. He wiped the blood off his hands and went into hiding. No one heard much more about him after Judy's death; it was over for him in Hollywood. His wife tried to keep him afloat, and he was hiding behind her. Everybody who knew anything about Freddie Fields came to despise him. He's just as guilty as the other one who put a bullet in his head.

———— ✺ ————

Judy was only forty-seven when she died, but she looked much older. The years of abuse had taken their toll on her tiny, frail body. Her death made international front-page headlines, and more than twenty-two thousand mourners filed past her glass-covered coffin at the Frank E. Campbell Funeral Home on Madison Avenue. James Mason, Judy's costar in *A Star Is Born*, gave the eulogy at her funeral on June 27, which I attended with the children. "I traveled in her orbit only for a while, but it was an exciting while and one during which it seemed that the joys in her life outbalanced the miseries," Mason said in that magnificent voice of his. "Her special talent was this: she could sing so that it would break your heart. What is a tough audience? A tough audience is a group of high-income-bracket cynics at a Hollywood party. Judy's gift to them was to wring tears from men with hearts of rock."

Judy Garland was a very rare mix of shattered nerves and insecurity, self-doubt, self-destructiveness, and suicidal tendencies—but also true genius. She was, to me, the greatest talent who ever lived.

I found it so easy to separate Judy the artist from Judy the person. The latter always came first, because she was so special as a person, so loving, especially to me. She really was truly in love with me, and I knew it. Every move I made, she wanted to know where I was. And she missed the sound of my voice, just like I missed hers. At least when she was herself.

Despite whatever bad things happened between us, I could never fall out of love with Judy. If anyone tried to save a woman who was breaking apart, I did. I know that I did the best I could do, and it still wasn't enough.

People used to say that Sid Luft was this Svengali who took over Judy Garland's life, but that's a lot of crap. I was no more a Svengali than any other husband. I was just a husband who loved his wife and tried to do what was best for her. That's all I was. I didn't tell her what to do or what not to do; Judy was always an independent woman who knew what she wanted and went after it. I invented things for her, though. And she respected my notions and thoughts about show business. I had proven myself to her by the things that I had done for her career. I was in love with her, she was in love with me, and that's the way it was.

Index